Paul Copperwaite has worked in book publishing for several years and is the author of twelve titles on a diverse range of subjects, most recently *Pop Charts* and *Movie Charts*. He began to research the criminal underworld while working as an editor in London.

The Mammoth Book of
Drug Barons

Edited by
Paul Copperwaite

ROBINSON

RUNNING PRESS
PHILADELPHIA · LONDON

Constable & Robinson Ltd
3 The Lanchesters
162 Fulham Palace Road
London W6 9ER
www.constablerobinson.com

First published in the UK by Robinson,
an imprint of Constable & Robinson, 2010

A copy of the British Library Cataloguing in Publication
Data is available from the British Library

UK ISBN 978-1-84901-306-2
1 3 5 7 9 10 8 6 4 2

First published in the United States in 2010 by Running Press Book Publishers

US Library of Congress number: 2009943386
US ISBN 978-0-76243-993-5

Running Press Book Publishers
2300 Chestnut Street
Philadelphia, PA 19103-4371

Visit us on the web!

www.runningpress.com

Printed and bound in the EU

Cover photo credits – **supplied by Alamy**: wrap of cocaine, Select Photo; Laboratory,
UK Science-Chris Ridley; Chopping out line of cocaine, Everynight Images; Police
raid, Mikael Karlsson; Opium poppy capsules, Phototake; Cessna aircraft, Colin
Underhill; Poppy pickers, Stuart Abraham; Pakistan Anti Narcotics Force commando,
Jeff Rotman. **Supplied by Press Association Images**: Gilberto Rodriguez
Orejuela under arrest, AP; Pablo Escobar Gaviria, AP; Howard Marks, Empics.

Contents

Acknowledgments

The editor would like to thank all those who made this book possible by allowing us to reprint the extracts listed below:

Charlotte Knight and Anna Watkins of David Godwin Associates for use of extracts from chapters 3 and 5 from *Mr Nice: an Autobiography* by Howard Marks, © Newtext Limited 1996, 1997 (Secker & Warburg, 1996). Kirsty Wilson at Canongate for permission to quote from the extract from the Introduction to *Snowblind; a Brief Career in the Cocaine Trade* by Robert Sabbag, © Howard Marks 1998 (Canongate, 1998). Extracts from chapter 7 of *Blowback: Rise and Fall of a Millionaire Dope Smuggler* by Michael Forwell with Lee Bullman, © Michael Forwell and Lee Bullman 2009 (Sidgwick & Jackson, 2009), reprinted by kind permission of Pan Macmillan and Creative Authors Ltd, with thanks to Isabel Atherton. Meghan Tillett at Hachette US, and Hodder and Stoughton for permission to quote from chapters 4 and 8 of *Escobar, The Inside Story of Pablo Escobar, the World's Most Powerful Criminal* by Roberto Escobar (© Roberto Escobar with David Fisher 2009, published in the UK by Hodder and Stoughton, 2010), first published as *The Accountant's Story* in the US by Grand Central Publishing reprinted by kind permission of the publisher in 2009, reprinted by kind permission of Hodder and Stoughton and Hachette Group US. Olivia Hunt at United Agents for help, advice and use of various extracts from *Bloggs 19 and Reefer Men: the Rise and Fall of a Billionaire Drugs Ring* by Tony Thompson, © Tony Thompson, 2000 and 2007 respectively (Warner Books, 2000 and Hodder & Stoughton, 2007 respectively), reprinted by kind permission of Sphere, an imprint of Little, Brown Book Group, Hodder and Stoughton, and United Agents (*www.unitedagents.co.uk*). Mark Bowden for use of extracts from *Los Pepes* and *The Kill* from *Killing Pablo: the Hunt for the Richest, most Powerful Criminal in History*, Mark Bowden, © Mark Bowden 2001 (Grove Atlantic Inc., 2001). Ron Chepesiuk for use of extracts from chapters 7, 8 and *What Goes Around* from *Drug Lords: the Rise and Fall of the Cali Cartel, the Richest Crime Syndicate in History*, Ron Chepesiuk, © Ron Chepesiuk, 2003 (first published as *The Bullet or the Bribe*, Praeger, 2003). Norman Parker for use of extracts from *Lucera, Guerilla Queen* and *The Cocaine Factory*, from *Dangerous People, Dangerous Places*, Norman Parker, © Norman Parker 2007 (John Blake Publishing Ltd, 2007). Extracts from *The Candy Machine: How Cocaine Took Over the World,* © Tom Feiling (UK: Penguin Books, 2009; entitled *Cocaine Nation* in the USA), reprinted by permission of Penguin Books Ltd and Pegasus Books LLC. With thanks to Tom Feiling and Broo Doherty for "running interference". Sharon Campbell at Mainstream for use of selected extracts from *Druglord: Guns, Powder and Pay-Offs* and *The Devil* by Graham Johnson, © Graham Johnson, 2006 and 2007 respectively (Mainstream Publishing Company Ltd, 2006 and 2007 respectively), together with use of various extracts from *The Happy Dust Gang*, David Leslie, © David Leslie, 2006 (Mainstream Publishing Ltd, 2006), reprinted by kind permission of the publisher. Chris Burrows of Milo Books for use of extracts from chapter 5 of *Cocky: The Rise and Fall of Curtis Warren, Britain's Biggest Drug Baron,* Tony Barnes, Richard Elias and Peter Walsh, © Tony Barnes, Richard Elias and Peter Walsh (Milo Books Ltd, 2001), reprinted by kind permission of the publisher. Extracts from chapter 10 of *McMafia: Seriously Organised Crime* by Misha Glenny, © Misha Glenny, 2008 (The Bodley Head, 2008), reprinted by kind permission of the Random House Group UK and Alfred A. Knopf, a division of Random House, Inc.

With grateful thanks to the following for their often immense support and patience:

Norman and Betty Copperwaite, Duncan Proudfoot, Laura Price, Mahesh Deol, Ben Ando, Jacqui Jackson; to Ron Chepesiuk for his generosity; to Norman Parker; and to Nick Wetton for being a gent.

Introduction

A million centuries ago, plants said "High" to animals. Roots and seeds seduced tongues and stomachs. Vine, leaf and resin interplayed with hand, heart and mind. Drinking, smelling and sucking were the order, but not the regulation, of the day.

And Nature said, "Higher".

A pyramid here and a pyramid there.

Gargling, sniffing, smoking, puking and starving for God, Siva and the Sun. Who'll have the booze? Who'll have the blow? Who'll have a line? Who gets the fun?

"I've got the dope. But stick to my brand. Use any other dope, and I'll kill you. Don't do this. Don't do that. That fruity stuff is verboten."

Nature asked, "Why?"

So fuck you, and let's smuggle cider into the Garden of Eden. Adam's apples are shite. Eve's cool. She calls it a scam. Smuggling cocaine, alcohol and marijuana. But is the snake a grass?

– Howard Marks, 1988

Since prehistory, humankind has applied its boundless ingenuity and questionable wisdom not only to filling its belly but to altering its mental state, too. It's not hard to see why. There you are, out on the Savannah – one of the Clovis people of North America, hunting the mammoth to extinction, not that you know it, living as you do some 13,000 years ago. After a hard day following the herd, keeping quiet, aiming your spear, your stomach is full.

It gets dark early in the colder seasons, and the fire is lit, keeping predators at bay. The flames lick logs and make momentary shapes in which you see the things from the world around you. Your mind wanders. You too could be like that fire – and you pick up a stick, dip it in some pigment, daub those shapes on a cave wall . . . And then one of your buddies from the hunt leans across with a gesture that says, "Wanna get high?" Well, what would you want to do? Besides, it would be churlish not to, and you need them to bring you along on the next hunt; none of you is any good alone.

Okay, there's no archaeological evidence for my Flintstones-like historical revisionism, but I'd suggest that this is not because it didn't happen, but because stashes, then as now, were notoriously perishable. Leaping forward to a century before the Christian era, ceramic bowls, together with tubes for snorting or inhaling, were in use in Mexico, South America and the Caribbean. Scientists believe that the peoples of these regions used cohoba, a hallucinogen extracted from mimosa beans, along with the mescal beans and peyote cacti that are still appearing in modern-day drug classics such as *Fear and Loathing in Las Vegas*.

Meanwhile, our ancestors in Asia and Africa cultivated corn, wheat, rice and barley, and not merely for food. It's a possibility that would warm Homer Simpson's heart with its rightness: as a species, we may in fact have settled down to an agrarian lifestyle for the sake of beer.

And yet today there's an expectation that we should be different. Where such behaviours are acknowledged to have taken place, it is as part of lives that were nasty, brutish and short. Sincere in the belief that it is for our own good, politicians and leaders of all but the most irresponsibly libertarian beliefs have sought to ban certain indulgences in pursuit of their particular shining city on a hill – to improve us.

But still, we do not evolve that fast, and in the gulf between reality and someone else's hopes for us, the law of unintended consequences has determined the existence of a relatively new economic sector – drug smuggling and distribution – and it has concentrated real, effective global power in the hands of the smugglers who rank most highly.

★   ★   ★

Men like Howard Marks or Michael Forwell belonged to an era of self-exploration. In the 1960s Bob Dylan had been freewheelin', then Leary had encouraged the young to turn on, tune in and drop out; to find out who they really were and what they really wanted, rather than what society had always told them they needed. These debonair dope-smugglers of the "me" generation facilitated fun. As they saw it, no one was ever hurt by cannabis unless they were hit by a truck full of the stuff. (Harm being relative, of course, and tobacco-smoking being commonplace and normal in the 1970s.) Even Zachary Swan (the hero of *Snowblind*, Robert Sabbag's insouciant, cult non-fiction book from 1976), though he dealt in cocaine, is a sympathetic figure if you can accept that people die in car accidents, and we don't ban cars. An ex-Second World War soldier who never got over his dislike of guns, Swan would reach into his empty briefcase if he needed to give the impression of being tooled up.

Swan was in his early forties when he began to import and supply cocaine, undertaking regular trips to Bogotá and distributing his wares to a select Manhattan circle upon his return. In the years before crack began to screw with the lungs of America's urban poor, and street prices for powder dropped a little meanwhile, coke was still a "champagne" drug, an after-dinner ice-breaker for the more adventurous of America's middle classes. It still benefitted from its reputation as a livener, the tonic that had made the 1920s roar.

For a few years, once borders had been crossed, dealers could rely on a measure of discretion from their customers, at least relative to other drugs (such as heroin, an epidemic of which gripped New York in the early 1970s), not that those customers were often the type police routinely lean on, in any case.

Swan was in his early forties when he first tried drugs at all, and it was after only minimal personal experience with coke that he began to import it. Nonetheless, his life experience and general caution paid dividends from the start. A square-jawed New York sales manager for twenty years before his brief diversification into importation, Swan undertook his own voyage of discovery, as chronicled Sabbag's book, while the youth around him turned on, tuned in and dropped out.

Often happily high on his own supply, he looked on with a wry puzzlement as those around him shuffled off the orthodoxies of the 1950s, and his attitude almost represents the reasonable response of straight, "breadhead" America to the emerging counter-culture: to facilitate its fun and reap the financial rewards. It's the American way.

The world of Marks, Forwell or Swan was miles away in spirit from the grim menace of Liverpool's John Haase or Curtis Warren for a single reason: back then, gangsters seldom touched the drugs trade. The Gambinos, Genoveses or east-London geezers all considered them a suspect business compared to the traditional grafts of racketeering or robbery. Try a scam like Marks' or Forwell's today, and you would soon find you were on someone's turf. Without the name of a firm to protect you, your stock or stake would be gone, and you would be lucky to keep your legs, hands or life intact. Surrender to the police would soon look like the lesser evil, were it not that prison affords little protection for the grass.

Some smugglers will traffic anything lucrative, others have scruples, and Paul Newman, for example, was one of the latter. A legitimate businessman who found himself the hapless subject of a fraud investigation in the 1979, he was found innocent of all charges, but in the meantime had incurred a lot of time, expense and stress, to say nothing of the cost to his business.

Having lost his respect for the law, and with a family to support, he began to traffic cannabis from Africa to the UK. Focussing his activities on the containerized shipping of Ghanaian weed, he met officials along the route corrupt enough even to organize an '"honour guard" for their dope-buying guests. Such was the cheerful if edgy atmosphere in which he managed to conduct a very lucrative business, and fund his daughter's Formula Ford racing career – until 1988, when he learned that one of the men working for him had organized a shipment of South African grass behind his back.

The man had offered work to two others at the operation's UK end at the cost of £50,000 each, which gives some idea of its size. Customs swarmed over the load and two of the men – the problem for Newman was that the scene was his business premises. At his Old Bailey trial, he pleaded guilty to conspiracy to import cannabis, and received a ten-and-a-half year sentence. Banged up in, variously, Brixton, Wandsworth and Parkhurst prisons, Newman frequently found himself in the company of well-known long-term prisoners such as "Mad" Frank Fraser and Charles Bronson, becoming well-versed in the lives and lore of the lags.

Sadly, Newman's case reflects what can go wrong when fear's not a factor in enforcing the smooth and discreet running of a covert importation operation. However, the hardest and most ruthless gangsters still come on top (get caught) in the end, and often faster than Newman's operation did. While it lasted, everyone was a winner!

The buccaneering spirits in the early part of this book did what they did because, though financially driven, they had an interest in their product. They were only a step away from the touring bebop musicians who were obliged to travel with their own heroin, and their main enemy was the law, not other gangs. Some, like Howard Marks, are positively evangelical about the benefits of their wares. Today's barons would handle the logistics of any scam if the returns were big enough, provided it was sufficiently illegal as to grant a monopoly to those hard enough to take the risks involved – capture, or, when there's no recourse to law for those who've been ripped off, competition of the deadliest kind. For example, even a regular drug user in London today would have to go quite out of their way to find LSD. However, it's not as if psychedelics (as opposed to the more commonly found opiates and coca-based products which do not produce sensory disturbances or a psychotic break) aren't popular, as is shown by the growth in the use of ketamine as a party drug (resulting in its classification as a class "C" drug under The Misuse of Drugs Act in 2005). The paradox is that "Special K" is more available because it is harder to make, and therefore worth procuring and trafficking in, at least for some. Though both are proscribed, acid is a simpler chemical compound, traditionally synthesized by idealistic chemists such as San Francisco's Owsley Stanley, the Grateful Dead fellow-traveller who gave away substantial batches of his squeaky-clean product for free. Even the four-hour party acid sometimes found in Britain's dance scene in the 1990s was still a quarter of the price of an E at that time (the same price that an Ecstasy pill commands now, after more than a decade of further prohibition and reclassification). Ketamine, on the other hand, is difficult to produce and requires professional facilities but is already supplied as an anaesthetic and a veterinary tranquillizer. This makes it more attractive to traffickers, who have another opportunity to employ their traditional skill set of intimidation, procuring, theft and distribution. By contrast, people do not deal in acid to make a fortune – they would be too easily undercut by student chemists who, unlike domestic cannabis growers, can produce acid covertly and quickly enough to minimize the risk of detection. Interestingly, K, as a hallucinogen that is usually snorted, allowing some control over its intensity, is perhaps closer to those powders the ancient Mexicans took than we might at first think.

Some, like Carlton Leach, spent the 1990s and early 2000s as a drug baron of a different kind. Like the guys who sell the pans and donkeys in a Gold-Rush frontier town, every stream of wealth attracts those who gather along its banks. Making money from the needs it creates is often a wiser way to riches than diving straight in, especially if you have the build of a young Arnie and have paid your dues manning the dodgiest doors in clubland.

Behind the smiley badges of Britain's "E generation", which began with "the second summer of love" in 1988, lay underworld menace from the start. After all, who else but someone with some balls and the ability to marshal a crowd was going to organize raves in the first place? Leave it to the DJs and artists and the fences might have come down, like they did at Woodstock. And that might have been beautiful, but the next event wouldn't have happened at all. It was the security that made the soul trains of house run on time. And made sure that, for individual club nights, there *was* a next time.

Ecstasy began to hit the streets, and importantly the terraces, in the late 1980s. It offered, or at least went along with, something of a thaw in the social tensions of the Thatcher era – it was not uncommon to see burly blokes of different races, creeds and football colours locked in an embrace and proclaiming the other a top geezer and their best mate. Not surprisingly, it had originally been synthesized as a potential psychotherapeutic aid.

Holland has always been the international centre of Ecstasy manufacture and distribution, and Britain, with its geographical proximity and its miles of unobserved coastline, a ready market. Inspired by corporate marketing, and the work-hard-play-hard ethos of a generation who embraced both the free market and personal freedom, early pills, such as Doves or Mitsubishis, were "branded", and were almost pure MDMA. As the 1990s "progressed", pills became more commonly mixed with amphetamines, and brand logos inevitably pirated. Prices began to drop, maintaining user acceptance of a pill that would at least keep them awake if not prove transcendental.

Anyone who attended an outdoor rave in the early 1990s may remember the hours spent cramped in the back of a friend's GTi on the way there, and the big guys with the dogs and the bats when they arrived. Carlton Leach was one of those who, like Dave Courtney, made his money running the rave scene – not a dealer, but someone who knew a heck of a lot of them and who held more than a handful of those in his palm. Club culture had ventured out to Essex, and the Essex boys followed it back into town. (Leach was an associate of the three victims of the Rettenden Range Rover murders, which feature in chapter 13.)

Drugs became weaker, the music sounded like more of the same, and those who had got together on "the love drug" were now having families and settling down, and could no longer stay out all night or afford to have a mid-week low. In more recent years, "X" has found new if limited acceptance on the techno scene across north America, which mirrors the movement of cocaine that began to occur a little earlier in the opposite direction, when the Cali cartel first sought to exploit the European coke market to compensate for a waning one in the US.

As the UK rave scene became more corporate, with super-clubs such as Cream and the Ministry of Sound becoming brands that would appear on merchandizing, street apparel and compilation albums, a problem became apparent; at some point, this squeaky-clean business-person's world had to rub shoulders with drug culture and the drug barons, as discreetly and tacitly as it could manage. Let's face it, those thousands of people waving their arms in the air, swaying their hips and describing imaginary shapes with their hands would not have wanted to do that for hours on end without the drugs – not unless you were paying *them*. And so the clubs would have been empty without the guys with the polythene coin-bags of pills in their pockets – those both known and unknown to the guys like Leach who managed the door.

Britain's "clubland" became a corporate half-world in which, though you may own the building as far as the law is concerned, someone hard still wants your turf; where it pays to speak softly but carry a baseball bat, and where menace became a matter of how things were put, of conveying a promise of violence so carnal that, as you make it, you hope it will remain unfulfilled.

★ ★ ★

Britain remains Europe's most druggy country. As of 2007, it had the highest levels of multi-drug consumption, and the second highest number of drug-related deaths. Around a quarter of 26–30-year-olds had tried class "A" drugs, and forty-five per cent of young people had smoked dope. In the 1990s, Noel Gallagher famously said that taking drugs was "like getting up and having a cup of tea in the morning", and in 1999 Liverpool's Robbie Fowler got up people's noses when he celebrated a goal against Everton by imitating the snorting of coke. However, widespread occasional use is rarely the cause of collateral social harm – statistically, the bulk of drug-related crime occurs among a hard core of heroin and cocaine addicts.

Among importers and suppliers, however, it's a different story. Largely due to changes in sentencing guidelines, the UK's prison population increased by sixty-six per cent between January 1995 and January 2009, from 49,500 to 82,100, with about a third of the prison population having been sentenced for drugs or violence-against-the-person offences (the Ministry of Justice appears to class these together). Around forty per cent of women in prison are there for drug-related offences, their ranks swelled by Caribbean cocaine mules, whom we "rehabilitate" only to deport once they have served their sentence.

The more statistically average the drug-taking population, the larger, more lucrative – and therefore heavier – the drugs trade becomes. As will become clear from the extracts here, profits are vertiginous, with mark-ups a hundred times larger than could be dreamt of for any legal commodity. Curtis Warren allegedly remarked to Customs officers, upon his acquittal of smuggling charges in 1992, that he was off to spend the £87 million he had earned from importing and distributing a single shipment of cocaine from Venezuela.

Traditionally, working-class boys had few routes out of the industrial grind to money and excitement – boxing, football – and only a few more out of the post-industrial wasteland including playing the guitar, maybe even deejaying. The fact that what grows by the roadside in one country is worth a fortune to the residents of another has provided one more avenue, albeit a deadly one for some, and as long as the profits remain so high, drug distribution will still seem to many like something that's worth a hell of a lot of sweat, adrenalin and fear.

The stories in this book span the world to connect the mighty and the meek, linking dodgy deals in far-away lands with that house over the road where a lot of people come and go. We have no reliable way of estimating the global profit from drugs as a commercial sector. So bear in mind that the barons in this book, whether dashing or downright evil, are just some of the ones who have "come on top". And they are just a fraction of the ones that exist.

Paul Copperwaite

1

Mr Nice

Howard Marks

Back in the 1970s in Britain, when the working classes still had places to work, tutting over a tabloid during a tea-break punctuated many people's morning and afternoon. There's a desire on the part of some of us who get up and pay our dues every day, facing the certainty of taxes along with the certainty of death, to look with Schadenfreude *at the misfortunes of people like Marks – the seemingly carefree chancers and scammers of life. Some people have a tendency to like it when these mickey-takers fall. So Howard Marks made great copy, especially when other newspaper pages featured the three-day week, power cuts, Britain's going cap-in-hand to the EMF, or the winter of discontent.*

But Marks' relentless optimism was also a way to cope with life on the run. He must have sometimes thought it would have been much easier to have settled down, and probably would have done just about anything for a quiet life, or certainly time with his growing family, especially when banged up in the hardcore Terre Haute prison in Florida. Then again, it must ease a lot of your melancholy to be sitting in a Swiss café, pondering your lot when you glance at the bank across the square, wonder for a second what is familiar about it, and then recall that you deposited rather a large sum of money in a numbered account there some years ago.

Marks was a guy for whom multiple passports were normal ("Mr Nice" being a black-market alias over which he had no choice), who experimented with changing his appearance like he was going after an academy award, and who wore the need to keep running lightly. A scholarship boy at Oxford's Balliol College and then a postgraduate student at Sussex University, he drifted into the drug culture of the late 1960s. Then, stepping into the breach to track down a drug-dealer friend who had gone missing, he was offered an opportunity too good to resist, that would change the course of his life and turn it into a roller-coaster ride that was by turns exhilarating and vertiginously scary.

This extract follows the start of Howard Marks' career, beginning with the normality of his life at the time and the conventional if lucky educational choices he faced. The languid world of a bright young man with options at the end of the 1960s seems like a good point of departure for the larger-than-life stories that follow, both in this extract and in the others in this book.

Marks embraced scamming, liked people, and relished the bizarre cast of characters to which he was being introduced (and about whom he writes so well). There's Mac, the shady "secret squirrel" from MI6 who recruits Marks as an asset, and the larger-than-life McCann, self-confessed PIRA contact from Northern Ireland who may turn out, one hopes, to be something of a Walter Mitty after all. There's Ernie Combs who, together with the mysterious drug-runner Eric, was Marks' freewheeling California contact, for whom hospitality was never too much trouble.

In fact, it was America's DEA who would put an end to Marks' years as a smuggler, organizing his arrest in Majorca in 1988.

America's tough extradition laws allow a request to be made to a foreign country not only for crimes committed on US soil, but also for crimes committed outside the US where the US government believes that collateral harm has occurred inside the country. American law enforcement had kept Marks on its radar ever since hashish had been discovered inside rock-band speaker cabinets in September 1973. DEA agent Craig Lavato's side of the story is covered in the book Hunting Marco Polo *by Paul Eddy and Sarah Walden.*

Marks' private life became necessarily peripatetic, putting a strain on his relationship with girlfriend Rosie, with whom he had a daughter Myfanwy.

Then there's Marks' ex-wife Judy, who married him while he was on the run and juggled raising their three children with the busy life of an international fugitive, often while Howard was away, whether on business or (for the lion's share) in custody. When the US sought their extradition from their Spanish island home, it ended with Judy Marks serving a prison sentence in a tough Madrid jail, after her own spell in custody in Miami, and Howard being spirited into the US without the necessary paperwork. Marks was sentenced to twenty-five years, of which he served seven and was paroled in 1995. He claims to have survived prison with his "usual trick of being excessively friendly and polite".

Judy Marks wrote her own memoir, Mr Nice and Mrs Marks, about her life on the run with Howard. A film based on both books is currently in production, reportedly starring Rhys Ifans and Chloe Sevigny.

Howard Marks' story is of its time, featuring tales of druggie derring-do that would not be possible now. One can read it with nostalgia for the era of travel before 9/11, when suitcases could be swapped on baggage carousels; when the idea of the nation state was still strong enough that countries did not routinely share information with each other, it was up to each country to regulate its own banking system, and privacy was still held to be an important part of customer service where those banks were concerned. As Iain Sinclair pointed out in the London Review of Books, "If he has revised the past, it is only to protect the guilty . . ."

I hated Sussex University. By this time, I had a firm idea of what a university should be like, and Sussex didn't come up to it. Every room had a number rather than a name. There was no romance about studying in an office-block library. One couldn't lie back and think that this was where, in the past, great minds produced great ideas. My supervisor was a Polish logician named Jerzy Giedymin. He was reckoned to be brilliant, but only in areas that no one else could test. I found him very difficult to understand, whatever he was talking about. He made it plain he had no interest in irrelevancies such as confirmation paradoxes. I made it plain I had no interest in studying his irrelevant obsessions. He said I should never have left Oxford. I said he was right.

I was still getting the Thomas and Elizabeth Williams Scholarship *[a school bursary for bright lads off to university, that Marks had secured]* and spent the first term's instalment on a new stereo system. The next few months were devoted to listening to Led Zeppelin, Blind Faith, Jethro Tull, and Black Sabbath. I decided to give up academic life and withdrew from the University of Sussex. Ilze's schoolteacher's salary was barely enough to live on but I managed to make up the shortcomings to almost survival level by getting more hashish from Graham Plinston, who often came down to Brighton for a weekend by the sea and a game of Go, at which we were both now becoming proficient. Graham had visited Morocco, where he met Lebanese Joe. Joe's mother was an entertainer in Beirut. Joe knew Sam Hiraoui, who worked for the Lebanese airline, Middle East Airlines. Sam also had a textile business in Dubai, the great Middle East gold- and silver-smuggling port on the Persian Gulf. Sam's partner in Dubai was an Afghani named Mohammed Durrani. Graham explained that through these people he was being delivered fifty pounds of black Pakistani hashish every month or so. For the first time, I imagined what an interesting and rewarding life a smuggler's must be. But Graham was merely treating me as a confidant. He was not making me any propositions. I was just another provincial dealer selling a couple of pounds a year to survive and not wanting to do too much other than survive.

Graham Plinston's wife, Mandy, telephoned. She asked if I could come up to London to see her as soon as possible. When I got there, Mandy was distraught and crying.

"Howard, Graham has disappeared. There's something wrong. I think he's been busted. Can you go and find out? You can have all the expenses you need."

"Where is he, Mandy?"

"He's got to be somewhere in Germany."

"Why do you want me to go?"

"You're the straightest of Graham's friends. You don't have a record or a file on you. Can you imagine what our other friends are like? Graham was meant to meet this German guy Klaus Becker in Frankfurt. He'll probably be able to help you find Graham."

"All right, I'll go."

I had never flown before, and I was excited throughout the flight. At his house, Klaus told me that there'd been a bust in Lorrach, a Swiss-German border town near Basle. He suspected the person busted was Graham. I flew from Frankfurt to Basle on a scary propeller plane. Not speaking a word of German hindered progress somewhat, but I was eventually able to get newspaper back-issues from the Basle public library and found a report of the bust. Graham had been driving a Mercedes from Geneva to Frankfurt. A hundred pounds of hashish had been stuffed under the back seat and in the door panels. At the Swiss-German border, the car had been searched and the hashish found. Graham was in Lorrach prison.

I took a cab to Lorrach and walked around the streets until I found a lawyer. He went to see Graham in prison and agreed to defend him. Graham had no messages. When I arrived back at London airport, I telephoned Mandy and gave her the Lorrach lawyer's particulars.

"Is he all right, Howard?" Mandy asked.

"The lawyer said he looked fine."

"Did he have any messages for me? Anything he wants me to do?"

"He didn't have any messages for anyone, Mandy."

"Howard, would you mind going over to see a friend of Graham's and telling him what happened on your trip? He's a good guy, but he's a bit concerned about what's happened and wants to hear everything from the horse's mouth."

"I don't mind, Mandy. Where do I go?"

"Mayfair, 17 Curzon Street. His name's Durrani."

Mohammed Durrani was the grandson of the brother

of the former King of Afghanistan. Educated in Delhi, he served eleven years on the Hong Kong Police Force and had several shady businesses throughout the East. One of them was supplying Pakistani hashish to Europe. Durrani let me in to his Mayfair flat. He had a hawk-like face, Savile Row suit, beautifully manicured fingernails, and wore strong aftershave. He poured me a Johnnie Walker Black Label whisky and offered me a Benson & Hedges from his gold, monogrammed cigarette case. He lit my cigarette with a Dupont lighter, introduced me to Sam Hiraoui, his Lebanese partner, and said, "Thank you, Howard, for agreeing to come. We have simple question. Has Graham talked?"

"He said he didn't have any messages for anyone," I answered.

"We mean to the German police."

"I don't know."

"The reason we ask, Howard, is that we have merchandise in the pipeline which might be compromised by our friend's arrest. You are best friend, Mandy says. Do you think he would let police know anything about our operations?"

"Not deliberately, obviously, if that's what you mean."

"That is what we mean."

"In that case, no. He hasn't talked. But here's all the newspaper reports, lawyers' papers, etc. Maybe these will help you."

"You have been very efficient, Howard, very efficient," said Durrani. "We are much in debt to you. It is possible, *inshallah*, that we may have merchandise to sell in England when Graham is in German prison. Are you interested?"

"I don't have any money, but I am honoured you ask me."

"We would give you 100 per cent credit," said Lebanese Sam. "Simply sell it, keep your commission, and give us the agreed amount of money."

"I'm not really that kind of dealer, Sam. Graham would give me a pound or two to sell every couple of weeks. That's it. I've never done any real business of any kind."

"Surely you must be knowing people who are buying merchandise?" Durrani asked.

"No, I don't."

"But you were at the Oxford University with Graham, no?"

"Yes, we were at Oxford together, but it's not much of a business school." *[That was then, of course. The Said Business School might contest that today.]*

"It is world's best, Howard. Graham sells his merchandise to people from the Oxford University."

"That's very probable. Can't you get hold of any of them to sell your stuff?"

"We know only David Pollard, and he is now crazy man."

I knew David Pollard. He was an exact contemporary of mine at some Oxford college other than Balliol. He too read Physics and was by no means crazy, though he was a little eccentric and had recently suffered tragic circumstances. In fact he was brilliant and invented all sorts of things from kidney dialysis machines to LSD manufacturing accessories, as well as pioneering the first British joint-sized rolling papers, Esmeralda. His girlfriend, Barbara Mayo, had gone hitch-hiking on the M6 motorway, and had been raped and murdered. The police never found the killer, but David was routinely grilled and treated as the prime suspect. The police finally let him go, and he threw his LSD manufacturing plant into the Thames. I had no idea he was Graham's main wholesaler.

"Jarvis once came out to Beirut to see me," said Sam, "but I have no idea where to get hold of him. Neither does Mandy. I don't think he was at Oxford University, but Graham sells to him."

I had met Jarvis a few times with Graham. He was a state-of-the-art London Sixties dealer: shaded glasses, pop-singer clothes, model girlfriends, and lots of new vocabulary. He hailed from Birmingham but spoke Chelsea.

"No, he wasn't at Oxford, but I could probably track him down."

"Good," said Durrani. "We look forward to good business. I will ask Mandy to call you when we are ready."

The German and Mayfair experiences filled me with a new kind of energy and excitement. So much of me longed for more of this adventure. I thought of things I could buy with a lot of money.

Back in Brighton, I saw lots more of Rosie and little of anyone else. I told her about my recent adventures and the proposition I'd been made.

"That's wonderful, Howard," said Rosie, "that's obviously what you should do. Get out there and be somebody in your one and only life. I think selling Durrani's hashish in London is a brilliant idea. It's what you've been waiting for, isn't it?"

"I don't know. I just don't have any money to set myself up. I'd need a flat in London, a car other than my beaten-up Hillman, operating expenses, all kinds of things, let alone money to live on."

"Howard, I don't know about you and Ilze. But Richard and I are not going to carry on pretending to be living with and loving each other. We're separating. My family has money. His family has a lot more, and they will certainly make sure that Emily, their granddaughter, will be properly provided for. I'm going to move to London. My parents will rent me a flat and buy me a car. You can stay there any time you want, use the car; and if you need to borrow a couple of hundred pounds to set up a business, I couldn't think of a better investment for me to make."

In a whirlwind of love, romance, and unlimited possibility, Rosie, her baby daughter Emily and I moved to a maisonette in Hillsleigh Road in the expensive part of Notting Hill. Richard would visit and play Go. We have remained very good friends. Ilze would also visit, and although we both felt somewhat betrayed by each other's infidelity, we remained on the very best terms.

During my postgraduate year at Oxford, I had met and liked a friend of Graham's called Charlie Radcliffe. He was from an aristocratic background, had an enormous collection of Blues records, chain-smoked marijuana, belonged to the Campaign for Nuclear Disarmament, and had been busted for forging a staggering quantity of first-class counterfeit United States one-hundred-dollar bills with the words "In God We Trust" replaced by an anti-Vietnam war slogan. He worked then for Robert Maxwell's publishing company, Pergamon Press, in Headington, just outside Oxford. Now Charlie, too, was living in London, and when he heard of Graham's bust, he tracked me down to get what news he could. I told him what I knew and mentioned the possibility of my being asked to sell Graham's hashish in his absence. I asked if he could help me out by either selling some or getting hold of Jarvis, whom Charlie knew quite well. Charlie was eager to make some money but explained that he had a partner, Charlie Weatherley, who would have to be involved. I had met Charlie Weatherley a few times when he was an undergraduate at Christ Church. He was now a heavy hashish-consuming biker and, when not pushing his Norton Commando to the limit, listened continually with amusement to The Grateful Dead. He was a joy to be around. Charlie Radcliffe and I decided that the simplest and fairest arrangement for all concerned was that Jarvis, the two Charlies, and I form a syndicate to market Durrani's hashish. My initial responsibility would be to receive the hashish from Durrani and store it at Hillsleigh Road. Jarvis and the two Charlies would sell the hashish to their various dealer connections. I would then be expected to take the money to Durrani after splitting the profit four ways. We were ready. All we needed was the hashish.

No hashish materialized. Durrani never got in touch, and Graham was released after serving a six-month sentence. Throughout that six-month period, however, partly because of the conveniences provided by the Hillsleigh Road maisonette and partly, I'm sure, by the continual hope of Durrani coming through with large amounts, our newly formed syndicate operated as arranged with hashish from other sources. Through these dealings, I became acquainted with Duncan Laurie, a major hashish importer who had set up the Forbidden Fruit chain of Sixties boutiques in the King's Road and Portobello Road, Lebanese Joe, the person responsible for Graham's knowing Durrani, and James Goldsack, David Pollard's dealing partner. Essentially, I was making money and connections by sticking Rosie's neck on the line and mercilessly using her accommodation, car, and telephone.

But I was also able to buy a few pounds of hashish at the best prices, and these I would sell in quarter-pounds and ounces to university dealers and friends in Oxford, Brighton, London, and Bristol, where my sister was doing a French degree.

Graham had hatched up several plans while incarcerated. Some were hindered by his inability to enter Germany without first paying his rather hefty fine. I agreed to take £5,000 of Graham's money to Frankfurt to give to Lebanese Sam. He would then take care of the fine. Currency restrictions made it illegal to take more than £25 out of the country, so I stuck the money down the back of my trousers and checked in at Heathrow. A couple of policemen did an unexpected anti-terrorist passenger search. Before I had time to realize the danger I was in, I had been incredibly inefficiently searched and motioned through the boarding gate. I didn't feel relief. I just felt a bit dazed and confused.

On the way back the next morning, I hid the receipt for the fine payment and £300 generously given me by Sam in my sock. I bought some duty-free perfumes for Rosie. Customs stopped me at Heathrow.

"Where have you come from, sir?"

"Frankfurt."

"Is this all your luggage?" he asked, pointing to my small briefcase and plastic bag of perfume bottles.

"Yes."

"Did you buy these perfumes duty-free?"

"Yes, at Frankfurt airport."

"Do you realize, sir, that it is illegal to buy duty-free items if out of the country for less than twenty-four hours?"

"Yes," I lied.

"How long have you been abroad?"

"Two days," I lied again.

"Would you mind opening your briefcase, sir? I would just like to have a quick look."

The briefcase contained only my used airline ticket, a toothbrush, and a book appropriately entitled *The Philosophy of Time.*

"Travelling light, sir?"

"I stayed at a friend's house. I didn't need to bring anything."

The Customs Officer picked up my used airline ticket and looked at the dates.

"I thought you said you had been gone for two days. This ticket shows you left London last night."

"Yes, two days: yesterday and today."

"Would you come this way, sir?"

The Customs Officer led me to a cold, breeze-blocked room.

"Let me see your passport. Thank you. Would you mind taking off your clothes?"

"Of course I mind."

"Mr Marks, if you have no contraband, you have nothing to fear."

"I have no contraband, and I have nothing to fear. But I'm not taking my clothes off."

I was beginning to worry about the £300 in my sock. If it was illegal to take £25 cash out, then it surely must be illegal to bring in twelve times that amount, or was it?

"Then you leave me no choice. I will hold you both for attempting to smuggle perfume into the United Kingdom and on suspicion of carrying other contraband. You either let me strip-search you now or the police will do so when I put you in their cells."

"I'll take the second option."

"That's up to you. There is another alternative. You declare what contraband you have to me and hand it over. If I accept your declaration as true, we'll deal with the matter without strip-searching."

"I've got £300 in my sock," I stupidly confessed.

"Show me."

I took off my shoe and sock and gave him the bundle of fifteen twenty-pound notes and the fine-payment receipt.

"Did you take this money out of the country, sir?" There didn't seem much point in admitting that fact.

"No. A friend gave it to me in Frankfurt. I didn't know what else to do with it. Is it illegal to bring back money, too, if I've been away for just a short time?"

"No, Mr Marks, bringing sterling into the country is not illegal, but taking more than a certain amount out of the country is. Why did you put it in your sock? So we wouldn't see it?"

"Just for safe-keeping, I suppose."

"Is this receipt also in your sock for safe-keeping? What is your occupation?"

"Well, I'm sort of unemployed at the moment, but usually I'm a teacher."

"Who is Kenneth Graham Plinston?" he asked, looking at the name on the receipt.

"Just a friend, really. He owed some money in Germany and asked me to sort it out."

"You always pay off his debts? Are you that well paid as a teacher?"

"No, I used his money. It was his friend who gave me the money in Frankfurt."

"What was this friend's name?"

"Sal." I knew I had to lie on that one.

"Italian, is he?"

"I think so."

"Just one moment, Mr Marks."

The Customs Officer left with the receipt. After several minutes, he returned with a senior official-looking man in plain clothes.

"Good morning, Mr Marks. I'm with Her Majesty's Customs and Excise Special Investigative Branch. We are going to charge you the duty on the perfume you bought. In the matter of the £300, we can't touch you. Here it is. We know your friend Mr Plinston. We know how he makes his money. We trust you aren't going the same way. Stick to teaching."

Graham seemed totally unperturbed when I got to his house and gave him the receipt and report of my brush with the law.

"I don't think there's much to worry about there, Howard. We're friends, and that's that."

"I'm not worried about it," I said. "I'm just telling you what happened. I really couldn't care less."

"That's good. Howard, something's just come up. Would you

like to make quite a decent sum of money by doing a couple of days' work in Germany driving some hash around to various friends of mine?"

"Graham, I've never driven abroad. I can't imagine driving on the wrong side of the road."

"There's always a first time."

"Maybe, but it shouldn't be when I've got dope in the car."

"Couldn't you hire someone, Howard, to be your driver? I'll be paying you plenty."

"Yeah, I'm pretty sure I could do that."

"Okay, Howard, I'll call you from Frankfurt in a few days when I'm ready."

Neither Jarvis nor the two Charlies were interested in venturing from the Royal Borough of Kensington and Chelsea. It was too much of a disruption. However, Charlie Radcliffe's attractive lady, Tina, had a New Zealand friend called Lang. He had years of all kinds of smuggling experience and was in London looking for work. He was more than happy with the German proposition. We agreed to split profits.

Lang and I met Graham in Frankfurt airport. Graham explained that a ton of Pakistani hashish was in a lock-up garage. The assignment was to rent an appropriate vehicle, go to the garage, load up the hashish, deliver some to a group of Californians in a predetermined lay-by, some to a couple of Germans in Frankfurt, and the rest to a group of Dutchmen at a pre-arranged location in the middle of the Black Forest. Lang and I would be paid £5,000 between us.

We rented an Opel estate car with massive space for baggage. The lock-up garage was in an expensive suburb of Wiesbaden. Inside the garage were twenty fifty-kilo wooden boxes with "streptomycin, Karachi" stencilled on each. The smell of hashish was overpowering. We loaded up the Opel, covered the boxes with a rug, and drove to the lay-by. A couple of Cheech and Chong lookalikes were waiting in a large saloon car. We pulled up alongside. One of the Californians jumped out and opened the boot. Lang and I opened the back of the Opel, and the three of us transferred five of the twenty boxes to the saloon. We shook hands. The saloon car drove off.

The Dutch and Germans were not ready to receive their hashish. Lang and I had to kill a few days. We drove the Opel from Wiesbaden, along the banks of the Rhine, to a village called Osterich.

There we checked into a hotel, curiously named, in English, The White Swan. We wined and dined and broke into one of the boxes. We got stoned.

The day before the rendezvous with the Dutch, we took a boat down the Rhine to Wiesbaden. Lang wanted to get some English newspapers. While we were crossing one of the city's main streets, a car came quickly round the corner, shot the red pedestrian light, and almost knocked Lang over. In a moment of understandable anger, Lang hit the back of the car with a rolled-up newspaper. The car screamed to a halt. A huge red-faced German jumped out of the car, ran over to Lang, gave him a tremendous thump across the head sending his glasses splintering on the road, ran back into the car, and drove off. It was all over in seconds. Lang was barely conscious and was blind without his glasses.

"You'll have to drive tomorrow, mate," was all he said.

The rendezvous with the Dutch was at a remote but accessible clearing in the Black Forest. With fear and apprehension, I drove the hashish-filled Opel into the country's wooded depths. It took no time to adjust to driving on the other side. We got to the clearing. There was no one there. After twenty minutes, two Volvos arrived. Inside one was Dutch Nik, whom I'd once met at Graham's. Inside the other was a man who introduced himself as Dutch Peter. We gave them thirteen boxes.

At an efficient German chemist's, Lang soon fixed himself up with a pair of new prescription glasses and was able to drive the Opel into Frankfurt for the final drop-off to an unnamed German in the car park of the Intercontinental Hotel. It passed without incident.

Graham had been supervising matters from his room in the Frankfurter Hof. He had bought a new BMW. He asked if we wanted to keep him company for a few days, after which he would pay us off. Lang wanted to get back to London and was happy to be paid there. I stayed with Graham, who was collecting bags of money. After a couple of days, we hid the money, a mixture of United States dollars and German marks, in the BMW, and drove to Geneva. Graham banked large quantities of German and American cash in his Swiss bank account after first giving me our payment. I asked what happened to the hashish we had distributed and was told that the German would be selling his hashish in Frankfurt, the Californians would buy brand-new European cars and ship them stuffed with hashish to Los Angeles, while Dutch Nik and Dutch Pete would be driving the 650 kilos of hashish they received to England. I asked who would be selling the hashish once it got to England. I presumed Graham would now revert to using David Pollard and James Goldsack. Graham smiled.

"You will be, Howard."

"But I know that in the past you've used Dave Pollard and James. I don't want to cause problems."

"Howard, I also used to use Jarvis and the two Charlies. London dealing is musical chairs. Anyway, Dave Pollard is out of business. You can keep James happy by letting him have some hash to sell at a good price."

Jarvis, the two Charlies, and I sold the 650 kilos of hashish and made about £20,000 profit between us. I had made £7,500 in just one week. For the first time ever, I felt rich and gradually began to get used to a lifestyle of fast cars, expensive restaurants and gadgetry. I bought a brand-new BMW, record- and cassette-playing equipment of all descriptions, and a waterbed. Rosie suggested we rent a flat in Brighton to use at weekends and other periods when I wasn't tied up moving hash around London. She still had friends in Brighton and missed the proximity of the sea.

We rented a ground-floor flat at 14 Lewes Crescent. One of Rosie's friends was Patrick Lane, ex-Sussex University English Literature graduate working as an accountant for Price Waterhouse Ltd. Patrick and I got on well with each other. He introduced me to his seventeen-year-old sister Judy. Her smile, her waist-length hair, and her long legs tantalizingly stayed in my mind. It wasn't long before I invited Patrick to participate with me in Graham's next proposal.

Mohammed Durrani had a variety of ways of getting hashish into Europe. The most common was in the personal effects of Pakistani diplomats taking up positions in Pakistani embassies and consular offices throughout Europe. Durrani would arrange with the diplomat to put about a ton of hashish into the diplomat's personal furniture and belongings before they left Pakistan. A diplomat's personal effects would be unlikely to be searched on arrival, and he could always claim diplomatic immunity or blame it on the Pakistani shippers if the dope was accidentally discovered.

On this occasion, the personal effects had been delivered to the diplomat's residence in Bonn. Patrick and I had to rifle through the cabin trunks, remove the hashish, and drive it to a disused gravel pit near Cologne, where Dutch Nik, Dutch Pete and other Dutch would pick it up and smuggle it to England. Everything went without a hitch, and after taking care of sales in London, I'd made another £7,500.

Graham had made a great deal more and was intent on legitimizing his hard-earned money in the form of respectable London businesses. He had met Patrick and liked him. He needed a bent accountant and felt Patrick would be ideal. I could see no disadvantage.

Soon Graham and Patrick had established a carpet shop, Hamdullah, and a property company, Zeitgeist, at 3 Warwick Place, Little Venice. They carried appropriate business cards, which they flashed at every opportunity.

My lifestyle went from expensive to outrageously flamboyant. In London, Brighton, Oxford and Bristol, I would pick up the tab at every bar and restaurant I visited. Any of my friends who wished to merely smoke hashish rather than sell it would be given as much as they wanted free of charge. There are few things that give me more pleasure in life than getting people very stoned and giving them good food and wine, but meanwhile I could see very well the sense of using some of my money to set myself up in the way Graham was doing. It would have to be on a smaller scale, but in principle it could be done.

Redmond and Belinda O'Hanlon were undergraduate friends of mine at Oxford. Redmond was now at St

Anthony's doing a D.Phil. on Darwin's effect on nineteenth-century English literature while Belinda was running a small dressmaking business with Anna Woodhead, the Spanish wife of Anthony Woodhead, another Oxford undergraduate friend. Their clientele were largely Oxford University ladies looking for suitable ball dresses. Anna and Belinda were badly under-capitalized. I gave them the impression that I had recently inherited some money. We agreed to go into business together from small, tucked-away premises near Oxford railway station. Using cash, I bought a bunch of sewing machines and formed a company, AnnaBelinda Ltd. It immediately did well, and we looked for suitable street-front rental premises to open up a boutique. We found them at 6 Gloucester Street, where AnnaBelinda still stands.

A few more Durrani scams occurred, but they involved significantly smaller amounts. Occasionally I would drive a stashed car across a European border. I'd get a religious flash and an asexual orgasm every time I did. Marty Langford and a couple of other Kenfig Hill school friends, Mike Bell and David Thomas, were also living in London doing boring and menial jobs. I gave each the opportunity of working for me moving and stashing hashish, taking telephone calls, and counting money. Each took it, and I was no longer exposing the London flat to the dangers inherent in street dealing: they were exposing theirs. The four of us were probably London's only Welsh criminal gang, and were jokingly referred to by our fellow dealers as the Tafia. It was dangerous fun.

But I was spending almost as much as I was earning. Thousands of pounds a month were not enough.

In early 1973, I decided to invest some of the cardboard boxes of money in dope deals that didn't involve McCann. An old Oxford acquaintance had a friend, Eric, who claimed he could smuggle suitcases from Beirut to Geneva through a personal connection in Middle East Airlines. Eric needed to be supplied with the hashish in Beirut. Furthermore, if given a boatload of hashish on a Lebanese beach, Eric was prepared to sail it to Italy. I discussed these possibilities with Graham, and we agreed to begin work on them. We gave Eric a couple of hundred grand and told him to get on with it.

Graham also mentioned an idea he had been presented with. A friend of his, James Morris, was responsible for manufacturing and arranging the transport of pop group equipment to and from the United States. In those days, British pop was at its peak of excellence, and groups such as Pink Floyd, Genesis, and Emerson, Lake and Palmer would frequently tour America with container trucks full of enormous speakers and amplifiers. The equipment, because it was only temporarily imported into America, underwent minimal examination by United States Customs. If the paperwork was in order, the equipment went straight through. Although source countries like Pakistan and Lebanon · were not hosting British pop concerts, European countries were. Hashish was three times more expensive in America than in Europe. The scam was obvious. Fill the speakers with hash in a European country. Airfreight them across the Atlantic. Take the hashish out in America. Put bricks back in the speakers to avoid the possibility of weight discrepancies appearing on air waybills. Bring the speakers back across the Atlantic, and wait to get paid. Let's do it.

Mohammed Durrani was still coming up with Pakistani and Afghani diplomats who were moving several hundred kilos of hashish with their personal effects as they took up their positions in various Middle Eastern embassies throughout Europe; Lebanese Sam was doing the same thing with Lebanese diplomats and, of course, he was only too glad to supply Eric with any of his needs in Lebanon. One of Sam's contacts had just smuggled a few hundred kilos into Paris, and in March 1973 the first transatlantic rock-group scam took place. None of James Morris' rock groups were actually due to tour America at the time, so four out-of-work musicians were hurriedly banded together to form a group called Laughing Grass and behave as if they had an engagement in California. Rock bands were continually splitting up and reforming with slight personnel modifications: there should be no grounds for suspicion.

The speakers were loaded with hashish in the remote French countryside and air-freighted from Paris to Los Angeles, via

New York. It worked like a dream. Graham's Brotherhood of Eternal Love contact, Ernie Combs, sold the hashish in California. I occasionally talked to him over the telephone when Graham was unable to. Ernie was invariably happy, witty and extremely sharp. We developed an excellent telephonic rapport with each other.

A few weeks later, Mohammed Durrani came up with some Pakistani hashish in Vienna. This time we didn't even take the precaution of finding or creating a suitable touring British rock group. A name was written in the appropriate place on the Customs form, that was all. The hashish was again sent to Philadelphia. No problems.

Eric was as good as his word and turned up at Geneva airport with a hundred kilos of Lebanese hashish that Sam had provided outside Beirut airport. It wasn't enough to justify a rock-group scam, so I asked Anthony Woodhead to drive it from Switzerland to England. He did so without a hitch. I paid everybody off and asked them to do the same again. This they did several times, until Eric had to concentrate on his Mediterranean boat scam.

He was now in a position to pick up hashish off Lebanese Sam at the port of Juni, Lebanon.

During Eric's air-freight scams, I occasionally monitored his passage through Geneva airport. I noticed that some international flights had stopped in Zurich before the last leg to Geneva, and further noticed that suitcases checked in at Zurich emerged on arrival at Geneva on the same carousel as suitcases checked in at airports outside of Switzerland. This was worthy of focused investigation and I was delighted to discover the existence of a Swissair flight whose itinerary was Karachi-Zurich-Geneva. I flew the flight's Zurich-Geneva leg. At Geneva airport the immigration police asked to see my ticket. They gave it a cursory glance and let me through to pick up my luggage. There was no Customs check after baggage pick-up.

Graham and I sent Anthony Woodhead to Karachi and asked him to catch this potential goldmine of a Swissair flight just to see what would happen. I waited at Geneva airport. When Woodhead showed his ticket, they took him to the luggage carousel to identify his suitcase, which they then thoroughly searched. We sent Woodhead back out to Karachi and arranged with Durrani and Raoul to fill Woodhead's suitcase with hashish. Woodhead got on the Zurich-Geneva flight. In Zurich, I got on the same plane with another suitcase, which had previously been filled with Woodhead's effects. I got off the plane first and showed my ticket to the Geneva immigration police, who waved me through. I picked up Woodhead's suitcase of hashish from the luggage carousel and carried it out. Woodhead showed his ticket. Swiss Customs wanted to see his suitcase. He showed them mine and displayed its innocent contents. Later on, I gave him back his suitcase, and he drove the hashish to London. We repeated this a few times until the Swiss changed their Customs procedures, rendering the scam impossible.

Much as Graham and I were enjoying the lack of business with McCann, it was difficult to resist. We planned to send 1,500 kilos, our biggest load yet, to Shannon and deliver it to Moone. Some we would move in the usual way on the ferry to England. The rest we would take to another house in County Cork, rented by Woodhead, whose location was unknown to McCann, and air-freight it from Dublin to New York in James Morris' Transatlantic Sounds rock-group equipment. We could take care of paying McCann and the Pakistanis out of the British sales, and McCann wouldn't know we were making heaps more money by selling hashish in California. I was soon sitting on a ton and a half of Pakistani hashish in the curious Moone property, loading up the first drivers for the ferry before dashing to catch the next flight to London.

We couldn't use the Winchester garage as the British de-stashing point [. . . but] James Goldsack had his own facilities, so the first two carloads were sent across on the ferry to him while a few other carloads went to the place in County Cork. While selling the first carload, James Goldsack was busted. The second carload of hashish had been parked outside Hammersmith Police Station. James was being grilled inside the police station. In an extraordinary display of pure courage, Patrick Lane broke into the car and retrieved the hashish. I took it from Patrick to Rosie's cottage in Yarnton. I repackaged the hashish from its plastic wrappings into suitcases and threw the plastic wrappings on to a pile of litter on the country roadside. Transatlantic Sounds' rock-group equipment was sent from London to Cork, filled up with hashish at Woodhead's Irish country place, and air-freighted from Dublin to the United States.

We badly needed new de-stashing premises in England, so Marty rented a farmhouse near Trelleck in Monmouthshire. Hashish from Ireland and Oxford accumulated in Wales. Jarvis sold enough to pay off McCann, Pakistan and the drivers. The rock-group equipment was de-stashed in California by Ernie Combs and the Brotherhood of Eternal Love. Ernie sold the lot at three times the price we would have got in London in just one day. Greatly impressed, we filled some more Transatlantic Sounds speakers with what hashish was left in Marty's Trelleck farmhouse and sent them from Heathrow to Phoenix. We took a week's breather.

There were worries whether James Goldsack would talk. Would he blow the Irish scam? In fact James was as solid as a rock. He admitted being a hashish dealer and refused to testify against anyone else. Nothing seemed to be compromised. The Irish scam was still unknown to the authorities.

During the week's inactivity, I invited my parents and grandmother to visit Rosie, me and the children at the cottage in Yarnton. It was a warm spring Sunday afternoon. My grandmother was doting over little Myfanwy. Emily was playing dressing up with my father. Rosie and my mother discussed maternal matters. I was trying to stabilize. A police car drove up the little lane and pulled to a halt outside the cottage. Two members of the Thames Valley Constabulary emerged holding a few of the plastic wrappings I had just discarded on the roadside. I remained seated, paralyzed. My mother looked at me, puzzled and worried. She could tell I was uneasy.

"Does someone called Emily live here?" asked one of the policemen, unexpectedly.

"Yes, that's my daughter. Why?" Rosie was unshaken.

"Is this envelope hers?" asked the policeman, pulling out a small envelope addressed to Emily at Yarnton.

I then realized what must have happened. Emily, in childish

innocence, must have stuffed one of her letters into the waste-bag containing the hashish wrappings. Instead of taking the wrappings to a rubbish dump or burning them, I had stupidly thrown them away at the roadside. Someone had discovered them. The wrappings were full of crumbs of cannabis, covered with my fingerprints and accompanied by an envelope which had been in my house. This could be serious.

"Yes, it is. Where did you get it?"

Rosie was still completely unshaken. Did she realize the danger we were in?

"It was with these, ma'am," said the policeman, holding up some plastic wrappings.

"Have you seen these before?" the second policeman addressed the family group as a whole.

"Well, no," said my mother.

"We've just arrived from South Wales, Officer," said my father. "How would we know anything?"

Dad was always firm with police.

My grandmother kept playing with Myfanwy as if the policemen did not exist. The first policeman looked me directly in the eyes.

"What about you, sir? Familiar to you, are they? Obviously, they came from here, didn't they?"

"No, I've never seen them before."

"Oh! Now I remember," interjected Rosie with first-class criminal inspiration. "The man who came to fix the damp course last week had a big bag of these wrappings left over when he'd finished doing his work. I suppose all the chemicals he used must have been in them."

"I don't suppose you have his name and number, ma'am."

"I certainly do; I was going to call him anyway. His work was so shoddily done."

Rosie gave the policemen the name and number. They shot off to harass some poor damp-course man. I excused myself on the pretext of having to attend to important matters at AnnaBelinda, sped off down the M40 to London, and checked into Blake's Hotel, Roland Gardens, under the name of Stephen McCarthy.

I was sure the police would return to Yarnton and was

haunted by images of Rosie in a police cell and two little girls crying in intense fear and sadness. Rosie was easily persuaded to leave the country, and in my BMW, she, the two little girls, and a wonderful nanny named Vicky drove to Ibiza and rented a house in Santa Eulalia. I stayed at Blake's.

I had to find out what was going on and thought maybe Mac would help. I called the Foreign Office and arranged to meet him. I told him what had happened at Yarnton. Later on the same day, we met again.

"Did you find anything out, Mac?"

"I certainly did. You can rest assured that the police are not minded to arrest you. Feel free to go home. But I want you to meet one of my superiors, tomorrow, if possible. He has some questions for you."

"What kind of questions?"

"He mentioned Ireland."

"Mac, I can't talk about that. It involves my dope-dealing business."

"Howard, I assure you we are not interested in your smuggling of cannabis. That is of no concern to us. Other matters in Ireland may be."

"Like what?"

"Donald will explain to you tomorrow."

Donald, a stern-faced, well-dressed spy, Mac, and I met for lunch at the Pillars of Hercules, just off Soho Square. Donald came to the point.

"We know you have been meeting a member of the Provisional IRA who supplies them with arms and know why you have been meeting him. We would like you to carry on meeting him to get some information from him."

"Well, I have no plans to see him again right now."

"That's fine. But when you do, let McMillan here know."

"Sure."

Mac and I went to his home in Putney. We had a whisky each in his sitting room.

"Howard, this might clear up any uncertainties," said Mac, producing a photograph. I looked at it. It was a picture of

McCann with his name underneath. Mac took it back from me
and went into his study to make a phone call.

There was no doubt in my mind that I had to let McCann
know MI6 were on his case. If MI6 knew he was dope-dealing,
the IRA would soon get to know, and McCann might get
executed. No more Shannon deals. They had to stop. It was
just too dangerous, too heavy. Where had all that peace and
love stuff gone? Arms smuggling, Bloody Sunday, executions
and kneecappings. Ernie's Brotherhood of Eternal Love came
far closer to traditional dope-dealing values of sex, drugs and
rock 'n' roll; and they could make far more money. No more
McCann. I would warn him of the danger, then get out of his
life. I wanted that photograph of him so he would know I wasn't
playing games.

Mac returned. I asked if I could telephone AnnaBelinda. He
motioned me towards his study, and I made my phone call,
letting my eyes roam over Mac's bookshelves. A book named
The Unconscious Mind snatched my attention. I picked it up,
opened it and the photograph of McCann fell out. I put it into
my pocket. That has remained the most inexplicable event in
my life. Feeling noble and resolute, I left Blake's and went back
to Yarnton. I cabled Rosie to call me and told her it was safe
for her to come back. She said she didn't want to come back.
Life in Ibiza was far more meaningful: sun, stars, beaches, and
lots of dope to smoke. She suggested that before I turn into a
money-making megalomaniac and lose all my friends, I should
join her in Ibiza. But I should promise not to bring with me any
of my fucked-up lifestyle. She'd made some wonderful friends
who wouldn't appreciate it. I could tell I was losing her. I went
to visit Fanny Hill and began a very clandestine affair with her.
At the same time, she was having a less clandestine affair with
Raymond Carr, the Master of St Anthony's College, Oxford's
CIA annexe.

I went to Ibiza and thought it would make a good neutral
venue to meet McCann.

"Why the fuck have you dragged me here, H'ard, in the
middle of all this hippie shit? You know I'm busy. Why couldn't
you have come to Ireland? This had better be important."

"It is, Jim. MI6 are on to you."

"Who the fuck cares? There's a war going on. And what the fuck's MI6 got to do with you, you Welsh cunt?"

"An old Oxford friend of mine works for them. They know you and I have been dope-dealing. If they know, other people know, like maybe the IRA."

Jim went white.

"Fuck off! Fuck off, will you! You're playing fucking games."

I showed him the photograph.

"You and Soppy Bollocks, I knew you were fucking Brit agents. I knew it. How can I know you haven't been setting The Kid up all along?"

"Try thinking, Jim,"

"Fuck you!"

"This is it, Jim. No more deals for a while."

"Okay, H'ard. But I'm staying here in Ibiza for a while for a holiday. My new Dutch girlfriend, Sylvia, and my old Irish girlfriend, Anne, are coming over. We'll stop with you."

"I thought you were busy, Jim."

In a couple of days, Rosie's Santa Eulalia holiday house had turned into a madhouse. McCann was playing musical beds with Sylvia and Anne, unsuccessfully encouraging Rosie and Vicky to do the same, and forever filling the house with various odd characters he picked up in the bars in Ibiza. He was making me laugh, so I didn't mind. I called AnnaBelinda in Oxford. There was a message to phone Eric in Athens. I knew Eric had picked up the hashish from Lebanon. He must have already landed it in Italy, where Johnny Martin had rented a villa in preparation to receive both the dope and Transatlantic Sounds rock-group equipment.

Great!

It wasn't great. Eric said that there'd been a slight problem. I should come to Athens now. I packed my bags, and Rosie exploded.

"That's right. Leave me in the middle of all this chaos you've brought to ruin my holiday. I told you not to do this. Where are you going?"

"Athens. Fancy coming? Vicky can look after the children."

The "slight problem" was that Eric had temporarily stashed 700 pounds of Lebanese hashish on a remote Greek island. A herd of goats had unearthed the dope, which was spotted by some Greek sponge fishermen. The sponge fishermen had taken the hashish to Crete and were selling it at absurdly cheap prices. I knew Eric was telling me the truth. Eric's solution was to launch a commando-style attack in Crete and recover the hashish. I told him to forget it, but if he ever did get it back, I'd like some. After a quick tour of the Acropolis, Rosie and I flew back to Ibiza.

Graham favoured a commando solution and wanted to proposition McCann. I persuaded him not to. With no other means at his disposal, he sent Patrick Lane to Heraklion. A week later, Patrick returned with a suntan, lots of tall stories, and no dope, but I'm sure he did his best.

Graham told Ernie that the Italian speaker shipment was off. Ernie said it wasn't: some friends of his were soon to arrive in Italy having driven from Kabul in a camper stashed with Afghani hash. One of his friends was a draft-dodging Californian Scientologist named James Gater. James Morris and I met Gater at Johnny Martin's rented villa in Cupra Maritima, near Ancona, on the Adriatic coast. We de-stashed the camper that had come from Afghanistan, put the hashish into Transatlantic Sounds speakers, and air-freighted it to Los Angeles from Rome. James Morris and I caught a flight from Rome to Zurich, where he introduced me to his Swiss banker. I opened up an account at the Swiss Bank Corporation. The banker assured me there would be no problem in my depositing large amounts of cash. Ernie gave me 100,000 dollars for my assistance. Graham said I could keep it all. He wouldn't interfere with any deal I made with Ernie as long as I did not interfere with deals he intended doing with McCann. We would remain partners on all other deals and could invest in each other's individual deals without participation. I agreed but couldn't help worrying about Graham. He was changing from a bourgeois, middle-class monarchist buccaneer to the exact opposite. That was okay, but he was doing it too quickly and doing it under the influence of McCann. God knows what

McCann had in mind but it wouldn't have been Graham's political development.

In Ibiza, Rosie had given up the Santa Eulalia holiday house and rented a *finca* in the middle of nowhere. She was going back to nature. There wasn't even a bathroom or toilet, and it was several miles from a telephone. I put up with it for a while. Rosie and I were getting on well again. We had confessed our infidelities and were pretending they didn't matter. She introduced me to one of many Dutchmen who had places on the island. His name was Arend, and he was a heavy-drinking, fun-loving dope dealer from Amsterdam. I asked him what sort of prices and quantities normally prevailed in Amsterdam. I reported them to Ernie. He sent over Gater and another friend of his, Gary Lickert, to Amsterdam with several hundred thousand dollars, and Arend and I invested some money of our own. Gater rented a flat in Maastricht, near Utrecht. A hired truck full of Transatlantic Sounds speakers was parked outside. Arend and I purchased 700 pounds of Lebanese hashish from an Amsterdam wholesaler friend of his. Gater and I stashed the speakers, and one of James Morris' people drove the truck to Schiphol Airport and air-freighted them to Las Vegas via New York.

It was early September 1973, and Ernie had invited me to come over to California once the Dutch load had been sent. I could pick up my own profit and maybe spend some of it. I was in Los Angeles before the speakers arrived at Las Vegas. Ernie and James Morris met me at the airport. Ernie was tall, thin, bearded, bespectacled, long-haired, and suntanned. He was Californian.

"Hi. How you doing? Have a good flight?"

"Yeah. It was long, though."

Ernie thought for a second, then machine-gunned a few sentences.

"Shit! I used to do that son-of-a-bitch once a week when I was working with Graham in the early days. What's his beef, these days? He's been really kinda rude to me. I get pissed with that. Well, we should pick up our load from Las Vegas airport tonight. You're booked into the Newporter Inn, an old Richard

Nixon hangout. Nixon cracks me up. What you like to do for fun? There's real good surf here. I got a shed full of surfboards."

"I've never tried surfing, Ernie."

"How about sailing?"

"Never tried that either."

"Not an ocean lover, huh? Okay. You want to go motorcycle riding in the desert? I got a bunch of real nice bikes."

"That's another thing I've never done. I've been a passenger but I've not ridden one. Not even a pushbike."

Ernie started laughing uncontrollably. I joined in.

"I guess it seems strange to you, Ernie, yeah?"

"You got that right. So what do you do when you ain't working, watch television?"

"Sometimes. But usually I just get stoned, read books, and listen to music."

"You'll like California," said Ernie.

I did, or what I saw of it, which was mainly the inside of a hotel room in Newport Beach. I wandered around the hotel complex, the bars, swimming pools and other public areas, and realized that American movies weren't about fantasy: they were documentaries about Hollywood. There were hundreds of radio stations and dozens of TV channels. In Britain we had only three. The radio stations were fantastic. I listened to a few hours of doo-wop and golden oldies before the commercials drove me mad. All the TV channels were showing sport, cop shoot-outs, sit-coms, game shows, or news. I watched the news. A reporter said, "Hey, one of you guys out there has just lost $5,000,000. Today, law enforcement officers seized Nevada's biggest ever haul of illegal drugs. Hashish, highly concentrated cannabis from the Middle East, almost half a ton of it, was discovered hidden in speaker cabinets. Over to Las Vegas." On the screen came pictures of the Lebanese hashish and the speakers Gater and I had stashed in Holland.

In the movies, the crook, usually a fugitive, always immediately switches off the radio or television when the relevant news bulletin finishes. I didn't. I stared at it blankly for at least an hour. Was this really happening? I was very jet-lagged from my first-ever long flight, and Ernie had given me the most varied collection of hashish and marijuana imaginable. I was as stoned as I'd ever been. This was Hollywood. It probably wasn't happening. There was a knock on the door. It was Ernie, and it was happening.

"Well, we lost that one. The cops . . ."

"I know, Ernie. I just saw it on TV."

"No kidding. That was quick. What you figure on doing next?"

"I think I ought to leave."

"That's smart. Here's 10,000 dollars. I guessed you didn't bring a bunch of money over with you. It'd be kinda dumb if you were coming to pick some up. Here's my new phone number. Call me."

"Thanks, Ernie. How did the load get busted? Do you know?"

"Sure I do. Didn't it say on TV? The load transited in John F. Kennedy Airport, New York. When the airport loaders put it on the plane to Vegas, they fucked up and left one speaker behind, which they stuck in some shed in Kennedy overnight, and a dog sniffed it. The DEA took the dope out of the speakers once they were in Vegas and let my guy, Gary Lickert, the kid you met in Amsterdam, pick it up so they could see where he was taking it to. I had that covered. I was watching Gary from a distance. I saw him being followed, overtook him, gave him the signal, and haularsed outa there."

"What did Gary do?"

"Drove in circles around the airport until the cops stopped him."

"Will he tell the cops about you and me?"

"No. He did a tough stint in Vietnam. He won't crack. But we should play it cool for a while, like a few days. I got friends in the FBI. I'll find out what they got on us. Take a limo from here to LA airport. When you get there, buy a ticket in some dumb English name like Smith for a flight to the East Coast, somewhere like Philadelphia, then fly in your own name to anywhere you want."

I flew to New York and stayed at the Hilton overnight, visiting Greenwich Village, Times Square, and the Statue of Liberty. Then I flew to London. Mac wanted to see me. We met at

Dillons bookshop *[Gower Street]* and took a cab ride to nowhere in particular.

"Howard; you know that recently we have had to suffer some embarrassment over the Littlejohn affair."

"Yes."

Kenneth and Keith Littlejohn were bank robbers who had claimed to be infiltrating the IRA at the behest of MI6. The claims had been substantiated, and the British public expressed outrage at their Secret Service's employing of notorious criminals for undercover work in the independent Republic of Ireland.

"For that reason, and that reason alone, you and I have to terminate our relationship. We can no longer liaise with criminals."

"Dope smuggling is hardly a crime, Mac."

"Of course it is, Howard. Don't talk rot. It's illegal."

"I thought you agreed hashish shouldn't be illegal. It's the law that's wrong, not the activity."

"I do. But until the law changes, you're a criminal."

"Don't you think, Mac, there's a duty to change laws which are wrong, evil, harmful and dangerous?"

"Yes, but by legal means."

"You would use the law to change the law."

"Of course."

"I suppose you would recommend saving a drowning man by telling him to drink his way out of it."

"That's sophistry, Howard, and you know it. This end to our relationship is not my decision. I've been ordered to tell you this."

I felt curiously cheated. My career as a spy was over without my having derived any benefit from it.

"Mac, if by abiding by my own decisions and beliefs, rather than those of others, I come across something which affects the security of this country, do I take it that I should now no longer bring it to your attention?"

Mac smiled. I've not seen him since.

After the Greek sponge fishermen fiasco, Eric was determined to make amends; he went to Beirut. He found his own source of supply who was prepared to give him a hundred kilos of hashish on credit. Eric offered to extend this credit to us and bring another suitcase to Geneva. The deal went ahead smoothly. Anthony Woodhead drove the hashish from Geneva to England. One of Mohammed Durrani's diplomats had turned up in Hamburg with 250 kilos of Pakistani hashish. Graham and I sent out one of the Tafia, who rented a car and a lock-up garage in the outskirts of Hamburg to store the dope.

James Morris rang from Los Angeles. Three of his workers had been arrested in London. He didn't know why. Neither did Graham or I. We knew American law had been broken, but we couldn't see how anyone involved had been guilty of breaking British law. Graham didn't want to bother to find out. He'd been to prison once; that was enough. He wanted to go to Ireland under a false identity to join McCann and supervise matters from there. It was safer. McCann had got him a false Irish driving licence. He left London that night.

Graham was right. Whatever reason was used to bust James Morris' workers could be used to bust us. I didn't want to rejoin McCann so soon after breaking from him, but Ireland was the only foreign country one could travel to from England without showing a passport. If there really was a danger of being arrested, I clearly shouldn't travel around under my own name: I had no choice but to seek refuge with McCann. I borrowed Denys Irving's driving licence, hired a car, stashed my passport, some dope, money and bits and pieces in the back panels, and drove to Fishguard. On the ferry I drank several pints of Guinness at the bar before it docked at Rosslare. Once I reached open country, I stopped and rolled a very stiff joint of Afghani. As night fell, I drove towards Drogheda, where McCann was now based. Cruising along at 50 mph, I totally missed a right-angled bend and crashed through a hedge into a field. I lost consciousness.

"Will he be needing a doctor or a priest?"

Two carloads of people surrounded the steaming, dripping vehicle. Although I was lying awkwardly, I felt no pain and could move all my muscles.

"I'm all right," I said.

"Don't you be moving now. We'll have an ambulance and tow truck here in no time. No time at all."

I thought of the dope and my inconsistent identity documents.

"No, look, I'm perfectly all right," I said, leaping out of the wreck. "If someone could give me a lift to the nearest telephone, I'll be able to take care of everything myself."

"That'll be at Bernard Murphy's down the road. Jump in."

Bernard Murphy's, which was actually named something like the Crazy Horseshoe, was heaving with serious Irish Saturday night revelry. A large group was energetically performing an Irish jig around the telephone. A few young lads were holding the phone and sticking fingers in their ears. I made a reversed charges call to McCann at Drogheda and told him I was stuck in the Crazy Horseshoe about ten miles outside Rosslare. Would he please come and get me? He arrived in a couple of hours.

"Some fucking operator you are. Can't drive a fucking car. Got nowhere to go. Can't even go back to selling dope on Brighton seafront, or dresses to fucking academics. Like a rolling fucking stone. Why don't British Intelligence help you out? You can't do things without The Kid, can you? This is war, H'ard. Soppy Bollocks has joined the struggle. You fucking better, too. You got two fucking choices: I'll lend you £500 and you fuck off, or, with a new passport that The Kid'll give you, you handle these two deals from Kabul and Lebalon, or whatever the fuck that place is called, that Soppy Bollocks told me you and him are in the middle of."

"What you mean by handle?"

"Soppy told me the Lebalon nordle is in London. Sell it. The Kabul nordle is in fucking Nazi land. I've already blown up a British Army base in Monchengladbach, and the Baader-Meinhof gang eat out of my fucking hand. I want you to give the Kabul nordle to my man in Hamburg. He'll sell it."

"How much do we all make?"

"We're partners, H'ard. Me, you and Soppy. Equal shares after everyone else has been paid off."

"That's fair enough for the dope in Hamburg if your guys are selling it. But why should you get anything from the Lebanese deal?"

"Soppy's already agreed, H'ard."

We picked up my belongings from the wrecked car and drove to McCann's Drogheda hideout. The false Irish passport took a few days, during which time McCann constantly berated me for incompetence. It looked perfect and was in the name of Peter Hughes.

"Is this a real person, Jim?"

"Peter Hughes is fucking real all right. He's a member of the Provos, and he's interned by the Brits."

"In that case, it doesn't seem to be a particularly good idea for me to pretend to be Mr Hughes," I said.

"Well, the cops are not fucking looking for him. He's in Long Kesh, and they fucking know that. They're looking for you, H'ard. Think, you stupid Welsh cunt."

McCann took me to the airport.

"Let me give you some advice, H'ard. Never fly to where you're really going. Do the last bit by train, bus or car. See, there's an Aer Lingus flight to Brussels. Go on it, then take a train to Hamburg."

On my arrival in Brussels, the Immigration Officer looked carefully at my Pete Hughes passport. He looked up.

"Howard?" he asked.

I froze. I'd been found out. But the Immigration Officer was smiling. Then I realized he was merely making a joking reference to billionaire Howard Hughes.

"You have a famous name, Mr Hughes."

After several hours on the train, I checked into the Atlantic Hotel, Hamburg, where I was meant to stay until McCann called with his friend's whereabouts. I had the keys to the car and garage.

Meanwhile, Marty Langford had checked into the International Hotel, Earls Court, London, with a carload of Lebanese hashish in the hotel car park. Charlie Weatherley was going to sell it. I called Marty. He wasn't in his room. I left my number with reception. I called again after a while. Someone else answered the phone in his room.

"Could I please speak to Marty?" I asked.

"Yes, this is Marty, go ahead."

The voice wasn't remotely like Marty's.

"This is Marty. Who are you?"

I put the phone down and rang again.

"Could you put me through to Mr Langford's room, please?"

"Hello, hello, this is Marty speaking."

It was now obvious to me what had happened. Marty had been busted, and the police were in his room finding out what they could. I had stupidly left my hotel number in Hamburg with the receptionist at the International Hotel, Earls Court. It was time to check out and scarper.

On the flight schedule board at Hamburg airport there were two flights leaving almost immediately, one to Helsinki and one to Paris. I couldn't remember in which country Helsinki was situated, so I bought a ticket for the Paris flight. At Paris I was able to get a flight to Barcelona, and from there to Ibiza. By the time I landed, I had a heavy fever. For the next two days, I stumbled around Rosie's primitive home deliriously searching for a telephone and a toilet. Rosie ignored me. When I recovered, I went straight to Ibiza airport and called Marty's, Weatherley's, and a host of other London numbers. No answer. I called McCann's in Drogheda. No answer. I caught the next flight to Amsterdam and went to Arend's flat. I called McCann's again.

"Don't you ever call this fucking number or show your fucking face in my country again. My Anne is in prison because of your fuck-ups. She's with those fucking Nazis, man. Marty and his two friends are over here. I've given them sanctuary. You promised them riches and gave them fucking ashes, you Welsh cunt."

The torrent continued. I was able to piece together what had happened. Charlie Weatherley had gone to Marty's rooms to get a sample of the Lebanese. He was stopped by a hotel security man on the way out, and when asked which room he had come from, gave Marty's. The security man hauled Charlie up to Marty's room to check. Marty, thinking that Charlie must have been busted, denied all knowledge of him. Marty panicked, packed his clothes, left his room, left the carload of

Lebanese and fled to Ireland, taking the rest of the Tafia with him. McCann had no idea what had happened to me. He sent his girlfriend, Anne McNulty, and a Dutchman to Hamburg to pick up the car from the lock-up garage with the spare keys that Graham had. They got busted by the Hamburg police.

'Jim, I'm genuinely sorry about Anne. Is there anything I can do?'

'I don't need your fucking help. I've already personally declared war on those fucking Nazis. They know what The Kid's capable of. Unless they want a fucking reminder of World War II, they'd better let Anne go.'

I called up Ernie. He said he'd come over to see me in Amsterdam during the next few days. The Paradiso, Amsterdam's first legal joint-smoking cafe, had just opened. I was beginning to like the city with its pretty canals, hooker window displays, and liberal dope-smoking policy. Perhaps I should settle here. One evening, I went to the Oxhooft, a nightclub, and ran into Lebanese Joe.

'Hey, Howard, man, it's good to see you. What are you doing here?'

'I might be living here from now on.'

'Same as me, man. It's a cool place. Give me your number. Here, have a smoke.' He put a piece of Lebanese hashish in my top pocket.

Ernie arrived and checked in under a false name at the Okura Hotel. I told him my tales of woe.

'Hey, don't worry. We're going to do something from this Amsterdam place real soon, even if we go back to our old way of taking new European cars to the States. It made me a bunch of money, I'll tell you. Here's $100,000. Start buying. And here's a sole of Afghani. I know there ain't nothing good to smoke in Europe. Can I give you a lift anywhere? I got a rent-a-car.'

'Yes please, Ernie. I think I'll open up a bank deposit box to put this money in and then get to Arend's.'

Ernie drove me to the Algemene Bank Nederland. I opened up a safe-deposit box in the name of Peter Hughes and placed the $100,000 and the Irish Peter Hughes passport inside. Arend was overjoyed at the idea of buying some more hashish in

Amsterdam. We made a pipe out of Ernie's Afghan. There was heavy knocking on the door. It burst open, and six Dutch police swarmed through the flat. I got up to leave.

"I don't live here. I have an appointment. I have to go," I stammered.

One of the police stopped me and searched me. He found the piece of hashish Lebanese Joe had given me. He asked for my passport. I still had my own. I gave it to him.

"Are you Dennis Howard Marks?"

"Yes, I am."

"We are arresting you and will now take you to the police station."

Three of them marched me downstairs and put me into the back seat of a car before climbing in. At the police station, they went through my pockets again and took everything away. They took down my particulars and led me towards the cells. Mick Jagger was singing *Angie* on the police-station radio. I was busted.

2

Blowback: A Dope Smuggler's Adventures From the Golden Triangle to the Golden Gate

Michael Forwell with Lee Bullman

Michael Forwell blazed the trail for the Bangkok smuggling ring that features in the following chapter, shipping vast quantities of Thai sticks (the high-quality, outdoor-grown cannabis from Thailand or Cambodia that is pressed around a central stem, like a cannabis kebab) to the USA. In fact, he owned the bar – the Charlie Superstar – in which Brian Daniels' motley collection of colourful characters met regularly to spend, enjoy the fruits of their labours, and hatch their next scam. Like Howard Marks, Forwell could play the unprepossessing Englishman abroad without a problem. In addition to having access to a jungle's worth of weed, it seems Forwell was possessed of a Raffles-like, devil-may-care approach that would stand him in good stead, and which makes his version of Bangkok sounds something like inter-war Shanghai, a world of pleasure-seeking intrigue. We'll see elsewhere the risk that drug distributors run, not merely evading capture but situations in which capture could be the least of their worries, including the turf wars, protection and chilling methods of compulsion that exist on the street. The smuggler, however, faces a different set of problems, which are perhaps more romantic to some, especially from the comfort of an armchair, but nonetheless can be equally chilling – literally – and no less lethal. Nature, as the saying has it, can be a cruel mistress, and many smugglers have been lost to the elements, just as they were back in the seventeenth and eighteenth centuries, when the product was rum and the object not to traffic in proscribed goods (a concept which wouldn't really have been understood at that time, except perhaps in the case of religious interdiction), but to evade paying duty.

As a smuggler, if you are doing your job well, no one but a trusted few will know even your most general whereabouts (and even then the best tradecraft suggests that any unnecessary sharing of information is by definition unwise). Who knows how many have perished, possibly in inadequate craft, realizing that no one else would even be aware that anything was amiss, let alone raise the alarm?

In waters smaller than the Pacific, where rescue is more realistic, there have been instances where smugglers in peril have issued a Mayday signal and faced the music rather than be lost at sea (see chapter 10*). In chapter 7, the writer comes across the wreck of one ill-fated light plane, and in chapter 13, a smuggling neophyte describes the fear he feels when crossing the English Channel on a semi-rigid craft not much larger than a double bed.*

Smuggling drugs by boat in Pacific waters held threats other than the sharks that Forwell makes light of, too. By way of a little context regarding the real risks facing smugglers in Asia during the 1970s, take the terrifying case of James Clark and Lance McNamara, two carefree counter-cultural scions of the US who set sail to Thailand from California in the summer of 1978. Both were hippies of the old school, a couple of the "volunteers of America" who had protested against Vietnam, grown their hair and discovered the delights of dope and the mind-opening possibilities of LSD. James Clark had stayed in the US and taken his two years' jail for dodging the draft like a man. Thai weed was the finest they had experienced back in the laid-back beachside enclave of LA's Santa Monica, and they were not the first to realize that if they were prepared to pay top-dollar for it in preference to the Mexican "cough-pot" that was their usual bread-and-butter fare, then many of their peers would be too. But when all is said and done, they were American sons who, by the end of their tragic experience, might have felt they had more in common with the thinking of Thomas Jefferson than Jefferson Airplane after all.

McNamara and Clark, at twenty-six and thirty-five years of age respectively, having successfully packed their craft, the Mary K, *with Thai sticks, set off for their return voyage, doubtless looking forward to a fast fortune and some more of that California dreaming. They were never seen again, at least not by anyone friendly.*

Smugglers, indeed sailors of all kinds, who left Thailand to travel east would have to navigate the coastline of Vietnam, keeping close enough to the shore to minimize the risks in these pirate-infested waters, but be cautious not to enter Cambodian territory. For Cambodia was at that time undergoing the infamous genocide wrought by the Khmer Rouge, a regime so murderously, insanely ideological on its own scale as to make Stalin look like a circus ringmaster.

Pol Pot's troops executed anyone they deemed an enemy of his regime – from those who failed to meet their quota of rice production, to those who wore spectacles. To be foreign was to be a spy. The hapless Clark and McNamara had strayed too far into Cambodian waters and compounded their error by mistaking a Khmer gunboat for a pirate launch. Each had taken a pistol along for their personal protection and so Clark began firing at their pursuers as McNamara desperately tried to get the most knots out of their boat before a fifty-calibre machine-gun tore a hole along the side of its hull.

The Cambodian troops dragged them ashore, threw them into a truck and, with Clark possibly wounded, delivered them to the horrific prison S-21, a former high school, which the Khmer had turned into a charnel house and an institution beyond all hope. Inmates were forced into tiny cells and forbidden to move without permission. Electric-

shock treatment was administered, toe- and fingernails removed with pliers and bones broken on a daily basis. Witnesses saw Clark and McNamara dragged across the ground by guards who took hold of them by the beards they had grown on their voyage.

The increasingly paranoid regime believed that Cambodia had been infiltrated by foreign agents and the story of two young men out to make a fortune by smuggling drugs from neighbouring Thailand tragically beggared belief where the Khmer were concerned. The prison's former director, Kaing Khek Leu, has confessed with regard to the western captives: "I knew from experience that if they were only tortured they wouldn't say anything. So torture had to be accompanied by psychological tactics. I told them they would be released if they talked. This was a lie, but it worked."

After a month of captivity, Clark issued a "confession" in which he claimed to have been recruited as a spy by the CIA at the Raffles Hotel in Singapore. "He [a CIA contact] wanted me to photograph essentially the central and southern parts of Cambodia. I was to photograph fishing boats and war boats, notice their speed, how they were painted and what they were made of (wood, steel, cement, etc.), whether or not they were doing military practice three or more at once, whether they had radio antennae.

"The key country to watch in South East Asia is Cambodia, the most successful communist country. Cambodia seems to be getting stronger every year. The US thinks that if Cambodia becomes strong enough, it will invade Thailand and turn it to communism. After Thailand, it would be easy to make Malaysia communist and then Singapore would be threatened ... This finishes my Cambodian job, and with that we have taken only twelve pictures. For this mission, my pay is about $700,000 and Lance's about $400,000. As to Cambodia, the CIA will keep on bringing its agents of all kinds to spy upon it.

"The CIA has men all over South East Asia to keep up with the political events there. Even though I was caught, there will be someone else to do the job. The CIA must know what is happening."

This chillingly stilted confession was signed with Clark's thumbprint. It betrays a Maoist peasant farmer's Mickey-Mouse idea of how the US would conduct its espionage, and is flattering in the importance it gives to Cambodia within the region, however much America adhered to its "domino theory". Whether paranoid or just plain cynical, the Khmer used Clark for just the kind of misinformation that was designed to make a terrified populace cleave more closely to the devil they knew.

As there is no confession from McNamara, it's likely he died from wounds received on the boat, or else under torture. Confession in hand, prisoners were of no further use to the regime. It's likely that Clark was taken to Cheong Ek, known to westerners more familiarly as the Killing Fields. Made to kneel blindfold in front of a burial pit, victims were hit on the back of their heads with a metal pipe, their throats were then slit for good measure. Foreign corpses were burned and their bones smashed to powder, to remove all trace of their existence.

Laid-back though they seem, it's worth bearing in mind when reading the following extract that Forwell and his crew would have had a varied list of very present dangers at the forefront of their minds ...

I was sitting in the bar one afternoon in early 1980 when Lietzman strolled in, back from spending some time in Kamal. He was looking pretty pleased with himself.

"The shopping was fine," he said, " bought us a great new boat."

I shook my head and smiled. This was becoming a habit. The vessel in question was the *Yellow Bull*, a forty-foot Thai fishing boat that Lietzman wanted to fill with dope and sail to America. He was enthusiastic about the vessel's potential but I wasn't at all convinced.

"A Thai fishing boat? You want to sail from here to Washington in a Thai fishing boat?"

"It's not as dumb as it sounds, Mike, trust me."

Hmmm. The boat was certainly sturdy enough to get us from Thailand to America and roomy enough to make the trip with four tons of dope hidden in the bows and front section. But there was a problem. Thai fishing boats are not designed with round-the-world trips in mind. A journey covering thousands of miles and lasting for anything up to three months aboard *Yellow Bull* would soon become very uncomfortable indeed. Obviously there was only one thing to do. We began to remodel the boat, making renovations that went far beyond those needed to hide and disguise the weed. We ripped open the centre of the craft and installed a cabin large enough for us to relax in and outfitted the new space with all the creature comforts of a well-appointed sitting room: couches, tables and unnecessary odds and ends. The alterations to the boat were completed over six months while she was moored in Singapore. Once the changes were made to the structure we outfitted the bridge of *Yellow Bull* with a few choice pieces of kit to help us navigate the boat halfway around the world: the latest radar, speedometer and radio communications equipment.

Once the cabin was outfitted for the journey we sailed to Thailand where we loaded on the last and most important of our supplies: enough cartons of Benson & Hedges to see us through months at sea, a few cases of Lietzman's favourite bourbon – oh, and four tons of Thai marijuana.

The night before we were due to set sail, I broke the news to May that I was off on a trip. "I've got to go away and do some business. I could be gone for a while."

She didn't look overjoyed at the news, her countenance falling as the conversation proceeded. "Michael, you're hardly ever here as it is. How long will you be gone?"

"Not too long," I said, "maybe three months."

May was hurt by the news, and my matter-of-fact delivery of it. For what would not be the last time in our marriage, she prepared to carry on without her new husband. As we kissed each other farewell the next morning, I was tempted to tell her the truth behind my voyage but decided against it at the last minute, figuring that divulging to my new wife that I was in fact a marijuana smuggler would cause more problems than it solved.

I soon forgot any lingering guilt as we set off in bright Asian sunshine on glassy seas, plain sailing. To cool off from the heat on deck we dived off the side of the boat and swam in the ocean, never straying too far from *Yellow Bull* though, just in case those left aboard had forgotten that one of their number had elected to take a dip and carried on without him. Another worry while swimming was the possibility that our progress through the ocean had attracted attention from below, the sharks that were not unheard of in the area could well have decided that that day, they fancied a smuggler for lunch.

The weather as we left the East and sailed towards California seemed to be on our side and boat and crew sailed along happily.

The first order of business, once a case of bourbon had been cracked open and a toast raised to the success of our newest venture, was to disguise our vessel. If the *Yellow Bull* mission had been compromised in any way, if we'd been ratted out in Thailand and anyone at the American end was waiting for us, then they would be looking for the distinctive white boat that had left Asia and not the rather poorly painted yellow one that would shortly be sailing proudly into San Francisco harbour.

While the sea remained calm and weather warm we began the task of repainting the vessel, covering the white with a coat of bright canary yellow. The facelift was achieved by hanging off the hull of the *Yellow Bull* while sitting on planks supported at each side by ropes secured on deck, like window cleaners on a skyscraper. With paintbrushes and bourbons in hand and cigarettes clamped between our teeth we spent a happy week or so covering ourselves and the boat in an evenish coat of yellow paint. At the time, ideas like that seemed normal, sensible even. The plan to repaint the boat while at sea was not seen as dangerous or foolhardy but rather as an example of our forward thinking. It's the kind of arrogance that can kill.

In order to make the journey to the States we needed to take on more fuel and had chosen the Marshall Islands in the Pacific as the perfect spot to fill up. We weren't the only customers shopping for gas that day and as we took on board the fuel we needed, we met a band of fresh faced young smugglers coming the opposite way. Not one of these guys could have been more than twenty-five years old. They were heading for Thailand in order to fill their small boat with dope and sail it back to America.

Eight shaggy-haired American kids in Adidas sneakers, faded jeans and skinny T-shirts on their merry way to make their first million. The boat the young men were sailing east was completely sterile, clean as a whistle, not a rope, net or fishing rod offered even the pretence of its being a working boat. To trained eyes their whole operation screamed out smuggler, and inexperienced ones at that. We wished the gang the best of luck and watched them head off.

"Fucking amateurs," Bobby said, shaking his head pityingly.

We all laughed at the idea of being so unprepared.

But there was one thing we hadn't counted on: the weather. Nor had we counted on the fact that the extensive renovations we had made to *Yellow Bull* had dramatically weakened the structure of the boat. In order to install our living quarters we had ripped out many of the large wooden bulkheads that kept *Yellow Bull* rigid.

That oversight was almost about to sink us. Literally.

As Hawaii, our next fuel stop, approached the weather began to turn nasty, with fierce storms blowing up. The boat began to sway at first, pitching slightly more than was comfortable, the smooth rock and roll we had been experiencing since leaving the Thai coast giving way to something far more worrying. Then the weather worsened and suddenly we were being thrown around inside the hull of the boat, fear leaking into our bourbon-soaked brains. The waves started to touch ten feet, the boat pitching dramatically. We were drinking now to keep us brave in the face of increasingly unsettling odds.

This was no time to be sober.

Then *Yellow Bull* began to make noises we hadn't heard from her before, noises you really don't want to hear from the only thing separating you from a mile or so of who-knows-what-infested watery depths. She came alive with a series of drawn out horror-movie creaks and shudders, the sudden loud cracks and low long moans audible even above the fury of the storm. The bow became progressively weaker under the incessant pounding. To my horror and bemusement, I saw a crack appear halfway along the deck in the middle of the boat.

"Guys," I yelled, pointing a shaking finger, "this doesn't look good, this doesn't look good at all."

The crack grew in front of our eyes, getting very bad very quickly as *Yellow Bull* rocked through the open sea.

Soon it looked as though the bow of the boat was threatened, like it was getting ready to snap and send our band of drunken sailors and our four tons of dope into the dark fathoms below. No joke. By now, with rain lashing the vessel and waves crashing into her from all sides, the only thing holding the boat together was the keel, and wishful thinking.

Thai fishing boats are traditionally built of wood and corking. As *Yellow Bull* fought her way through the storm some of the corking had worked itself loose and as a consequence the boat had sprung a series of leaks, taking on so much water that the pumps we carried were struggling to contain the problem. Lietzman's mechanical fix-anything skills came to the fore as he battled desperately to fix the pumps, drenched from head to foot. Soon we were ankle-deep everywhere. It was then that the journey went from bad to worse, and everything on the boat that possibly could go wrong did.

Lietzman was flying by the seat of his pants, making repairs that would have been difficult enough in a shipyard under the most unholy of circumstances and, I suspected, rather enjoying himself while he did it. We stood by and tried to make ourselves useful while he worked, handing him the tools he would scream out for while trying to save the boat, our lives, and the dope.

"The wrench! Someone get me the fucking wrench . . .

And while you're at it, get me another drink."

At one point, above the noise of the storm, I thought I heard him singing. We were repairing the boat as we sailed, high on bourbon nerve and bravado. Somehow we managed to navigate *Yellow Bull*, barely still in one piece and as ragged and tired as its small crew, into Kona, near Hawaii.

Once in Kona the weather settled and our hangovers cleared a little. Lietzman took off for a little much-needed rest and relaxation while Bobby, Terry the deckhand and I enjoyed the brief respite from our ordeal. As it happened, the seas around the Kona coast of Hawaii where we had elected to stop a while and take on supplies were playing host to a fishing competition, a big one, with a fleet of boats of all different shapes and sizes taking part, all trying to hook marlin. I was still a keen fisherman and had brought along my new rods and reels, upgraded to the best that money could buy. So we cast off and started fishing.

We weren't enrolled in the competition, we hadn't registered or paid the nominal entry fee but didn't see minor details like that as excluding us from the fun. We cast off our lines and began to fish. Since arriving in the area, the radio aboard *Yellow Bull* had been tuned to Channel 16, the international distress channel, which meant that we could keep up with any sudden news concerning the area we were sailing. We also knew that as a matter of course the Coast Guard would also have their radio tuned into Channel 16 on the lookout for any maritime emergency that required their immediate attention.

Before long we began to attract unwanted attention, one of our fellow competitors taking exception to what he assumed was a Mexican fishing boat plying its trade in American waters. He put in a call to the Coast Guard and ratted us out. Fortunately for us he made the call on Channel 16 and we could listen in to every word. The last thing we needed after the trials of our journey so far was unwelcome attention from the authorities, with four tons of dope still on the boat. We reeled in our lines quick time and headed out for the safety of the open sea until things had cooled off a little, not returning until later when we could safely pick up Lietzman for the final leg of the journey.

I disembarked in Hawaii and made my way by air to San Francisco to finalize arrangements for the offload.

We were the lucky ones as the *Yellow Bull*'s problems weren't over. The boat still had 2,000 miles to go before she reached the safety of San Francisco harbour and on the way there the crew, now reduced to Lietzman, Bobby Colflesh and Terry, were hit by yet more storms.

By now the boat simply couldn't take the constant battering it was being subjected to by the elements and the leaks were getting progressively worse. The two pumps on board were clearing water for all they were worth but were simply not up to the job. If the shipment was to get through and the crew were to survive then something had to be done. Desperate times were calling for desperate measures.

As soon as they were within radio range of the California coast they called the Coast Guard on Channel 16 and reported themselves as a vessel in distress, supplied their co-ordinates and waited. Before too long a Coast Guard helicopter battled its way through the storm and lowered a pump down on to the deck of *Yellow Bull*.

Once the pump was safely on deck the Coast Guard wished the crew good luck and went on their way, blissfully unaware that they had just helped four tons of dope make the final stretch of a long and tiring journey.

The new pump worked a treat, able to evacuate more water than the two that were already on board combined.

Yellow Bull finally limped into San Francisco harbour where Sam and I were waiting to meet her. The once-proud vessel had all but given up. Its crew, doused in bourbon and tired to their bones, under cover of night offloaded the dope into the warehouse we still kept on a long-term let, then loaded the Coast Guard's pump aboard the trusty Camino and returned it to them, with sincere and heartfelt thanks.

Yellow Bull ended her journey abandoned on the mudflats of San Francisco, battered and bruised by the trip, but having served us admirably.

A lot of dope had been brought into America that year, so much that the two thousand dollars a pound we could usually expect had dropped by almost half. We weren't pleased by the news to put it mildly, but even at a reduced selling price the four-ton load had still grossed us close to ten million dollars, ensuring that the cost of buying, fitting out and abandoning the fishing boat was hardly noticed when we got to the bottom line.

Delivering such a large amount to Rod and the hippie connection meant that we would have to hand the weed over to them at a series of different pick-up points. Over the next four days we met with Rod or members of his commune at car parks dotted around the city. Payment for the load was received piecemeal too, with hundred-thousand-dollar Halliburton suitcases handed over to us in twos and threes once or twice a day for the next three weeks. Once the money had all been collected, we moved it back to Thailand and Singapore, sent as hand luggage in Halliburton cases on a number of expensive and luxurious first-class flights. I bought May a necklace, a peace offering to make up for my prolonged absence, and presented it to her as soon as I returned home. "Michael, it's beautiful," she smiled.

"It's no less than you deserve. It's just a little something to make up for all of the time I've spent away."

"You didn't need to. Does this mean that you're here to stay for a while now?"

"Well, actually, no," I said uncomfortably. "I've got a flight booked back to Thailand this evening."

I told myself there was nothing I could do, I had to get back to the gang. By midnight I was at Superstar, drinking with Lietzman and the Colflesh brothers.

Because we had no truck with outsiders the four of us socialized and worked together exclusively, and as a consequence our family lives began to suffer. Our wives and partners were never privy to the more shadowy aspects of our ever-growing business, and were never invited on our long drinking sprees. We would book ourselves hotel suites – Hong Kong's Mandarin Oriental was a particular favourite –and hole up for weeks on end, planning, drinking and growing more convinced of our invincibility.

The women in our lives were treated well materially but no amount of money can compensate for the levels of secrecy and absence necessary when you're related or married to a smuggler, even one living the supposed "clean" life of a prosperous ex-pat bar owner.

The history of the Thai dope trade at that time is littered with accounts of busts and rip-offs. Boatloads of dope were routinely intercepted and held for ransom and the danger of double-cross was everywhere. There were stories of pirates operating off the coast of Thailand believed to be responsible for the half-dozen yachts that had gone missing in that stretch of water in 1978 alone.

In nearby Cambodia the Khmer Rouge were constantly on the lookout for foreign spies, their paranoid vigilance bringing them into contact with smugglers who had strayed into their waters and whose ugly destiny at their hands was one of slow torture and eventual murder.

Unlike the scams of some of our contemporaries, ours were all working, all of our weed was getting through.

Our 100 per cent success rate may have made us overconfident but it didn't mean we grew slipshod. Lietzman and I had always kept our dealings to ourselves. And the Colflesh brothers were ex-Special Forces and both knew well the importance of secrecy and a strong, authored chain of command; loose lips bust ships.

As far as the illegal side of the business was concerned we had completely assimilated a clandestine approach into our working practices. As far as possible we carved up the duties in preparing and moving shipment between the four of us. On the occasions when we had to take on extra hands for loading and offloading the dope and crewing the *Yellow Bull* voyage to America, we employed the same old faces; western workers Bobby knew from the nearby oilfields supplementing their wages, or Thai locals, also sourced and recruited by Bobby. All were well paid for their efforts, they were put on salary and we gave fat bonuses to one and all when loads got through. Any staff employed was made aware of the premium we put on absolute secrecy and loyalty as a matter of course.

Operating from a permanent base in the form of the nightclub meant that we had the luxury of getting to know people gradually, watching potential employees in action before deciding whether or not to employ them.

Bobby had taken up Thai boxing; he was good at it and eventually reached competition level, and his sparring sessions and gym workouts offered another ideal opportunity to get to know potential help. But no matter how many auxiliary staff we employed, only the four of us had an overall picture of how the scams worked, so we stuck together like glue and kept our mouths shut. No outsiders.

As a further security precaution, the various sides of our business were each kept strictly autonomous. We never brought dope or the cash it earned through the bar.

And despite having homes in different countries we were officially registered nowhere, which had the added bonus that we paid no taxes.

For someone whose main income was supposedly derived from a go-go joint on the Patpong Road, I was moving around an awful lot in Asia, Europe and America. When we divided up the duties involved in a particular scam I would push myself forward to take on any that involved travel, flying into America to pick up cash or secure the vehicles or boats we needed at that end. In order to travel and remain safe I needed a new identity to hide behind.

Just to be on the safe side, I got four.

First I became Michael Charles Young, an alias I would use on and off for years and for which I eventually acquired a full suite of supporting documentation that helped to flesh out the identity and add a fictional back-story.

Michael Young was a tombstone name – that is to say the name of someone of roughly your own age who had died young, usually as a child, before ever applying for a passport. Once you'd found the name – in my case through a guy I met in a bar who had some useful connections – you could obtain a birth certificate by filling in a form and sending it to the local registrar. The birth certificate could be used to apply for a passport, which could then be used to begin a collection of credit cards and memberships. *Voilà*, one new identity.

As well as the Young identity, which was British, I also used the tombstone method to turn myself into Rodney Wayne Boggs, an American identity for which I collected another full suite of supporting documentation. The Boggs identity, though, needed a back-story. Although I tried to tone down my English accent when using it, it would have been obvious to anyone spending more than five minutes in my company that I was not an American.

I made Rodney Wayne Boggs an antiques dealer who had spent the last ten years working in England, loving the country so much that he'd picked up the accent. Though not quite as well supported as the Young identity, the Boggs name proved real enough for me to use it to buy a house in San Francisco, a modest family dwelling on the outside but inside an extensively remodelled luxury pad.

The Young and Boggs identities were the most well rounded but I used other names to a lesser extent. I was also Michael Escreet and Michael Leslie Stocks, each identity having enough supporting documentation to be plausible. Wherever possible I would create new identities using my real first name and a fictitious surname.

Sometimes, just remembering who I was supposed to be proved a full-time job.

As a nickname, my three partners had crowned me "Fox", a reference to the fact that my real surname, the one I was using less and less, began with the letter F. As a nod to my newly secured alias I occasionally signed in and out of hotels under the name Michael Reynard, after the French for Fox.

I soon became very adept at altering passports. I experimented long into the night, listening to the sound of the street while curlicues and question marks of smoke rose up from the tip of my Benson & Hedges as I trained myself in the fine and ancient art of forgery.

I worked at faking the passports alone, in my office at home in Singapore or in the office above the club, at tables strewn with bottles, visa stamps, passport photographs and blank pages. It was trial and error at first and many early attempts ended up in the wastepaper bin.

But I kept going, because altering passports and travel documents was thrilling: it harked back to the spy stories I had enjoyed as a boy and appealed to the watch-maker within.

Through tireless application I found that when I used the steam from a boiling kettle to heat a passport I could, very slowly and very carefully, remove the document's hard cover, which would in turn expose the spine of the document's inner page.

Once I had access to these pages I noticed that they were stitched together rather than glued. I set about sourcing the thread used to bind the pages and practised, practised, practised, honing my sewing skills until I was confident that I could replace or swap pages, lose a travel stamp here or add one there, with no sign the passport had been tampered with. I had a collection of entry and exit visa stamps for all of the countries I visited on business and pleasure, thanks to the services of a local Thai forger Bobby had found and enlisted.

A passport stamped with multiple visas in and out of Thailand would have been guaranteed an unwanted pull in Europe or America by Customs officials who were by now wising up to the Thai dope trade. Once a page in any particular passport began to appear overburdened with entry and exit visas it was simply removed and replaced with one which recorded a far less hectic travel schedule. By replacing pages I could make my passport, in whichever alias I was travelling under, read like that of a first-time tourist or a businessman whose work took him to the East once or twice a year. My passports became pure fiction.

In the days before the war on terror and the shrine to government-sponsored paranoia that modern air travel has since become, you could, if you desired, board a plane under one name and disembark in another country as someone else entirely. All you needed was the passports and the balls, and I had both. I began carrying at least two passports with me at all times and was soon slipping effortlessly between my growing collection of bought-and-paid-for identities. On one memorable occasion preparations for a smuggle called for me to visit five countries in a single day. Beginning the mammoth journey in

Singapore at 8 a.m, I flew to Hong Kong to collect the cash to pay Kamol for that year's weed, and from there straight to Thailand where I handed the money over to our supplier in the early afternoon. Once Kamol was paid I flew to Jakarta in Indonesia to finalize arrangements for the onload of the dope shipment. Once my business was complete in Indonesia I flew back to Superstar to deliver the news that the crew was prepped and ready to go. Finally, as midnight approached, I boarded my last plane of the day to take me back to Singapore. Throughout the whistle-stop tour of South East Asia I used all of my fake names and began to wonder once I arrived home exhausted, if I couldn't do with a few more besides.

I made the most of a world in transition. On the one hand the world was moving towards a bright new technological age – progress, they called it – on the other it was still run without the use of high-speed accessible international communications and full co-operation between nations. With my passports in hand, I slipped through the gaps between the old world and the new.

I loved to travel, whoever I was. Michael Young, Rodney Boggs, Michael Escreet, all of my aliases had in common a growing affection for the luxury afforded while flying first class on the world's premier airlines.

Boarding planes to America to pick up cash or meet with our buyer became an exercise in self-amusement, part method acting, part subterfuge. Walking through Customs with the trusty Halliburton stuffed to the gills with used dollar bills was a kick in itself. On top of the cash, I'd lay a couple of T-shirts, a sweater maybe, as a token attempt at concealing the fact that I was carrying up to a quarter of a million dollars out of America and back to the East. Quite how I thought a layer of cashmere would disguise the money should Customs decide to take a look is an issue I chose never to fully explore.

By the time 1981 rolled around, we were ready to go again with another scam and, having learned our lesson the previous year, this time we had something more substantial than the *Yellow Bull* to rely on to help us achieve our objectives. We had the *Cape Elizabeth*.

Cape Elizabeth had begun life in the sixties as a cargo vessel. Lietzman had found the boat in England the year before and gladly paid the $100,000 asking price. Once he and a friend of his had got drunk aboard the new boat and sailed her around for a few days, he was sure she was just what we needed.

One of the plus points of the vessel, apart from its size and durability, was the heavy-duty winch installed to lift cargo on and off the main deck. We intended to use the winch to lift and drop our two new cigarette boats. This time Lietzman and I had gone top of the range, buying forty-foot speedboats, *Kim Ono* and *Mariposa*, rather than the twenty-eight-footers we'd started with. Cigarette boats weren't cheap, each one setting us back $250,000, even though *Mariposa* wasn't a true cigarette; owning four meant that we had almost a million dollars tied up in speedboats alone. Things were edging towards crazy but, as yet, no one had noticed.

The back end of *Kim Ono* had been ripped out and replaced. The decking which covered the back end of the boat would usually be short enough to allow two rows of seats, much like the front and back seats of a car. I had the decking on my boat lengthened until it was brought up flush with the back of the first row of seats, nudging the driver's shoulders. This gave me a forty-foot hull where I could secrete up to three tons of dope. No one watching it speed by would be any the wiser. I had the boat decorated with the number 88 at May's suggestion, go-faster stripes and decals. I'd even invented the *Kim Ono* logo, featuring an oriental Geisha in traditional dress, which decorated the sides. As a final touch, I went so far as to have a bomber jacket made up featuring the same logo which I wore to drive the boat. Lietzman's *Mariposa*, though not a true cigarette, had been built to our exacting specifications and was able to hide as much dope as *Kim Ono*, and between the pair of them they could hold six tons without any trouble whatsoever.

The smuggle started with the *Cape Elizabeth*, captained by Samuel Colflesh, sitting off the coast of Phuket.

The weed was packed and pressed in Thailand. Bobby had rented a local warehouse in which to get the shipment ready and it became a hive of activity as we toiled, vacuum-packing and baling machines working day and night to turn the two tons of marijuana into waterproof bricks. They had to be compact enough to be hidden in twelve-inch PVC piping, the kind seen running down the sides of houses all over the world as rainwater pipes . . . The pipes measured eight feet in length and again came complete with waterproof endcaps, which ensured that nothing secreted inside the tubing was visible. Once the pipes were packed with weed they were painted yellow up to the mid-point, the words THIS WAY UP and FLOATING LEVEL HERE were carefully added with stencils and, as a final touch, an aerial was added, left dangling uselessly from the endcap at the top of this curious item.

Ten days of hard work later and, hey presto, one shipment of electronic marine buoys, destined for California.

The "buoys" were then loaded into the speedboats and driven out to the *Cape Elizabeth*.

The buoys were packed four to a crate and stacked in the far corner of the hold, which was then covered with wooden slats and a sheet of tarpaulin, secured by lengths of rope and ready to be transported to Singapore, from where they would complete their journey to America as normal freight.

The shipping lanes around South East Asia, those we shadowed but never stuck to completely, were often awash with hidden obstacles that meant our onboard forward-looking radar system became a necessity rather than a luxury. Huge cargo ships sailed the area, picking up and dropping off hundreds of tons of freight at a time in steel containers. Often the containers were stored on deck, loosely secured as they made their way around the world.

It was not unheard of, in bad weather, with the cargo ships tossed this way and that by the huge waves that could blow up, for one of the containers to simply slide off the deck and into the sea. Because airtight containers were sealed and often not completely full, they held enough air to keep them afloat. Even if the crew of the ship that had lost the container knew it had gone overboard, their tight schedules would not allow them to turn back and retrieve it, so these small steel icebergs were simply left bobbing in the ocean. The forward-looking radar system we had fitted on the boat gave us enough prior warning to divert us from any potential hazards, though it could not tell us whether those hazards were a large school of migrating fish, a whale making its slow heavy way from here to there or a container full of training shoes and tractor parts waiting to sink us.

The other major hazard of our journey was the other ships we would encounter en route. As soon as another boat appeared on our radar or line of sight we immediately began to speculate. Who are they? Where are they from? And what do we look like to them? We always purposely stayed just far enough off the major shipping lanes to avoid such run-ins and most of the other boats that appeared in the twelve miles between us and the horizon were probably there for the very same reason as us.

Cape Elizabeth sailed into Singapore harbouring her illicit bounty. Once there we arranged for the buoys to be shipped into America as commercial freight using one of our spurious company fronts. When the paperwork was finished and the waybills needed to collect the product at the other end were in order, it was simply a case of flying to America to meet the ship carrying our dope, signing for it, and selling it on. Happy days.

By 1981 the American dope market had stabilized and the price of Thai weed was back up to between $1,200 and $1,700 per pound, ensuring that our overall gross receipts from the *Cape Elizabeth* smuggle nudged a very respectable nine million dollars.

Once you're counting money in hundreds of thousands, in million-dollar increments, it becomes something abstract. Dollars in Disneyworld amounts, Mickey Mouse money. We had so much that some of it was left collecting dust in boxes stored in our various homes around the world. (I certainly always had a million or so in cash handy in a suitcase under the bed, should I need it.) Most of the cash was deposited at the Singapore branch of an international bank, giving us access to our money in that city and also, should we need it, at their branch in the Far East Trading Centre in Hong Kong (also favoured by Howard Marks). Luckily, we had found a bank that was content to take suitcases full of cash from us and not ask any questions whatsoever. Perhaps we weren't so out of the ordinary, maybe they were used to dealing with millions of dollars handed over by half-hungover nightclub owners in sandals and jeans with brand-new Jags parked out front; perhaps they had us marked out as respectable businessmen with an unconventional approach.

In 1982 we remodelled the *Diver's Delight* landing barges, cutting the decks open and taking out the foam that lined them. The space left in each could easily accommodate the two tons of dope we had ordered from Kamol.

Once the dope was packed and hidden, the craft were crated up and shipped to San Francisco. The crates travelled as normal freight with the accompanying paperwork filled out in fictitious names representing non-existent companies. I picked them up from the Customs clearing at dockside and moved them to the warehouse to unload.

We made another nine millions dollars, cash. It was that easy. Of course the money wasn't pure profit; the costs of running the operation were big, and getting bigger. We had the rent on the warehouse in San Francisco. A journey from Thailand to America and back on a vessel like *Cape Elizabeth* could cost half a million dollars in fuel and crew alone. We'd put our casual team of helpers on salary and were routinely paying them huge cash bonuses, as much as a hundred thousand dollars per man, when the money from another successful shipment rolled in. But still we were left with roughly two million dollars each. Cash.

As if that wasn't enough, Superstar's popularity was such that on a bad day we could reasonably expect to take thousands of dollars in cash. And that was on a bad day.

Annually, the bar was turning over a huge amount of money. We were charging to get into the place and our drinks weren't cheap. Of course, the money going through the bar wasn't all profit, there were running and staff costs, but, even so, selling legal intoxicants was definitely giving the weed business a run for its money. In cash.

With that kind of money in such large and endless supply, the best thing to do is spend it, because the next smuggle will bring in more.

3

Reefer Men: The Rise and Fall of a Billionaire Drugs Ring

Tony Thompson

In the 1970s and 1980s, before skunk flooded the European cannabis market, Thailand was the byword for a quality smoke, good enough to justify a separate price point from either Afghani hash (where Europe was concerned) or "domestic" Mexican weed in the US. It's often sold as Thai sticks, which are themselves often imitated, with weaker strains of grass being dried and bundled to look like Thai (the stick adding weight, of course).

Tony Thompson's Reefer Men *chronicles the high lives of the sometime denizens of the Superstar Bar on Bangkok's Patpong Road (see chapter 2), a shady collection of mostly American sailors, ex-servicemen and scammers, who probably did more than anyone else to give Thai weed the outstanding reputation it's always enjoyed in dope-smoking circles.*

Their luck eventually ran out after around eighteen years of very lucrative activity, and neither were they blessed when plans for a major Hollywood movie about the gang, to star Brad Pitt soon after his appearance in Ocean's 11, *appear to have been shelved in 1999. In their heyday, Brian Daniels and his partners, Chris and Bill Shaffer, moved unimaginable quantities of weed to Australia and California by yacht and helicopter, approaching the matter with the attitude of an American corporation: they pioneered the vacuum-packing and compacting of large batches of weed to a state of the art, ensuring they maximized their storage capacity and minimized mould, and even printed "passed by" stickers to affix to them, so that they would know which tame official to kickback to upon receipt.*

This is very different in method from today's skunk-farming, where intensive hydroponic grow ops in suitably discreet premises can obviate the need for crossing borders. Currently, it is thought that Vietnamese gangs produce the majority of the UK's skunk in this way. Sadly, there has been at least one case where this appears to have involved indentured child labour.

If the Superstar-Bar gang were different in method, they were also very different in spirit; for a while, Brian Daniels guaranteed Thai farmers a market, and also helped to introduce new farming methods. He even continued this kind of work with legitimate crops, like an unofficial Peace-Corps volunteer, while on the run, partly to create a good impression should he come to trial, and partly because that impression would have been accurate.

A motley collection of hippies, draft-dodgers, helicopter pilots and ex-marines, the gang's mutual need for skills and contacts overcame one of America's great social divides, post-Vietnam. However, in an operation so large, employing so many, it was perhaps inevitable that the centre would not hold. This extract is from early in the gang's tale, chronicling the creation of the US arm of its operation, and how these carefree Californian college kids discovered a lucrative supply of weed from a surprising source ...

September 1969

He sat on the edge of the kerb at the corner of Second and St Marks, shirtless and shoeless, the soles of his feet flat in the gutter, his skinny arms resting limply in his lap. Weeks of neglect had turned his hair and beard into a bushy black mane and you could tell from his eyes that he had spent most of the day crying.

"No weed in a month!" he sighed. "I guess I might as well accept that athletics scholarship to Notre Dame and study business economics after all."

This forlorn young hippy first appeared in a cartoon titled "The legendary dope famine of '69", published in an underground newspaper in September that same year. By that time everyone was ready to see the funny side of the situation, but just a few short weeks earlier, the chronic shortage of marijuana across America had been no laughing matter.

Supplies had all but dried up in several major cities and the price of what little was left had risen to an all-time high, while the quality had fallen to an all-time low.

"There's just not any available," a New York dealer nicknamed Porky Pig sobbed to the Associated Press after three fruitless trips to the West Coast in search of the elusive weed. "If I had a bunch of grass I could take it to New York or Miami and make a million dollars!"

The seeds of the shortage had been sown months earlier when the usual heavy spring rains that fall across central Mexico – the source of around eighty per cent of all the marijuana smoked in the US at the time – failed to appear. By the end of May the crop had been ruined, drying out to little more than matchwood. In Sinaloa, one of the main growing regions, the local police chief took advantage of the situation and ordered his men to set fire to around fifty acres of fields containing the few remaining viable plants.

For the growers, already considerably out of pocket, this proved to be the final straw. Before the day had ended, the police chief had been shot dead .

The response of the Mexican government was immediate.

Martial law was declared and the army flooded into Sinaloa carrying out house-to-house searches in a bid to track down those responsible. All cars heading for the American border were forced to pass through heavily guarded roadblocks, and search-and-destroy squads were travelling deep into the countryside to torch every marijuana crop they could find . Within the space of a few days, more than one million plants had been destroyed.

Prior to the crackdown, grass had been flowing through the US-Mexico border like water flowing through a burst dam. But once the leak was well and truly plugged, it was only a matter of time before supplies began to dwindle down to nothing.

It could not have come at a worse time. In the weeks leading up to the shortage, the popularity of pot had grown beyond all expectations. In July the film *Easy Rider* had been released to massive commercial success and critical acclaim. Featuring dozens of scenes in which its stars Peter Fonda and Dennis Hopper smoked pot, and fuelled by rumours that the actors had been getting stoned for real, the film helped to popularize marijuana almost as much as it popularized motorcycling.

The fast-growing anti-Vietnam movement had adopted marijuana as one of its sacred tenets and its use by well-to-do middle-class college students was also soaring.

At the Woodstock festival in August 1969, an estimated ninety per cent of the 400,000 attendees smoked marijuana over the course of the event. The drug was rapidly making inroads into mainstream society to the point that even those considered otherwise "straight" had begun using and selling it.

This soaring demand, combined with the sudden shortage, meant that the few dealers lucky enough to have stock in reserve found themselves making serious money. Selling marijuana became something more than just a way to get your own dope for free or "stick it to the man"; it became a way of making a living.

A few chancers tried to jump on the bandwagon, selling alfalfa, oregano and even lawn grass as the real thing, but for those with access to the genuine article, profits were high and the risks were low.

For one student, the son of a wealthy ranch owner, the situation seemed to represent nothing less than a golden business opportunity.

"The way I see it," twenty-one-year-old Ciro Mancuso told his friends that summer, "is that anyone with a bit of sense who can get hold of some pot is going to be in a position to get real rich, real fast."

Mexican grass may have been off the menu but for those willing to put in a little effort, there was an abundant source of marijuana far closer to hand.

During the Second World War the US government urged farmers throughout the Midwest, from Kansas and Nebraska to Ohio and Indiana, to sow the botanical equivalent of marijuana's first cousin – hemp – with a promise that, in return, both they and their sons would be exempted from military service.

Just five years earlier the plant had been labelled "the assassin of youth" and all cultivation had been banned. But the war in the Pacific meant vast quantities of hemp were needed to replace supplies of cheap foreign fibres that had been cut off by the Japanese.

An inspirational film, *Hemp for Victory,* showed how the plant could be used to make rope to rig battleships, fire hose, thread for army boots and parachute webbing – all essential to the war effort. Special permits were issued, millions of free seeds were handed out and soon . . . ten-foot high hemp plants.

Once the war ended the farmers switched back to corn and other grains, but the "wild marijuana" continued to spread. Some called it "loco weed" because it made farm animals that nibbled on it giddy, even though the plants contained barely one-tenth the amount of the active ingredient, delta-9-THC, found in Mexican marijuana.

Local pot dealers used it mainly as filler, but once imports of the good stuff started to dry up many users decided that, in this hour of great need, bad grass was better than no grass at all.

Unlike the hard-to-find Mexican marijuana, the domestic variety was plentiful. That summer, Kansas alone had some 52,000 acres growing wild and the university town of Lawrence soon became a Mecca for eager potheads. The local hippy hang-outs the Gaslight Tavern and the Rock Chalk Café even sold hand-drawn maps giving directions to the prime sites down by the banks of the Kaw river, alongside politically active fare like "fascist pig burgers" at thirty-five cents a pop. But the maps were hardly necessary – college campuses along the East and West coasts buzzed with whispered tales of the fact that, so abundant was the marijuana, all you had to do was stick your arm out of the window as you drove through town and you would come away with a handful.

One July weekend, lured by the promise of easy money, Ciro Mancuso and his college room-mate Brian Degen loaded up a

car with sacks and machetes and set off on the forty-eight-hour
drive to Kansas.

The pair were party-loving students at the Paradise College,
an unremarkable liberal arts school on the south shore of Lake
Tahoe. Classmates remember them as the kind of guys who
were so laid-back they were practically horizontal. Mancuso in
particular was friendly and outgoing, but although he had bags
of charisma and a strong personality, he kept his distance and
was never part of the "in" crowd.

Exceptionally bright and quick to learn, Mancuso excelled
at anything he put his mind to. During the summer he played
defensive halfback for the Patterson Tigers, in the winter he
joined the wrestling team, while in the spring he worked the
running track. But skiing was by far his favourite pastime.

He and Degen had met after initially enrolling on a course at
the University of Reno but transferred to Paradise at the end of
their first year on skiing scholarships. The move suited them, as
their achievements on the slopes had long overshadowed their
achievements in the classroom and Paradise College was just
minutes from at least three ski resorts.

The pair had smoked and traded small amounts of dope
for kicks since their school days and bonded over their equally
desperate desire to find an escape from small town life. And
now, for the first time, they had stumbled across it.

In Kansas, under cover of darkness, they hacked down plants
until their backs ached and their palms were red raw. Back at
Lake Tahoe they cured the stems by placing them inside pillow
cases which in turn were placed inside dryers at the college
launderette.

One- and five-dollar bags were then weighed out and, as an
added touch, wrapped in pages torn from Mexican newspapers.

The dope sold like hotcakes.

That first trip was so successful that Mancuso and Degen
spent the next few weekends driving up to Kansas and Nebraska
for more supplies.

They were not the only ones. Police officers in the Midwest
were initially puzzled at what seemed to be a vast increase
in the number of birdwatchers that summer. When they

decided to investigate, they realized that this new breed of ornithologist invariably failed to bring binoculars, had long hair and usually drove vans with flowers and peace signs painted on the side.

Across the Corn Belt, arrests for illegal harvesting of marijuana more than tripled that summer, with the vast majority of those caught coming from out of state. A single sheriff in Cloud County, Kansas, bagged forty-three suspects in the space of a few weeks, all but three of them from California. Every nightshift, if things got a little too quiet, he and his deputies would head down to the river and almost always return with at least a couple of collars.

It was only a matter of time before Mancuso and Degen's luck ran out and on 8 August they were arrested in Kansas and charged with attempting to illegally possess marijuana. They spent a couple of nights in jail but the money they had made from their previous drug runs was more than enough to pay the $1,000 they were fined before being sent back to California.

Some might have taken such an arrest as a sign that it was time to get out of the trade, but Mancuso was already hooked.

He and Degen would not return to Kansas, but it had nothing to do with the fear of being caught again. The drug runs had been profitable, but the work had been slow, tedious and physically exhausting. Selling marijuana was, they decided, the way forward. All they needed now was to find a way to make it even more lucrative.

By the middle of the summer the weather had achieved something that tens of billions of dollars spent on the war against drugs had failed to do: reduce the marijuana traffic across the Mexican border to a trickle.

Six months into his first term, President Richard Nixon spied an opportunity to strike a decisive blow against the trade. A loser in the 1960 election that saw John F. Kennedy take the White House, Nixon had won through this time round thanks to millions of votes from the so-called "silent majority" – blue-collar Americans deeply opposed to hippy counter-culture, anti-war demonstrators and, in particular, marijuana smokers.

At 2.30 p.m. Pacific Daylight Time on Sunday 21 September, Nixon launched Operation Intercept. More than 2,000 Customs agents were moved down to the American side of the border with Mexico and given orders to stop the marijuana trade.

Timed to coincide with the September harvest, Nixon's plan was to hit the trade hard at a time when supplies were already running extremely thin.

Within an hour of the operation's launch, traffic at the main border posts was backed up for more than two and a half miles. By the end of the afternoon the tailbacks stretched out for six miles.

The chaos continued in the days that followed. In theory every vehicle was supposed to be subjected to a three-minute inspection.

In reality not all vehicles were searched, many of those that were received only a cursory glance, but the odds of being caught had shifted enough to ensure that few smugglers were willing to risk the trip.

Supplies of freshly harvested marijuana began to pile up in the stash houses on the south side of the border and the price, already high, began to rise higher still.

After the Kansas debacle, Mancuso and Degen had begun looking for new and innovative ways to stay in the marijuana business. As Operation Intercept began to bite, the pair quickly realized that the increased retail value of their chosen product meant that a method previously deemed too costly and impractical had suddenly become feasible. Rather than taking a chance by driving through the border, they would simply fly over it.

It was a possibility the Nixon administration had already considered. As part of the crackdown, the Federal Aviation Authority had installed mobile radar equipment on trucks positioned at strategic points along the border, while the air force stationed a fleet of intercept planes nearby. Within days of the blockade, blips of light moving south to north appeared on the screens, but by the time the interceptors had been scrambled, the blips had already vanished.

Mancuso, Degen and dozens of other smugglers had realized that small planes were able to dip between the mountain ranges and canyon corridors that made up much of the border, and thus travel underneath the radar blanket.

Each flight required nerves of steel. In Mexico the landing strips were heavily disguised to prevent them being spotted from the air by the military. In many cases, the sole difference between a patch of treacherous rough ground and an official landing strip was that, on at least one occasion, someone had managed to land there. By the same token, the only difference between a landing strip and a crash site was that the same aircraft had subsequently managed to take off.

The journey back was little better, with the planes flying low and navigating through the potentially deadly mountain peaks by moonlight before landing in the desert where trucks would meet them to carry away their precious cargo.

Within days of the crackdown Customs agents estimated that at least ten planes a night were crossing the border, and admitted there was virtually nothing they could do about it. "They are developing their own air force," noted one official, "and it's getting bigger and bigger."

After just two weeks, Operation Intercept was abandoned amid growing protests from employers fed up with workers arriving late, and from legitimate businesses and traders on both sides of the border who had experienced a seventy per cent drop in sales.

But the new techniques devised by the smugglers soon became the norm.

Having fast discovered the profitability of their new enterprise Mancuso and Degen dropped out of college, joined forces with a team of "crossroaders" – professional casino cheats – and began using a variety of small aircraft to smuggle marijuana. Over the next two years the pair helped to organize more than fifty flights that brought in a total of 35,000 pounds of dope.

Selling at around $225 per pound, the gross profits amounted to almost $8 million. It was a small fortune but Mancuso and Degen received only a modest share due to the large number of others involved, the high cost of running the planes and the money spent hiring the trucks and drivers.

It was clear to Mancuso that the only way he would ever be

able to keep more of the money for himself was if he found a way to cut out the middlemen.

It was time to head south.

Fluent in Spanish ever since his schooldays, Ciro Mancuso took his profits from the airborne smuggling operation and bought a run-down ranch near Guadalajara. After a few essential renovations the ranch became Mancuso's permanent home and he and Brian Degen began contacting local growers and suppliers before launching themselves on to the market as marijuana brokers.

Each month tons of the drug would arrive at the ranch for processing and buyers from America and beyond would visit to select the goods they wanted to purchase. The customers would then choose their own way of getting the drugs across the border or, for an additional fee, have Mancuso make arrangements on their behalf.

The pair bought a caravan and had it fitted with a cleverly concealed secret compartment where large amounts of marijuana could be stored. This could then be towed back and forth across the border to get the drugs into California.

The drugs were so well concealed they were virtually undetectable but as an extra precaution, the mobile home was always towed by pick-up trucks driven by late middle-aged men or couples – far less likely to arouse suspicion from border guards than young men like Mancuso and Degen.

Within weeks hundreds of pounds of marijuana had made their way north, but the scale of the operation soon attracted the attention of the local authorities who were still under pressure from the US government to help stem the tide of pot flowing across the border. Even tucked away in the boondocks of Mexico, the combination of a luxury lifestyle with no visible form of employment made Mancuso stand out like a sore thumb.

In March 1972, while Mancuso was in the middle of negotiating a price with a group of American buyers, Mexican police raided the ranch, arresting him and nine others, including four key customers. Brian Degan, running his end of the operation from back in Lake Tahoe, missed the swoop.

After a swift search the Federales seized more than two tons of marijuana from the property as well as a plane.

Transferred to prison that same day, Mancuso refused to allow what he saw as a relatively minor setback to have any effect on his fast-growing smuggling empire.

Mexican prisons in the early seventies were notorious for being run by guards willing to turn a blind eye to almost anything, just so long as they were properly compensated. Mancuso started out in a bare, filthy cell but was quickly upgraded to a beautifully decorated "suite" where he had his choice of meals, regular female companions, a guitar and a host of other creature comforts.

All inmates were required to carry out some form of work and Mancuso was no exception. He set up a furniture factory in the prison with the intention of creating cut-price products for the American market.

It was a front of course. Each item the factory produced featured a specially made secret compartment, and after leaving the prison the goods were taken to a nearby warehouse run by junior members of Mancuso's gang. There the compartments would be filled with marijuana. The furniture was then shipped up to California or Nevada where Degen would extract the drugs and sell them on.

Smuggling operations with the caravan also continued while Mancuso was in prison. In October 1972 the gang's regular driver, Harry McKeown, towed the vehicle across the border and made his way up to San José where the drugs were to be dropped off.

No sooner had McKeown arrived at the rendezvous and spotted his contact than dozens of police officers swooped down and arrested them both.

"They knew all about the trip we made," McKeown later recalled. "He told me all the officers had come up from Los Angeles and had been following me all day." McKeown and his contact were taken to jail, certain that, like Mancuso, they would now be spending a long spell behind bars. But to McKeown's surprise it was not to be.

"The next morning, ten o'clock or so, they took me down,

took me to the desk, gave me my things and said 'get out', so I left. The other guy was nowhere to be seen and they didn't say anything about anything. I went back to Reno and got my lawyer to call the police station and they said 'well, the truck and caravan is sitting right here in the parking lot, get it out'. So I flew back."

The caravan was in tatters, having been torn apart by the police officers looking for the concealed drugs. All the wall and roof panels had been pulled off, the floorboards had been ripped up, the cushions had been slashed open and each and every interior fixing had been removed or smashed. The search had been comprehensive and the officers had even brought in sniffer dogs to ensure every last nook and cranny was explored.

"I can't even begin to describe all the damage done to this thing," says McKeown. "This was a disaster. I took it to a repair place and the guy had an estimate of like $4,000-plus to get it fixed. He was amazed. He couldn't understand what possibly could have happened to it."

McKeown drove the wreck back to Reno and left it parked on his driveway. It sat there for three or four days before a couple of Mancuso's men came over to assess the damage for themselves.

Their faces, initially grim, soon burst into broad, radiant smiles as both they and McKeown realized the almost unbelievable truth:

"It was still loaded."

After just over a year in prison, Ciro Mancuso returned to his ranch in Guadalajara to find that the Federales who had raided it had somehow failed to uncover the full extent of the renovation he had made to the property.

Several rooms in the main building had been given false walls that he had used to conceal vast amounts of drugs. Despite an extensive search by dozens of officers, more than two tons of marijuana remained behind these panels.

But while the drugs were safe, Mexico itself was anything but, and Mancuso soon packed his bags and headed back to Lake Tahoe. While he had been locked away, an increasing number of marijuana suppliers had switched to heroin, which was proving more profitable. By 1974 Mexican interests controlled two-thirds of the US heroin market.

Those dealers that had stuck with pot were facing increased competition from each other and from Colombian dealers who were fast moving into the trade. Violence, once a rarity, was now becoming commonplace and the once-congenial atmosphere in which deals had taken place was a thing of the past.

Members of the Coronado Company *[Mancuso and Degen's front, named after their old high school]* experienced this new, darker mood first-hand when Louis Villar decided to cut out the middleman and deal directly with Joe the Mexican's suppliers for their biggest load to date – twelve tons.

When the new supplier arrived to meet Villar and the others, he was accompanied by ten heavily armed bodyguards.

It was a chilling sign of the times. Rip-offs were becoming increasingly common, but not the kind of rip-offs that the mostly docile American hippies had been used to. Everyone had stories about being burned, deals where you came away with a lower grade of dope or got home to discover half the weight was made up of packaging rather than product. Deals like those were seen to be part of the territory but the new rip-offs didn't just cost money, they cost lives.

Around the time the Coronado Company was entering negotiations for their twelve tons, a teenage smuggler, a Mexican–American by the name of David Ortiz, had a lucky escape.

Ortiz had started out dealing lids – ounces of marijuana – in high school and had spent ninety days in prison after being caught at a checkpoint in a fully loaded car. Through a contact in Mexico he met a pilot named Loren Smith and the two men arranged to fly a load of dope up from a town called Guerro.

David was also supposed to fly down to act as ground crew and oversee the loading but he had to pull out at the last minute.

Desperate to find someone he could trust, he persuaded his close friend Glen to take his place. The flight down to Mexico went smoothly and Smith managed to land the plane on the makeshift strip in the middle of the jungle, but the pair never made it home.

Exactly what happened has never been fully established but it is known that the plane took off again with both Smith and Glen on board, but with no marijuana. Shortly after take-off, the plane crashed into the ocean killing both men instantly.

It was an early example of what would become an increasingly common scam among Mexican merchants. A crucial element of all the deals involving aircraft was that, as well as supplying marijuana, the growers would have to procure aviation fuel to top up the plane's tanks for the return journey.

It didn't take long for the less scrupulous drug cartel bosses to work out that withholding the drugs and replacing half the kerosene with diesel or water would make the plane stall and crash soon after take off. The Mexicans would get to keep both the money and the drugs and the buyers would be left in the dark. Dozens of drug planes had crashed after being overloaded and they would simply assume they had been hit by bad luck.

Ortiz only found out his friend's fate because Glen's father flew down to Mexico and spent months diving in the ocean until he found the empty plane and identified his son's body still in the cockpit.

Ortiz was left deeply shaken by the loss of his friend and tried to quit the drug business altogether. He stayed out for a while but then was all but forced back in by his younger brother, Brian.

When David had been selling, Brian had been one of his biggest customers. Once David stopped, Brian had been forced to go elsewhere but had been repeatedly burned in deals and even had threats made against his life. Fearful for his brother's welfare, David decided his only option was to return to dealing in order to keep his brother safe.

Mexico was out of the question. One possible alternative was Morocco, an annual Mecca for thousands of hippies, surfers and backpackers, and firmly established throughout the counterculture underground as a good place to buy top-quality hash.

But just as he started putting out feelers, Ortiz came across a new source of supply that put both the Central American and North African products to shame. The natives were friendly and completely in tune with the hippy ideal, the prices were low and the quality of the pot was better than anything he could have ever imagined. Best of all, the trade was being pioneered by a group of individuals that no one in law enforcement, not even the eager agents of the Drug Enforcement Administration, had the slightest interest in seeing inside a courtroom.

From the moment they arrived in Vietnam, the leaders of the American military found they were fighting a war on two fronts.

The first involved the action against the Vietcong, the second an ongoing series of battles to keep the troops from getting high.

Marijuana had been a small yet integral part of Vietnamese culture long before the arrival of the Americans, but as soon as the first trickle of soldiers began to arrive during the 1963 advisory period, entrepreneurial farmers realized they had a lucrative new cash crop on their hands. By 1966, there were twenty-nine fixed stalls selling marijuana in Saigon alone. The drug could be bought loose or in the form of ready-made cigarettes delivered in neat, cellophane-wrapped packs of twenty.

Recreational drugs were frowned upon in the field because of the risk of enemy contact, but back at the fire support bases it was another story. Attacks here were infrequent and many young draftees took full advantage of every opportunity to relax.

At first Army officials were willing to turn a blind eye – alcohol abuse was, after all, a far greater concern – but with so many journalists embedded with the troops, reports of the fast-growing problem soon found their way back home.

Newsreel footage shot at Fire Support Base Ares from the summer of 1969 shows Vito , a twenty-year-old draftee squadron leader, demonstrating a technique called "shotgunning". The stem of a pipe loaded with marijuana was inserted into the chamber of an empty shotgun, and air was blown through the bowl. The members of Vito's squad then took it in turns to suck in the concentrated smoke from the end of the barrels. "You get really stoned," explained one miserable soldier, "and then, who cares about this war."

In April 1970 nineteen-year–old Specialist 4 Peter Lemon of Company E was serving as an assistant machine-gunner at Fire Support Base Illingworth in Tay Ninh province when the base came under heavy attack by more than 400 Vietcong. Despite being hopelessly outnumbered, Lemon took on the waves of enemy soldiers first with his machine gun until it jammed and then with his rifle until that too malfunctioned.

The attackers began to focus on his position and Lemon was wounded by a hand grenade. Despite this he used his only remaining armaments – his own hand grenades – to kill all but one of those pursuing him. He then chased after the last enemy soldier and killed him with his bare hands.

Lemon moved back to his foxhole where he picked up a more seriously wounded colleague and carried him to an aid station.

Returning to his foxhole, a mortar shell exploded, killing the man next to him. Lemon was wounded a second time but ignored the hail of bullets and grenades and took up his fighting position.

He then realized the area was in danger of being overrun and once more took on the enemy with hand grenades and hand-to-hand combat, eventually managing to drive them back. Finding a working machine gun, Lemon stood out in the open and fired on the enemy until he passed out from loss of blood. When he came to at the aid station, he refused treatment until his more seriously wounded comrades had been evacuated.

Lemon was awarded the highest possible military award, the Congressional Medal of Honour, and it was only after he had received it that he revealed that he had been as high as a kite throughout the whole ordeal.

"It was the only time I ever went into combat stoned," he told CBS evening news a few months later. "You get really alert when you're stoned because you have to be. We were all partying the night before. We weren't expecting any action because we were in a support group. All the guys were *[pot]* heads. We'd sit around smoking grass and getting stoned and talking about when we'd get to go home."

He was not alone. In one study of 1,064 soldiers, sixty-seven per cent admitted smoking marijuana in the previous month.

No longer able to simply ignore the problem, the army set about trying to wipe it out. Education campaigns and compulsory lectures were introduced to highlight the dangers of the evil weed; helicopters and fixed-wing aircraft were diverted from other duties to fly out in search of marijuana fields; sniffer dogs were introduced to search billets and property.

Soldiers caught with even a small amount of marijuana faced court martial and, at the height of the eradication campaign, arrests for possession were running at a thousand per week. As a direct result of the campaign, many soldiers switched to heroin and by the end of the war one in five would be addicted to the white powder. *[White, because it would have been sourced from the "Golden Triangle" trade, which originated with CIA-backed anti-communist Chinese nationalists, rather than brown, as with the Afghan variety usually found in Europe.]*

But by the time the marijuana crackdown was introduced, soldiers weren't just smoking the stuff; they were bringing it back with them. Some was simply posted home using the military's own mail system; larger amounts were being brought back hidden among the personal belongings of returning soldiers.

Authorities on the West Coast noticed that huge amounts of South East Asian marijuana flooded the market hours after the docking of each homebound troopship. There were even rumours that some marijuana was shipped back inside sealed HR boxes [the large aluminium chests used to hold unidentified human remains], but prosecutions were rare. No one wanted to face the political repercussions that would follow the large-scale prosecution of veterans freshly returned from an increasingly unpopular war.

The marijuana coming out of Vietnam was good but that which came out of neighbouring Thailand, where many of the troops were sent for their R&R, was even better.

Not only did Thai marijuana look unique – the premium buds and leaves were skewered on stems or tied to thin bamboo reeds or sticks using animal hair – but it was also considerably more potent than anything else available at the time. Two or three puffs of Thai would produce the same effect as smoking an entire joint of Mexican and the high the drug produced was smoother and longer lasting.

Thai marijuana was so good that many believed the effects could not be attributed to THC alone. The story was that the real reason for the stick design was that it allowed the buds to be dipped in opium-infused water. No definitive answer about whether this actually happened has ever been produced but the rumours helped spread the popularity of the new brand as increasing numbers of Thai sticks found their way to America and beyond.

Profits were huge and overheads were low: $75 worth of Thai sticks purchased in Bangkok sold for more than $4,000 on the streets of San Francisco. Smuggling became so rife among certain members of the United States Marine Corps that many suggested the initials USMC actually stood for Uncle Sam's Marijuana Club.

In April 1974 the DEA issued its first public warning about potential imports of Thai sticks, following a modest bust in Hawaii, but the unintentionally enthusiastic tone they used served only to boost demand for the new product. Thai marijuana was, an unnamed official noted, at least three times more potent than the regular stuff and anyone smoking a joint made of it would invariably "go on one hell of a trip . . . could stay up for a couple of days." And although the price was considerably higher than the regular stuff, the official pointed out that this was justified as Thai sticks were effectively "the Cuban cigar of the marijuana world".

That summer, David Ortiz became one of the first major dealers to tap into the potential of this new product, obtaining regular supplies from a Bangkok-based soldier who used military post to mail home packages of up to twenty pounds at a time.

As Ortiz's imports found their way across California, demand for the potent new strain rocketed and canny dealers began exploring ways of obtaining supplies of their own.

By pure coincidence, Paradise College, where Mancuso and Degen had studied, had been taking part in an ongoing cultural exchange programme and Mancuso had played host to a young man from Thailand a couple of years earlier. It took only a few phone calls for a source to be arranged. Mancuso and Degen then purchased a brand new Air Stream caravan, complete with a custom-made secret compartment, and dispatched it on the lengthy voyage to Bangkok.

Once there, the vehicle was met by Sunthorn Kraithamjitkul,

a local businessman also known as "Thai Tony". The owner of a Bangkok automobile dealership, Sunthorn also had extensive contacts among the dope growers and was thus able to secure the highest quality product for the lowest possible price.

The caravan, driven by Harry McKeown's brother, Joe, spent several weeks on an extended sightseeing vacation before returning to Bangkok where 1,200 pounds of Thai sticks were concealed inside . It was then shipped to Canada where Joe collected it and drove it down through British Colombia back into California.

Back at Lake Tahoe, the drugs fetched around $1,500 per pound, at least four times more than Mexican pot could have generated.

Eager to present a legitimate front, Mancuso invested the money into the small construction company he had launched when he returned to Lake Tahoe. Contractors soon began to develop suspicions that some of his funds were being sourced from outside the traditional banking system – one noted that Ciro always paid his bills in cash and that the money often smelled as if it had been dug up out of a hole in the ground but no one complained too loudly.

The construction company was the real deal and all the projects it embarked upon were genuine but Mancuso had no intention of going straight. He had found the perfect product and the perfect way to disguise his income. All he needed to do now was find a way to get hold of a great deal more.

Back in Thailand, Mancuso's supplier, Sunthorn Kraithamjitkul, eager to exploit growing demand for his country's finest export, was in the process of signing up another young American as a customer.

Robert Lahodney was a keen sailor who, after graduating high school, had spent his time travelling around the world on the *Pai Nui,* a small yacht belonging to his father, before ending up in Thailand for several weeks. Lahodney was yet another former member of the Coronado High swim team and his best friend was none other than Eddie Otero.

Returning to Coronado, Lahodney was eager to tell Otero and the rest of the company of his discovery. "You guys can make the same money from two tons of Thai sticks as you'd make from twenty tons of Mexican pot, and it will only cost you a tenth as much up front!"

Otero and [his associate] Weber were eager to switch to the safer, more lucrative source but Villar resisted. Despite concerns about violence and safety, the Coronado Company's importation of twelve tons of Mexican marijuana had gone without a hitch and had been closely followed by an equally successful consignment of fifteen tons.

They were making plenty of money and had managed to keep the risks to a minimum. Why change a system that was working so well? In truth, Villar's reasons for objecting were far more selfish. He had been brought into the enterprise purely because of his ability to speak Spanish and this remained the cornerstone of his role. If the gang stopped using Spanish-speaking suppliers, he feared they might no longer need him.

But with his being the only dissenting voice, he was out-voted and arrangements were made to transfer money to Kraithamjitkul in Thailand to pay for the upcoming shipment.

Lahodney was not a member of the Coronado Company so the profits would not be shared equally. Instead he would effectively hire the company to perform the offload and hand over a third of the drugs as their payment.

In December 1976 the *Pai Nui* and its precious cargo sailed into a small natural harbour just south of San Francisco. This time around, instead of using the Zodiac boats and rafts, Weber had come up with a brainwave and bought a DUKW, an amphibious military vehicle capable of reaching ten knots on water and fifty m.p.h. on land. DUKW is a US Army acronym, with the D meaning the vehicle was first introduced in 1942, the U standing for "Utility", K referring to all-wheel-drive and the W designating twin rear axles. The vehicles have always been affectionately referred to as "Ducks".

Instead of bringing the drugs in by boat and then loading them on to the truck, Weber took the Duck out to the *Pai Nui* and tied up alongside her while the drugs were transferred. The Duck then returned to shore, drove straight up the beach, on to the main road and made its way to the stash house. It all worked perfectly, significantly reducing the time the drugs spent on the beach – the most vulnerable part of any offload operation.

Even with their small share of the load, the Coronado partners still made more than $150,000 each and it was clear that Thai marijuana was the way to go. The Company offered Lahodney the chance to become a full partner, in return for a one-off payment of $85,000. It was a token gesture, nothing more. By then each of the partners had each made more than $1 million from their smuggling activities. Now, thanks to the switch from Mexican to Thai, they were set to make many millions more.

4

ESCOBAR: The Inside Story of Pablo Escobar, the World's Most Powerful Criminal

Roberto Escobar

The introduction to the next extract, by Mark Bowden, gives more detail of the professional life of Pablo Escobar – still the world's most legendary and larger-than-life drug baron, and possibly the most paranoid, vengeful and divisive, even from among the fearful company to be found in the latter half of this book.

The details of Escobar's surreal private life, however, are best found courtesy of his brother's hagiographic memoir. Pablo Escobar may have been many things, something of a Robin Hood among them, but that doesn't mean that he doesn't also remain a cold-blooded killer. So to read about Escobar the family man, generous on his own terms, is to experience a kind of cognitive dissonance. Until you realize that the contradiction between personal loyalty and warmth, and professional zero-sum brutality – the theme of The Godfather *books and films (that Escobar loved) – is the same contradiction that features in the lives and lore of so many gangsters real and fictional.*

Among his "business assets" Escobar counted two large submarines besides his fleet of aircraft large and small, and a jungle cocina settlement in which the houses could be moved on wheels to cover its runway. How do you live

when, through fear and intimidation, you have unified a
national industry full of disparate sole traders into a large
national operation, so that even your closest competitors are
paying you for your "assistance"? What material wealth
can possibly reward such an achievement? It seems the
family made it their mission to find out – if Escobar took
the cocaine business on to a grand scale, his personal toys
were no less life-size.

I know that as the pressure on Pablo increased, as people who
had profited from him betrayed him, to protect himself and
his family and the business, Pablo became vengeful against
those who deceived him or his organization. But for as many
people who will tell you that Pablo killed someone himself
there are as many who say that he only gave the orders. Pablo
wouldn't kill anybody himself and of that I am sure. The Lion
(*a leading Medellin* sicario) remembers being there when
Pablo made his decisions. "When Pablo talked it was an order.
Everybody knew that what he said was going to happen. So
he would say, 'You have to kill this guy,' like it was nothing. He
would say it as if he was asking for more water. But I never
saw Pablo doing anything himself. None of the executives ever
saw that.'

There are people who tell stories about things they supposedly
saw at the Hacienda Napoles. George Jung, the original partner
of Carlos Lehder, said that he was at Napoles when a man was
brought there by two bodyguards. Later Jung was told the man
had been caught providing information for the police. This man
believed that if he had escaped his whole family would have
been killed so instead he gave himself up. Jung claims that as he
watched, Pablo got up from the table, walked over to the man,
and from a few feet away shot him in the chest.

This is typical of the stories told about Pablo, but like most of
them I don't believe it to be true. I know what the world believes
about my brother and I know his legend has been built on tales
of brutality like this one. People have their reasons for telling
these stories. And I know that when I protest against them

people think that I am protecting my brother. But I am telling the truth as I know it to be.

The violence was always part of it, but it was never the soul of Napoles. Napoles was Pablo's favourite home, it was his finest possession, it was loved by the family and all our friends, and it was a place unlike any that had ever been built in Colombia.

Hacienda Napoles was a drive of several hours or a brief flight from Medellín. Far enough away from the problems, and the people, of the city. Pablo and Gustavo [Escobar's cousin, who began and ran the smuggling business with him] bought the land and began building their dream kingdom in the late 1970s. It was ready in 1980, almost 7,500 acres of beautiful land, with a river running through the property.

The land was spread over two departments, or political regions.

Eventually it would contain several houses in addition to the large main house, a complete zoo opened for free to the people, as well as some runways for airplanes to do business. For someone who had been raised as simply as he had, Pablo somehow understood and appreciated great quality in all parts of his life. And Napoles was the fulfilment of all his material passions.

There are two things that everyone who was ever there remembers: above the entrance gate he had mounted that first Piper airplane that he used in the business. He believed that airplane had started his fortune. After passing through the strong security at the gate, people would drive on a winding road past fields of lime trees, lemon trees, and all sorts of tropical fruit, past the open meadow with several thousand grazing purebred Braham cattle, for almost two miles until they reached the zoo. The zoo was another crazy dream of Pablo's that came true. Who builds a zoo at his house?

This was a real zoo with many big animals, including hippopotamuses *[sic]*, rhinoceroses, giraffes and ostriches and elephants, emus, a pink dolphin, zebras, monkeys, and a kangaroo that liked to kick soccer balls. There were also many types of exotic birds. Pablo loved birds, especially parrots, and wanted to have a male and a female of every species. He had a favourite parrot, Chinchón, who could name most of the great soccer players of Colombia, However, Chinchón also liked to sip whisky and would fall asleep. Unfortunately, one evening she fell asleep on a table and one of the cats ate her. After that Pablo prohibited cats from Napoles – even big cats like lions and tigers.

Pablo bought the animals from the circuses that performed in Colombia as well as from the United States. It was legal to buy them in America, but not legal to import them into Colombia without a special licence. Bringing those animals in from America was a big problem, a very big problem. How do you smuggle a rhinoceros?

Pablo was careful, and a veterinarian travelled with each animal to advise our keepers about the proper care of the animal. Usually they were landed on our business runways and transported by our disguised trucks to Napoles. One time, though, a rhino arrived illegally in Medellín but it was too late to drive it to Napoles. The journey would take them through guerrilla territory and they did not want to make that trip at night. That left Pablo with a great problem. How do you hide a rhino overnight? Even in Medellín where people have become used to some unusual sights, that was hard to do. It was suggested they put it in a private car garage and so that's what they did. The trucker put the cage inside this garage and a keeper stayed with it. The family kept its car on the street that night, although they could not explain to anyone that it was necessary to do so because there was a rhinoceros in their garage. The next morning it was put on a truck and driven to Napoles – here it joined the herd. There was a whispered saying that came from that: "If he is willing to hide an illegal rhinoceros there is no question he would hide cocaine anywhere."

The only animals that I kept at Napoles were my horses, my beautiful horses. From the time I was a boy I have loved riding and when it became possible I started buying horses to ride and to breed.

Pablo didn't share my passion for them. He never bought one for himself, only for the ranch. But he would often joke with me,

"Oh, what a beautiful horse. You spend all your money on these expensive horses. That's a crazy thing to do." I would respond to him, "You know, Pablo, at least I enjoy riding my horses, but you and all those animals . . . You don't enjoy the animals. Try to ride a hippo and see what happens."

Pablo did keep some horses at Napoles. He had four horses that pulled a silver carriage slowly around the property, and he also had miniature ponies to entertain the children who visited.

The zoo at Napoles was open for the public to enjoy. Pablo explained to a Medellín newspaper, "Napoles zoo belongs to the Colombian people. We built it so that children and adults, rich and poor, can enjoy it, and owners cannot pay for what is already theirs."

One day three years after the zoo had been open an official document from the Institute of Renewable Resources arrived and told Pablo he possessed eighty-five animals and he did not have the proper licence: "This is all illegal. You have these animals without permits. What are you going to do about it?"

Pablo was polite. "Please, if you want, take them,' he said casually.

"But you know the government doesn't have the money to feed them all and take care of them. So you should sign this paper and I'll take care of them." The government fined Pablo about $4,500 but left the animals at Napoles. In addition to his real animals, Pablo had five full-size cement prehistoric animals, including a T-rex and a woolly mammoth, all constructed for the children to play on them.

Beyond the zoo were the houses. There was intense security on every part of the property, some of it easily seen, but more of it concealed. No one could get through the gates to the house unless they were cleared personally by Pablo. If you didn't have an invitation the armed guards turned you away. Even if people did have invitations the guards faxed them to the house for Pablo to check. Near the house was a lit runway for the transportation planes to land. By the runway was Pablo's collection of cars, and among them was an old bullet-holed car that he told everyone had belonged to Bonnie and Clyde and an old Pontiac that supposedly had belonged to Al Capone. The Bonnie and Clyde car had been sold to him by our friend in the United States who introduced us to Frank Sinatra.

Frank Sinatra was real, I wasn't so certain about those cars.

By the main house were the lit tennis courts, swimming pool, and basketball courts, the outdoor dining areas, and the games room.

Everything for pleasure that could be wanted was there: the river on which we often held races with wave runners, spaces to play soccer and long open pastures for my horseback riding and hiking. There were stables where the riding horses were kept, even a bullring where visiting matadors entertained our guests. For transportation and to race we had cars and motorcycles, some of them with sidecars for passengers; we had Jet Skis, boats, even hovercraft.

The houses offered even more pleasures, swimming pools, Jacuzzis, large dining rooms, a theatre for watching recently released movies, even a discotheque for parties. The professional kitchen was always open and if we wanted a special meal in the middle of the night it was prepared for us. The meals were so nicely prepared that for each meal there was a menu. During the meals Pablo would move among the tables, sitting with his workers, his guests, his bodyguards, and the family. He would stand up and recite poems, which he loved, or even sing tango music from Argentina to the music that seemed to be always playing, just like he always loved to sing opera in the shower.

Every member of the family had their own bedroom and bathroom on the first floor, which were named for the letters of the alphabet.

The second floor was the private floor where Pablo and Gustavo lived. There was always noise and life going on in the house. It was always fun. Pablo liked to have people around. He would sit with Gustavo or the Mexican *[José Rodrígues Gacha, who, like Carlos Lehder, had been an independent cocaine smuggler before linking up with the Medellín cartel.]* relaxing and sometimes they would bet a lot of money. They would bet fifty or 100, but that meant thousands of dollars and they would not bet on the usual winning or losing, but instead it would be $100,000 if at 1.27 of the first half

Nacional had the ball. The money meant nothing to any of them. There was more than they could spend.

The parties were like those of Hollywood or even better. The performers would be the best singing groups from Colombia as well as all over South America. The most beautiful women were at these parties, the beauty-contest winners. People from business. Artists.

And, always, the people he worked with in the business. There was no better place for the politicians of Colombia to raise money for their campaigns. But remember, at that time Pablo's true business was still hidden and he was accepted by the public as a successful real-estate investor.

There was also business done at Napoles. When those public crowds were gone, Pablo quietly entertained important people for the business. This included Colombian politicians; government leaders from nearby countries, people on the upper levels of the operation.

This was one place where everyone could relax in complete privacy and safety. Flights to transit points took off from the runways.

One incident I remember well was the afternoon an old friend named Walter came to visit. When Pablo was just starting out in contraband he had earned $10,000. This was right at the very beginning.

"Do me a favour," he had told Walter in 1973. "Hold this money for me. I'll ask you for it in a couple of weeks."

When Pablo needed the money he reached out for Walter – who had taken the money and moved to the United States. He had disappeared.

Ten years later Pablo was informed that Walter had returned to Medellín. Pablo said to a friend who knew them both, "Tell Walter you're going to invite him to a nice farm for the weekend. Tell him it's going to be a great party. But don't tell him it's me."

Walter came to Napoles. When he learned he was *on* the ranch of Pablo Escobar he was shaking worse than leaves in a hurricane.

They brought him to the dining room, which easily sat fifty people.

But only Pablo, myself, Walter, and the person who brought him there, our cousin Jaime, and an aunt and two daughters were there in the big room. "Long time no see," Pablo said. "How are you?"

We were laughing to ourselves to see this guy shaking. He'd stolen money from the wrong person.

Walter could barely speak. "I'm sorry for the $10,000. I'll find a way to pay you back. Just give me time, please."

"No, no, don't worry about it," Pablo said casually; his whole attitude was not angry. Then Pablo asked one of the bodyguards, "Hey, please bring me my gun." Pablo's favourite gun was a big Sig Sauer.

When the bodyguard returned, Pablo stuck the gun in the waistband of his jeans.

Walter's eyes popped open. "Are you going to kill me?"

Pablo's exact words were, "No, listen. I don't kill anybody for money, and especially you because you were my friend when we were kids."

They ate lunch, but naturally Walter didn't eat too much. After, Pablo offered to show him around the ranch. "That's okay," Walter said. "I already saw around."

"Come," Pablo said.

"I don't want to go, Pablo." He was afraid to leave the dining room.

Pablo insisted, and when they stood up Pablo touched his gun.

We thought Walter was going to jump through the ceiling. Pablo showed him his collection of beautiful cars, but still sometimes touching his gun. When they finished Pablo said, "Come to my bedroom upstairs. I want to show you something."

Walter was convinced that was where he was going to be killed.

As they walked up the stairs Pablo asked him what he was doing. "I have a taxi in Medellín that I drive. I just bought a house. I promise, Pablo, I'll pay you the money little by little."

Instead, when they reached the bedroom Pablo opened up a suitcase filled with cash. He reached and took a pack of bills. I don't know how much it was, but a lot. "Here," he said, handing it to Walter.

"But listen to me. Don't ever, ever steal anything from me again, because I won't take it." Walter was crying, but he wanted to get out of there. He couldn't believe Pablo would let him go. He did a kind of walk that was really running, and went back to Medellín with the money Pablo gave him. We never heard a word about him again.

In August 1990, Cesàr Gaviria became president of Colombia. Negotiations began to end the drug wars that had long since been spilling blood far beyond that of the cartels' own sicarios. Mindful of the punishment handed down by the USA to the extradited Carlos Lehder – life plus 135 years, in one of those illogical, compound sentences with which federal courts like to set examples – Escobar's sticking point for surrender was the prospect of his extradition to the USA. The Ochoa brothers (see chapter 6) had surrendered and received tolerable sentences. Archbishop Dario Castrillón of Perreira helped to convey Escobar's surrender terms to the government, while the police hunted him with extreme prejudice, killing his cousin Gustavo in the process.

Escobar would accept a thirty-year sentence (which he estimated would realistically result in around seven years being served) if Colombia's extradition agreement with the USA were repealed. At this point, forty-one traffickers had been extradited, and coupled with Escobar's promise of surrender was the ransom-demand of an end to the country's street violence. In Escobar's mind, he was achieving political progress (in the cause on which, after all, he had politically campaigned, in the brief and ill-advised political career that first drew major national police attention to the Medellín cartel) on behalf of all traffickers, who would now owe him even more than they already did for the use of his routes and facilities.

In the event, George Bush Sr needed support among the world's nations at the UN Security Council for a resolution allowing the expulsion of Saddam Hussein from Kuwait. Perhaps because of this, the US did not protest when

Colombia approved a new constitution in 1991, clauses
in which precluded the extradition of Colombian citizens.
Colombian daily life rapidly became more peaceful.
　　Roberto Escobar picks up the story of Pablo's paradoxically
triumphal committal to prison. But the stasis described in
the following passages was not to last. Escobar's continuing
business activities – in particular the grisly events detailed
at the end of this extract – pressured the authorities to act. In
June 1992, the government attempted to move Escobar to
a secure facility and, fearing extradition once more, he was
able to organize the leisurely escape that was nonetheless the
beginning of his life's final chapter.

With the agreement to end extradition the rest of the terms
of surrender were finalized over several months. The terms
that Pablo arranged allowed him and other members of the
organization to plead guilty to at least one crime, and the other
crimes would not be prosecuted. Pablo would be permitted to
keep most of his property.

The people who hated him most could be kept away from
him, and in particular Maza *(Miguel Maza Màrquez)* would
step down from his post as chief of the DAS *(Departamento
Administrativo de Seguridad)*. The government wanted to put
Pablo into its highest security prison in Medellín, but of course
that was not possible. He would pay for his own prison. As part
of the agreement he insisted on approval of the guards. After
searching for several weeks Pablo informed the government that
a suitable prison could be made from a vacant building sitting
on top of a mountain just outside Medellín. The building looked
like a small school surrounded by tall electrical wire fences, but
it had originally been built as a rehabilitation centre. It was
known as *La Catedral*, the Cathedral.

Pablo owned the building and all the land, although his name
did not appear on the ownership papers. To hide that fact from
the people it was registered in the name of a friend of the family,
an old ironmonger, who exchanged it to the government of
the city of Envigado in a completely legal arrangement and in
return was given a smaller but desirable tract of land. It was

not traceable to Pablo. The area measured about 30,000 square meters.

Pablo had been very careful in selecting this place. The government had suggested two others, including Itagui where the Ochoas were doing their sentence, but the Cathedral offered many advantages. The location was on the top of a hill overlooking Medellín, 7,000 feet above sea-level, which gave us a view of anyone approaching from below. It would take considerable time for anyone to get up the mountain. It also gave Pablo a complete view of his beloved Medellín. As I said to him while we stood on the top of the mountain, "With a telescope, from here we could see the whole city." In addition, for security, Pablo purchased a small bodega at the base of the road going up the hill and gave it to an employee, Taro, on his wedding day. But inside was a phone wired directly to the prison, so people stationed there instantly could give us warning if anyone passed. I built an electronic system that was laid across the roads and gave us a warning signal. The buildings also were bordered by a forest, which provided good coverage from the air and also would allow us to hide among the trees if we had to escape. From the first, we knew that we might have to escape quickly, so Pablo planned for it. In the agreement Pablo signed with (President) Gaviria the government was prohibited from cutting down any trees.

Pablo also was concerned that Cali or another enemy might attempt to bomb us and a big advantage of the Cathedral was that early in the morning and late in the afternoon it was hidden in fog. The prison was surrounded by a 10,000-volt electric fence. As much as it was to keep the prisoners inside, the purpose of the security was to keep people out of the prison.

After the terms were negotiated the only problem remaining was the extradition treaty. So in June 1991, the constitution was changed to forbid extradition. From then on Colombians would always be tried for crimes committed in Colombia in Colombian courts. Or until the law was changed again long after Pablo's death.

In addition to the government, Pablo also made arrangements with the other drug-traffickers. He believed he was serving his sentence for all the traffickers who would be helped by the new laws.

It was agreed that during his time in prison he was to be compensated by them from the business. This was just as had always been done when one person gave up his freedom for others. "I am the price of peace," he told them. "I am making this sacrifice for you, so you should compensate me."

To get safely into the jail all of us had to plead guilty to a minimum of one crime, which would serve as an example for all of the crimes committed. Pablo confessed that he had participated in one deal that had smuggled twenty kilos of cocaine into the United States. Twelve of our men went into prison with my brother and me. Pablo helped them invent the crimes for which they pleaded guilty. Three of them agreed that they had collaborated to transport 400 kilos of drugs. Pablo told each of them, "You confess that you borrowed a blue Chevrolet. You say you put the package together. And you say you drove the car. Remember, a blue Chevrolet."

During their confessions the three men described the colour of the car differently. It didn't matter; these crimes were just for the record.

By informing on each other as drug dealers each man was entitled to a reduction in his sentence for turning in a drug dealer.

I was the last person to surrender. At first, I didn't see a good reason for me to be with them in the prison. The police had listed no crimes against me, and I could be more helpful outside. I could watch our family and pursue whatever legal work had to be done.

But Pablo called me and said that for me the safest place was with him inside the Cathedral. "They are looking to kill you," he said. I assume he meant Cali. But it could have been any of our enemies.

"You'll be safe in here so give yourself up quickly."

When I presented myself to the government I was asked to which crime was I confessing. "I will confess to my crime," I told them. "It's Rh."

The people in the room were puzzled. The female district attorney said, thinking I was referring to some code used to identify a crime, "That's not a code. What are you trying to tell me?"

I smiled. "No, doctor," I said. "It's not a code. My crime of Rh is that I have the same blood as my brother Pablo."

*   *   *

On the morning of Pablo's surrender he woke up much earlier than usual, at 7 a.m. We ate breakfast with our mother, then Pablo began making plans to meet the helicopter that would take him to the Cathedral. The surrender would begin as soon as the Assembly voted to outlaw extradition. That vote was taken right after noon.

The war was won. We all got ready for the move.

I think the whole country was waiting.

We drove in a convoy to a soccer field in Envigado. A big crowd of our people was waiting there to offer protection. Pablo was dressed as always in blue jeans, blue socks, sneakers, and a simple white shirt.

He was wearing a Cartier watch and carrying his Sig Sauer and a Motorola radio with two bands of twenty-five frequencies. By the time we got to the field the helicopter was landing. He hugged me and climbed on board for the flight. Father García [Father Rafael García Herreros, the priest who had helped to broker Escobar's deal with Gaviria's government via secret signals on his nightly TV show] and the journalist Luis Alirio Calle were waiting inside to fly with him. There was still great danger; there were many groups that did not want Pablo free to talk to the government. So the defense minister closed all the airspace in the region, writing in his own diary, "Not even birds will fly over Medellín today."

When the helicopter reached the top of the mountain Pablo got off and walked directly to the entrance. He handed a soldier his pearl-handled gun as a symbol of the end of the fighting. But people who were there told me that as soon as he got inside he took another gun. It took a few more days before all of us had surrendered and were safely inside. Officially there were fourteen of us.

The first few days there were very busy. Among our first visitors was our mother, who arrived with a rosary and a pot of cooked meat, Father García, who took our confession – we asked God to allow us to get out of this situation and protect our family – and friends like Colombia's famous soccer star Rene Higuita. Pablo had helped discover him as a young player and brought him to the notice of the professional teams. They had stayed loyal friends. The media tried to make a scandal from Higuita's friendship with us, but no one paid attention; he didn't even lose his TV endorsements of products.

There were many other things that had to be done quickly. While Pablo's people living outside would continue the business and pay whatever bribes had to be paid, we needed to have our own access to money. As much as $10 million in cash was packed tightly into ten milk canisters, which were covered with salt, sugar, rice and beans, even fresh fish. We told the guards that these canisters contained our weekly food ration, so they let them inside. Eventually they were buried near our soccer field. Other money was stored in tunnels hidden under our bedrooms that could be reached only by trapdoors under the beds. Weapons that we might need to protect ourselves were also brought in that way.

To communicate with our associates outside we also installed eleven telephone lines, a cell telephone system – which was now available – a radio-telephone system, and nine beepers. It was written that we had carrier pigeons to carry messages, but that wasn't true. We had the lighting system prepared for our needs, so that if planes flew overhead we could quickly turn out all the internal lights with a remote control that I built – or when we needed to slip outside we could do the same thing.

Security was always the primary concern. In addition to our bodega watching post, there were four guard stations along the twisting mountain road to the Cathedral. These were manned by the army, who were never permitted inside the gates, but in truth we were allowed to hire half of the jail guards, and the good mayor of Envigado hired the other half so these guards mostly were friends of ours. The government paid them very little, so they were often persuaded to work with our needs in exchange for additional cash payments, good food, and coloured pieces of paper. An arrangement had been made so that these pieces of paper could be exchanged in Envigado for home appliances, electronics, clothes and even Colombian cash, and the owners would be paid by our people.

When our protection was done, we prepared the Cathedral for our pleasure. When we arrived it was a simple place. It wasn't like a regular prison with bars and cells, but it wasn't especially comfortable either. With the help of my son Nico, we changed that situation. Nico had acquired a soda truck and received permission to bring cases of soda to the prison. But the crates of soda formed walls and inside those walls was whatever we wanted. He brought in Jacuzzis and hot tubs, television sets, the materials needed to build comfortable bedrooms, whatever we wanted – including the first of the many women to stay there. It was a hectic period and much was done to transform the prison into a much more tolerable place.

I also brought two bicycles inside with me, a stationary bike and one of my own Ositto riding bikes, so I could keep in shape. Among the things that Pablo brought with him was a large record collection, including classical music, Elvis' records he'd bought when we had visited Graceland, and his signed Frank Sinatra records that we'd received when visiting Las Vegas. For reading he brought in a collection of books, from five Bibles to the work of Nobel Prize winners. The books I brought included a text on having a super-memory, and books on horses, cancer, AIDS and bicycles. We also had a large collection of videotapes, naturally including the complete set of *The Godfather* movies and Steve McQueen movies, including *Bullitt*.

Eventually we turned the prison into a comfortable home. We had all the necessary electronic devices, including computers, big-screen televisions with video systems, beautiful music systems, even a comfortable bar with the best champagne and whisky. Outside we had a good soccer field with lights to play at night, paths to walk where we could be hidden from the air by thick trees, and good places to exercise. Within a couple of months we had made it a reasonable place.

Immediately there were stories written that we were living in luxury, that the faucets in the bathroom were gold. That it was just like Napoles. That wasn't true at all. It was safer for us than moving between hiding places, and we made it comfortable – it wasn't an ordinary prison, but still it was a prison. We no longer had the freedom to make our plans – to go where we wanted or see whoever we wanted when we wanted to see them. Everything required planning.

But soon we had settled in. We fixed the kitchen and brought in two chefs to prepare international foods for us – we knew them as the Stomach Brothers. We had sufficient entertainment, sports and exercise facilities, security, arms and a lot of money.

But it was not luxury. Some of our mattresses were on cement.

The furniture was simple; the walls were decorated mostly with paper posters, although Pablo did have a couple of nice paintings. And our clothes were basic. In Pablo's closet, for example, were his jeans and shirts, and many pairs of sneakers – some of them ready with spikes on in case we had to move quickly.

The difference between this prison and the world we'd lived in for the past few years was that now our enemies knew exactly where we were, but they couldn't get to us. Instead of tracking us and trying to kill us, the government was responsible for protecting us. It was a difficult political situation.

President Gaviria had his own needs. To restore Colombia as a safe place for foreign companies to do business the Gaviria government had to have peace in the streets. People had to feel safe to come here. Ending the war was the beginning of that.

I spent the first months there without being charged with a true crime. After several months a government prosecutor came to the prison to accuse me. "The charge against Roberto is that he has accounts outside Colombia with millions and millions of dollars in them."

At that moment there was no law in Colombia against keeping money in foreign banks. I told the judge, "That isn't illegal, and if you read the law you see that I have the right to negotiate an agreement with you. I'll give you half the money and then you make the other half legal for me."

The judge refused this offer. Instead the Colombian government made an agreement with other countries to freeze the bank accounts. Some of these accounts are still frozen.

Meanwhile, outside the prison the drug business continued to prosper. The arrest of the legendary Pablo Escobar did nothing to change that. Members of our organization continued to do their deals, the Cali cartel stayed in serious business, the other cartels kept working. When someone fell, other people stepped forward to take his place. What was different was that the violence had abated.

While we were there we did try hard to change our situation.

Pablo had as many as thirty lawyers working most of their time in our effort inside the judicial system. The soccer star Higuita volunteered to try to make peace between us and Cali. Eventually with the help of Father García he spoke with the Rodriguez Orejuela brothers *(see chapter 6)*, but to no good. They were too stubborn. Pablo told me, "I don't believe in the word of those two." As we discovered later there was good reason for that. A DAS agent who was helping run the prison security discovered that Cali had bought four 250-pound bombs from people in El Salvador and was trying to buy a plane to drop them on us. They were not able to, but on occasion our guards suddenly would begin firing their weapons at airplanes hovering too long in the area or coming too close to the Cathedral.

Time passed very slowly. I exercised, rode my bicycle; continued to read everything possible about AIDS and making my research, and I worked with my brother. Pablo would spend his days on the telephone, reading and visiting with his attorneys. He even began studying Mandarin. In the evenings we would sit in rocking chairs watching the lights come on in the buildings of Envigado. At those moments, when we watched the normal life of others, it was hard not to think about people being with their families in an ordinary but comforting way.

As before, Pablo continued to try to help the people who most needed it. He received hundreds of letters every day. The world knew he had surrendered and wrote to him with their requests. Letters came from around the world, from Europe, Asia and basically everywhere else, and most of them asked for money or advice on how to make money. Four or five of our employees did nothing but organize these letters. They were put in piles for family, for friends, for people who needed help with their health especially with cancer, for students needing money for education, and for business letters.

Pablo would read most of these letters and often send a crew to investigate the cases and verify the information. If it was real they would hand money to the people.

I remember a few of the letters. One odd letter came from a man in Africa who owned the elephant that was the mother of the elephant we'd had at Napoles. It was his idea to have the mother and daughter together living at Napoles. He included a picture of his elephant and his request for money.

A person wrote from America that he had seven different bank accounts and would be very happy to hide Pablo's money in his accounts. There was a letter addressed to myself and Pablo; it included a photograph of a gorgeous seventeen-year-old blond wearing a wedding dress. She wrote something like, "I'm a good girl and have just finished high school and my dream is to be an attorney but I don't have the money. I am a decent girl, but it would be an honour if one of you can take me. I am a virgin and that is all I can offer. I am not a whore, but I need the money for my college career."

Pablo sent a representative to her house. Although we never became involved with her in any way, we did pay for her college. But that was typical. The pleading letters were hard to read: I am dying and my children have nothing ... I need an operation so I can walk and support my family ...They are coming to take away our house ...The government helped none of these people, so their only hope was Pablo.

Countless other people would gather at the first gate at the bottom of the mountain and send handwritten notes, *boletas,* with the guards to ask for assistance. Sometimes they wanted money but other times they just wanted Pablo's advice about the problems of their life. To them, Pablo was a man of the streets like they were who had risen to the very top of the mountain.

Most important for our daily lives was the fact that we were able to receive visitors regularly. This was not supposed to happen, the only official visiting days were Wednesday and Sunday when our families came, but it seemed like there were always people there. We had bought two trucks, a Chevrolet and a Mazda van. In the back of them we built a fake wall, leaving a space we called the tunnel that was big enough to hide as many as twenty people. The people who used this method to come see us were those who did not want their visit known publicly, others who had committed crimes and were not legally allowed to be there, or people we did not want our enemies to know were there. Usually they would be picked up in the night and driven to our bodega. From there those people who could show ID to guards were placed in the seats and those who could not were put in the hidden tunnel. At the checkpoint the guards would ask, "What are you taking there?"

The password was "Materials".

Each time a truck left the bodega we were called and told who was coming up.

In addition to our family and friends, politicians visited us, businessmen, priests, the greatest soccer players, and some of the most beautiful women in the world. There were many parties and in attendance were the beauty queens of Colombia and other countries, including famous actresses, models and the prettiest girls at the universities.

We would see a beautiful woman on television or in the newspapers and she would be invited. There was never any danger to them and for their visit they would receive a very nice gift. Often, by their own choice, they would stay the night, and leave after breakfast the next morning in the tunnel. In fact, between many of our bedrooms we had built small hideouts, so the girls could stay there without anyone being suspicious.

No one was ever pushed to come if she felt uncomfortable. One of the girls at the university remembers being approached by a friend who asked her if she wanted to go to a lovely party, for which she would be well paid. "What do I have to do?" she asked.

"Nothing. Just be beautiful."

There is a magazine in Colombia called *Cromas* that publishes pictures of beautiful women. We would pick out women from the pages and invite them to the parties. One of the very first women to stay at the Cathedral was a twenty-year-old beauty who had just been fourth in the Miss Universe pageant who I had invited – she arrived there and stayed for five days. From these visits several people fell in love and there were some marriages at the Cathedral. And one of these women I fell in love with, she was a beauty queen and we had three beautiful children together before our marriage had a bad end. As I learned eventually, she had not fallen in love with me, but instead with my bank account.

It should not be surprising that there was a lot of sex at the Cathedral.

We were young men, many of us rich, and confined inside the walls of a prison. Who could protect a woman better than the men of Pablo Escobar? Even our parties were moderate, with nice music and dancing.

Later, photographs found at the Cathedral after we'd escaped, of blow-up sex dolls and some of our men dressed as women, were printed in magazines to try to embarrass us. The impressions of those photographs were not true at all; these toys were jokes, the dress-up part of a costume day we had as our entertainment.

The beautiful women were never invited there during the weekly family visits. During the years we'd been running we had only been able to spend brief periods with our families. Being in prison allowed us to finally spend time safely with our wives, children and families.

In fact, Pablo had three beds put into his bedroom so his whole family could sleep in that room with him when they visited. He even had a small playhouse built for his daughter and a go-kart for his son.

★   ★   ★

We spent 396 days inside the Cathedral. We celebrated many events there, including holidays, marriages and birthdays. Pablo turned forty-two there and we enjoyed a feast including caviar and pink salmon. Musicians played for the guests and our mother gave him a special Russian hat she had bought during a recent trip there.

But when I think of it all maybe most memorable were the days Pablo's beloved soccer teams visited us there.

Rene Higuita's *Nacional* team arrived first, on the celebration of Las Mercedes, the patron saint of prisoners. Pablo wanted us to play a real game against them, except as he warned them, "Games here last about three or four hours, without rest and only two changes are allowed. A tie is settled with penalties." They wore their official uniforms; we wore the colours of the German team. Pablo was a good player but he was guarded hard by Leonel Alvarez, and when Pablo complained, Alvarez told him, "This is how we play soccer, brother."

Nacional went ahead 3–0, but eventually the game was finished 5–5.

In penalty kicks I believe Rene helped us, missing his own attempt; then allowing my brother's left-foot kick to get into the goal for our victory. There was no consideration of the fact that maybe they had played easy with us. We won, that's what mattered.

Within a few days the professional teams from Medellín and Envigado also came to the Cathedral to play against us – and they also could not beat us! From those days until our stay there ended, the flag of one of those teams always flew outside the perimeter. And if that flag was not that of Pablo's favourite Medellín team, after everyone went to bed he would quietly make certain that it was.

Pablo believed he was serving his time for all the people in the organization. He had given himself up to end extradition. With Pablo Escobar in prison the government could say the war against drug trafficking was being won. This really wasn't true.

Because we were in the Cathedral did not mean our business stopped totally. Pablo continued to know what was going on in Medellín and throughout Colombia. People would call him and tell him what was happening. Not one single load left that he did not know about. But it was expensive being there; there were still people on Pablo's payroll who expected to be paid. Sometimes helicopters from the outskirts of Medellin would land in our prison and fly away carrying money to keep the business operating. But all of that stayed possible because the people doing business paid Pablo his fees in cash.

Two of the biggest organizations paying their percentage belonged to Pablo's friends Fernando Galeano and Kiko Moncada. They were making a lot of money using the route through Mexico, called Fany, opened by Pablo, and thanks to him without fear of extradition. But then Pablo found out that they had done five loads without paying him a cent. They had cheated him out of millions of dollars. As business that made no sense. They were earning millions of dollars, the money they needed to pay Pablo was nothing for them. So Pablo knew that this was much more than the dollars and the lack of respect, this was an attempt to take control of the whole business. But Galeano and Moncada were friends, men he had trusted. In Pablo's mind, men he had gone to jail for.

Pablo found out from a friend where Galeano had hidden the money and he sent people to collect it. It was more than $20 million in the *coleta [hiding place]*. Galeano and Moncada wanted it back, denying what Pablo knew to be true. He told them to come to the Cathedral to discuss the business.

They died as expected. Probably they thought they were safe coming to the prison. They were killed after they left the Cathedral. The *sicario* Popeye confessed that he killed Moncada and claimed that Otto killed Galeano. It doesn't matter who killed them, they were still dead. Their families pleaded to have their bodies and they were told where to dig them up. Pablo then called all the accountants for those people and told them from now on they were responsible to him. All the properties of those families, the boats, the planes, the cash, were put in the names of Pablo's loyal people.

5

Killing Pablo: The Hunt for the World's Greatest Outlaw

Mark Bowden

"Don" (Uncle) Pablo to many Colombians in his lifetime, Escobar remains a legend to some today, and a bi-word for high-rolling organized crime throughout culture low and high. The airport in "Grand Theft Auto: Vice City" is named after him, while he features in a novel by the grandfather of South American fiction, Gabriel García Márquez's News of a Kidnapping. *Rappers and rockers invoke his name, and he is more than touched on in films such as* Blow. *Based on George Jung's autobiography and starring Johnny Depp and Penelope Cruz, the film chronicles a smuggling career spent trading with Escobar and Carlos Lehder, along with Jung's eventual swingeing sentence in the US.*

But those who weren't alive, or old enough, to be even a casual follower of the daily news during Escobar's "reign", may still not appreciate the extent to which many of his actions lay behind the headlines of his day, as if he really were the politician he in fact so wanted to be, and really had the popular mandate he behaved as if he had (not that that even then would have justified his megalomaniacal extremes).

Wealthy enough to face down or co-opt the authorities, Escobar is not so much a drug baron as drug royalty, the man who single-handedly brought Bond-villain bling to an area that had been sleazy, secretive or at least discreet. He was also a torturer and killer who reinforced the "life *is cheap" cliché of South America. Escobar did not only kill those who stood in his way, nor even simply those who annoyed him, nor only those who were related to someone like this. He issued instructions to kill to whoever would listen and whoever wanted to curry favour, and those were instructions to kill not on account of who the victim was, but for the uniform they wore or for what they represented. In other words he was a terrorist. For example, in 1991, at the height of Escobar's fight with the Cali cartel, there were 7,081 murders in Colombia, making it the world's murder capital for the year. Over 600 police officers alone were killed by poor youths on his promise of payment (of a rumoured $4,000 US per head) if they did so.*

In 1989, the Medellín cartel exploded a bomb at the DAS (Department of Security) headquarters in Bogotá, killing fifty-one and injuring around 1,000, but this was trumped by the downing of an Avianca Airlines internal flight to Cali in November of that year, with the loss of all 107 travellers. There are differing theories as to how it happened, neither of which suggest that Escobar wasn't responsible, but which differ as to motive: the assassination of Louis Carlos Galán in August 1989 has been attributed to the Medellín. Galán was the front-runner in the forthcoming presidential election, campaigning on a promise to get tough with the barons, and to honour Colombia's controversial extradition agreement with the US. Had he been elected, Escobar would have been the key target of this high-profile initiative.

Therefore one theory suggests that the Medellín believed that Cesar Gaviria would be aboard the flight, though in the event he wasn't. Gaviria had been a key aide to Galán and was now standing in his own right. He would go on to win the Colombian presidency in 1990 and, ironically should this theory about the motive for the explosion be true, in the event had to allow Escobar to surrender himself into police custody on the condition that he would not be extradited. This was because Colombia's legislature, the Constituent Assembly, ratified a new constitution, one which prohibited extradition, in 1991, once again making it the subject of legal debate. It's alleged that they were influenced by the Medellin and other cartels in so doing. (Previously, in 1985, the M-19 guerrilla movement had stormed the Supreme Court and murdered half of its judges – just as it had been debating the constitutionality of extradition. It was rumoured that Escobar had funded the attack.)

It was at this point that Escobar was famously housed, on his own terms, in the magnificent and luxurious jail, La Catedral, *along with his family. Against the terms of his surrender, he carried on his activities, even luring employees that he suspected of being on the take – the Galeano and Moncada brothers – inside the jail and having them killed. In July 1991 he escaped, fearing that he would be extradited after all.*

A key Escobar sicario, *Dandeny Munoz-Mosquera, was extradited to Florida and convicted of organizing the bombing, prosecution being possible because some of the plane's passengers were found to be US passport-holders. Sentenced to ten life-sentences plus forty-five years, he shares a federal "supermax" jail with Ramsi Yousef (responsible for the first World-Trade Center bombing) and the Unabomber, and it is said will never again see daylight.*

A cold-blooded assassin, Mosquera however denies he was involved in this particular carnage. It has been suggested that another Escobar sicario, *Carlos Alzate, arranged for a* suisso *– a suicide – to be aboard the plane and to flip the catch on a briefcase, setting off five pounds of dynamite. He may have done this by threatening to harm the victim's loved ones – which happened in other episodes of narco-terrorism, as it did during the Troubles in Northern Ireland – or by duping him that he was going to tape-record the conversation of the passenger next to him.*

A girlfriend of Miguel Rodriguez Orejuela, key member of the Cali cartel, had been on board the flight when, after all, Gaviria hadn't been. (And we only have the Medellin members' word for the fact that their intelligence had said he would be. He had already in fact stopped taking commercial flights on account of the risk to himself but also to other passengers. It's not known whether the cartels knew this at the time of the bombing.) A previous Cali assassination attempt on Escobar had left his daughter, Manuela, partially deaf owing to an explosion. Escobar would not have been above bearing what is, in the larger-than-life context of Colombian public affairs, this kind of small-minded grudge.

The Avianca bombing did more than any other single thing to turn the tide against the cartels and their collective attempt to render Colombia into a narco-state along every corridor of power. It empowered the Gaviria government to implement extradition policies without looking to their own electorate that they were doffing their sombreros to the gringo imperialists, and made the idea of technological assistance from the CIA acceptable to the elite Search Bloc police units charged with the seemingly impossible hunt for Escobar. After his death, it enabled the seizure of assets and extradition proceedings with which the US pursued the members of the Cali cartel.

Within the drugs business, Escobar did more than any single individual to turn the trade into the chillingly ruthless zero-sum game we know it as. As the old drug-lore adage has it, don't get high on your own supply, and Escobar was driven by far deeper personal influences than drugs, even though the moustache and the megalomania perfectly complement today's idea of how the Boogie Nights-era was. Driven by the hurt that extreme poverty has on a bright mind, Escobar was a force of nature enough without the added stimulation of coke. This was a man who decommissioned the Piper plane in which he had made his own first cocaine run to the US so that he could have it mounted above the gates of his ranch, Hacienda Napoles, in Antioquia, about two hundred miles northwest of Bogotá.

Besides the private airport, classic-car and bike collections and go-kart racing track, the estate also featured some actual dinosaur-bone statues for the kids to climb on, together with a zoo that put the one at Michael Jackson's

Neverland Ranch to shame, as seen in the previous extract. The surviving animals have since been dispersed to zoos around the world, with the exception of the hippopotamuses, now contained in nearby jungle – it can therefore be said that Pablo Escobar introduced the animal to South America.

Escobar's largesse did not end at home. At the height of his power, he was estimated to be worth around $25 billion dollars, the seventh wealthiest man on Forbes' *worldwide rich list. Football and the Church were two consolations from his poor background that he continued to adhere to and wrote large in his life, building sports grounds and sponsoring little-league teams. This and his funding of churches in Medellín added something of a Robin-Hood touch, though the local Roman Catholic hierarchy subsequently attracted criticism for this. Grateful townsfolk marched to show their appreciation, while its business community would be well aware of the methods Don Pablo put to use in his day job, demanding loyalty with his motto, "silver or lead?" and torturing and killing on the merest suspicion of disloyalty, knowing it paid to be paranoid. He was responsible for around eighty per cent of Colombia's cocaine trade, and even farmers in other regions of the country had to give twenty to thirty per cent of their profits to him.*

It's said that he was a master at public-relations, but it's hard to tell how many he could have persuaded, for example when he campaigned publicly on behalf of the Extraditables, *when so many feared him anyway. He spoke often to the press and appeared at rallies, and this reputation is partly down to the fact we don't expect a drug baron to do that. But if you have the chutzpah to smuggle drugs, you have the front – or deluded self-belief – to do just about anything. To be surprised would also be to overlook the political nature of the cocaine trade in South America: extradition was a hot political issue because the US's desire to pursue the cartels was interpreted as having a colonial edge (especially when the demand for cocaine that made the trade such a concern also came from within the US),*

*and pro-extradition administrations knew it could easily
bring South Americans together in a Bolivarian spirit that
overrode their other differences, strengthening the cartels
and allowing them to corrupt their own pro-US power base.*

*At the height of his powers, Escobar managed to exploit
this popular fear of US imperialism and of foreign
meddling in Colombia's internal affairs, but events such
as the Avianca bombing exposed the lie that this* paysan
*Colombian, a simple flower-exporter and one of their own,
deserved their protection. He was shown not merely to
dispose of his enemies but to kill indiscriminately to sow
division and discord from which he could benefit. He could
no longer claim to have Colombia's interests at heart, merely
his own in avoiding possible extradition.*

*Following Galán's assassination and at the height of his
bombing campaign, he issued press releases that nonetheless
betray a tone of victimhood that seeks to hoodwink the
reader into thinking him the patriot, like the messed-up
school bully who steals your lunch and then wonders why
he can't be your friend. By the time of his imprisonment, his
methods were already being superseded by the quiet cruelty
of the men from Cali, who by contrast to Escobar saw the
wisdom in setting their enemies against each other rather
than blowing them to bits and trying to cover up that it was
you, as they did when they tacitly assisted the Colombian
police in finding Escobar right-hand-man José Rodriguez
Gacha,* El Mexicano.

*Escobar had certainly come from the poorest of backgrounds.
In his brother Roberto's unapologetic biography of him* (see
chapter 4), *he recalls how Pablo was sent home from school
for having no shoes. The son of a farmer and a schoolteacher,
he was bright enough to gain entry to the University of
Antioquia to study political science, but had to drop out on
account of the fees. This early disappointment might explain
why he so enjoyed addressing appreciative crowds later in life.*

*Roberto Escobar writes: "My brother and I were born
into a civil war between the Conservatives and the Liberals,*

a period known in Colombia as La Violencia. *In the decade ending in the mid-1950s peasant guerrilla armies murdered as many as 300,000 innocent people, many of them hacked to death with machetes." Roberto Escobar describes how, "in what became known as the* Corte Florero, *the Flower-Vase Cut, limbs were cut off and then stuck back into the body like a macabre arrangement of flowers." He describes one such guerrilla attack from which his family spent the night cowering. With such personal experience of terror under his belt, it's no wonder Pablo Escobar understood its value as a means of controlling others.*

Escobar believed his own hype, but he was right about one thing. He brought fear, pain, suffering and grief directly to hundreds, even thousands of people – but he wasn't killed because of that; he was hunted because he satisfied America's demand for cocaine. Had he continued to do that without attempting to influence Colombia's political elite through violence, the man who instead became the world's most famous criminal might even now be still doing so ...

In time, no one in Colombia knew Pablo Escobar better than Colonel Hugo Martinez of *La Policia Nacional de Colombia (PNC)*, even though the two men had never met. The tall, taciturn man who was nicknamed "Flaco" (Skinny) knew Pablo better than even the drug boss's closest family members and henchmen, because there were things he would say and do before his associates that he would not before his family, and there was a side of him that his family saw that he showed to no one else. The colonel saw it all. He knew Pablo intimately. He recognized his voice, knew his habits, when he slept, when and how he moved, what he liked to eat, what his favourite music was, how it was that criticism written or broadcast against him infuriated him but how he delighted in any political cartoon that portrayed him, no matter how crudely. The colonel knew what kind of shoes Pablo wore (white Nikes), what kind of sheets he liked on his bed, the preferred age of his sexual partners (girls of fourteen or fifteen, usually), his taste in art, his handwriting, the pet name he had for his wife ("Tata"), even what kind of toilet he preferred to use – since he had new facilities installed in all of his hideouts, and they were always the same. The colonel felt he understood Pablo, could see the world through his eyes, how he felt unjustly hounded and persecuted (mostly, nowadays, by the colonel). Martinez understood this last part so well he could sympathize with it, at times.

There was truth even in the world-view of a monster, and the colonel believed he was chasing a monster. He never grew to hate Pablo, although he did fear him.

On 18 August, 1989, the same day that Pablo's *sicarios* killed front-running presidential candidate Luis Galán, another group of his hit men killed *PNC* colonel Waldemar Franklin, chief of the Antioquian police. Franklin and Colonel Martinez had been friends. They had come up together through the ranks. When Franklin was assigned to Antioquia, Martinez and the other top officers in the *PNC* knew there would be trouble for the Medellín cartel. Franklin couldn't be bought or bullied. He had steered the raid that rousted Pablo in his underpants from the mansion outside Medellín that spring; one of his closest calls yet, and Franklin's men had recently raided a cartel laboratory and seized four metric tons of cocaine. This was bad enough but Franklin sealed his fate when his men stopped Pablo's wife, Maria Victoria, and his children, Juan Pablo and Manuela at a road block. The drug-boss's family was taken to police headquarters in Medellín, where they were held for hours before Pablo's lawyers negotiated their release. Pablo would later complain to Roberto Uribe that Maria Victoria had been refused permission to give Manuela a bottle of milk. Pablo had always denied ordering the murder of Galán but to Uribe he admitted that he had ordered Franklin killed over that bottle of milk.

Galán's killing had the anticipated effect. President Barco launched an all-out war against the cartel. He suspended *habeas corpus*, which meant people could be arrested and detained without being charged with a crime, and once again he authorized army and police to seize the cartel leaders' luxurious *fincas*. Shadow ownership of property was declared a crime, which made it harder for Pablo and the other *narcos* to disguise their holdings. But the biggest step Barco took was to invite further American help in this growing fight.

[. . .] The *narcos* could see the United States government closing in on them. The kingpins had all been indicted by the US Justice Department, most of them, like Pablo, more than once. They knew the DEA had been active in the country for years. Having long since compromised the Colombian police and military, they were holding their own at home, but President Bush *[Snr]* had campaigned in 1998 saying he favoured taking direct military action against traffickers in other countries. It was clear which other country he had in mind. Colombia was the source of nearly eighty per cent of the cocaine making its way to the United States.

[Famously, President Reagan had designated the influx of drugs into the US to be "a national security threat", which made US military involvement overseas permissible in US law and public opinion. The Bush administration coined the phrase "war on drugs", and authorized an increasing spend from under $300 million in 1989 to more than $700 million in 1991 on fighting it.]

Indeed, in August of that year *[1988]* the army's counterterrorism Unit, Delta Force, had prepared to raid a house in Panama where Pablo was reported to be staying. The plan called for Delta to seize him and then turn him over to DEA agents who would arrive after the drug boss was in custody. The raid was called off when agents discovered that the reports were false; Pablo had not left Colombia. Nevertheless, the aborted mission showed how much the rules had changed under Bush. Over the next five years, the United States would basically underwrite a secret war in Colombia . . . The US might have been considering acting unilaterally, if necessary, but Bush clearly preferred co-operation from Colombia. Barco had resisted opening that door until Galán's murder. That had changed everything.

[Galán's murder took place between this event and those following, on 18 August 1989.]

In the four months after Galán's death, Barco's government shipped more than twenty suspected drug traffickers to the United States for trial, and with the new bonanza of American assistance, Barco created special police-units, one of which was based in Medellín and was dedicated to hunting down José Rodriguez Gacha, the Ochoa brothers and Pablo Escobar. It was called the *Bloque de Basqueda* or Search Bloc. This was the command given to Colonel Martinez. It was a position he'd neither sought nor desired. Nobody wanted it. It was considered so dangerous that the *PNC* decided the command would be rotated monthly, like a hot potato.

[. . .] Pablo practically owned Medellín, his home city, including enough of its police force that one of the rules for this newly constituted Search Bloc was that it could not contain even one native Antioquian, or *paisa,* for fear he would secretly be on Pablo's payroll. Instead, the national police had assembled a collection of men from different units, including Colombia's FBI, the *DAS,* and its special branch of judicial police, the *DIJIN (Dirección Central de Policía Judicial e Investigación).*

All were considered elite and incorruptible. Some were used to working in uniform under straightforward military command, and others were essentially undercover cops who worked in plain clothes as civilians. None of them was familiar with one another or with the city, and they had no local sources or informants. They didn't dare ask the Medellín police force for help, because it was known to be largely on the cartel's payroll. The whole of Search Bloc, even its plainclothesmen, stood out sharply because none spoke with the thick *paisa* accent. On their first foray out into the city, eighty men in ten vehicles, they got lost.

Within the first fifteen days, thirty of the colonel's 200 men were killed. Despite elaborate precautions to protect the men and hide their identities, Pablo's army of *sicarios* picked them off one by one, often with the help of the Medellín police.

They shot them down on the street, on their way home from work, even at home with their families when they were off-duty.

The funerals for the slain officers left the *PNC* reeling. At police headquarters in Bogotá the top command considered pulling the plug on the Search Bloc. The colonel and his top commanders asked that they be allowed to stay. While the killings grieved and frightened them, it also angered them and hardened their resolve.

Instead of withdrawing, the *PNC* sent the colonel another 200 men. Martinez was proud that, as bad as things were in that first month, his men had managed to mount one impressive raid.

Informed that Pablo was staying at a *finca* in the jungle that was about a two-hour helicopter flight from Medellín, the Search Bloc planned an assault. But the maps showed that on the way to the targeted *finca*, the choppers would have to fly over a Colombian army base. If they attempted to do so without getting permission from the base commander, it was likely the base defence forces would try to shoot them down. Martinez suspected that if he informed the commander of an army base in Antioquia of their mission, Pablo would be tipped off immediately. So he risked it. To avoid radar they flew over the base fast and low; so low that the colonel feared they would hit electric and telephone wires. But they made it. They hit the jungle *finca* from the air, co-ordinating the assault with ground troops who had moved in quietly the night before. Pablo escaped, but only narrowly.

Under the circumstances, the colonel considered the raid a triumph.

Still, at the end of October 1989, according to the rotation plan, the colonel asked to be replaced. He was told he had done such a good job, the department wanted him to stay. His request the following month was similarly rejected.

Pablo's response to the Search Bloc's initial raid was swift and pointed. A car bomb was discovered in the basement of the apartment building in Bogotá where the colonel's family lived.

Martinez' oldest son, Hugo Jr., was now a cadet at the national police academy, but his wife, daughter, and two younger sons had been home. The bomb had been found after someone telephoned a tip to the police, so it probably had been just a warning. But it was a chilling one. Pablo should not have been able to find them.

Nearly all the residents of their building were high-ranking national police officers, the only ones who knew of the colonel's dangerous new job. Obviously someone among them had passed the word. The betrayal was aggravated when, instead of rallying around their besieged colleague, the other families in the apartment building held a meeting and voted to ask the colonel and his family to leave.

The day after the bomb was found, the colonel boarded a helicopter in Medellín and flew home to help his family pack.

He told only his commander, General Octavio Vargas, where he was going that morning.

He was stuffing boxes bitterly in the apartment when a retired police officer, someone he had known since his days in the academy, arrived at his door. The colonel was surprised and alarmed. How had this man known to find him in Bogotá?

"I come to talk to you obligated," the retired officer said with a pained expression. Martinez asked what he meant.

"If I did not agree to come talk to you, they could easily kill me or my family," he said.

Then he offered the colonel $6 million, a bribe from Pablo Escobar to call off the hunt. Better yet, the officer explained, "Continue the work, but do not do yourself or Pablo Escobar any real damage." Pablo also wanted a list of any snitches inside his own organization.

Sometimes the fate of an entire nation can hinge on the integrity of one man. The bribe came at the lowest point in the colonel's career. He had been given a suicide mission, one with little chance of success. He attended funerals almost every day.

The national police had constructed special funeral chapels in Medellín and in Bogotá just to handle the demand. The bomb in the basement of the apartment building had made it clear that Pablo could find the colonel's wife and children. This move was not going to protect them; it was designed to protect the apartment building's other residents. His own department was, in effect, abandoning him and his family to their fate.

And for what? Martinez could not even *see* the wisdom in going after Escobar. Cocaine was not Colombia's problem; it was the *norte americanos'* problem. And even if they did away with *El Doctor,* as the United States insisted, it was not going to curb the cocaine industry.

Here was a generous ticket out. *Six million dollars.* Enough money to support himself and his family in luxury for the rest of their lives. But the colonel did not consider the bribe for any longer than it took him to have those thoughts. His gut rebelled against it. He cursed at his former friend, and then his anger turned to pity and disgust.

"Tell Pablo that you came but did not find me here, and then leave this matter as if it had never occurred," he said.

Martinez had known other police officers who took bribes, and he knew that money was just the hook on *El Doctor's* line.

Once he had accepted the bribe, Pablo would own him, just as he owned his friend who had approached him with the offer – *I come to talk to you obligated.* Martinez could see himself forced into a similar humiliating betrayal somewhere down the road. It would be like handing over his whole career, all the years of work and study, all the things he took professional pride in, to this thug.

It would be like turning over his soul.

After he dismissed his old friend, Martinez drove to police headquarters and informed Vargas of the bribe. They agreed it was a good sign.

"It means we're getting to him," said Martinez.

[. . .] In the fall of 1989, the US embassy in Bogotá was not sure exactly how the Medellín cartel worked, or even who was in charge.

Pablo was considered just one of the big names. The Colombian authorities believed he was the boss, but information from the local police and army was regarded with suspicion by the Americans.

All of the cartel leaders were now infamous. *Fortune* magazine listed them annually with the richest men in the world, but José Rodriguez Gacha, "El Mexicano", the fat man who often sported a Panama hat with a snakehead on its band, was thought to be the richest and most vicious of them all. *Fortune* had put Gacha on its cover, estimating his worth at $5 billion. Before Centra Spike *[the name given to the CIA's top-secret surveillance staff, installed covertly within the US embassy in Bogotá]* landed, their briefing indicated that Gacha was the real power atop the cartel. US intelligence agencies believed it was he, not Pablo, who had ordered the hit on Galán.

So the fat man was Centra Spike's first target, and it didn't take them long to find him. He had been hiding from the national police ever since they had seized his estate north of Bogotá immediately after Galán's murder. A well-placed police informant revealed that Gacha had regular phone conversations with a woman in Bogotá. That information was passed to the US embassy through the DEA, and Centra Spike started listening for the calls. They found him immediately, in a *finca* on a hilltop southwest of Bogotá. It was the only dwelling on the hill and was conspicuously elegant for a such a remote spot. Jacoby passed on the location to the CIA station chief, and it was given to President Barco.

The response was immediate and surprising, and answered any uncertainty the Americans had about Barco's intentions.

The co-ordinates were given to the Colombian air force, which launched a squadron of T-33 fighter-bombers on 22 November to destroy the *finca* and everyone in it. Embassy officials were taken aback. No one had anticipated that the Colombians would simply kill the people Centra Spike had helped them find.

As it happened, the bombing sortie never forced the issue, because the lead pilot, a Colombian colonel, noticed that just beyond the *finca*, over the lip of the hill, was a small village. If any of the bombs overshot by even a small margin, they were certain to hit the thirty or forty smaller homes below. To avoid a tragedy, the colonel called off the bomb run at the last minute, but not soon enough to stop all four fighters from streaking about fifty feet over the rooftop of a severely startled Gacha. The cocaine boss was on the phone (with Centra Spike listening in) when the jets boomed overhead. He shouted with surprise and anger and immediately fled. A number of his key lieutenants stayed, however, and were arrested the next day when a police unit assaulted the house from helicopters. The army seized $5.4 million in cash at the *finca*. A judge promptly found fault with the legal basis for the raid, and most of these men were released; some of them would later be identified by Centra Spike as key figures in the cartel.

The last-minute decision to abort the bombing brought heavy criticism on the pilots and on the air force, which was accused of selling out, of letting Gacha get away. There was some reason to suspect this because he had long-standing friends within the Colombian military who had collaborated with his paramilitary squads against the Communist guerrillas. The national police who were the most serious go-getters in the war against the cartel, accused the air force of intentionally bungling the mission, tipping off Gacha and enabling him to escape. The US embassy found itself adjudicating the dispute, reviewing imagery of the hill, approach speeds, and likely bomb trajectories. The air force even offered to fly Jacoby in the backseat of a T-33 over the site. He declined. The review concluded that the colonel had been prudent.

The hunt for Gacha and the other cartel leaders assumed an even higher level of importance to the United States when, just five days later, an Avianca airliner was blown out of the sky shortly after taking off from Bogotá for Cali. The bombing had been planned two weeks earlier at a meeting attended by Pablo, Gacha, and some of their top lieutenants and *sicarios*. They'd discussed two bombings, the most important of which was an attack on the *DAS* building in Bogotá. Plans for this were set in motion, and then Pablo suggested the Avianca bombing. He wanted to kill César Gaviria, the candidate who had taken up Galán's standard and was now the front-runner in the campaign for president.

Gaviria had been serving as Galán's campaign manager, and at the funeral Galán's son had asked him to finish off the run.

This session also produced a new communiqué from the *Extraditables [the barons selected by the US as candidates for extradition to face trial]*, written by Pablo: "We want peace. We have screamed out loud for it, but we cannot beg for it . . . We do not accept, nor will we ever accept, the numerous arbitrary raids on our families, the ransacking, the repressive detentions, the judicial frame-ups, the anti-patriotic and illegal extraditions, the violations of all our rights. We are ready to confront the traitors."

Carlos Alzate, one of Pablo's veteran *sicarios*, recruited a young man in Bogotá to do a job for them. He was to carry a briefcase on the flight that they told him contained a recording device. Once aloft, he was instructed to secretly tape the conversation of the person seated next to him. In fact, the briefcase contained five kilograms of dynamite. The hapless bomber – Alzate called him the "*suisso*" or suicide – was instructed, once in flight, to flip a toggle switch on top of the suitcase to activate the recorder. All 110 passengers were killed. Gaviria was not on the plane. He had a ticket, but his staff had decided weeks earlier to avoid all commercial flights, for safety reasons, but also because Gaviria's presence on a commercial flight tended to panic the other passengers, who did not want to fly with someone who was so clearly a target for assassination.

Ever since the downing of Pan Am 103 over Lockerbie, Scotland, the year before, threats to air travel had been elevated to a primary concern by the United States and other world powers.

International air travel was regarded as vital to the civilized world and also highly vulnerable to anyone unscrupulous enough to attack it. Deterring and punishing those who would take aim at commercial airplanes had become a priority in the counter-terrorism community worldwide. Concern about the Medellín cartel heightened when some of Pablo's men were caught trying to buy 120 Stinger anti-aircraft missiles in Florida.

Weeks after the Avianca bombing, President Bush released a strenuously reasoned opinion by the US Justice Department's Office of Legal Counsel concluding that it *would not* violate the Posse Comitatus Act for the army to be used against criminal suspects overseas. The Avianca bombing was significant for another reason. In the eyes of the Bush administration, it marked Pablo Escobar, José Rodriguez Gacha, and other cartel leaders as a direct threat to American citizens. Two of those on the doomed flight had been American citizens. As such, the *narcos* were now men who, in the eyes of the Bush administration, could legally be killed.

[. . .] The opinion eased concerns among soldiers in the covert ops community, including the men of Centra Spike, that their work would not someday be labelled criminal. If the Colombians were going to simply kill cartel leaders that Centra Spike found, so be it.

The situation in Colombia was clearly war. On 6 December, just nine days after José Rodriguez Gacha fled his mountaintop *finca,* the second of the two bombings planned with Pablo weeks before took place. A bus loaded with 500 kilograms of dynamite was detonated outside the *DAS* building. It carved a crater four feet deep in the pavement outside the building and tore off its front. Seventy people were killed, hundreds more injured, and the explosion caused more than $25 million in property damage. One target of the explosion was General Miguel Maza, who had miraculously survived the car bombing in May.

He emerged from the ruins of the building, again unscathed.

The blasts were swiftly avenged. Centra Spike traced Gacha over the next few weeks as he fled north from *finca* to *finca,* but he never stayed in one place long enough for the Colombians to launch a raid. He settled eventually into a cabin in the *departamento* of Chocó, in a remote, heavily forested area near the border with Panama. He was picked up on a radio phone arranging for women to be trucked to this remote spot. The location wasn't precise – the portion of the intercepted call had been too brief – but elite police units were deployed to search the area. They were finally led to Gacha's *finca* by a man named Jorge Velasquez, a cocaine smuggler from Cartagena who had been working as a spy for the Medellín cartel's rivals in Cali. The Cali cartel leaders had a lot to gain by the destruction of their Medellín rivals and had begun quietly assisting the Colombian police. Once Velasquez pointed out Gacha's precise location, a coordinated assault was planned for early the next morning, 15 December, 1989. Just in case, the United States readied a task force of Delta Force operators and SEALs on the USS *America,* sailing just off the coast. As the police assault helicopters, AH-6 Little Birds armed with Israeli miniguns, descended on Gacha and his teenage son Freddy and five bodyguards, they fled the house and ran for a nearby banana grove. According to the official report, they fired on the choppers with automatic weapons and the miniguns cut them down. Their bodies were placed on display afterward. The lower half of El Mexicano's face had been shot completely away. It was a grotesque way of serving notice that this time, the drug war was for keeps.

Gacha was publicly mourned by thousands in his hometown of Pacho, about twenty-five miles north of Bogotá. At his estate there police found a working gallows, machine guns, grenades, and a gold-plated, personalized 9-mm pistol with monogrammed bullets. His death would do little to curb the flood of cocaine leaving Colombia for the United States, but to the vast majority of Colombians, cowed by years of bombings, kidnappings and assassinations, it marked a major victory for the state, for President Barco, and, quietly, for the United States.

A curious thing happened after Gacha was killed. His death prompted a torrent of phone calls to and from Pablo Escobar. One of the other things Centra Spike did, besides finding people, was track communication patterns. A fairly comprehensive chart of the power structure of any large organization can be built by monitoring the flow of electronic communication over time.

None of the top people in the cartel used standard landline telephones, the central Colombian telephone network. The police and the secret police, both the *DIJIN* and the *DAS*, were both known to monitor it closely. But none of the cartel leaders apparently suspected that anyone was listening in on their cell phone and radio calls.

It was during those days that Centra Spike got its first chance to listen to Pablo. The intercepted conversations were recorded in the Beechcrafts [*the CIA had chosen two of these typical twin-prop charter planes to kit out with surveillance equipment*] by Centra Spike's technicians, who would then forward the tapes to the embassy, where Jacoby and his team would study them. Unlike Gacha, who was uneducated and crude, Escobar appeared to be a man of some refinement. He had a deep voice and spoke softly. He was very articulate, and even though he could slip into the familiar *paisa* patois, he usually used very clean Spanish, free of vulgarity and with a vocabulary of some sophistication, which he was fond of sprinkling with English words and expressions. He was painstakingly polite and seemed determined to project unruffled joviality at all times, as though trying to keep things light, even though it was very clear that everyone who spoke to Pablo was afraid of him. With his intimates his standard greeting on the phone was *"Qué mas, caballero?"* or "What's happening, my man?"

Both the pattern of these calls and the content changed the unit's understanding of the Medellín cartel. Instead of scrambling to fill the leadership void or feuding between those thought to be José Rodriguez Gacha's equals or underlings, what Centra Spike heard was Pablo Escobar coolly at work, like a chief-executive officer who had lost a key associate. People called him to make decisions; and he did so calmly, redistributing Gacha's interests and responsibilities. The more Centra Spike listened over the next few weeks, the more they realized that Pablo had been the man in charge all along. Always deeply concerned about his public image, he had evidently been content to let Gacha be perceived as the chief bad guy.

What also came through was Pablo's casual cruelty. It hit home when, not long after Gacha's death, Pablo ordered his men to kidnap a Colombian officer, a commander in the army's Fourth Brigade. Angered over his associate's killing, Pablo ordered that the officer be not just killed but tortured to death slowly, just to make a statement to the Colombian government.

Pablo was infuriated by Gacha's death. The government had clearly upped the stakes. In one intercepted conversation with his cousin Gustavo Gaviria, he was captured in a rare unguarded rant that offered insight into how he saw his predicament. He viewed himself as a victim, caught in a class struggle between the power elite in Bogotá and the common people of Medellín.

He intended, he said, to use the public's weariness with violence to his benefit. He planned to turn up the violence until the public cried out for a solution, a deal.

"We will begin to go for the oligarchs and burn the houses of the rich," Pablo said. "It is very easy because the house of a rich person has only one watchman and one goes in with three gallons of gasoline, and with that we shit on them and make them cry and beg for mercy . . . You know, brother, that is the only way. This country is asking for peace and every day there are more people asking for peace. So we have to apply much harder pressure."

A communiqué from the *Extraditables* not long after hammered home the point:

We are declaring total and absolute war on the government, on
the individual and political oligarchy, on the journalists who
have attacked and insulted us, on the judges that have sold
themselves to the government, on the extraditing magistrates
. . . on all those who have persecuted and attacked us. We will
not respect the families of those who have not respected our
families. We will burn and destroy the industries, properties
and mansions of the oligarchy.

[. . .] Trouble at once began closing in on Pablo. Three tons of
dynamite planned for his stepped-up bombing campaign were
seized in a police raid on a warehouse in Bogotá. Five more
tons were seized at a *finca* owned by Pablo near Caldas. In
February, the day before President Bush arrived in Cartagena
to attend a hemispheric anti-drug conference, police raided
three big cocaine labs in Chocó, the state just south of
Antioquia. In the two months after José Rodriguez Gacha's
death, the *PNC* seized $35 million in cash and gold. Pablo's
men started falling, too.

Pablo concluded that there was a spy in his inner circle.

Clearly somebody was informing the police of his
whereabouts and plans. Pablo had a number of his security
force tortured and executed in his presence in early 1990 to
set an example.

In one intercepted conversation, Centra Spike recorded the
screams of a victim in the background as Pablo spoke calmly
to his wife.

The US embassy jealously guarded the secret of Centra
Spike. Jacoby and his staff literally worked in a vault, a secure
room on the windowless fifth floor of the embassy building.
The vault had reinforced walls and a six-inch-thick steel door.
There was strict secrecy even within the building. The Centra
Spike men employed there had cover jobs on the ambassador's
staff, and the entire area where they worked was off-limits to
most embassy employees. So long as Pablo and the other cartel
leaders didn't know anyone was listening, they would continue
to talk freely on their radios and cell phones.

But Pablo did find out that his calls were being overheard.

In March 1990, the Colombian government inadvertently tipped him off.

It happened because Centra Spike intercepted a phone conversation between Pablo and Gustavo Mesa, one of his *sicario* gang leaders, plotting the murder of another presidential candidate.

"What's up? How's everything going?" Pablo asked.

"Everything's going fine," said Mesa. "What you ordered to be done is going ahead well."

"But don't you do it, because you're in charge of one and only one job. Understand?"

"Yeah, I've got the people who will do the job. I'm doing well with the task and I've already presented the bill. They'll pay me Friday, everything's fine."

They went on to discuss the payment (about $1,200), promising that the young killer's family would be provided for in the event he was killed in the attempt. Mesa explained that other gunmen would take care of the bodyguards around the candidate, that the assassin need only focus on the main target. Half of the money would be paid in advance, the other half when the job was done. They mentioned the exact date and time of the hit but, maddeningly, never mentioned which candidate was to be killed or where the hit would take place.

The embassy decided that this information would have to be shared with the Colombian government, so a transcript of the tape was given to President Barco, and the government began scrambling to prevent the killing. The most likely target was assumed to be Gaviria, because he was the front-runner, he had spoken out in favour of extradition, and he was the only candidate who had publicly ruled out negotiating with the traffickers (a promise, as it happened, that he wouldn't keep). Several more attempts had been made on his life since the Avianca bombing.

So Gaviria and several other likely targets were given intensive security on that day. When the appointed hour came, the victim was the least likely candidate: Bernardo Jaramillo, the minor Union Patriotica candidate, was gunned down in the lobby of El Dorado Airport. The police immediately blamed drug traffickers for the killing, but the link was not apparent. Jaramillo had not been an outspoken opponent of extradition, nor a likely winner in the election. Through his lawyers, Pablo immediately issued a denial. But the government had the recording and it found the opportunity to publicly link Pablo to the killing too hard to resist. The transcript was leaked to the press.

There was a swift, outraged public response. Pablo was revealed to be, despite his denials, a killer, someone who was now ordering candidates killed just to sow discord. He lost whatever credibility he'd gained by his years of skilful public relations.

So the leak from Barco's office had its desired effect. But it also had an undesired one. Pablo now knew that conversations on his cell phone were being overheard. His voice vanished from the airwaves. He would never again hold an unguarded conversation on a radio or cell phone.

[It was a phone conversation, albeit a very guarded one, that led to Escobar's eventual demise. By November 1993, Escobar's family were in an immigration limbo, attempting to flee to safety as the Colombian authorities negotiated to block entry to their familiar haunts of London and Frankfurt. With control over his empire ebbing away (handing victory over the Colombian drug-war grudge match to the Cali cartel, rather than doing anything to diminish the amount of cocaine, and by now crack, in the US) Escobar, a man who had treated the families of his own victims as so much collateral damage, had his eye on the safety of his wife and children. He alternated between threats – such as his threat to kill German nationals in Colombia if his family were not given asylum in Germany – and misguided appeals to any lingering sense of post-colonial injustice the Colombian people might still have on behalf of the Extraditables. *With his family in jeopardy, the need for PR was enough to make him break telephone silence, and he arranged a call from his son, Juan Pablo, in order to answer a journalist's questions that his son relayed.*

In the manner of a thriller, or maybe a South-American

soap opera, the son of another player in this tale also plays a key role in its conclusion: second lieutenant Hugo Martinez Jr. The place of Col. Martinez's eldest son in a crack police unit was coincidence not nepotism – in fact, the colonel had tried to get his son transferred somewhere other than Medellín, given that Escobar had once threatened to kill all of his family "up to the third generation". Had the common- sense suggestion that he made his unit a target been heeded, however, it would not have been Colombia.

Thursday, 3 December 1993:] Hugo had driven out of the *[police station]* parking lot in pursuit as soon as his friend on the switchboard at the Hotel Tequendama *[Bogotá, where Escobar's wife and children were staying]* had alerted him that Pablo was on the line. They had recognized his voice right away when he'd called, even though he was still pretending to be a journalist. Per instructions, they had delayed, then finally put the call through.

All of the men at Hugo's parking lot followed him out. The rest of the Search Bloc were converging from their positions.

Hugo felt terribly excited and nervous. He could feel all of his father's men, hardened veteran assaulters, close on his heels.

He knew that if he failed now . . . with all of these men awaiting his direction, he would never live it down.

The tone in his earphones and the line on his scanner directed Hugo to an office building just a few blocks from the parking lot.

He was certain that was where Pablo was speaking. No sooner had he named it than the assault force descended, crashing through the front doors and moving loudly through the building.

Pablo continued to speak calmly, as though nothing was happening.

Hugo was amazed. How could his equipment be wrong?

Clearly he was not in the office building where the men had just launched the raid. Hugo felt panicked. He took two long, deep breaths, forcing himself to calm down. So long as Pablo was talking he could still be found. In the passenger seat of the white Mercedes van, he closed his eyes for a moment and then looked again more carefully at the screen. This time he noticed a slight wiggle in the white line that stretched from side to side. The line spanned the entire screen, which meant the signal was being transmitted close by, but the wiggle suggested something else.

From his experience he knew that this vibration meant he was picking up a reflection. It was very slight, which was why he hadn't noticed it before. When the reflection was off water, the line usually had a slight squiggle in it, but this line had no squiggle.

"This is not it! This is not it!" he shouted into his radio.

"Let's go!"

To his left was a drainage ditch with a gently moving stream in a deep concrete gully. To cross over to the other side, where Hugo was now convinced the signal originated, his driver had to go up a block or two and turn left over a bridge. When the van had crossed the bridge and arrived on the other side of the ditch, Hugo realized that only one car had followed him. Either the others hadn't heard or were ignoring him.

Pablo's conversation with his son continued.

Juan Pablo repeated the journalist's question about why so many other countries had refused to allow him and his mother and sister entry.

"The countries have denied entry because they don't know the real truth," said Pablo.

"Yes," answered Juan Pablo, taking notes as his father spoke.

"We're gonna knock on the doors of every embassy from all around the world because we're willing to fight incessantly," Pablo continued, "because we want to live and study in another country without bodyguards and hopefully with a new name."

"Just so you know," said Juan Pablo. "I got a phone call from a reporter who told me that President Alfredo Christiani from Ecuador, no, I think it is El Salvador —"

"Yes?" Pablo got up and moved to the window, mindful that this conversation had gone on for several minutes. Twenty seconds was usually the rule. Pablo looked down at cars moving on the street below as he listened.

"Well, he has offered to receive us. I heard the statement – well, he gave it to me by phone."

"Yes?"

"And he said if this contributed in some way to the peace of the country, he would be willing to receive us, because the world receives dictators and bad people, why wouldn't he receive us?"

"Well, let's wait and see, because that country is a bit hidden away."

"Well, but at least there's a possibility, and it's come from a president."

"Look, with respect to El Salvador."

"Yeah?"

"In case they ask anything, tell them the family is very grateful and obliged to the words of the president, that it is known he is the president of peace in El Salvador."

"Yeah."

Pablo stayed at the window looking out. When Juan Pablo related a question about the family's experiences under government protection, his father answered, "You respond to that one."

"Who paid for maintenance and accommodation? You or the attorney general?"

"Who did pay this?" Pablo asked.

"Us," said Juan Pablo. "Well, there were some people from Bogotá who got their expenses paid . . . but they never spent all of it, because we supplied the groceries, mattresses, deodorants, toothbrushes, and pretty much everything." Juan Pablo rattled off two more of the questions, but his father abruptly ended the conversation.

"Okay, let's leave it at that," Pablo said.

"Yeah, okay," said Juan Pablo. "Good luck."

"Good luck."

The signal pointed Hugo straight ahead. The line of the screen lengthened and the tone in his earphones grew stronger as they proceeded up the street. They drove until the signal peaked and then began to diminish, the line pinching in at the edges of the screen and the tone slightly falling off. So they turned around and crept back the other way more slowly. The line stretched gradually until it once again filled the screen.

They were in front of a block of two-storey row houses.

There was no telling which was the one that housed Pablo.

They cruised up and down the street several more times. Hugo stopped staring at his screen and instead stared intently at the houses, one by one.

Until he saw him.

A fat man in the second-floor window. He had long, curly black hair and a full beard. The image hit Hugo like an electric shock. He had only seen Pablo in pictures, and he had always been clean shaven except for the moustache, but they knew Pablo had grown a beard, and there was something about the man in the window that just clicked. He was talking on a cell phone and peering down at traffic. The man stepped back from the window.

Hugo thought he had seen a look of surprise.

The face of Pablo Escobar assembled slowly in Hugo's brain.

For a split second he was confused, disbelieving. Him! He had found him! Years of effort, hundreds of lives, thousands of futile police raids, untold millions of dollars, countless false leads and man-hours, all of the false steps, false alarms, blunders . . . and here he was at last, one man in a nation of thirty-five million people, one man in a rich, ruthless, and regimented underworld he had virtually owned for nearly two decades, one man in a city of millions where he was revered as a legend, a task literally more difficult than finding a needle in a haystack.

Hugo leaned out of his van and called to the car behind him, "This is the house!"

It was in the middle of the block. Hugo suspected Pablo had been spooked by their white van cruising slowly down the street, so he had told his driver to keep on going down to the end. Shouting into the radio, Hugo asked to be connected to his father.

"I've got him located," Hugo told his father.

The colonel knew this was it. Those were words he had never

heard before. He knew Hugo would not be saying it unless he had seen Pablo with his own eyes.

"He's in this house," said Hugo.

Hugo explained excitedly that only he and one other car were there. He thought Pablo had seen him and that his gunmen were probably on their way. He wanted to clear out, fast.

"Stay exactly where you are!" Colonel Martinez ordered his son, shouting into the radio. "Station yourself in front and in back of the house and don't let him come out."

Then the colonel got word to all his units in the area, including those still thrashing through the office building blocks away, and told them to converge on the house immediately.

Hugo's two men got out of the car and positioned themselves against the wall on either side of Pablo's front door. Hugo drove the van around the block to the alley, counting the houses until he could see the back end of Pablo's. Terrified, with weapons ready, they waited.

It took about ten minutes.

There was a heavy metal front door. Martin, one of the lieutenants assigned to the Search Bloc assault team, stood ready as his men applied a heavy steel sledgehammer to it. Martin had not worn his bullet-proof vest today, and he had a moment of anxious regret, just as the hammer crashed into the door. It took several blows before it went down.

Martin sprinted into the house with the five men on his team, and the shooting started. In the din and confusion, he quickly sized up the first floor. It was empty, like a garage. There was a yellow taxi parked toward the rear, and a flight of stairs leading up to the second floor. One of Martin's men stumbled on his way up the stairs, and everyone stopped momentarily.

They thought the man had been hit.

Limón [one of Pablo's men] leaped out a back window to the orange tile roof as soon as the team burst through the front door. The way the house was constructed, there was a back roof surrounded by walls on three sides that could be reached by dropping about ten feet from a second-storey window. Limón hit the tiles and began running, and as he did the Search Bloc members arrayed in the street behind the house opened fire. There were dozens of men up and down the block with automatic weapons, some of them standing on the tops of their cars. One Search Bloc shooter had climbed to the second-floor roof of the house next door.

Limón was hit several times as he ran. His momentum carried him right off the roof. He fell to the grass below.

Then came Pablo. He stopped to kick off his flip-flops, then jumped down to the roof. Having seen what had happened to Limón, he stayed close to one wall, where there was some protection.

The shooter on the roof overhead could not get a clear shot directly down at him, so there was a break in the firing momentarily as Pablo quickly moved along the wall towards the back street. No one on the street had a clear shot at him yet. At the corner, Pablo made his break.

He went for the crest of the gently sloping roof, trying to make it to the other side. There was a thundering cascade of fire and Pablo fell near the crest. He sprawled forward, dislodging orange tiles.

The shooting continued. Martin's team inside the house had found the second floor empty. When he stuck his head in the open window to look out on the roof, he saw a body and then heard an eruption of more gunfire. He and his men fell prone on the floor and waited as rounds from the street below crashed through the window and into the walls and ceiling of the room. Martin believed he and his men were taking fire from Pablo's bodyguards. He shouted into his radio, "Help! Help us! We need support!"

Everyone was shooting on automatic from below. Rounds chewed up the brick walls around the enclosed rooftop. It felt as if it took minutes for the shooting to die down, for the Search Bloc to realize they were the only ones shooting. Finally, it stopped. The shooter on the second-floor roof shouted, "It's Pablo! It's Pablo!"

Men were now scaling the roof to see. Someone found a ladder and placed it under the second-floor window, and others climbed down to the roof from the window. Major Aguilar grabbed the body and turned it over. The wide bearded face was swollen, bloody, and wreathed in long, blood-soaked black curls. The major grabbed a radio and spoke directly to Colonel Martinez, loudly enough for even the men on the street below to hear.

"Vivá Colombia! We have just killed Pablo Escobar!"

6

Drug Lords: The Rise and Fall of the Cali Cartel

Ron Chepesiuk

"The Colombian government hunted down and killed Pablo Escobar because he was a terrorist, not [*because he was*] a drug trafficker."

– Mark Eiler, DA intelligence analyst

"Pablo Escobar, Carlos Lehder and the other Medellín cartel godfathers are called the Henry Fords of cocaine trafficking. We need to go one step further with the Cali cartel and call it the McDonald's of cocaine trafficking because its godfathers turned drug trafficking into a major corporate enterprise. The Cali cartel had a set formula and knew how to make it work."

– Lou Weiss, DEA agent

"Mr Escobar is sick, a psycho, a lunatic . . . he thinks that a criminal can win a war against the state. I think that is absurd."

– Gilberto Rodriguez, "chairman" of the Cali cartel

Where Escobar, a familiar public figure with his cruise-ship entertainer's moustache, exploited the traditional sympathies of Colombia's poor, the Cali cartel members blended into the business communities of their region, building links through their legitimate businesses as much as with other traffickers. Where Escobar spoke the emotive language of loyalty, treason and his own persecution at the hands of the state, the Cali were very much gangsters of the "nothing personal" school of crime, not that that meant they gave any quarter, eliminating many, quite possibly, simply for knowing too much, including some killings that have been attributed to the paramilitary death squads who slaughtered hundreds of desechables, or "disposables" – drug addicts, gays, transvestites and transexuals, prostitutes and petty thieves in Cali, Medellín and Bogotá towards the end of the last century. The Cali men were quite capable of ordering the execution of those who crossed them, as well as of those whom it simply suited them to kill. They were meanwhile too wise to stir the brutal beast of government other than with bribe in hand. Death for them was a means of elimination, pure and simple, rather than a public statement designed to instill fear into a ghettoized population with no means of escape.

The Cali was therefore able to make inroads into the US, and later Europe, under the noses of the authorities, before their operations even began to come to light. Their attitude to the emerging technologies of the 1990s also marks them out as having stolen a march on the men from Medellín: while Escobar tortured haplessly loyal employees to death before twigging that his phones were bugged, the six major players of the Cali cartel – the Rodríguez Orejuela brothers, Gilberto and Miguel; the Urdinola Grajales brothers, Jairo and Julio; José Santacruz Londoño and Hélmer Herrera Buitrago – were communicating by then untraceable cellular technologies.

The technological and counter-intelligence sophistication of the Cali rivalled the resources available to a first-world state. Following a raid in 1995, the Colombian authorities discovered that the cartel had been able to monitor all telephone traffic in and out of Cali and Bogotá, including the Ministry of Defence and the US embassy. Whether through bribery or threat, they cultivated contacts in official ministries, seemed to know when their phones were bugged, even by remote, and had complete copies of Colombia's up-to-date car-registration records. They possessed encryption software that outfoxed the knowledge of Colombian and DEA IT experts. In short, much as a modern nation-state's intelligence service would, they understood that blanket coverage was less hit-and-miss than the old ways of intrigue and espionage.

On their payroll were a rumoured 5,000 Cali taxi-drivers, who yielded precise details of the comings and goings of the officials they were contracted to drive, together with news of who was entering and leaving the city as a whole. Time *magazine ran a story in 1991 about how DEA and US Customs agents were monitoring a cocaine shipment being offloaded in Miami, while themselves being under surveillance by the Cali cartel.*

One thing detailed in the following extract is how the cartel changed importation methods, in their early days "living over the shop" or rather the lab, by bringing cocaine manufacture north of the Mexican border and establishing a factory in New York State, allowing for the importation of the drug as base rather than as blocks of powder.

However, the greatest change they brought about in distribution patterns, and through it geopolitics, was to recruit Mexican gangs to move the drug on to its market in the US. Traditionally, the Cali cartel had dominated the cocaine route into Florida from their tame state of Panama, while Escobar and Lehder had operated out of the Bahamas. But when the Colombian government bowed to US pressure over extradition, the Cali came up with the solution of cutting in the Mexicans because, by no longer exporting directly to the US, they hoped to avoid eligibility for extradition under the terms of the relevant legislation.

In so doing, the Cali have been partly responsible for the growth of Mexican gang warfare (having raised the stakes over and above those provided by the traditional Mexican crops of cannabis and heroin) and the social disorder that parts of the country are currently undergoing. The gangs around Cuidad Juárez, for example, include the Aztecas, Mexicales *and* Artistas Asesinos. *Fights between these gangs in the city's prison have turned into bloodbaths, killing around 160–180 prisoners a year. Outside, the drug wars alone are believed to be responsible for over 6,000 killings in 2008. Nor is violence limited to Juárez. On 21*

January 2010, twenty-three inmates were killed in a prison rampage near Durango, Sinaloa.

Further evidence of this delegation of US distribution to Mexican gangs, this time on the part of the heirs to the Medellín cartel, came in early February 2010, when, in Operation Frontier, Medellín police arrested twenty-one traffickers including twelve pilots with over 5,000 hours each of flying time, spent taking multi-kilo loads of cocaine into Mexico and into the hands of Sinaloa's Joachim "El Chapo" Guzman. Mexicans gangs have established border-smuggling expertise, as well as seeming to lack the fear of extradition, Mexicans being traditionally more used perhaps to America deporting them than seeking to bring them in.

At their height, the Cali were already dwarfing and threatening Escobar's business before his spell as a fugitive and his eventual killing, with ninety per cent of the cocaine market. With this unimaginable wealth came the need to launder it. Gilberto Orejuela became chairman of a bank, Banco de Trabajadores, and in offering account facilities to the Medellín (the need to wash money being a problem big enough to make any gang member swallow their pride), he made money out of them, as well.

It was Gilberto who founded the First InterAmericas Bank, operating out of Panama, which first tipped the US authorities to the cartel's immense wealth. Gilberto also started the radio network, Grupo Radial Colombiano, and – ironically – the pharmaceutical chain Drogas la Rebaja, which employed around 4,200 people, with over 400 stores, worth an estimated $216 million dollars.

An example of their corporate approach was their understanding of the need to expand, to not stagnate. If you manufacture cola, you address the "problem" of continued growth with new ways to market your product – different packaging, new sizes, suggestions that the consumer orders or buys it in situations where they'd usually drink something else. If you manufacture cocaine, a similarly unchanging product, you look for new markets.

Therefore, in the 1990s, it was the Cali cartel's cocaine that could be found in London, Liverpool, Manchester and Glasgow among many other British and European cities. The burgeoning European trade was developed largely by the networking of the Ochoa brothers. From their base in Holland, they negotiated with, among others, the old British lags who had taken up residence on the Costa del Sol in the days before Britain's extradition treaty with Spain, Curtis Warren (see chapter 10), *and were not above dealing directly with those who had found their way into the trade via smaller city-based networks, such as Brian Doran from Glasgow* (see chapter 14).

Their timing was good: the quality of Ecstasy was on the wane, and young European professionals were ready for another party drug. With its plentiful supply, the street price of a gram of cocaine dropped from £100 in the 1980s to roughly £60 in the 1990s and £50 and even £40 thereafter. It became more accessible than it had been in the 1980s. Robbie Williams was photographed with a nosebleed, lads' mags such as Loaded *were talking up druggie hedonism, 1970s chic was in fashion,* Snowblind *was back in print, and Europeans were probably consuming more cocaine in the 1990s than they fondly imagined their 1970s counterparts had been in the disco era, despite the legends of Studio 54.*

The cultural – and, sad to say, political – influence of the Rodríguez-Orejuela brothers, now languishing on multiple life-terms in a federal US penitentiary, has been immense – in Colombia, Mexico, the US, Europe and around the world. But these anonymous men would doubtless rather you didn't know of them at all – all they ever wanted was the money. In his comprehensive source book not just on the Cali men but on Colombia's cartels as a whole, Ron Chepesiuk details the downfall of its leaders through the US's persistent following of their paper trail. Too centralized, they remained managed from the centre as they grew, incriminating themselves. Subsequent to their downfall, other Colombian gangs took note, and have not repeated this mistake.

The Cali men lived and worked by the phone system.

Police had wiretapped the Cosa Nostra, but that was like wiretapping the Boy Scouts compared to what was involved in bugging the Colombians. It turned out that wiretapping, especially of pay phones, would require a lot of manpower – interpreters, technicians, detectives – to watch the pay phones to see when the suspected criminals got the call, and people to sit around and tap the phones at the right moment. There were legal considerations as well. The police needed a court order to wiretap a public telephone, and the wiretap conversation had to be related to the persons named in the court order. "If a certain part of the phone conversation was irrelevant to our investigation, we had to shut down the wire," explained Louis Velez, a former member of the NYSP [. . .]

"We could go back on the wire tap when the parties started talking about the alleged crime again," he said. Calls between the caller and his counsel were privileged. The strategy was to identify and gather evidence against customers, couriers and managers.

"Very difficult decisions had to be made as to when to arrest and seize contraband," said Terrance Kelley, the attorney the NYDETF assigned to the investigation. "We had to be careful not to expose too prematurely the existence of electronic surveillance on a particular phone."

The investigators on the street were free of paperwork, but the wire-intercept crew had to document all the calls they made by writing a short synopsis of each call and noting the time it was made and where. Case 86055 set up a huge wiretap room in early 1986 in the Whitestone section of Queens. The Organized Crime Task Force had identified the Cali cartel as an emerging organized crime syndicate and provided funding for the wiretap operation. The Whitestone building was where Velez and his seventeen-member wiretap team operated for the next six years, twenty-four hours a day, 365 days a year. In some years they got lucky and made it home for Christmas dinner.

Mante's and Velez's close working relationship helped to co-ordinate better what was happening in the wiretapping room and on the street. Mante, the son of a New York City police officer, joined the NYSP in 1974. Velez, the son of a chief who grew up in the tough Lower East Side of Manhattan, joined three years later. They both started out as uniformed officers at the Somers Barracks in Westchester County, about thirty miles north of New York City. In the late 1970s, the two were assigned to the Troop K narcotics unit as undercover detectives, initially investigating street-level drug operations involving mostly heroin, PCP, marijuana and pills.

"As undercover cops, we also bought illegal guns on the street, sold fenced stolen property, and bought the real proceeds from burglaries," Mante recalled. "We propositioned hookers and pimped them. Basically, we did whatever our cover required." At the time, Mante noted, "cocaine was fresh on the streets and was selling for a hundred dollars per gram, but most of our targets could not afford the luxury." Over the years, he and Velez continued to work the streets undercover until they joined case 86055. "We clicked and kicked some serious ass when it came to narcotics enforcement," said Mante.

The investigation had a chronic problem that was giving Velez headaches. Reports of the intercepts needed to be written, but almost all of the cartel operatives spoke in Spanish. New York in the mid-1980s lacked police officers fluent in Spanish who could translate the intercepts. Finding them wouldn't be easy. Indeed, Velez could identify just one Colombian on the NYSP force, and he was stationed on an Indian reservation near the Canadian border. The officer was transferred to Velez's unit overnight and began working as a translator.

Through documents obtained by its lawyers in discovery, the cartel learned that the authorities were bugging the pay phones. So, as it did throughout its history, the cartel adjusted its strategy, and by 1985 it was using faxes to communicate with headquarters and to conduct business. The cartel used so many faxes, in fact, that they actually had apartments whose sole purpose was to serve as stash houses for their fax machines.

The switch prompted the NYSP to begin wiretapping faxes, becoming the country's first law enforcement agency to do so.

The investigation became a cat-and-mouse communications game, as the Cali cartel tried to outfox the authorities and stay one step ahead of them. About four years later, the cartel switched again – this time to cell phones. "They started using banks of cell phones and we said, 'Oh shit!'" Mante recalled.

He explained: "Wiretapping cell phones was really tough at first because NYNEX [the New York Telephone Company] had only seven ports available at a time. So imagine the number of people in the New York metropolitan area and then consider that only seven phones at a time could be tapped. Also, the US government had set aside a number of the phones for national security purposes, and it never allowed anybody else – including law enforcement – to use them."

Fortunately, that barrier was an issue only for about a year.

The government started using a different system, and law enforcement had unlimited access for court-ordered eavesdropping.

As a result of the fax wiretaps, Hernando Rizzo, an important Cali cell manager, whose codename was "Tio" ("uncle" in Spanish) and five other traffickers were arrested in Queens for possession of 2,014 kilos of cocaine and about $2.3 million in cash. "To this day, it's the largest cocaine bust ever by US law enforcement without the use of CIs," Mante said.

The Rizzo bust was only one of two times that Bill Mante saw the price of cocaine jump during the investigation.

"Making the price jump was a sure sign we were hurting them," Mante explained. "The Rizzo bust drove up the price of cocaine to $30,000 from about $15,000 a kilo for six to eight months. It has a trickledown effect and can make their business customers go to other suppliers. It doesn't kill their business, but it lets them know that we're on to them."

By 1987, the investigation began to broaden, as the Cali cartel network expanded, and the DEA, NYSP, and NYDETF coordinated intelligence, surveillance and wiretap operations.

"We realized that we couldn't just rely on the wiretaps," said Robbie Michaelis, who joined the NYDETF right out of the DEA academy in 1987. "We also had to use the knowledge of the old-timers who had worked the investigation, such as Ken

Robinson and Bill Mockler. We did surveillance and continued trying to develop informants."

As the wiretaps revealed, the flow of cash and cocaine never slowed. Jaime Orejuela, who had overseen the US processing labs for Chepe Santacruz, fled the United States after authorities uncovered them in 1985. Now he was working the phones from Cali, giving instructions to the regional managers. In early 1986, the first wiretap intercept relating to the cartel's distribution in New York City involved a call between Jaime Orejuela and Marina Montoya, a distributor for the cartel in Queens. Orejuela informed Montoya that he was sending her ten kilos of cocaine. On 5 June, Nelson Tapias delivered approximately $1.2 million in cash to a buyer in Queens. On 2 January 1987, Gerardo Garcia, also known as "Puntillon", told Jaime Orejuela that he had "something", meaning money, to give to Orejuela.

On 29 February 1988, Orejuela instructed Jorley Arbelaez to "change your house, don't go back there, go and move now! Move from where you live, grow a moustache, a beard, whatever."

Kenny Robinson, now working closely with the case 86055 investigators, was getting so familiar with the financial records that he could tell from Guzman's ledgers that Freddie Aguilera was next in line to take over as the cartel's regional manager. That was why he had him under surveillance and tailed him to a location near the Minden lab in 1985. *[In April 1985, a barn in this sleepy upstate New York farming town exploded accidentally, leading police to a new phenomenon in the US – a cocaine lab. The incident was the first revelation of the existence of the Cali ring in north America.]*

In September 1987, the NYSP received information that Aguilera had re-entered the country and was in the Miami area and, most likely, was hanging out at a bar called the Bakery Center. Robinson, Mante and three other agents from the Task Force and the DEA began surveillance of the Bakery Center. On 28 September, the investigators followed Aguilera to several bars into the wee hours of the morning. Aguilera emerged from the bar blind-drunk and, when they moved in to arrest him, he struggled violently. The officers had to pull him out of his 1987

Cadillac Seville. They brought him back to the DEA's Miami office for questioning and got a warrant to search his apartment on Biscayne Boulevard. There, they found forty-one kilos of cocaine stashed in various places and a Colombia passport in the name of Victor Martinez. On 7 October, the US Attorney's Office indicted Aguilera for possession of cocaine with intent to distribute.

When the NYDETF seized the José Justo Guzman ledgers in 1984, they identified two brothers, Humberto El Pintor Sandoval and Francisco Sandoval, as cartel members. Twenty-four-hour surveillance of Francisco (Humberto was out of the country) over several days led them to an individual who they identified as Luis "the Shrimp" Ramos, a forty-year-old Colombian illegal alien whose real name was Alvaro Ivan Neira. Task Force investigators followed him to quiet residential streets in middle-class neighbourhoods, a cemetery, street corners, and several other locations, where they saw various people give Ramos suitcases and duffel bags. They believed the Shrimp was handling the money for the cartel's drug sales, and they applied for a search warrant for his house, located in a well-to-do section of Bayside, Queens.

On 20 February 1988, the Task Force decided it was time to execute the search warrant. The detectives hit the apartment door, rushed into the living room, and hooked left to the master bedroom. There was the Shrimp coming out of the shower. He dove for the bed but two officers tackled him and put him in handcuffs. Underneath the bed was a fully automatic and loaded Uzi machine gun. Also within Ramos' reach were an AR-15 assault rifle and an automatic pistol. Both the Uzi and AR-15 had the safety off and were in fire mode.

A search of the house revealed several other weapons – a .44, two .38s and Chinese martial arts throwing stars – and a drug ledger on the coffee table in the living room. They found the duffel bags that Ramos had received and discovered that they contained $7.8 million in cold cash. Back at the office, investigators had to push four desks together to stack the money. An analysis of the evidence connected Ramos to Santacruz and the Cali cartel.

Using the windfall of records and documents confiscated

in the Ramos arrest, investigators continued to identify the cartel's operatives and customers in New York City. Meanwhile, law enforcement in other areas of the United States, especially Miami and South Florida, were also targeting Cali smuggling operations. "Any ongoing investigation in New York City had a South Florida connection on it," said Tom Cash, an administrator at the DEA's Miami office in the late 1980s. "South Florida became Cali's staging area for getting their drugs into the country and their money out of it. It seemed that, at times, we had more people in South Florida from Cali than there were people living in Cali."

When Gilberto Rodriguez was arrested in Miami in 1984, he had the name of Michael Tsalickis, along with his home and work phone numbers, in his address book. Tsalickis, a Florida businessman from Tarpon Springs, owned an import–export business and had sold monkeys from Colombia's Amazon jungle to research laboratories. "CIs had told us that Tsalickis had been involved in importing cocaine since 1983 and we suspected him of using his business to launder money for the Cali cartel," said Rich Crawford, who was assigned to the case. As part of the investigation, Crawford journeyed to the Amazon region of Colombia, about 150 miles east of Leticia, to a Tsalickis-owned sawmill, which informants told the DEA was a major centre for cocaine production and distribution.

In February 1987, an anonymous letter written in Spanish and postmarked from Cali arrived at the DEA's Miami office.

The letter claimed that a shipment of 4,000 kilos of cocaine valued at a mind-boggling $1.7 billion would be arriving in St Petersburg, Florida, aboard a ship named *Amazon Sky*. On 20 April, customs agents boarded the ship to inspect the cargo. One of the cedar boards broke and an agent became suspicious. He got a power drill from his office and drilled into the broken board. Pay dirt! The drill came out tainted with cocaine. They discovered that the boards holding the cocaine were holed out to neatly hide one kilo in each hole.

The authorities decided to stay put. They carefully glued the boards back together and sanded them down to hide the seams. Federal agents knew that the traffickers had been shipping their cocaine in lumber since 1976, but they still marvelled at the sophistication of the organization. "You had to look hard to find the seams," Crawford recalled. "It was unbelievable how professional the job was." Tom Cash later estimated that it must have taken an army of about 800 to 1,000 workers to load the boat.

The authorities watched as the *Amazon Sky's* crew moved the boards over a period of four days to Tsalickis's office and warehouse complex in St Petersburg. The authorities obtained a search warrant allowing them to videotape the warehouse and wiretap the telephone. Federal agents saw about 700 boards of the cocaine-filled lumber being carried into trucks for the drive to Tsalickis' warehouse. Two weeks after the surveillance began, authorities arrested him and two Colombian associates for cocaine smuggling.

By the end of the 1980s, authorities had a good understanding how the Cali cartel operated. From its headquarters in Cali, the high level "executives" would direct the managers and other traffickers, which federal officials estimated to number between five and six thousand. The executives kept in daily contact with their people in the United States.

"Decentralization is not a word in their vocabulary," Tom Constantine, administrator of the DEA, told Congress in October 1994.

The cartel sold its cocaine wholesale through the use of cells or "customer groups", each headed by a manager.

Overseeing the cells were regional managers, such as José Justo Guzman, who oversaw the distribution of cocaine, the collection of money from customer groups, and the acquisition and maintenance of storage and commercial facilities.

The regional managers had to attend periodic business meetings in Cali. In 1984 Jorge Salazar became head of the cartel's Los Angeles office. In January 1988, he attended a meeting in Cali presided over by Jaime Orejuela. Arriving with twenty bodyguards, Chepe Santacruz greeted Salazar and told him to relax while he made some calls to the United States: "How are things going in L.A.?" Chepe asked Salazar when he had finished making the calls.

"Everything is going well," Salazar replied.

Chepe then took out the books and did a check to be sure there was no missing drugs or money and no money owed.

Good, the books were in order.

"You're in Cali for a short time, so enjoy it," Santacruz told Salazar. Then he gave his employee a $12,000 cheque in Colombian pesos as a bonus for having done a good job.

The NYSP compared the cartel in its style of management to a fast-food chain, such as McDonald's or Dairy Queen, which provided franchisees with supplies of hamburgers or ice cream. Cell managers were treated like the employees of a franchise in that they were given financial incentives to sell the product. Santacruz, for instance, paid Salazar $500 for each kilo he distributed. Just as a corporation would, the Cali cartel transferred its workers from one city to another. "If the heat was on one of their employees in New York City, the cartel would move them to L.A.," Diaz said.

Employees would get regular vacations and other company benefits. In return, they were told to act like regular Joe and Jane America. For instance, those workers maintaining stash houses were expected to leave the house every day, as if they were going to work. On 11 December 1992, investigators hit a home on a quiet street in the city of Yonkers, New York. It was the residence of Orlando Jaramillo, a Miguel Rodriguez operative. Jaramillo left his home every day just like many of his neighbours. His wife shopped in the local supermarkets and his children attended the local Catholic elementary school.

Jaramillo told his neighbors that he worked on Wall Street.

Inside the Jaramillo residence, police found the typical financial ledgers showing that Jaramillo had collected $5 million over the previous few weeks. They found a large box in the basement containing more than $100,000. They looked for the Cali cartel's trademark hidden vaults and, when they moved a flowerpot, a door opened, allowing access to a room, approximately three feet by twenty feet. Inside were U-Haul boxes, floor to ceiling, each stuffed with cash and marked on the outside with amounts totalling $5 million.

Still, there was a big difference between the Cali cartel and a franchise. Each cell or franchise operated with little or no knowledge of other cells. So the takedown of one cell would not compromise another. Once inside the United States, the cocaine was transported from a central distribution point to markets throughout the country. The mob used trains, buses, private vehicles, airlines, the postal service, and concealed compartments within vehicles, such as trucks and vans, much in the manner that the Aguilera gang moved cocaine from Minden to New York City in 1985. Using perishable cargo to conceal and move the cocaine inside the US was a favourite smuggling method. In June 1994, thirteen metric tons of cocaine were discovered behind the false wall of a tractor trailer transporting thirty pallets from Edinburg, Texas to Immokalee, Florida.

The drug lords retained a team of "corporate" lawyers in the United States to handle legal problems and a team of private investigators to vet potential business partners. When the Task Force busted Hernando Rizzo, the cartel made him go to trial to see what it could learn from the discovery phase.

"They analysed us like we analysed them," Mante observed.

Still, despite the cartel's well-planned organization, law enforcement was taking down its cells with regularity by the early 1990s. "The cartel was having to send substantial numbers of Cali operatives to the US from Colombia," Robinson said. "That showed we were making a dent in their organization." By 1991, the Case 86055 investigation had resulted in the arrest of nearly 200 defendants and the seizure of more than 5,700 kilos of cocaine and nearly $24 million in cash. Additional property confiscated included seventy-five vehicles, numerous weapons and property valued at $1 million. The NYSP had done a major hit on the gentlemen from Cali.

Other major cartel distribution rings in New York City and Miami went down hard. Two of the most successful investigations focused on the Pacho Herrera and Ivan Urdinola-Grajales organizations. Like the other three Cali godfathers, Herrera kept a tight rein on his business through the use of coded telecommunications from Cali. But over the course of a one-and-a-half-year investigation, the NYDETF broke most of his codes and penetrated Herrera's wireless communications through the use of eighty-four court-ordered wiretaps. In all, they investigated 71,403 calls, 40,000 of which pertained to drug-trafficking activities. At one point, in what turned out to be the largest eavesdropping campaign ever waged by US law enforcement against an international narcotics trafficking organization, the NYDETF simultaneously bugged twenty-one cellular phones, five pay phones and thirty-five pagers.

The Herrera crew became paranoid about the eavesdropping and tried to further encrypt their communications using aliases, cryptic language and numeric codes. The names of their distribution centres were coded. "The Towers" was used for New York; "la Tia" (the aunt) for Los Angeles; "la Playa" (the beach) for Miami; and "the Town" for Cali. The drug business was going so well for Herrera's people that they had no time to change their modus operandi. They got sloppy and kept using the same words, phrases and code names over and over again. Micromanager Pacho Herrera was referred to in the wiretapped phone calls as "Abuelo" (grandfather) and "Don Pacho". Over the course of an hour's conversation, several of his team would continually refer to cocaine as "shoes", "checks" or "shirts".

On 26 November 1991, the NYDETF arrested Ramiro Herrera Buitrago and a federal grand jury in the Eastern District of New York indicted Ramiro and his brother William Herrera Buitrago, who remained in Colombia. On 8 December 1991, Ramiro Herrera was sentenced to thirty years in prison. Eleven months later, Pacho Herrera and brothers William and Alvaro were indicted in the Eastern District of New York, and the United States presented warrants to the governor of Colombia for their extradition.

Meanwhile in Miami, law enforcement took down the network of Jairo Ivan Urdinola-Grajales, a Cali drug dealer who had a close business relationship with Miguel Rodriguez.

He regularly purchased a part of Miguel's multi-ton shipments.

The DEA in Miami wiretapped lengthy conversations among Urdinola's cell workers to build its case. In 1992, its High Intensity Drug Task Force concluded Operation Wizard 11, seizing 13,000 kilos of cocaine and $15 million in US currency, and indicting and arresting sixty-five people in the US and Colombia who worked for the Urdinola-Grajales organization.

Authorities had found the Achilles' heel of their target. As the Cali cartel grew into a multinational enterprise during the 1980s, it became more reliant on telecommunications to co-ordinate its activities. Yes, they used the best and latest technology available on the market, but law enforcement was not standing still either. It, too, refined its investigative techniques and methods as it learned more about the organization. The bosses in Cali, however, couldn't let go, and as the criminal enterprise expanded not just in the United States but globally, their management style became a major liability.

"All important decisions were made from Cali – whether it involved distribution, security or whatever – and that made the cartel dependent on communications technology," said DEA agent Michael Horn. "They were planting the seeds for their own downfall."

The major drug of choice in Europe in the late 1980s was heroin supplied by the Asians. But the Cali cartel showed up on the DEA's radar screen, and we began seeing substantial increases in cocaine seizures.

– John Constanzo, retired DEA agent

Successful money-laundering investigations in the early 1990s exposed the global reach of the Cali cartel.

Federal agents working undercover on Operation Green Ice provided laundering "services" for the cartel in Europe, Colombia and the Caribbean. In the UK, authorities seized about $6 billion, arrested three cartel members and confiscated forty-three kilos of cocaine. Italy's Servicio Centrale Operativo (SCO) and the Internal Security Service (SISDE) seized $1 million and arrested twenty-one members of two Italian Mafia families who worked with the Cali cartel.

The Spanish National Police arrested four cartel members, while the Royal Canadian Mounted Police arrested one individual and seized another $1.6 million. The international community had never co-operated on drug trafficking cases as it had on Operation Green Ice, and the investigation showed that more of that type of co-operation needed to be done in the future, given the growing reach of the Cali cartel.

In Operation Dinero, authorities in the United States, Italy, Spain and Great Britain had used a clever sting to follow the cartel's money trail and unravel a web of organized crime syndicate connections in Italy, Russia, Great Britain and several other European countries, and as far away as the Orient. Dinero also exposed a strong alliance between Cali and the Italian Mafia when authorities arrested Italian crime boss Pasquale C. Locatelli in Spain on 6 September 1994. The Locatelli organization, which had operations in France, Romania, Croatia, Spain, Greece, Italy and Canada, sent ships to the Colombian coast to pick up cocaine and transport it to North Africa, where it was transferred to smaller boats and smuggled into Europe.

By the early 1990s, the cartel had grown into a true crime multinational. It made its money illegally, but that was about the only difference between the Cali cartel and IBM or any other multinational corporation. In terms of structure, marketing and distribution, the drug mafia had as much in common with the giants that made *Fortune* magazine's annual list of top 500 companies as it did with its rivals in the drug trade. The Cali cartel, in fact, became the poster syndicate for multinational crime. It had the ability to challenge state authority. It employed a workforce spread around the world.

It was constantly opening up new markets.

As a multinational commonly does, the cartel began decentralizing and moving some of its operations out of its home base of Colombia. By the early 1990s, it had cocaine processing and distribution operations in a dozen Latin America countries. Tom de Renenteria, a drug expert with the Andean Commission of Jurists, told *Newsweek* that "Latin America as a whole is sliding into the drug war. Argentina and Brazil can see their future in Bolivia. Bolivia sees its own 'future' in Peru ... Peru in Colombia ... it's an endless cycle." *Newsweek* also noted that "Bolivia and Peru, which have long been prime sources of raw coca for Colombia's cartels, were becoming major producers of finished cocaine as well."

The Cali drug lords began using Latin American and Caribbean countries in a variety of dynamic ways. Guatemala became the largest warehouse for cocaine in Latin America, and, according to US officials working in the country, most of the cocaine trafficking there was Cali-related. Analysts at the US Department of Justice and the US State Department's Bureau of International Narcotics Matters calculated that traffickers were using Guatemala to move fifty to seventy-five tons of cocaine annually to the United States.

In 1990, customs officers began seeing a significant increase in the number of Haitian couriers smuggling large quantities of cocaine out of Haiti for the Cali cartel on commercial airlines and air cargo planes. In one three-month period, they arrested about thirty Haitian drug couriers or mules, trying to smuggle sixty kilograms of cocaine into Miami and San Juan, Puerto Rico. Ecuador became a drop-off point for precursor chemicals, while in Brazil the cartel worked closely with Italian organized crime groups based there to form dozens of bogus companies that they used to launder drug money.

In Venezuela, the cartel worked with the Contrera family, which had moved to the country from Sicily in the 1970s and made it an important conduit for the Colombian-Sicilian drug connection. One Venezuelan official, Guillermo Jiminez, the head of the country's organized crime unit, estimated the Contrera network was responsible for eighty per cent of all the cocaine being exported from Colombia.

In terms of marketing strategy, the alliances the Cali cartel forged with Mexican traffickers were its most important in Latin America. Mexican and Colombian drug traffickers had collaborated on a small scale since the early 1970s, when the Colombian traffickers "piggybacked" their drug loads on smuggling routes that their Mexican counterparts had set up for heroin and marijuana. Still, most of the Colombian cocaine entering the United States from the 1970s through the mid-1980s came by way of the Caribbean. As the United States stepped up its so-called War on Drugs in the 1980s, law enforcement intensified the pressure on this smuggling corridor, forcing the cartel to seek new routes through Central America and Mexico and across the United States' Southwest border. In reality, the shift was inevitable. Mexico had what the cartel needed – a 2,000-mile expanse of border that offered unlimited smuggling possibilities, experienced smugglers eager to collaborate and a ready-made infrastructure to meet its needs.

To further its changing distribution strategy, the Cali cartel helped organize a crime federation in Mexico, which consisted of experienced traffickers who could provide safe and reliable smuggling services. According to DEA intelligence, to meet the cartel's transportation needs, "major Mexican traffickers united their operations, which resulted in the formation of a loose federation".

By the early 1990s, sixty to eighty per cent of the cocaine entering the United States came through the Mexican connection, while only twenty to thirty per cent continued to be smuggled via the Caribbean. The 1989 seizure of more than twenty-one tons in Sylmar, California, illustrated how important the Mexican connection had become in the Cali cartel transportation scheme of things. The shipment, at the time the largest cocaine seizure on record, crossed the Mexican border at El Paso, Texas, and then was moved by truck to the West Coast. In making the big bust, law enforcement officials boasted that they had prevented an even larger amount of cocaine from reaching the streets but on further investigation they learned that it had merely dented the drug smuggling.

"We realized our encouragement was premature when we analysed seized records," conceded Tom Constantine, the DEA administrator from 1994 to 1998. "What we found was even more astounding. We learned that during only a three-month period, the organization had succeeded in smuggling fifty-five tons of cocaine into the United States. This cocaine had been trucked to the United States and had already been distributed on the streets."

Several Mexican drug traffickers became key players in the cartel's Mexican connection, but one of the first was actually a Honduran named Juan Ramon Matta Ballesteros, who, from the mid-1970s to the mid-1990s, worked with the Guadalajara cartel, the group responsible for kidnapping and killing DEA

Special Agent Enrique Camarena in 1985. Matta Ballesteros was arrested and jailed in Colombia but he escaped after paying a bribe estimated at between $1 million and $2.5 million. He fled to Tecucigulpa, Honduras, where he bought a home and moved openly in public. The drug lord thought he was safe in Honduras because it didn't have an extradition treaty with the United States but Honduras, under pressure from the United States, deported him in 1988. Two years later, he became the first person convicted of Camarena's murder. The following year, Matta Ballesteros was sentenced to three life-terms in prison.

Until his arrest in January 1996, Juan García-Abrego, the first international drug trafficker to be included on the FBI's Most Wanted List, smuggled drugs for the Cali cartel from the Yucatán region in Mexico to South Texas and on to Cali's New York market. García-Abrego also helped move bulk shipments of cash. During one four-year period, from 1989 to 1993, US authorities seized $53 million from the García-Abrego organization. The personal fortune of García-Abrego, nicknamed "the Doll" because of his youthful appearance, was placed at $2 billion, and he reportedly owned eighty-six homes. He had close ties to leading Mexican politicians, including Raul Salinas de Gortari, the brother of former Mexican President Carlos Salinas de Gortari. Salinas was seen at a lavish party given by García-Abrego at his ranch near Monterrey in 1992. The authorities captured García-Abrego in Mexico, and, since he was an American citizen, Mexico extradited him to the United States. In October 1996, García-Abrego was convicted on federal drug-trafficking charges in Houston and was given a life sentence.

The cartel forged its most important alliance in Mexico with Amado Carrillo Fuentes, nicknamed "the Lord of the Skies" because of his pioneering use of old passenger jets to move multi-ton loads of cocaine from Colombia to Mexico.

Carrillo Fuentes was born in 1953 in Mexico's northwestern state of Sinaloa, an area from which many traffickers came.

Legendary Mexican drug kingpin Pablo Acosta Villareal schooled Carrillo in the basics of the trade, and as part of his training he had to work with the Colombians to develop them as a source of supply. Carrillo Fuentes' mentor was his uncle Ernesto Fonseca Carrillo, who was jailed in 1985 for the murder of DEA agent Enrique Camarena. The drug lord assumed leadership of the so-called Juarez cartel in 1985 after its leader, Raphael Aguilar Guajardo, was gunned down in Cancún. Carrillo played an important role as liaison between the Mexican Federation and the Cali cartel. As one analyst told *Time* magazine, "He has the ability to form alliances."

Alberto Ochoa-Soto, a major Colombian money broker who operated in Mexico, was one of the first Colombians to work with Carrillo. They began collaborating when Carrillo operated in the Ojinaga, Chihuahua area, and maintained close ties as Carrillo-Fuentes' organization grew in power and he became the "premier patron [boss] in Mexico". The DEA arrested Ochoa-Soto on 9 July 1994 for conspiracy to distribute six tons of cocaine, but US authorities released him from their custody on 11 February 1995. Ochoa-Soto walked across the Stanton Street Bridge in El Paso and was never seen again. According to a DEA intelligence report, "recent reporting indicates that ACF [Amado Carrillo Fuentes] may have had Ochoa-Soto killed shortly after he returned to Mexico because Ochoa-Soto was moving large quantities of cocaine through Ciudad Juárez without co-ordinating the movements with Carrillo."

Hoover Salazar-Espinosa, an important Cali transportation co-ordinator and money launderer, was also Carrillo-Fuentes' close associate. The Lord of the Skies provided protection for cocaine shipments that Salazar-Espinosa brokered and transported and even helped to move the coke to crossing points along the US–Mexican border and across the border with the help of appropriate members of the crime federation.

Once the cocaine was in the States, Salazar-Espinosa assumed control of the load and continued moving it to its destination.

According to DEA intelligence, this scenario "showed ACF's power and the flexibility of the Mexican drug-trafficking alliances. With ACF's approval and protection, Salazar Espinosa has the ability to smuggle and stage drugs along the entire length of the United States–Mexican border."

Carrillo-Fuentes allowed Grupo Union, a Mexican money-laundering group, to operate in his area. Grupo Union members reportedly travelled to Colombia to co-ordinate the arrival of aircraft on their ranches in the Mexican State of Tabasco. The group then used Mexican rental vehicles to transport the cocaine across the US–Mexican border. The traffickers' sealed the powder in plastic and sprayed it with butane gas to mask the odour from cocaine detection devices.

As perhaps Mexico's most powerful drug lord, Carrillo-Fuentes established a close working relationship with another patron – Miguel Rodriguez. The two reportedly talked about business almost every day. Rodriguez paid Carrillo-Fuentes a "transportation charge" of one kilo for every two kilos of Colombian cocaine successfully delivered to the United States.

Despite their relationship, the two bosses constantly haggled over money, largely because Carrillo-Fuentes was chronically overdue on his payments for cocaine that he bought from Miguel. Once Carrillo-Fuentes had to send three Mexican hostages to Miguel as a guarantee that he would pay him for a lost shipment. The Mexicans were freed after Carrillo-Fuentes paid Miguel millions of dollars and turned over some property in Mexico to him.

Carrillo-Fuentes adopted the Cali cartel's use of high-tech gadgetry, including beepers, fax machines, cell phones and encryption, as well as its terrorist-like cell structure, which compartmentalized each of the organization's functions.

"Amado Carrillo-Fuentes learned from the Cali bosses," said Tracey Eaton, a former Mexico City bureau chief of the *Dallas Morning News* who has written extensively about Carrillo-Fuentes. "He ran his operation much like a corporation and got into profit-sharing before it was fashionable. He bribed Mexican police chiefs and politicians. He also had the touch of Tony Soprano of the HBO TV series, *The Sopranos,* in that he could go from polite gentleman to ruthless thug in a minute."

By the mid-1990s, however, Carrillo-Fuentes was under intense pressure from Mexican and US law enforcement.

He tried to disguise his appearance through cosmetic surgery and planned to retire after relocating some of his operations and resources to Chile. In July 1997, he went to Mexico City to have some plastic surgery done. His surgery appeared to have gone well but then he was injected with Dormicum, a post-operatory medicine. The drug lord's blood vessels contracted and he had a fatal heart attack. After his death, a violent struggle broke out in Juárez for control of his drug empire.

The US market for cocaine was starting to become saturated by the mid-1980s. The street price had dropped nearly two-thirds, while cocaine was selling for four times as much in Europe. The Cali cartel saw that the European drug market was ripe for penetration. When Gilberto Rodriguez and Jorge Ochoa moved to Spain in 1984, they bought a large ranch in Badajoz, near the border with Portugal, to serve as a base of operations from which they could analyse the potential for trafficking cocaine in Europe. The Cali cartel reached out to tobacco smugglers from Galicia in Spain, who had a good knowledge of the region's coastline and storage facilities that could be used to smuggle drugs. The cartel began to use boats to pick up the drugs from ocean-going vessels and bring them ashore. To launder its money, it set up a network of accounts between Spanish and Panamanian banks and invested in real estate.

Jorge Ochoa sent one of his key lieutenants, Teodoro Castrillon, to England, Germany and Holland to establish contacts with the local Colombian communities and to see if they could develop the infrastructure and distribution networks similar to those they had in the United States. Gilberto and Jorge and their wives, however, were arrested near Rodriguez's apartment in Madrid. The United States sent a lawyer to Madrid to secure the extradition of Rodriguez and Ochoa, but the Spanish court extradited the two to Colombia instead.

Another important potential market was the UK, which had seen an explosion in heroin consumption from the late 1970s onwards but did not as yet have a significant coke problem. In 1985, a female cousin of the Ochoas opened up a supply line with her English husband Keith Goldsworthy, a pilot. Goldsworthy would fly hundreds of kilos into the US in his private Cessna and then ship it to England. A parallel supply route was opened up by Fabio Ochoa personally on a visit to London. Within a year, cocaine seizures in the UK had doubled.

Goldsworthy was eventually caught in Miami and jailed for twenty-two years but by then the genie was out of the bottle.

Four years after the arrival of Rodriguez and Ochoa in Spain, the Cali cartel had made significant inroads in a drug market long dominated by heroin. "The major drug of choice in Europe in the late 1980s was heroin supplied by the Asians," said John Constanzo, a DEA agent who worked in Italy in the 1980s. "But the Cali cartel showed up on the DEA's radar screen, and we began seeing substantial increases in cocaine seizures."

Surveys conducted in the countries of the European Community verified these observations. Cocaine seizures skyrocketed from 900 kilograms in 1985 to thirteen tons in 1990.

Two years later Miguel Solans, a government delegate for Spain's National Plan on Drugs, commented, "Although it is obvious that even if heroin is the drug that produces the most instability and deaths in Europe, the level of cocaine traffic and cocaine consumption has been rising at an alarming rate in recent years." Three years later, the cartel had so refined the European smuggling network that they were using many of the major commercial ports in Europe, including Hamburg, Liverpool, Genoa and Rotterdam.

Operating on foreign terrain, the Cali godfathers, being the shrewd businessmen they were, understood their limitations and the importance of strategic alliances for getting a foothold in the European market. To meet their strategic objectives, they established a close working relationship with the Italian Mafia. "The Cali cartel and Italian organized crime had an understanding," said Michael Horn, a former DEA agent and the current director of the National Drug Intelligence Center in Johnstown, Pennsylvania. "Cali supplied the cocaine and the Italians would handle wholesale distribution."

The Italian mob and the Cali combine got along well, their relationship strengthened in part by their common love of soccer and the Cali men's respect for the Italian Mafia's criminal style. "The Cali cartel modelled its organization on the Italian Mafia," Constanzo said.

Group Five's investigation revealed that the cartel had cultivated the Mafia connection for some time. When Rich Crawford searched Chepe Santacruz's apartment in Bayside, Queens, in 1979, he found some shirts and original wrappers with the sale tags showing that they had been bought in Italy. In 1981 the DEA discovered that Santacruz had spent several months in Milan learning Italian and setting up the infrastructure for the cartel's cocaine pipeline from Colombia to Europe.

According to Constanzo, it was the Camorro branch of the Mafia that worked the closest with the Cali cartel. "The Camorro had a well-established heroin network in Europe that could handle cocaine," Constanzo explained. "The Cali cartel didn't have to invent the wheel." The Camorro services for the cartel included money laundering. In one case, authorities discovered that the Camorro had laundered $40 million for the Colombians by first depositing the money in the account of an elderly grandmother in Mantua and then having her transfer the funds to a dummy corporation in New York. From there, the money was moved to an account of another firm in Brazil.

Several cocaine busts documented the budding relationship with the Italian Mafia. In 1989, the dismantling of two laboratories in Italy resulted in the seizure of 267 kilos of cocaine base and cocaine hydrochloride and confirmed that Colombian traffickers and the Italian mob had established links. In the same year, the FBI convinced Joseph Cuffaro, a Sicilian drug dealer, to become an informant and he confessed to arranging a 590-kilo shipment of cocaine from Colombia to Sicily.

The growing ties between the Mafia and Cali concerned US legislators and Italian authorities. "If these two criminal organizations successfully join forces, the results could be disastrous in the US and Europe," warned Charles B. Rangel, chairman of the Select Committee on Narcotics Abuse and Control at the House of Representatives, in a letter to Secretary of State James A. Baker.

One of the last cases that legendary Mafia investigator Giovanni Falcone supervised involved the smuggling of 600 kilos of cocaine from Colombia to Sicily. In May 1992, Falcone, his wife and three bodyguards were blown to bits on a road outside Palermo. In the following weeks, speculation abounded about who was responsible, and there were even suspicions about a Colombian connection. The FBI, Falcone's close ally in previous transatlantic mafia investigations, sent a team of six agents to help with the investigation. "We had our suspicions," said John Moody, an FBI agent, in reference to the Cali cartel's suspected involvement in Falcone's murder.

"But the connection was never made."

Ironically, it was their love of soccer and connection to Italy that almost did in the cartel. In June 1990 the DEA, in collaboration with the Italian police, set up an elaborate sting operation called Offsides during the World Cup in Italy. The objective was to catch several fugitive traffickers who had fled to Colombia after being charged and convicted in the United States. The Colombian national soccer team had qualified for the World Cup for the first time since 1962, and the DEA had received intelligence from sources in Colombia that several important figures, including perhaps Chepe Santacruz and Miguel Rodriguez, were going to attend. Ken Robinson went to the World Cup as part of the investigation and thought he had spotted Chepe, but lost the surveillance of him. Miguel's wife and mother-in-law came to Rome but Miguel and the other Cali godfathers were no-shows, evidently scared off by the threat of capture.

By 1992, two important events dramatically increased the cartel's potential for expansion in Europe. The first was the collapse of Communism, which followed the fall of the Berlin Wall in 1989 and the dissolution of the Soviet Union on 1 January 1993. Second was the advent of a continent without borders after European trade barriers were erased in 1992, in accordance with the terms of the Single Europe Act of 1987. Immediately after the fall of the Berlin Wall, the first links established between East and West were those of organized crime syndicates. "Western Europe crime groups are better organized than those in the East, and they forged alliances for certain activities," said Robert Moroni, the former Interior Minister of Italy." The Cali cartel and other major crime groups, such as the Russian and Italian mafias, began holding summits in the early 1990s to see how they could better co-operate to further their criminal interests.

It took a little while for the collaboration to bear results.

"European law enforcement have been warning the United States for some time about the coming cocaine blitz of Western Europe, but that blitz didn't materialize until 1993 and 1994," wrote Professor Phil Williams, director of a think tank, the Ridgeway Center. "In the first three months of 1993, about 2,300 kilos of cocaine were seized. In a corresponding period for 1994, that figure jumped to 4,200 kilos of cocaine."

[. . .] There seemed to be no geographical limits to the level of international criminal co-operation. European traffickers were even travelling to Colombia to exchange information with local traffickers about the methods of refining and producing heroin. This reflects one of the major developments in Colombian drug trafficking in the early 1990s: the country's increasing importance as a producer and distributor of heroin.

By 1992 law enforcement had no doubt that Colombians had the "capacity to competently produce high quality heroin".

There is disagreement among analysts and officials, however, over how involved the Cali cartel was in the heroin trade.

Some experts said there was a strong connection. Robinson believes that Cali began dealing in heroin in the early 1980s.

He recalled that informant Robert Lafferty had even brought the NYDETF heroin samples from Colombia. The cartel had a Japanese chemist to teach them how to manufacture heroin, according to Ken Robinson. There were press reports, too, that they had co-operated with heroin distributors in New York and invested in heroin shipments smuggled to the city, although they did not get directly involved.

In 1994, Tom Constantine told Congress that "DEA intelligence suggested that the Cali cartel would be the dominant group in trafficking South American heroin. The Cali cartel had better access to the predominant opium poppy growing areas in Colombia. The Cali cartel has displayed a significant involvement in the South American heroin trade from its outset. It appears likely that large-scale involvement of the Cali cartel would make it difficult for small independent, trafficking groups with limited resources to compete for the market."

[. . .] By the beginning of 1993, nearly a decade after Gilberto Rodriguez and Jorge Ochoa had journeyed to Spain, the Cali cartel had a global reach that was perhaps unparalleled in organized crime history. In Colombia, the Medellín cartel was on the ropes. Pablo Escobar was in hiding, the Ochoa brothers were in jail, and Rodríguez Gacha was dead. The Cali cartel, on the other hand, looked untouchable. It dominated cocaine trafficking and it appeared to have no limits on its growth as a crime multinational.

In successfully flooding the world with the white powder, the cartel had steadily expanded, opening up new markets. Its ambitions were boundless. The criminal entrepreneurs had even begun moving into the lucrative Japanese market. "Why go to Japan?" said Robinson. "They are like successful businessmen. They need to conquer new markets to thrive."

One Joint Intelligence Center report noted that the main factors for targeting Japan are "almost certainly excesses of cash in Japan and excesses of cocaine in South America". But the Center doubted the Colombian cartels could make inroads into the Japanese market; given the power of the local mafia, the *yakuza*. Agents who had investigated the Cali cartel for years weren't about to bet that it couldn't happen.

During the Colombian drug trade's formative period, the Cali and Medellín cartels operated in their home country with virtual impunity. However, by the mid-1980s the United States government was pressuring Colombia to abandon its laissez-faire policy. President Ronald Reagan had declared the War on Drugs in 1982, and the US shifted the focus of its interdiction efforts from heroin in Asia to cocaine in Latin America. Uncle Sam recognized Colombia as the hub of the region's drug trade.

Two years later, Rodrigo Lara Bonilla, Colombia's justice minister, reopened the case involving Pablo Escobar's arrest in 1976 on drug possession charges. Escobar was at the time serving as an alternate delegate to the Colombia Congress, but he had higher political aspirations. As a criminal with a fervent desire for acceptance by Colombia's elite social class, Escobar presented himself as a sports promoter, industrialist, philanthropist, building contractor and defender of natural resources. For many poor people in Medellín slums, he was a folk hero, a kind of Robin Hood who stole from the rich and gave to the poor. Escobar shrewdly curried the common man's favour by doing good works. In the early 1980s, he built 1,000 small brick houses complete with plumbing, electricity and gardens in a poor barrio that bore his name.

The Rodriguez brothers and Santacruz, on the other hand, kept such a low profile that few knew who they were. They tried to blend into the Cali business community and quietly established legitimate ventures as a means of forging ties with key people from the country's media, politics, legal system and business community. They enjoyed their wealth but didn't make a public spectacle of it, unlike Escobar, who led a flamboyant lifestyle that made him a celebrity. His sprawling 7,000-acre estate, Hacienda Napoles, was the stuff of royalty, a country house that could accommodate 100 guests, surrounded by twenty-four artificial lakes, a swimming pool flanked by a marble Venus, and a zoo populated with hippos, giraffes, elephants and other exotic animals. At the entrance to Hacienda Napoles, the owner arrogantly displayed the aircraft that reputedly carried his first load of cocaine to the United States.

When the 1976 case was reopened, Don Pablo, as many now respectfully called the drug baron, suddenly found himself in the harsh and uncomfortable glare of public scrutiny.

Stripped away was the image of Don Pablo, leading citizen.

Exposed was the reality – Pablo Escobar, drug lord. Escobar sued Lara for libel, sniffing, "I'm a victim of a persecution campaign," but eventually dropped out of public life, humiliated and fixated on revenge. Lara Bonilla received death threats, but ignored them. He was determined to investigate Escobar and go after the country's mafia.

In 1984, Lara authorized the spectacular raid on Tranquilandia, the major cocaine processing plant in the Amazon region. He paid for it with his life. A few months later, *sicarios* machine-gunned him to death on a residential street in Bogotá. The justice minister's murder compelled president Belisario Bentacourt to declare a "war without quarter" against all drug traffickers, and the Medellín cartel godfathers did a disappearing act from public life. The Cali godfathers didn't approve of Lara Bonilla's assassination, but they were forced to go underground as well. That's when Gilberto Rodriguez and his friend Jorge Ochoa left for Spain, and Santacruz travelled to Mexico and sent some his lieutenants to the United States to investigate possible locations for new cocaine processing labs.

At 11.40 a.m. on 6 November 1985, approximately thirty-five M-19 guerrillas stormed the Colombian Palace of Justice, located on Bogotá's central Plaza de Bolivar. Within minutes, the guerrillas had 250 hostages, including Alfonso Reyes Echandia, the chief justice of Colombia's Supreme Court, and many of the twenty-four Supreme Court justices. For the next twenty-four hours, thousands of soldiers and police tried to retake the building, but the heavily armed and well entrenched guerrillas fought them off. When the government finally prevailed, twenty-five hostages lay dead, including Chief Justice Reyes, and apparently all the guerrillas.

It is widely believed the Medellín cartel paid the guerrillas to take the Palace and burn the extradition case files in the court archives, which contained incriminating evidence against them. The justices, many of whom favoured upholding the extradition treaty with the United States, were scheduled to vote on the issue in the near future. The shocking attack on the heart of the Colombian legal system set the tenor for the rest of the decade. By 1990, more than 200 court officials and at least forty Colombian judges had been murdered.

Colombian President Virgilio Barco, who took office in 1986, implemented the Colombia–United States extradition treaty. The Medellín cartel responded by launching a ruthless terrorist campaign against the state. Calling themselves "the Extraditables", the cartel vowed "better a grave in Colombia than a jail in the United States", and began to target prominent supporters of extradition, as well as get-tough-on-drugs officials. On 17 November 1986, *sicarios* murdered Colonel Jaime Ramirez Gomez, the head of the Anti-Narcotics Unit of the Colombian National Police. The following month, a killer on a motorcycle wove through the downtown Bogotá traffic and shot to death Guillermo Cano, the crusading anti-drug editorial writer for *El Espectador,* Colombia's second largest newspaper. In January 1988, near the Medellín airport in Rionegro, gunmen ambushed an automobile carrying Carlos Mauro Hoyos Jiminez. After killing Hoyos' bodyguard and chauffeur, the thugs dragged the bleeding attorney general from his limousine, put him in a car, and sped away. President Barco ordered a manhunt, and authorities found Hoyos' body a few miles away from where security forces a few hours earlier had freed the kidnapped Andres Pastrana Arango, the Conservative party candidate for mayor (and future president of Colombia). Pastrana told the author in 1988 that Hoyos' killers had planned to kidnap Hoyos and others to dramatize their opposition to extradition.

The Medellín cartel did not direct its warring efforts on the Colombian state alone. In 1981 the Cali and Medellín cartels had participated in a meeting that organized *MAS* to deal with the guerrilla threat, and for the next three years, their members met in Colombian bars, discos and haciendas to discuss business. When Gilberto Rodriguez and Jorge Ochoa left for Spain together, they trusted each other and worked together to explore new markets without fear of a double-cross. But relations went steadily downhill as the two powerful mafias expanded their operations and tension developed between them.

Colombian and US officials are unsure as to what caused the rift, but relations were not helped by the events following the extradition of Gilberto Rodriguez and Jorge Ochoa from Spain to Colombia in 1986. Rodriguez went to trial in March 1987 on cocaine-smuggling charges that could have led to his extradition to the United States, but it took place in the company town where the Cali cartel owned everything, including the legal system. Agent Rich Crawford, who was now in the DEA's Tampa office, travelled to Colombia to testify. He had no illusions about the trial's outcome but was eager to testify as a way of showing that the DEA wasn't afraid to go into the cartel's home territory and rip off its phony cover of respectability. Crawford arrived in Cali on 17 March and became the only DEA agent ever to testify at a trial in Colombia. His testimony was never allowed in court, however, and after three days, the judge acquitted Rodriguez.

As a result, Rodriguez could not be extradited to be tried for the same offence, thanks to the double jeopardy clause of the US Constitution.

Jorge Ochoa returned to Colombia in July 1986 to face a tougher legal situation than his friend Gilberto. He would first have to stand trial in Cartagena for smuggling 125 bulls into Colombia in 1981 and then face a drug charge in Medellín. If convicted, he could be extradited to the United States. Ochoa was found guilty and sentenced to two years in jail, but pending the appeal, the judge released Ochoa on a $11,500 bond, conveniently overlooking the fact that he faced a more serious criminal charge in Medellín. The judge ordered Ochoa to report to the court every two weeks. The drug lord thanked the judge and opted to walk away.

Ochoa remained a fugitive until November 1986, when police stopped him at the tollgate near Palmira in the vicinity of Cali. He was on his way to a summit meeting called by Pablo Escobar to work out the details for creating a single, supercartel that Escobar would head. According to reports, Rafael Cardona, one of the Cali's contacts to the Medellín cartel, tipped off police that Ochoa would be driving a white Porsche in the Cali area. Cardona wanted to get even with Ochoa for having an affair with his girlfriend. When a police officer stopped Ochoa's car, Cardona's girlfriend was seated in the front seat. The drug lord casually offered the officer a $10 bribe; he refused, the bribe offer climbed to $400,000, but to no avail. Ochoa was arrested and put in a maximum security prison in Bogotá. Meanwhile, the United States requested his extradition.

The police had arrested Ochoa while the drug lord's surveillance helicopter circled above. Obviously, the threat of arrest didn't concern Ochoa. He was in Cali country, and his good friend Gilberte Rodriguez would get him out quickly.

The Cali godfathers knew everything that went on in their stronghold, so they must have been aware that Ochoa was in the area. Yet they made no attempt to get him released.

Ochoa was finally freed on 30 December, but the damage was done and the seeds of distrust were planted. The Medellín godfathers wondered: did their Cali friends supply the information that got Ochoa arrested? And why didn't they try to get him out of jail quickly?

Meanwhile at his "supercartel" meeting, which included the men from Cali, Escobar laid out his proposal. Under his leadership, the unified cartel would co-ordinate political and economic strategy for all drug-traffickers in Colombia. Moreover, he would not only approve every shipment made, but would get thirty per cent of the wholesale value of each one. Two to three years earlier, such a proposal made by the powerful and ruthless bully might have intimidated the Cali godfathers into agreeing to such an outlandish arrangement.

But that was then. The Cali men were now in a much stronger competing position to reject Escobar's demands categorically and tell the Medellín boss that they wouldn't pay him anything. According to journalist Simon Strong, "Almost speechless with rage, Escobar was reported to have simply muttered, 'But this is war then,' before he immediately left the ranch."

Several scenarios have been put forth to explain why the deteriorating relations erupted into open warfare. One theory popular with many sources is that the two mafias were locked in a power struggle over the New York market. They say Cali had dominated the cocaine market since the mid-1970s, but when the market was glutted and prices began to drop in the late 1980s, Medellín's more aggressive element, led by José Rodriguez Gacha, started muscling into the lucrative New York market. It is known that Rodriguez Gacha visited New York City in 1988, but other sources say that he went to Queens to mend fences, not to break heads. The Colombian government may have tried to encourage the feud. One communiqué from the United States embassy in Bogotá to the US State Department stated that General Jaime-Ruiz Barrera, commanding general of the Medellín army brigade, and the mayor of Medellín, "are strongly pushing this line, perhaps to keep the cartels at each other's throats".

Bill Mante, a former New York detective who spent ten years investigating the Cali cartel, believes it was the Medellín cartel's anger at Cali's decision to shift their distribution network to Mexico that led to war. "We can't say for sure; it's purely speculation," Mante said. "But we knew that the Cali cartel had meetings with the Guadalajara cartel about shifting their distribution route to Mexico. That was Jaime Orejuela's brainchild. He had a good relationship with the Mexicans. It was a business decision but it led to war."

The mutual hatred of Pablo Escobar and Pacho Herrera, the result of a dispute over a worker for one of Escobar's New York distributors, is another plausible explanation for why the cartels went at each other's throats. While in prison during the early 1980s, Herrera befriended a Colombian named Pina, a worker for Jaime Pabon, who was a major cocaine distributor for Escobar. But Pina angered Pabon when he philandered with a member of his family and had to flee and seek support from the Herrera organization. At first, Pacho Herrera balked at hiring Pina because he knew Pabon was a close associate of the powerful and violent Escobar. He didn't need to rile the Patron.

That didn't satisfy Pabon though, who wasn't going to be happy until he had Pina killed for dishonouring his family. He asked Escobar for help. No problem. Escobar figured that a single call to Chepe Santacruz to complain about Pacho Herrera's protection of Pina would be enough to persuade him and the other Cali bosses to use their influence on Herrera and get him to turn Pina over to Pabon. The Rodriguez brothers, Pacho Herrera and Santacruz had a meeting. They knew the consequences of defying Pablo, but they decided that maintaining a united front was the best response to his intimidating threat. "We have no quarrel with Pina," was their terse reply to Escobar.

Pina wouldn't let the matter go. He lied to Escobar. The Cali cartel plans to kidnap you, Pina told Escobar. The enraged Escobar called Herrera and demanded that Pina give up Pabon within twenty-four hours or he would kill Herrera's entire family.

Rather than being intimidated, Herrera took Escobar's demand as a slight to his honour. There are times in the cut-throat world of drug trafficking when honour takes precedence over business. Pacho called his brother Ramon, who was managing his cell in New York City, and ordered him to hire Pina immediately.

Just before dawn on 13 January 1988, a huge bomb exploded outside the Monaco, a luxury eight-storey apartment building owned by Escobar in the upscale El Poblado barrio of Medellín. The, drug lord was not home, but his wife Victoria and their twelve-year-old son, Juan Pablo, and daughter, Manuela, were sleeping in the penthouse apartment.

The blast killed two nightwatchmen, dug a thirteen-foot hole in the street, and smashed the windows of nearby buildings.

Remarkably, Escobar's family was unhurt, although the explosion partially deafened daughter Manuela.

The attempted assassination shocked Escobar. No one had ever challenged his authority before. All he had to do was threaten and bully and people would knuckle under. At first he thought the DEA was responsible, but then he concluded that his upstart rivals from Cali were making a power play to take over his distribution networks. Escobar sent *sicarios* to Cali to find his enemies and kill them. Figuring that the best defence is a good offence, the Cali godfathers sent their own hit squads to Medellín. The war of the cartels was on.

In the following months, the casualties inexorably mounted.

On 11 July, authorities discovered the bodies of five ex-military men outside Medellín with a note explaining that the mercenaries were killed because they were *sicarios* for the Cali cartel. Three weeks later, police captured José Luis Gavria, Escobar's cousin, and charged him with participating in the killings. On 18 August, arsonists torched the biggest Medellín outlet of Gilberto Rodriguez's Drogas La Rebaja chain of drug stores. In mid-August, Colombian military intelligence officials reported that sixty members of the Cali cartel and eighteen of the Medellín cartel had been killed since the Monaco bombing. The US embassy noted in a cable that "their intelligence against each other appears to be very good, especially that of the Medellín cartel against the Cali cartel."

Both sides realized that war was bad for the drug business and tried to negotiate a truce, but there was too much bad blood. "They tried to meet several times, but it never happened," revealed Javier Pena, a DEA agent who played a major role in the hunt for Pablo Escobar. "They were just too big for the same territory."

Instead of working toward peace, the two mafias got increasingly vicious in their attacks. One 200-pound bomb planted inside a Renault exploded outside a Rebaja outlet in Cali, killing seven people, wounding twenty-four more, destroying a supermarket and damaging twenty other business and seven houses. The war spread to the United States, and, in the last week of August, the media reported on several dozen bombings in New York and Miami. According to the *New York Times,* law enforcement officials were saying that "there was evidence that the two cartels . . . had begun informing the police about each other's shipments" and that, "as a result of the anonymous tips, police made several large seizures during the year." The Cali cartel also sent more than ten professional killers to the United States from Colombia, according to the *New York Times.* New York City officials worried that their city would experience the same kind of out-of-control violence that ravaged Miami in the late 1970s and early 1980s.

Both cartels went even further and hired foreign mercenaries. Yair Klein, a retired Israeli Defence Force colonel, helped arrange a shipment of 100 Uzi submachine guns, 460 Galil automatic rifles and 200,000 rounds of ammunition to Rodriguez Gacha, and trained some of his men, including his son Freddy. The weapons were manufactured in Israel and believed to be a part of a shipment sold legally in 1988 by state-owned Israeli Military Industries to the Government of Antigua. The Antiguan authorities said they never ordered the arms for their defence force, which numbered just ninety personnel. They were later able to determine that the guns had been off-loaded from a Danish ship to another ship at an Antiguan port in 1989 and then smuggled to Colombia. An Israeli bank had financed the deal.

Yair Klein was a former lieutenant in the Israeli army, who, in the 1980s, established a paramilitary company named Sparhead Ltd, which he used to funnel guns and provide training in South America. He was accused of training cartel *sicarios* and of involvement in the infamous 1989 Avianca Airline bombing ordered by Pablo Escobar. It was also suspected that some of his weapons were used to assassinate Luis Carlos Galan, a leading Colombian presidential candidate, in 1989. The Colombian authorities charged Klein and several former Israeli officers with providing arms and training to drug traffickers. Klein denied the charges, but in 1991 an Israeli court convicted him of exporting arms to Colombia and fined him $13,400. In early 1991, a US Senate Governmental Permanent Subcommittee strongly criticized Israel for Klein's role in arming and training José Gonzalo Rodriguez Gacha and other Medellín cartel leaders. The Committee charged that Israel knew what Klein was doing in Colombia, but it took no action until after media publicized Klein's activities.

It took another seven years before the Colombians officially indicted Klein. One of the major pieces of evidence against him was a training video used to instruct death squads. That did not stop Klein from arms smuggling and paramilitary activities. In January 1999, he was arrested in war-torn Sierre Leone on suspicion of supplying and training rebels. Klein claimed to be in Africa looking for diamond mines. The Sierre Leone government did not extradite Klein to Colombia; instead, Reuben Gross, a Israeli parking garage magnate nicknamed the "Parking King", helped to obtain his release.

He promptly disappeared.

The Cali cartel, meanwhile, brought in a team of eleven British mercenaries in August 1988 to plan an operation that would kill Escobar. The mercenaries trained for three months in preparation for an assault on Escobar's ranch, Hacienda Napoles, but the operation turned into a fiasco when a helicopter carrying the assault team crashed into a mountain, aborting the mission.

As the war dragged on, the attitude of Colombia's security forces increasingly frustrated and angered Escobar. Rumours circulated that Escobar believed Gilberto Rodriguez had worked out a deal with the DEA. In April 1988, General Ruiz told the press that Escobar was plotting to eliminate the top members of the Cali cartel, but he failed to mention the similar plan the Cali men had for Escobar and his associates.

From Escobar's perspective, the Colombian government seemed interested only in taking down his cartel, not the one in Cali, and he suspected that the security forces were in bed with his bitter rivals.

Today, former Colombian officials confirm what Escobar suspected, but make no apology for focusing their attention and resources on him and his Medellín associates. "We viewed Escobar and the Medellín cartel as the worst of two evils," explained César Gaviria Trujillo, the president of Colombia from 1988 to 1992, and currently the president of the Organization of American States. "That's why the Colombian government directed all its attention and resources against the Medellín cartel."

The DEA office in Colombia had to follow the Colombian government's lead, said Joe Toft, a DEA agent who joined the agency's office in Bogotá in 1988. "We were concerned about the Cali cartel, of course," he said. "We had agents working on both cartels, and the group assigned to the Cali cartel worked just as hard as the Medellín group. But the Colombian government's focus was on Medellín, which had declared war on the state. So we couldn't get the Colombian government to do much on Cali."

Escobar saw plenty of evidence documenting the collusion. In June 1989, for example, police seized government documents from former army captain Luis Javier Wanomen and José Rivera, a civilian, showing that top government officials Raul Orejuela, the interior minister, and Colonel Oscar Pelaez, director of the F-2 intelligence agency, were collaborating with Cali by passing on information from agencies staffed by high-level Colombian officials.

The Colombian government could not have cared less about such revelations, so Escobar decided to take care of his problems. He targeted Miguel Masa, the head of DAS (Administrative

Department of Security), Colombia's equivalent of the FBI, whom he believed was on the Cali payroll.

Escobar flooded the streets with leaflets, offering $1.3 million for Masa's head. When Escobar seethed, Colombia shivered.

On 25 May 1989, a 220-pound car bomb exploded near a convoy carrying Masa and his bodyguards through downtown Bogotá, killing six people and injuring more than fifty.

[Galan's murder took place between this event and those following, on 18 August 1989.]

The terror blitz culminated in two spectacular attacks. On 27 November, Dandenny Munoz-Mosquera (nicknamed "Tyson"), a Medellín *sicario* believed responsible for killing fifty police officers, judges and other officials, arranged to have a bomb planted aboard Avianca's Flight 203, en route from Bogotá to Medellín. The plane exploded over Bogotá, killing all 107 passengers aboard, including two Americans.

The "official" explanation of the bombing was that Escobar wanted two informants on board the plane dead, but sources revealed that the shocking incident happened because Escobar wanted to kill a girlfriend of Miguel Rodriguez, who was aboard the plane, in revenge for the bomb blast that partially deafened his daughter Manuela. The flight was due to take less than an hour, over partially mountainous terrain. When the plane reached 13,000 feet, an explosion ripped through the cabin, causing a fire on the plane's right side. A second explosion blew the plane apart, showering the ground with wreckage over a three-mile radius.

During Escobar's campaign of narco-terrorism, which he began in the mid 1980s, the Colombian government continued its pursuit of the Medellín cartel bosses, including Carlos "Crazy Charlie" Lehder. Rumours abounded about Lehder's whereabouts. Finally a tip came in to stake out a farm about twenty miles outside Medellín, near the small town of Rionegro. A *campesino* had been watching the farm and noticed a "bunch of men" shouting, playing music and raising hell for a couple of days. At daybreak on 3 February 1987, a twenty-man elite police squad moved in. A gunfight broke out and half an hour later all fifteen men inside the farm were arrested. Only when the police looked at the suspects' papers did they know who they had captured.

"We've caught him!" shouted police major William Lemus excitedly, pointing to the suspect dressed in a T-shirt and blue jeans. "This is Carlos Lehder!"

Lehder muttered: "This is the one place I never expected you'd catch me."

Back at the Rionego police station, the phone began to ring off the hook. The general message was: "Lemus, whom do you think you are? You are dead." Ten days later, the DEA had Lemus and his family on a plane in Bogotá and out of the country. Meanwhile, Lehder had been taken to Bogotá and police headquarters. A DEA turboprop was waiting at the airport to whisk Lehder away to the US. The US government had its biggest prize in its War on Drugs.

Carlos Lehder's dramatic extradition made big headlines, for never before had a drug trafficker of his stature been brought to the US, and the authorities expected some kind of retaliation. Police placed sharpshooters strategically around the Jacksonville courthouse for his first appearance four days later. The metal detectors were so sensitive that many spectators in the court room had to remove their shoes because the nails in them set off an alarm. At the hearing, Lehder's public defender claimed that Pablo Escobar had set up her client. A few days later, a letter from Escobar arrived at the offices of Colombia's leading newspaper in which he denied the allegation.

Meanwhile, the IRS filed a $300 million lien against Lehder, estimating that he had earned $300 million smuggling cocaine in 1979 and 1980 alone. As a sign of how dangerous Lehder was viewed, he was sent to the federal maximum security prison in Marion, Illinois, becoming one of the few pre-trial detainees in Marion's history. Lehder was then moved to a federal prison in Alabama to make it easier for his lawyers to visit, but he was still kept in isolation. He was finally transferred to Atlanta, again so that he could be closer to his lawyers.

Lehder hired the best lawyers his money could buy, but delays pushed the trial date back from the spring to the early fall. The prosecutor said that Lehder had sent a letter to President George Bush, offering to co-operate, but Lehder's attorneys denied he wanted to turn informant. The story, though, made headlines in the *Miami Herald*. George Jung, Lehder's old associate, read the story and was angered. He had always wanted to get even with his ex-friend. Jung would be the subject of Bruce Porter's bestselling book *Blow*, and the movie of the same name, which starred Johnny Depp. The federal authorities had approached Jung in 1986 while he was prison with a proposal that he travel to Colombia in an attempt to lure Lehder into a trap. But before the plan could be implemented, Lehder was captured. Now if Lehder was going to snitch, Jung had a few things to say about him. He sat down and wrote a letter detailing what he knew about his former boss and the drug trade.

By the time Lehder's trial began, in November 1987, the prosecution had amassed an impressive body of evidence documenting Crazy Charlie's criminal career, from his early days at Danbury to the mid-1980s. Prosecutor Robert Merkle portrayed Lehder as "The Henry Ford of Cocaine", the gangster largely responsible for the coke plague in America.

Jung, Barry Kane, Winny Polly and the many other associates testified; in all, the prosecution presented 115 witnesses over seven months. It must have seemed to Lehder like a nightmarish verson of *This Is Your Life*. On 20 July 1988, he was sentenced to the maximum: life without parole, plus 135 years.

Carlos Lehder had become the first foreign drug lord to face the full force of American justice, but he had already been cutting a deal that would get him into the Federal Witness Protection Program. How could a man who had been characterized as the Henry Ford of drug trafficking wind up as a federally protected witness? The answer was politics.

General Manuel Noriega, the military dictator of Panama, had outserved his usefulness to the US and had become its latest foreign policy bogeyman. Indicted in 1988, during the peak of the drug hysteria, Noriega was portrayed as a drug kingpin and a corruptor of American children. In December 1989, determined to show his resolve against the drug threat,

President George Bush, Sr, launched Operation Just Cause, an invasion of Panama by 23,000 troops. The operation was a success. Noriega was captured and whisked to the US.

During his trial, Lehder had been portrayed as the monster who had been largely responsible for the drug epidemic in America. At Noriega's trial in 1992, he was turned into the star witness. Never mind that Lehder acknowledged that he had never met Noriega. For his testimony, Lehder got special treatment in prison, a drastically reduced sentence (down to fifty-five years) and protection in the US for his family. Moreover, only a small fraction of his estimated $3 billion cocaine-built fortune was seized. Prosecutor Robert Merkle, who had thought he had put Lehder behind bars for good, was outraged.

"First of all, Lehder's testimony was entirely gratuitous and unnecessary for a conviction of Noriega," Merkle told one reporter. "Second, they gave a deal to the guy (Lehder) who was directing the bad activities to convict someone who was following directions (Noriega)." Many observers wondered if Lehder had conned Uncle Sam and would some day be free.

Ledher was the first Colombian drug baron to face the full force of Uncle Sam. A decade later, another would follow. In 1991, while Pablo Escobar waged war with the state, the Ochoa brothers – Jorge, Fabio, and Juan David – escaped with their lives and fortunes by turning themselves in to the authorities and serving a few years in jail. After their release in 1996, they promised never to get involved with drug trafficking again. It looked as if Fabio would keep that promise, as he retired to the life of a cattle rancher and horse breeder. But the Colombians and their DEA allies were monitoring his movements, and they began collecting evidence revealing that Fabio was involved with a smuggling syndicate. He attended key meetings of the drug ring, and he was due to receive a million dollars for his role in it.

The one-time member of the Medellín cartel's inner circle was arrested in 1998, along with thirty others, accused in a US federal indictment of being the chief financier of the highly sophisticated drug ring run by Alexandro Bernal, one of Fabio's former underlings. Ochoa's lawyers later claimed that Fabio was merely fraternizing with syndicate members and that the DEA had targeted him because he had rejected a deal with the US government in which he would have provided information in return for immunity. Unfortunately for Fabio, his arrest came at a time when the political climate had changed. In 1990, he was the first Colombian trafficker to surrender in return for a pledge that his government would not extradite him. As we have seen, the Colombians had declared extradition unconstitutional but it was reinstated in December 1997, and the Colombian government was showing that it had every intention of sending drug lords to jail in the US. Fabio, however, did not go without a fight.

He and his high-priced legal team fought his extradition in court, through appeals and on the Internet, where he had a web page proclaiming his innocence. Billboards sprung up in Bogotá and Medellín that pleaded, "Yesterday I made a mistake; today, I am innocent."

By the time Fabio was extradited to the US in September 2001, the Colombian government had already extradited three dozen drug traffickers. Ironically, Fabio's extradition order was signed by Colombian president Andres Pastrana, the former mayor of Bogotá whom Ochoa's Medellín cartel had kidnapped in 1988. The cartel's slogan at the time was, "Better a tomb in Colombia than a jail cell in United States."

In August 2003, a US federal court sentenced Fabio Ochoa to more than thirty years in prison, even though Ochoa's defence lawyers argued that giving their client a sentence longer than twelve years would violate the conditions of his extradition. "We are truly confident in our assertion that we honoured our agreement," said Ed Ryan, the lead federal prosecutor. "In this world of narco-trafficking and what it did to this country, the defendant is one of four or five people who literally changed the world as we knew it at the time."

[In 1991, US Customs agents had busted a shipment of cocaine hidden in cement posts. The bust launched Operation Cornerstone, in the course of which, in 1995, DEA agents "turned" Jorge Salcedo, a key member of the

> *Calis' surveillance and security "department" who, as a CI – Confidential Informant – expressed concern about his friend, Guillermo Pallomari, whom he had implicated – and with good reason. What happened next provides just one example of the way in which, though much quieter and publicity-shy in their approach, the cartel was no less chilling than the Medellin, and had no compunction about involving the innocent as a means of hitting their enemies where it hurts.]*

By the summer of 1995, Pallomari had become the Man Who Knew Too Much. As the cartel's chief accountant, he had sat in on most of its important meetings and kept track of hundreds of legal and illegal documents. At the end of March 1995, he turned over his position to William Rodriguez, and the following month the Colombian government called him for questioning for the crime of serving as a frontman for a criminal enterprise. Miguel Rodriguez thought Pallomari was going to crack and knew time was short. If police caught Pallomari, he would be a devastating witness against him.

Miguel put a contract out on his former accountant's life, but Pallomari had time to go underground in Cali.

Pallomari realized his only chance to stay alive was to defect, so he called the US embassy in Bogotá to make arrangements. His wife Patricia Cardona agreed to join him, but first she needed to take care of some business matters. The DEA's agents Mitchell and Feistl visited Cardona and urged her to turn herself in to the US embassy. "We have intelligence that your life is in danger," they told her. In August, Pallomari arrived in Bogotá at the US embassy and met with the DEA to arrange details about his surrender and co-operation. In return for his testimony, Pallomari would join the witness protection program. The day after the DEA agents had visited Cardona, Pallomari tried calling her at their home, her office, and her family's residence. She was nowhere to be found, but her sister-in-law had received a call from the Cali cartel when she wasn't home. There was no message.

The cartel tracked Pallomari to the US embassy, and Bruno Murillo, one of its *sicarios*, called him. "Your wife has been kidnapped because you have not obeyed Miguel's orders," was Murillo's chilling message.

Pallomari became frantic. "What can I do to get my wife back?" he pleaded.

"Go to the Cali cartel. Don't co-operate with the authorities. Don't participate or get involved with the DEA," were the cartel's specific instructions.

But that was now impossible, given Pallomari's commitment to surrender. He never saw his wife again. On 16 August 1995, Cardona and Freddie Vivas Yangus, her employee, vanished without a trace. They were never seen again, although there is a record that Cardona left Colombia and travelled to Lima, Peru. "That's a tough task for a dead person," said DEA agent Chris Feistl. "Actually, the cartel was up to its old tricks. They were kidnapped from Cardona's business, tortured and eventually killed."

A few days later, Pallomari and his two sons made their way to an undisclosed location in the United States via a commercial airline with the DEA's assistance. He was brought before a judge in Miami, and on 15 December 1998, he pleaded guilty to racketeering, conspiracy and money laundering charges. He co-operated with US authorities and was placed in the Federal Witness Protection Program. One senior administration official told the Washington Post, "he may turn out to be the biggest witness of international drug trafficking that we've ever had."

The DEA spent days debriefing Pallomari. The US attorney general's office wanted him to work with their prosecutors in cases involving the Cali cartel. A tug of war ensued over who would have first crack at debriefing him.

Assistant US attorney generals Bill Pearson and Ed Ryan were constantly on the phone trying to get access to Pallomari for their work on Operation Cornerstone.

In the weeks after arriving in the United States, Pallomari worked long hours decoding the financial records taken from an office of José Santacruz Londoño on 18 May 1994. The authorities also confiscated from Chepe's office an IBM AS/400 computer worth one million dollars, the most sophisticated piece of technology the DEA had ever taken from drug traffickers. The DEA computer experts spent months trying to break into it. When they finally did, they found computer files containing information on thousands of bribes the cartel paid to Colombians from all sectors of society , as well as telephone and motor vehicle records of the cartel's real and potential enemies, including the US embassy and the DEA's offices in Colombia. Stunned DEA analysts found that the supercomputer contained Colombia's entire motor vehicle records.

"If you were a Colombian. and wanted a US visa, you might call the embassy in Bogotá once or perhaps twice for information," explained Steve Casto, a DEA intelligence agent who did analysis on the computer. "But what if you were an informant and were calling once or twice a month?

"The Cali cartel could find this pattern by analyzing the telephone records. Its computer analysts could go to the telephone records without leaving Santacruz's office and find out more information on the caller. Then the cartel could wiretap the calls that the person was making to the US embassy."

[. . .] In May 2002, the forty-nine-year-old Uribe had won the presidency in a landslide by campaigning on a law and order platform. He would get tough on the drug traffickers and tough on the guerrillas, Uribe promised the Colombian electorate. In winning by more than twenty percentage points over his nearest rival, Liberal Horacio Serpa, Uribe became the first presidential candidate to win outright on the first ballot in a Colombian election. Boyish-looking and educated at Harvard and Oxford, Uribe, with his wire-rimmed glasses, looked more like a bookworm than an ambitious politician.

A close examination of his resumé, however, would reveal a determined candidate who had an ultra-right-wing philosophy and had exhibited paramilitary sympathies in the past.

In August 2004, the National Security Archive in Washington, DC, announced that it had obtained a newly declassified Department of Defense intelligence report dated September 1991, which listed more than 100 people, including Uribe, who were believed to be associated with the Medellín cartel. The US government, which needed a strong and stable Colombia as an ally in its War on Drugs, moved into damage control mode. "What I can tell you is that this was a report that included information . . . based on input from an uncorroborated source," said a State Department spokesman.

"It's raw information . . . not fully evaluated intelligence, and my understanding from Department of Defense [DOD] colleagues is that it did not constitute an official DIA [Defense Intelligence Agency] or DOD position."

Written at the top of the report was a note cautioning that not all the intelligence had been "finally evaluated", but the report also stated, "Uribe is a close personal friend of Pablo Escobar Gaviria. He has participated in Escobar's political campaign to win the position of assistant parliamentarian to Jorge [Ortega]. Uribe has been one of the politicians, from the senate, who has attacked all forms of the extradition treaty." In 1983, FARC guerrillas gunned down Uribe's father at the family ranch in Antioquia province. Uribe denied that he held any grudges against the guerrillas, but during the 2002 election, he vowed to end the country's thirty-eight-year civil war by destroying their movement.

In the six months prior to his election victory, FARC put a contract on Uribe's life and tried to assassinate him at least three times. In one of the attempts, Uribe was travelling in the coastal city of Baranquilla when a bomb exploded, killing three people and wounding sixteen others passing by. The armour from Uribe's vehicle saved his life.

At the age of twenty-six, Uribe became mayor of Medellín, at a time when the city was the capital of the Colombian drug trade. According to reports, Mayor Uribe launched two programmes, "Civic Medellín" and "Medellín Without Slums", both of which were financed by drug lord Pablo Escobar. From 1980 to 1982, Uribe served as Colombia's Director of Civil Aviation, having, among other duties, responsibility for granting pilot licences. According to investigative journalist Fabio Castillo, Uribe "granted most of the licences to the mafia pilots when he was Director of Civil Engineering." While in that position, Uribe had as his deputy César Villegas, an associate of the Cali cartel, who was later sentenced to five years in prison for accepting several millions of dollars from the cartel during Ernesto Samper's 1996 political campaign.

Despite these explosive revelations, the question of whether Uribe had ties to drug traffickers has never been definitively answered. Writing in her book *More Terrible than Death: Massacres, Drugs and America's War in Colombia,* Robin Kirk noted that no one had been able to prove Uribe had such links "beyond the inevitable contact that anyone living in Antioquia during the 1980s might have had, particularly if that person had interest in land and politics". Kirk is the main researcher in Colombia for the US-based Human Rights Watch.

Even if it could be proved beyond doubt that Uribe had narco links, it would not have mattered to the US government. Alvaro Uribe was their key ally in the War on Drugs and a welcome successor to the corrupt Samper and the soft-on-guerrillas Pastrana. Despite questions about his past views towards extradition, no Colombian president has sent more traffickers to the US for trial than has Uribe. In the first ten months of 2004 alone, Colombia extradited close to 250 individuals for drug-related crimes. Uribe also had no problem with having large numbers of US military personnel in Colombia. In April 2004, 400 US military personnel and another 400 US contractors were operating there, but Uribe asked the US to double the number. Delighted officials agreed. "We are building on success," enthused Roger Pardo Maurer, the US Deputy Assistant Defense Secretary for Western Hemisphere Affairs. "President Uribe has really done all the right things. The Colombian people are backing him . . . and his military has an eighty-seven per cent approval rating."

All of Uribe's power and popularity, however, could not keep Gilberto Rodriguez in jail. Uribe tried to stall the court decision, ordering a stay on the release of Gilberto and his brother Miguel, both of whom got time off for good behaviour and for participating in work-study programmes. The Uribe administration accused Judge Pedro Suarez of obstructing justice, and its prosecutors questioned the judge as part of an investigation into his decision. Colombia's legal profession did not take kindly to Uribe's interference. The National Judicial

Employees Associations filed criminal charges against Uribe for the offence of "perverting the course of justice, abuse of authority and fraud regarding a court ruling". There was one consolation for the Uribe administration, though.

Judge Amanda Moncada declared that Gilberto's brother Miguel would stay in jail to serve another four years for bribing a judge.

The Colombian government and its US allies did not give up. On 12 March 2003, police arrested Gilberto as he was leaving his house in Cali. The authorities had been hard at work digging up new charges against the Chess Player.

This time they charged him with being involved with the trafficking of 330 pounds of cocaine to the US from Costa Rica in 1990. The drug lord could not be extradited on this charge because the alleged crime had occurred before 17 December 1997, but at least they could put him behind bars in Colombia. The authorities transferred the Chess Player from Cali to police headquarters in Bogotá, where he gave testimony. Once again, US officials began looking for a way to extradite him.

The authorities had jailed the Rodriguez Orejuela brothers in 1995, and criminals had killed Chepe Santacruz Londoño in 1996 and Pacho Herrera in 1997. Yet the US government never relented in its aggressive pursuit of Cali cartel money and assets. The Office of Foreign Assets Control (OFAC) in the US Department of the Treasury became the lead agency in the financial investigation of history's richest trafficking organization. The use of economic sanctions against the cartel's assets would be its punitive tool.

[. . .] OFAC's main legal instrument was executive order (EO) 12978. According to R. Richard Newcomb, OFAC's former director, the office's primary mission is to "administer and enforce economic sanctions against targeted foreign countries, and groups and individuals, including terrorist organizations and narcotics traffickers, which pose a threat to the national security, foreign policy and economy of the United States." In implementing the executive order, President Clinton announced that he was declaring a national emergency because he found that "the actions of significant narcotics traffickers centred in

Colombia, and the unparalleled violence, corruption and harm that they cause in the United States and abroad, constitute an unusual and extraordinary threat to the national security, foreign policy and economy of the United States."

[. . .] OFAC identified the four Cali cartel kingpins as targets: the Rodriguez brothers, Chepe Santacruz and Pacho Herrera.

"President Clinton told us to go and find the front companies and the people related to them," explained one OFAC official. "Even though the Rodriguez Orejuela brothers were in jail at the time, we began to go after their finances, identify their assets, name their companies and family members who controlled them." OFAC was not starting from scratch. "The FBI, DEA and other government agencies had been investigating the Cali cartel for years and had files and files," said one official. "We started our investigation by going to those government agencies and asking them: 'What do you know? What can you tell us? What can you share with us?'

"Before long we had a mass of information and could tell what belonged to Miguel, what belonged to Pacho . . . Then we began to build on that information."

According to the indictment resulting from the OFAC investigation, which was filed against Gilberto and Miguel in Southern District Court of New York in February 2004, OFAC learned that the cartel was involved in "all aspects of the cocaine trade, including production, transportation, wholesale distribution and money laundering. From about 1982 to 1995, the Cali cartel transported and sold at least 30,000 kilos of cocaine and ultimately amassed an illicit fortune with $1 billion." US officials concede that the amount of money stated in the indictment is not close to the amount the Cali cartel actually garnered from the drug trade.

"The amount is a conservative figure, but it's an amount that's beyond dispute in terms of the Cali cartel's assets," said one US Department of Justice official close to the probe.

As head of the Norte Valle del Cauca mafia, Ivan Urdinola Grajales, together with his brother Julio Fabio Urdinola Grajales, organized and distributed multi-ton shipments of cocaine throughout the US and expanded into the production and trafficking of heroin. According to the DEA, Ivan Urdinola was responsible for the torture and murder of more than 100 people in Colombia, although he was never charged with any of those killings. Ivan was known to kill vagabonds in the hope of bringing good luck to his syndicate. He was arrested in 1992 and imprisoned. In August 2000, the US Treasury's Office of Foreign Assets Control put Ivan on the list of Specifically Designated Narcotics Traffickers (SDNTs), which makes him subject to economic sanctions under Executive Order 12978. Julio Fabio surrendered to Colombian authorities in March 1997 and was imprisoned.

After Ivan Urdinola's death, a vicious gang war broke out in the Valle del Cauca, the territory that the Cali cartel dominated nearly a decade before. It was the worst violent confrontation between Colombian drug gangs since Cali and Escobar went to war in the late 1980s. More than 1,300 people were killed in the first ten months of 2004 alone. So serious was this "war of cartels" that the Colombian National Police sent 500 members of its elite Search Bloc unit (*see chapter 6*) to the valley to restore order.

The three major drug lords involved were Diego Leon Montoya (aka Don Diego), Wilmer Alirio Varela (aka Jabon, meaning "Soap") and Luis Hernando Gomez-Bustamante (aka Rasguno). They are godfathers of the Norte Valle del Cauca, an offshoot of the Cali cartel, which has been described as "the last of the big Colombian drug cartels". A Colombian National Police colonel told *Jane's Intelligence Weekly,* "The world of narcotics trafficking is now in crisis. What was once known as the Norte Valley del Cauca has now fractured into about three great blocks." No one knew for sure how the drug war started, but according to the *Jane's Intelligence Weekly* report, there has been speculation that after Victor Patino was extradited to the US in December 2002, he "began to sell out his comrades and this led to a circle of bloodletting".

On 14 March 1998, hitmen believed to be employed by Miguel Rodriguez shot Varela five times as he travelled to the Palmira airport. Although seriously wounded, he somehow made it to hospital two days later, but before too long Varela checked himself out, figuring that if he stayed put, the hitmen would return to finish him off. Varela sought revenge and ordered the killing of Pacho Herrera in November 1998.

Gilberto and Miguel Rodriguez retaliated by contacting Pacho's half-brother José and asking him to kill Varela associate José Orlando Henao Montoya, which he did. Rumours circulated that people working for Don Diego's and Rasguno's organizations, together with associates of Miguel and Gilberto, founded a group called *Peporva* ("People Persecuted by Varela") to go after Varela.

Described by the DEA as a "Cali cartel kingpin", Juan Carlos Ramirez-Abadia (aka "Chupeta") surrendered to authorities in March 1996, apparently because he feared for his life and hoped to be eligible for a shorter prison term. In December 1996, Chupeta was jailed for twenty-four years.

The DEA reported that Jorge Orlando Rodriguez (aka "El Mono") assumed control of the trafficking operations of Chupeta's organization while he was in prison, although Chupeta remained involved in making major decisions. A DEA source put his net worth at $2.6 billion. The US Treasury Department added Chupeta's name to the list of SDNTs in August 2000. In May 2004, the US government indicted Chupeta and eight other reputed members of the Norte Valle del Cauca drug organization under the RICO (Racketeering Influenced and Corruption Organizations) Act as operating a cocaine trafficking enterprise.

William Rodriguez Abadia, Miguel's son, played a key role co-ordinating the Cali cartel's still formidable trafficking network while his father and uncle were in jail. According to several government witnesses, in addition to handling the money of the cartel's daily operations, William also undertook efforts to retaliate against successful law enforcement operations. Salcedo told Kacerosky that William made it known the cartel had to identify and kill anyone providing information to the authorities, especially Guillermo Pallomari, who, as a foreign national (he was Chilean), could be extradited to the US and cause a lot of headaches for the cartel down the road. Later, when the godfathers learned that Salcedo had betrayed them, William offered money to Vicky Giron if she helped to locate Salcedo and other members of his family so they could be murdered.

Flores described William's second office on the top floor of an office building adjoining the El Coral restaurant in Cali as a "secret location . . . equipped with a false wall that accessed a hidden stairway that ran parallel to an adjoining discotheque in the building to provide an escape route for Rodriguez Abadia." Flores also stated that he received Miguel's approved monthly salary and expense payments at this office. How much money was William handling for an organization thought to be defunct, or at least on its deathbed? William received millions of dollars in the first eight months alone, according to Flores.

[. . .] In December 2003, the US authorities initiated a legal action that they confidently expected would lead to one of the biggest victories in their War on Drugs. They announced the indictment of Gilberto, Miguel and nine other suspected associates on three charges: drug trafficking, money laundering and the continued obstruction of justice through murder and payment of hush money to associates and their families. As part of the indictment, US authorities said they would seek the extradition of all eleven suspects and the forfeiture of $2.1 billion. "A decade ago, the Rodriguez brothers were at the top of their criminal game," said Roger P. Mackin, the Department of Homeland Security counter-narcotics officer. "The drug trafficking empire netted them billions. They owned vast properties and exercised great influence. They were the Colombian Untouchables. Now, because of the commitment of President Uribe, they are awaiting extradition to America to pay for their crimes."

Three US grand juries had indicted Gilberto and Miguel before, but given Colombian law, the cartel's ability to corrupt and the army of top-notch lawyers it had at its disposal, the godfathers had always managed to avoid extradition.

Colombian law, however, changed. The two countries signed an extradition treaty in 1997 making it possible for the brothers to be sent to the United States to stand trial for crimes committed after 17 December 1997. Colombia's President Uribe was a tough law-and-order president, and had been signing extradition orders that were sending suspected drug traffickers to the US *en masse*. When Colombia sent thirteen drug trafficking suspects to the US in early November 2003, Cesar Garcia, an Associated Press reporter, wrote, "So many Colombians are being extradited to the United States on drug trafficking charges that a shuttle flight of sorts is taking them to America for justice." The report went on to note that Colombia had extradited sixty-three nationals to the US in 2004, while another seventy-seven who faced extradition had been captured.

US officials were so confident that the Rodriguez brothers would join the streaming exodus that in August 2004 they held a conference call to discuss what would be the best jurisdiction in which to try them. No one doubted what the decision of America's strong ally in the War on Drugs would be, and one day after the US announced its indictment, Colombian prosecutors filed court papers allowing the extradition of the eleven suspects.

Judgment day for Gilberto Rodriguez arrived on 4 November 2004, when the Colombian Supreme Court ruled that the government could extradite him to the United States for trial. The high court said it was up to the government to decide if it wanted to put the Chess Player on a DEA plane to Miami. That was hardly an agonizing decision for Uribe. On 9 November, he announced he would approve the drug lord's historic extradition.

[. . .]Held in solitary confinement awating trial, Gilberto faced charges that he imported and distributed more than 200,000 kilos of cocaine from 1999 to July 2002, concealed in items such as concrete posts, frozen vegetables, watermelons and ceramic tiles. He was also accused of killing or bribing witnesses and of conspiracy to launder money. The indictment sought to seize $2.1 billion which prosecutors said was made from drugs. Meanwhile, a Colombian judge ordered the seizure of dozens of properties, businesses, bank accounts and vehicles belonging to the founders of the once-mighty cartel.

The assets included seventy-three houses, apartments,

parking lots and plots of land in Bogotá, Cali and on the Colombia-owned Caribbean island of San Andres.

As the Chess Player's criminal career headed towards its sordid conclusion, the remaining question was whether brother Miguel would follow him. "There was speculation that Colombia would not extradite Miguel because he was on dialysis. US officials were confident, however, though as one explained the day after Gilberto's extradition, "I doubt that the Colombian government will want to skip any legal steps to speed things up, so that everything is by the book."

In March 2005, President Uribe finally ordered Miguel's extradition, and "El Senor" was flown from Palanquero Air Force to Florida, where the stocky sixty-one-year-old was held without bail. Like his brother, he denied charges of drug trafficking.

[...] The Cali cartel was now on life support. Gilbert and Miguel Rodriguez were safely in a US prison awaiting trial.

Operation Cornerstone, the long, complicated investigation that began one hot humid summer morning in August 1991 with the discovery of twelve tons of cocaine hidden in concrete fence posts at the port of Miami, was about to conclude.

[...] In interrogating Gustavo Naranjo, the smuggling operation's leader, investigators learned that he worked for Miguel Rodriguez and communicated with him directly.

They persuaded Naranjo to call Miguel, his boss, and implicate him in the smuggling operation. From phone records seized in the bust's aftermath, US Customs was also able to identify Harold Ackerman as the cartel's "ambassador" to the US.

Ackerman was arrested and sentenced to six life-terms in prison, but he co-operated with authorities for a reduced sentence. This encouraged other arrested cartel workers to snitch, and was a major turning point in the case. US officials were able to tape-record hundreds of hours of conversations between Miguel, the "Señor" and micromanager, and his workers and lawyers. In total, Customs agents devoted more than 91,855 case hours to Operation Cornerstone, and by 1996 investigators had uncovered six major trafficking routes used to smuggle thousands of pounds of cocaine in shipments of coffee, lumber, frozen vegetables, and of course, concrete fence posts. By the time the brothers were extradited to the US, more than 100 individuals had been prosecuted and 50,000 kilograms of cocaine and about $15 million in currency had been seized. "It was remarkable investigation and the most significant in the history of the War on Drugs," said one official. "It took an incredible amount of resources and manpower, but we were finally able to take down the leadership of the most powerful drug organization ever."

[. . .] So after a thirty-year investigation, Gilberto and Miguel Rodriguez were finally paying for their crimes. The Cali cartel was as dead as Pablo Escobar and his Medellín cartel.

Yet did anything really change in the War on Drugs? Gilberto Rodriguez once offered a depressing but prescient take on the cocaine trade. "Economics has a natural law," he declared.

"Supply is determined by the demand. When cocaine stops being consumed, when there's no demand for it . . . that will be the end of that business." That end may be nowhere in sight, but it is safe to declare that at least one major battle in the War on Drugs has been won. Ironically, the end of what was left of the multinational-like Cali cartel, history's most powerful drug trafficking mafia, came with a whimper, not a bang.

After law enforcement finally took down Pablo Escobar at the end of 1993, it became inevitable that the men from Cali would become the focus of law enforcement's attention.

Always a little ahead of the curve, the Cali godfathers saw the writing was on the wall and realized that it was only a matter of time before they would be in a grave in Colombia or a jail cell in the United States. So they began using their legions of lawyers to negotiate their way out of the drug trade before they became law enforcement's principal target.

By the early 1990s, they had forged a crime multinational too huge to ignore. It had a global reach and thousands of employees and was involved in every aspect of the drug trade.

As drug trafficking expert Rennselaer Lee pointed out, "The sheer size of mafia operations require their explicit co-ordination of many transactions, as well as a system of information-gathering and record keeping. Cocaine syndicates are too big and too complex to escape detection, and they are too vulnerable to penetration by law enforcement agents."

The Cali cartel began appearing more frequently on law enforcement's radar screen as it mushroomed into a multinational enterprise. By the time authorities discovered the huge cocaine shipment in concrete cement posts in August 1991 in Miami, law enforcement had discerned a pattern to the cartel's criminality. As law enforcement successfully investigated its operations, the cartel found it increasingly difficult to hire the talent it needed to fill the ranks of its depleted managerial pool. Given its problems, its members even began breaking some of its well-thought-out rules, evident in the move that allowed Harold Ackerman, its so-called ambassador to the United States, to wear three hats.

This made it easier for law enforcement to penetrate the cartel's financial structure once Ackerman was caught.

The investigation was furthered by the enormous volume of records the cartel generated as it grew. It didn't help the cartel that the wrong CEO was running affairs at the most critical juncture in its development. Miguel Rodriguez, who took over day-to-day management about 1990, was a micromanager who couldn't seem to let go of business matters or didn't know how to delegate responsibility. Micromanaging affairs in the United States and Europe from headquarters in Cali could work early in its history when the cartel was small and law enforcement had little inkling about its activities, but not when it became the size of an IBM or General Motors. In fact, Miguel's micromanaging style became a liability . . . Sooner or later, communication is bound to break down.

The takedown of the Cali cartel and its Medellín predecessor provided a wise lesson for other Colombian drug traffickers; namely, becoming too big and complex an organization will make you more vulnerable to a takedown. So today, we see a radically different type of Colombian drug-trafficking organization. Gone is the huge octopus as represented by the Cali cartel, which employed thousands, had a global reach, smuggled large-scale shipments and earned *Fortune 500*-like revenues that reached $7 billion annually. Instead, we have the so-called *cartelitos* or baby cartels, which try to operate as discreetly as the Cali combine did, but don't rely on the sophisticated organizational structure and communications systems that it employed.

"Today's *cartelitos* have learned from the past," explained Pedro M. Guzman, a DEA special agent based in Bogotá since 1999. "In the days of the Cali cartel, drug traffickers relied on the cell phone to manage their day-to-day business activities. Today's criminals are using the Internet and push-to-talk radios as their main means of communication. They sell directly to the Mexicans so the United States won't be able to make extradition cases against them, no matter where the cocaine ends up. They like to have face-to-face meetings; which obviously alleviates the need for micromanaging and the constant need to monitor cell phones in the United States."

This change began in the early 1990s, well before the Rodriguez brothers were captured and their empire began to crumble. By July 1993, an estimated 200 trafficking groups were operating throughout Colombia, at least 100 of which were located in the Cali strongholds of the northern Valle del Cauca area. Six years later, a PBS *Frontline* show reported that "the DEA and Colombian National Police believe there are more than 300 active drug smuggling organizations in Colombia. Cocaine is shipped to every industrialized nation in the world and profits remain incredibly high."

[. . .] Even with the downsizing, the flow of drugs out of Colombia has not diminished. As Bruce Bagley *[professor of international relations at the University of Miami]* pointed out, "despite the US government's provision of almost one billion dollars in aid to Colombia over the decade of the 1990s, by 1999 Colombia had become the premier coca-cultivating country in the world, producing more coca leaf than Peru and Bolivia combined."

The *cartelitos* have not only downsized, they've diversified, and cocaine and cannabis are not the only drugs trafficked from Colombia today. As early as 1995, Colombia became the largest producer of poppies in the Western Hemisphere, producing a third more of the crop than Mexico. By 1999, eighty-five per cent of the heroin seized by federal authorities in the northeast United States was of Colombian origin.

Meanwhile, law enforcement is increasingly concerned about the growing role of Colombia in the trafficking of the popular drug Ecstasy, especially to European markets. "Putting the Colombian and Medellín cartels out of business caused only minor disruptions to the flow of illicit drugs from Colombia to the US and European markets," Bagley noted.

7

Dangerous People, Dangerous Places

Norman Parker

Lads' mags such as Front *and* Loaded *published some great "gonzo journalism" (named after Doctor Gonzo in* Fear and Loathing in Las Vegas*) in the 1990s and early 2000s, much as* Playboy *had published literary luminaries back in its early days. The following essays were collected in Norman Parker's* Dangerous People, Dangerous Places, *having appeared first in magazines, and they really give the reader a sense of life on the ground in Colombia, among the people for whom the drug barons featured in the previous chapters are myths as far away from their lives as any celebrity. Their whims and allegiances nonetheless set the grim terms of everyday life at the height of the cocaine wars, when terror and death could pay a visit as suddenly as a shower of rain in dear old Blighty.*

From fascinating insights into FARC (The Revolutionary Armed Forces of Colombia) to the specifics of cocaine production conducted at a remote and inaccessible cocina, the following passages – besides capturing a journalist's hunger for a story – show that justice as it was administered on the streets and in the villages of 1990s Colombia, whether by cartels or communists, could be summary and chilling . . . You can check out other books by Norman Parker at www. parkerstales.com

Now that I had my assignment, I set about doing some serious preparation. My first stop was the British Airways travel clinic in Regent Street. I was aware that I needed vaccinations against various diseases before I would be allowed to travel. What I didn't realize was just how many. Not only was Colombia one of the most dangerous countries from the point of view of political violence, but it seemed that the very environment was inimical to human life.

Next I considered what I should wear. No doubt professional journos in the field wore safari suits and other tropical kit. However, I didn't want to advertise my assignment to the Colombian government, because there might be restrictions on foreign journalists travelling to guerrilla-held territory. Jeans and T-shirts should be sufficient to allow me to blend in with the natives.

Finally, I read up on the current political situation to try to determine who the main players were. FARC were thoroughly Marxist-inspired.

Their political agenda called for agrarian reform, protection of natural resources from multinational corporations and democratization. With up to 20,000 men and women under arms, they were the biggest force in the field, apart from the Colombian Army. So successful had their military campaign been that the previous year the government had granted them a demilitarized zone the size of Switzerland in southern Colombia. This was where I was headed. FARC responded with an attack that reached the outskirts of the capital Bogotá.

The National Liberation Army, or ELN, was inspired by the Cuban revolution and had up to 5,000 men and women under arms. Although mostly fighting against the government, at different times and in different provinces they had been known to fight with FARC.

No South American revolution would be complete without its right-wing death squads, and this function was enthusiastically performed by the Autodefensas Unidas de Colombia, or AUC. An illegal paramilitary army, they numbered up to 5,000 men and were the sworn enemies of FARC and ELN. Although they were supposedly independent, informed sources said that they were merely an extension of the Colombian military and had close links with the drugs cartels.

Guilty of many human-rights abuses, they were widely known as the "head cutters" for their habit of decapitating victims after torturing them to death.

The Colombian Army largely comprised undertrained and unmotivated young men on national service. Regularly outfought and outgunned by FARC, they too had been accused of human-rights abuses by, among others, Washington's Human Rights Watch.

If every South American revolution is incomplete without its death squads, then it is similarly incomplete without the US. Sure enough, there was ongoing heavy US financial and military involvement. Under Plan Colombia, they were in the process of giving $1.6 billion in aid, seventy-five per cent of it in military assistance. They were currently training and equipping two elite Colombian anti-narcotics battalions.

All this added up to a very dangerous country indeed. The previous year, 5,000 people were killed in political violence, out of a total annual toll of 30,000 violent deaths. Journalists were not immune to this violence, either. Forty-six had been killed in the last ten years, and all sides frequently took journalists hostage. I assumed that I wouldn't be bumping into too many other foreign journalists in the field.

The air ticket provided by *Loaded [a British "lads" mag popular in the 1990s]* allowed me twelve days for the trip.

However, it would take a day to get to Colombia and another day to get back. Once I was in Bogotá, it would take a further day to get down to FARC's jungle capital and another day to get back. Then there was the fact that Trent would be arriving from another assignment a day after I arrived. So, if everything went absolutely like clockwork, I would have a maximum of five, maybe six, days with the guerrillas, not a lot of time to do a detailed piece. [. . .]

I must have checked, packed and unpacked my travelling bag six times. I was carrying Trent's camera and forty rolls of film to give to him in Bogotá. For the umpteenth time, I wrapped the camera in tissue to protect it from in-flight damage.

Just as I was as sure as I could be that I had everything, my phone rang. An official-sounding voice informed me that they would like to speak to me concerning a matter at Kensington Police Station. The voice wouldn't be drawn on the nature of the matter, but I was told to ask for DC Keith Brown on arrival.

Now my mind really was racing. What could it be that they wanted to see me about? I racked my brains about anything I might have done, but couldn't come up with anything. I reassured myself that, if it was really serious, they wouldn't have bothered to phone: they'd just have come and arrested me. It wasn't a lot of consolation.

Resignedly, I considered the possibility that it must be about the Colombia trip. I knew that everyone who travelled to Colombia, a drug-trafficking hotspot, was "flagged" by having a note made of the fact. No doubt the combination of Colombia and my being on life licence had provoked them. At best, I could expect a stern warning; at worst, I might not walk out of the police station and might instead be on my way back to a prison.

With considerable trepidation, I approached the front counter of Kensington Police Station and asked for DC Brown. There was no pressing of alarm bells or frantic phone calls. In fact, the desk officer hardly looked up at me. "DC Brown works out of the office directly across the street," he said, before returning to what he was doing.

"Across the street" was entirely more hospitable, in that there were large glass windows and a modern-looking reception area. On asking for DC Brown, I was politely asked to take a seat and promised that he would be with me very shortly.

Keith Brown was surprisingly young, hardly out of his twenties. He was also polite and very laid-back. Apologising for keeping me waiting, he led me into a small office. I declined the offer of a cup of tea and settled back in a manner that I hoped would indicate that, while not being unduly worried, I would like to know what was going on.

"Your name's come up in connection with the Jill Dando murder," said the detective constable.

My immediate reaction was one of relief. The murder of the television presenter was nothing to do with me. I very nearly said, "Oh I thought it was something serious," but realized that would sound flippant and insensitive.

Perhaps reading my expression, the DC added, "We're not taking it too seriously. The computer's just thrown up your name."

I mused on the fact that, whatever my journalistic pretensions, I would always be "Norman the Murderer" to the police and their computers.

He then asked me where I was on 26 April the previous year, 1999, the date of Dando's death. I confessed that I hadn't a clue. I didn't keep a diary and, unless something significant had happened in my life on that day, I wouldn't ever be able to remember. The DC admitted that *he* couldn't remember where he had been on that day, either, a further indication that he wasn't taking this enquiry too seriously. And with that the interview was over.

The final surprise came as I was leaving. He asked me what my personal theory was about the Jill Dando murder. I remembered reading that she had been killed by a single pistol shot to the head. I opined that the killer was either an amateur or didn't really intend to kill. Many victims had survived one shot to the head. A professional would have administered the second shot to make sure.

By now, I was beginning to see just what a responsibility taking on this assignment had been. It was all very well my progressing one step at a time towards the goal of a successful piece, but there would be no prizes for *almost* getting there. If at any stage of the journey I fell, then there would be no story and I would have taken *Loaded's* money and wasted it. [Loaded *had given Norman Parker his assignment.*] In such circumstances I didn't expect them to sue me, but I was sure that would be the end of assignments for them. Further, no doubt word travelled quickly in the world of the lads' mags, and I wouldn't get any more work from any of them. Thus, my whole future as a journalist hung on the success or failure of this Colombia trip.

The flight was uneventful enough, although it was difficult to settle back and get comfortable with my arm still sore from a host of injections.

Nascent paranoia troubled me as I contemplated my coming encounter with Colombia's CIA-trained Customs police. Would they question me about the camera and forty rolls of film? Did ordinary people travel with forty rolls of film? A small voice inside told me that it was all academic, anyway, since they would undoubtedly know exactly who I was.

In the event, I breezed through Customs without so much as a word exchanged and, within minutes, was in a battered taxi making my way through the equally battered streets towards my hotel. Bogotá was a revelation, a large city in terminal stages of urban decay. Virtually every building looked tumbledown or seriously in need of repair. The roads were badly potholed so that, every now and again, drivers would have to slow and navigate around a particularly large chasm.

The hotel was a welcome surprise. While being a long way from five-star standards, at least it was clean and efficiently run. With an absolute minimum of fuss, I booked in and was soon in my room, the only troubling event being that the receptionist said she would have to keep my passport and return it to me later. Seriously tired now, I barricaded the door with a heavy table, positioned a heavy bedside lamp within easy reaching distance to clobber any intruder, and immediately drifted off into a dreamless sleep.

Even though out of jail over two years now, I sometimes woke up thinking I was still in a cell. The Bogotá hotel room spared me that, though. As consciousness dawned, I was immediately aware of the awful cacophony rising from the streets below as rush-hour drivers leaned on their horns. Then there was the heat. Bogotá is up in the mountains and is supposed to be cool. Virtually the whole of the rest of the country is down in the jungle. Acclimatization was going to be a problem for me.

Trent wasn't due to arrive from Miami till the evening.

Dangers or none, I wasn't going to skulk in my hotel room until then. Bogotá was there to be explored. As I mentally prepared myself for the foray into the unknown, I noticed the printed pamphlet on the bedside table. In passable English, it advised guests to leave all valuables in the hotel safe and warned that, in the event of their being approached by people claiming to be the police, they should not go with them but return to the hotel instead. Very reassuring! Coming on top of the official warnings by both the British and US governments for their nationals not even to travel to Colombia, it served to concentrate the mind wonderfully.

Trent had given me the number of a good friend of his, an English guy who had lived in Colombia for twenty years. Danny was in the music business and his club, London House, had been the first acid-house club in Colombia. He had married a Colombian woman and, after the club closed, had eked out a living importing CDs and deejaying. I remembered that Trent had told me that Danny was fluent in Colombian Spanish. I had already discovered that hardly anyone in Colombia spoke English.

Within twenty minutes, Danny was at my room. Or, rather, twenty minutes later, "Hurricane Danny" hit my room. A big-built, rangy-looking guy in his early forties, he entered almost at a run. Everything was a hundred miles an hour with Dan, his body movements, his walking, his talking.

I considered myself a good judge of men and weighed him up quickly. There was a decidedly mad look in his eyes, but that was no disbarment, since many of my closest friends were quite mad. He had a bluff, easy-going personality and a ready wit. He soon had me laughing. The East End accent was reassuring, as was the quickly announced fact that he was a West Ham supporter. He confessed to having run with their hooligan arm, the Inter City Firm, for a couple of years when he was younger. For me, this was even more of a recommendation. Not that I had any time for football hooliganism.

There were plenty of things to fight over, and I just didn't consider football to be one of them. However, an immature outlook notwithstanding, the ICF were known for courage and loyalty to their mates. I was very big on loyalty.

Minutes into our conversation, I discovered the reason behind Dan's hundred-mile-an-hour approach. "Want a quick line, Norm?" he asked, whipping out a small tin, flipping its lid and revealing its contents of white powder.

Back in London, where coke had found its way into every stratum of society, this was the prelude to many social encounters. But it wasn't for me. I wasn't arrogant enough to think that I could control it where so many others had failed. And I liked to be in control. Especially on this, my first journalistic assignment.

My "No thanks, Dan" rebuffed him a bit and he looked closely to see if I had been offended. "But you carry on, mate," I added to show that there was no offence.

Dan needed little encouragement. In one fluid movement, he pinched some powder out of the tin, placed it on the back of his hand and snorted it up his nose.

Just for a second, as its effects hit him, he wasn't with me.

Recovering quickly, he shook his head, refocused his eyes and broke into a crazy laugh. "It's only about one pound fifty a gram out here, Norm. It keeps me going through the day." He laughed again.

No doubt it did. I was laughing with him now. This Dan was quite a character and I would enjoy his company. However, with the serious business of the assignment always in the background, I pressed him on his knowledge of FARC's jungle capital. For a guy whose main interest was music, he was remarkably well-informed about the politics. But, then, as he explained to me, the civil war was so much a part of every Colombian's life that they followed its twists and turns almost like some TV soap.

Dan confessed he'd never been deep into guerrilla-held territory himself, although he had been stopped several times by guerrilla roadblocks on routes leading to Bogotá when he'd been out doing DJ gigs. He said that they were easy enough to get on with, unless they thought you were working for the government. He also said that the people were very tired of the war and wanted peace, almost at any price.

Over the next couple of hours, Dan took me on a guided tour.

His base, which he used almost as an office, was a record shop in an arcade just across the street. The owner was a close friend and the three assistants were all sometime party companions. Everywhere he went, everyone seemed to know and like him. As we sat drinking the strong Colombian coffee, Dan mentioned my assignment down in San Vicente, the guerrilla capital.

Universally, everyone we spoke to was shocked. They strongly advised against it, saying that I must be mad even to consider it. From a social perspective, it was all very interesting, but from a professional point of view it was quite depressing. It seemed that my assignment was going to be anything but straightforward.

That evening, we collected Trent from the airport. For Dan and Trent, it was a reunion of old friends and fellow West Ham supporters.

The little tin and its contents took a right hammering. If nothing else, it helped them relax in the company of someone who, just a short while earlier, had been a complete stranger.

The following morning, it was down to business. To give credit where it was due, Trent knew when to party and when to work. At his suggestion, we made the rounds of all the agencies for further news of the situation. Reuters and a French news agency dismissed us out of hand as journalistic delinquents, pausing only to warn us of the seriousness of the situation. Clearly, *Loaded* didn't carry much weight with them. The lady at Médecins Sans Frontières tried to be more understanding. She warned us to stay close to the centre of San Vicente, as the roads surrounding it were contested and, should we be stopped by the "wrong" group, we could expect to be murdered out of hand.

As we sat talking later that evening, Danny was clearly concerned for our safety. We'd had a busy and constructive day, as well as a lot of laughs. Already, a kind of camaraderie had sprung up between us, as often happens between Londoners in strange places. With it also came the rivalry. There was always friendly ribbing between East and West Londoners. At times, I had been hard pressed to keep up my end of it with both Trent and Dan from the East, but in general I gave as good as I got.

"Look, I've been thinking," said Dan in a manner that

suggested he was on the verge of something portentous. Trent and I stopped whatever it was that we had been doing and looked at Danny in expectation. "You're my mate, Trent, and you, Norman, you're a fellow Londoner. I can't let you go down to San Vicente on your own. I'd never forgive myself if something happened. I'll come with you. You badly need someone who can speak the language. Trent's Costa Spanish will get you nowhere." He stopped abruptly.

It was an emotional moment. Danny was a loyal guy. He, probably better than anyone, realized the dangers of our trip. Yet he was going to put himself in harm's way just to help us out. We both thanked him warmly and, with that, we all stumbled off to our beds.

Early next morning saw the three of us back at the rather inaptly named El Dorado Airport. This time, though, it was in the "national" section. Through the large glass windows we could see the massive international jets and, dwarfed by them, the tiny twin-engined planes we were to travel in. As we booked three seats to San Vicente, we were immediately confronted by one of the many ironies of the Colombian situation. SATENA (Servicio Aéreo a Territorios Nacionales), the airline that would fly us to the guerrilla-held town, was run by the Colombian military. So much for our low profile!

The next shock came as we were about to board our little twin-engined twenty-eight-seater Fokker. We passed on the German jokes as we saw our luggage, and that of all the other twenty travellers, stacked on the runway around the plane. Each person had to identify his luggage (there were no female travellers) and carry it with him on to the plane.

Danny told me that this was to ensure that no one managed to sneak a bomb on board. As I settled into my seat, I noticed that everyone of the other passengers turned to look at us three foreigners.

The take-off seemed to take ages. We didn't seem to be going fast enough. I remember thinking that I hoped we wouldn't run out of runway. Just as I was becoming seriously concerned, we bumped into the air and skimmed over the green canopy of a forest. The experience of cruising smoothly at 30,000 feet hadn't prepared me for the roller-coaster ride of flight in a small plane. As we dropped down from the heights of Bogotá, the warm updrafts from the jungle below buffeted us unrelentingly. Sometimes we dropped by as much as fifty feet, leaving our stomachs behind to catch up with the rest of us. At the same time, the pitch of the engine would change from a piercing screech to a halting, throbbing sound. Never once were we able to escape the knowledge that we were on a plane.

Below us, the Amazon rainforest stretched out in every direction, with no other distinguishing features whatsoever. There were no roads, no buildings, no electric pylons, no sign of any human presence at all.

Occasionally, there would be a dark scar where a river intersected the jungle. I reflected that, should we come down, it would take hours, if not days, for help to reach us.

We made one stop, at a little jungle town whose name was as hard to pronounce as it was to find on the map, then it was on to San Vicente. This was the point of no return; there was no going back now.

San Vicente Airport was little more than a concrete strip in a jungle clearing. As we taxied after landing we saw a group of about eight guerrillas in military fatigues just beyond the perimeter fence. We had been warned that they would be expecting us, as they monitored the flight lists closely.

As we left the plane, the heat hit me. It was like being enveloped in an invisible hot mist. Within seconds, I was sweating from every pore on my body. My underwear was quickly saturated and I felt rivulets of cooler sweat running down my arms and legs. My love affair with the jungle was off to a very shaky start. I realized that this would be a very uncomfortable place to live, especially for someone used to mild European climates.

The terminal buildings were a collection of half-finished sheds. We stood in a group with several other travellers who we suddenly discovered were Colombian journalists. I had been so busy trying to keep my own identity a secret that it hadn't occurred to me to find out who else was travelling to San Vicente. "There's no one here to talk to you, you know," said the man from *El Tiempo,* the high-circulation Colombian daily. "All the leaders are in Spain at a big peace meeting."

It was not a particularly auspicious start. With fledgling feelings of impending doom, I climbed into a taxi and set out for nearby San Vicente. I consoled myself that it wasn't a particularly political piece I would be doing. So whether or not I managed to talk to any guerrilla leaders wasn't crucial. Just so long as I got some good background stuff on the guerrillas in general I'd be OK.

San Vicente was something more than a one-horse town. There were at least six of them standing in the high street. One urinated enthusiastically as we alighted from our taxi outside the hotel. It would have been nice to think that the Hotel Malibu had seen better days, but I feared it had always been a slum. At $8 a day, it was the best hotel in town. Unfortunately, that was no consolation whatsoever. The small dilapidated room with adjoining shower/toilet was rudimentary in the extreme. There were two ways of looking at it. It was either the worst hotel room I had ever been in, or the best cell. I decided to adopt the latter approach and set out to make the best of it.

With absolutely no incentive at all to sit in our rooms and sweat, the three of us soon congregated on a small veranda that overlooked the street. Unfortunately, it also overlooked the urinating horse, which suddenly decided to complete its ablutions by having a crap. As the stench of horseshit drifted up to the veranda, we decided that this was the cue for us to explore the town.

Carrying everything of value with us, we set off. The dusty streets, surrounded by broken-down two-storey buildings, looked like the Mexican towns in the old cowboy films. Higher up on the surrounding hills could be seen the tumbledown clutter of shanty towns. As we walked, sinister, suspicious faces seemed to stare out at us from every doorway. It soon became apparent that we were the only gringos in town, and the first for a long while.

Danny and I had already fallen into an easy familiarity. His irreverent humour complemented mine in many ways. And we continued the rivalry that often springs up between Londoners from different areas of the city. It was especially keen between those from the East – that is the East End – and its environs and the rest. They definitely thought that they were sharper dressers, better money-getters, could pull more women and were cleverer thieves. There was nothing malicious in it. In fact, it was all part of the rivalry to be funnier and cleverer with your mouth.

"Reminds me a bit of the East," I said out of the corner of my mouth, as if I were afraid of being overheard. "Definitely a touch of Brick Lane over there, so you two boys should be feeling quite at home."

Their reply of "bollocks!" was long and drawn out. "You West London mob've got a few slums of your own, mate," rejoined Dan.

"Yeah, but we ain't got all those outside toilets that you lot have still got." My reply was met with another chorus of "bollocks!" from the pair of them.

Suddenly, the narrow dusty streets opened out into a wide central square that was a riot of colourful graffiti and banners expressing revolutionary slogans. And there, right in front of us, was a one-storey slum, similarly bedecked with banners and slogans, which was obviously FARC's local office. A guerrilla in jungle fatigues, his weapon close by, lounged in a chair outside.

For melodrama, all that was missing was the strains of the theme from *High Noon* as the three of us advanced on the office. I reflected that this would be a crucial encounter. This would determine how much assistance, if any, we would get. In the event, Danny's fluent Colombian Spanish and ready wit proved invaluable. Soon he had the guerrilla laughing. He stood and shook hands and offered us a cup of coffee. Then he explained that there was no one here at the moment to talk to us and asked if we could come back in the morning.

Right next door to the office was the Yokomo Café. It was clean and the staff were friendly. We decided to make this our centre of operations.

Nine o'clock the following morning saw the three of us sitting outside the café eating breakfast. Jungle-fatigued guerrillas, with bandoleers of bullets around their chests and carrying automatic weapons, bustled in and out of the office. Strangely, FARC seemed to own few cars, for most came and went on trail bikes or in the yellow town taxis.

We soon saw that nine a.m. was quite late by San Vicente standards.

The town and, of course, the guerrillas had been up for hours and many had already gone off on their assignments for the day. We would have been there at least an hour earlier, but we had been held up by Trent.

Jungle or no jungle, he clearly felt that there were certain standards to be upheld. His fastidiousness didn't come without a price, either.

Danny and I had sat about for over an hour while Trent had washed, shaved, done his hair and generally attended to every detail of his toilet.

Dan summed it up nicely. "My old woman gets ready quicker than he does," he muttered *sotto voce.*

But now we were ready to get down to business. There were real live heavily-armed Marxist guerrillas to interview. However, on closer inspection, these guerrillas seemed considerably underwhelmed by our interest. It wasn't so much that they ignored us, just that everything else they had to do had a higher priority.

Then Lucero appeared. The Colombian journalists had told us of this beautiful guerrilla who held high political and military rank. She was married to a top FARC negotiator and had a seven-year-old daughter who was looked after by her family. Short, with eyes that seemed to flash and sparkle with amusement, Lucero was a veteran of many battles with the Colombian Army and had achieved almost legendary status. She listened while Danny explained what we wanted, but politely declined, saying she had important things to do. She suggested that we speak with Comandante Nora, who was out in the back of the office.

Leaving Trent and me outside, Danny went in search of Comandante Nora. Within seconds, he was back, a pained look on his face. "She's busy at the moment. We'll have to wait for a while," said Dan. But there was something in his attitude that made me curious.

"What's she doing, then?" I asked querulously. The combination of the stifling jungle heat and the lack of co-operation was making me tetchy.

"Her fucking ironing," replied Danny in similar vein.

There was something in his manner that indicated that he wasn't joking, but this I had to see. I walked inside and peered through a dusty window. Sure enough, there was Comandante Nora, AK-47 propped against a table, ironing her blouse.

While we were waiting, a portly, heavily moustachioed guerrilla called Comandante Mauricio came up and introduced himself. He had been sent to show us around the town. You didn't have to understand Colombian to discern that Mauricio was less than pleased with his assignment. But, as far as we were concerned, it was the most positive step so far. As Mauricio headed off on foot, we followed in his wake.

Over the next couple of hours we got an in-depth look at most of San Vicente's roadworks and municipal improvements. We trudged for miles along a network of hot dusty streets, none of which was paved or tarmacked. A few looked absolutely impossible to navigate in anything less than a tractor. Suddenly, we came across a road that was precipitously steep and deeply rutted. It may not have been the worst road in the world, but it was certainly in the top ten. Frustration must have made me blasé. Turning to Dan, I said, "Definitely a touch of the Mile End Road there, mate." The three of us laughed.

Mauricio may not have understood the language but no doubt sarcasm is internationally recognizable. His face like thunder, he advanced on me. With his finger, he beckoned for me to follow him. We had passed hundreds of tumbledown hovels in our progress through San Vicente, but had looked into none of them. Suddenly, I was standing inside one.

The floor was of bare earth, with a couple of pieces of plastic matting scattered about. The roof was a patchwork of rusty and holed corrugated tin. The walls were made from an assortment of timber of different sizes, colours and types. The windows were just holes in the walls with torn material in the place of curtains.

There was one large room, with what must have been a bed in the middle. On this sat a tired-looking woman in her early thirties dressed in rags. At her breast a small infant was feeding. Around her feet sat several other small children. This was abject poverty in the extreme.

Mauricio spoke to Danny for him to translate, but his words were clearly for me. "The government have never, ever done anything at all for these people. These are the ones they have given up on."

It was meant as a rebuke and it had its desired effect. I was instantly both ashamed and embarrassed for making fun of such a situation.

What had I been thinking of? I prided myself on having a social conscience. I wholeheartedly supported revolutionary movements such as FARC. I told myself it was the effect of the *Loaded* factor. Their readership wouldn't be the slightest bit interested in civic reconstruction in rural Colombia. *Loaded* was an irreverent, lighthearted read. Everything had to be a laugh or a putdown.

So how did I justify my writing for them? The answer to that was that, while the style of writing might appear to be light-hearted, the message was still there. Because the establishment controlled the media, socialist revolutions never got a fair press. This was an opportunity for me to get the message across to several hundred thousand people, who might normally baulk at the idea of reading a serious political piece about Colombia. Anyway, all ideology aside, I resolved to treat everything much more seriously from here onwards.

Then a little incident occurred that further defined what I was already discovering to be a difficult relationship with Trent. Danny and I had been strolling ahead, pointing things out to each other and talking, while Trent had been hanging back to photograph whatever took his interest. Suddenly he called me over. I thought it was to point out something. "Look, Norman," he said in a very level tone, "this is your first assignment, so I'm really the senior man. When we're out like this, you should walk behind me."

For a long second, I thought he was joking. Neither of us had completely relaxed with the other, so humour would have been difficult anyway. But as I stared into his face it dawned on me that he was serious.

Perhaps the rebuke from Mauricio had curbed my normally ebullient personality. Perhaps I was still striving to be as professional as possible.

Maybe I was temporarily lost for words. As I turned and walked over to Danny, Trent struck out ahead.

Danny screwed up his face as I drew near and shook his head. "He can be a bit of an arsehole at times," he offered. If anything, it served to bring Danny and me closer. He was a decent guy who was embarrassed by such behaviour.

That evening, tired, uncomfortable in the suffocating evening heat and frustrated by our lack of real progress, we sat in what passed for the lounge of the Hotel Malibu. Occasionally we glanced at the one TV set, high on the wall. Suddenly, it had all our attention. There, all over the national evening news, was San Vicente Airport. And at the forefront of the screen, waiting to meet what looked like some sort of official delegation as they descended from the aircraft, was Lucero.

With Danny translating, we learned that this was FARC's official delegation returning from a peace conference in Spain. Travelling along with FARC's delegation were top ministers of the Colombian government. We had missed what was probably the biggest news event in the history of San Vicente, out looking at roadworks with Mauricio.

With a growing feeling of impending doom, I retired to my room for the night.

The following morning I was up with the lark. If I was going to go down, I might as well go down fighting. If I upset a few guerrillas in the process, then so be it, but today I would get a few decent interviews no matter what. After I had rousted Danny from his room, we headed for the Yokomo Café.

Danny was like a child sneaking off from under a parent's control.

"What about Trent?" he asked, looking back over his shoulder. "He's not going to like us going off without him."

"Fuck Trent!" I replied. "If he wants to lie in bed while there's work to be done, then that's his lookout. Anyway, I'm beginning to get the hump with his bad attitude."

Danny didn't look convinced. He had a worried look on his face all through breakfast. I had brought my own camera with me, as had Danny. Neither of us was a photographer, but we had taken scores of photos of everything of interest. If Trent really threw a tantrum, I was looking at a situation of life without him.

I had just finished telling Dan that Lucero was top of the interview list when, as if on cue, she appeared. She collected a cup of coffee from inside FARC's office, then settled down to drink it in one of the chairs on the veranda outside, her AKA7 leaning against a nearby wall. I beckoned Dan to accompany me and we sat down in two chairs close by. In quick succession I showed her my National Union of Journalists card, a copy of my first book, *Parkhurst Tales,* complete with my photo on the back, and a copy of February's issue of *Loaded.*

I was slightly concerned about her reaction to the last of these. While being very professional and impressive in its layout, with well-written features and stories, there was no getting away from the fact that there were numerous photos of young scantily clad women in provocative poses. You didn't get much more liberated than a female guerrilla in FARC. Would Lucero be offended by what she might feel to be such less-than-serious treatment of women?

As she leafed through the pages, a broad smile spread across her face, revealing her perfect white teeth. She obviously couldn't understand the words, but the photos spoke for themselves. For several minutes, she was lost in the magazine. At last, she looked up, her eyes sparkling with humour. She pointed to the picture on the cover and asked Danny about it.

February's issue had the former Spandau Ballet member Martin Kemp on the cover and a story inside about his role as one of the Kray twins in the 1990 film *The Krays.* As Danny explained that he was a film star playing the role of a gangster, she suddenly pulled a .45 automatic from her waistband and held it to Kemp's likeness. "This is what FARC does with gangsters," she announced, still smiling broadly.

It was a great moment and just what I needed for the story. After asking her permission, we photographed her in several poses with the *Loaded* cover and the .45. It led nicely into the interview, too. On being asked how long she had been in FARC, Lucero replied, "I was born a revolutionary." From anyone else it would have sounded trite and would have smacked of melodrama, but, delivered with her beaming smile and sparkling eyes, it sounded just right from Lucero.

I mentioned the US involvement and asked if she was worried about the Americans and their superior technology. "They are tall, with blue eyes. They will make good targets," she retorted. When I asked about the reception for the delegation at the airport the previous day, she stopped for a moment and looked at me as if she were weighing me up.

"That was FARC's peace delegation returning from peace talks in Madrid. We were concerned that the Americans would try to assassinate them, so we insisted that several Colombian government ministers travel with them on the plane."

So perhaps that explained why Mauricio was taking us out to see the roadworks. Not really knowing who we were, maybe they just wanted us out of the way.

I asked if being a guerrilla in FARC meant that a woman had to give up any hopes of a husband, children and family life. Lucero explained that many of the female guerrillas were married, with their children being looked after by relatives. That was her own situation. Her husband was one of the peace negotiators and their seven-year-old child was being looked after by her mother's family in her home town.

At this point, another uniformed guerrilla came out of the office and whispered something to Lucero. She quickly made her apologies and said that she had to leave, because she was wanted elsewhere.

Without further ado, she mounted one of the several motorbikes parked outside the office and roared off in a cloud of dust, AKA7 strapped across her back.

In the absence of Lucero, Danny's thoughts now turned to

Trent. "I suppose I'd better go and see where Trent is," he said, a concerned look on his face.

"He'll still be in the bathroom, mate," I replied with the beginnings of a smile on mine.

Danny responded with a weak grin and, shaking his head, set off towards the hotel.

In no time at all, he was back. "He's got the right fucking hump, Norm. I'd better warn you." Now Dan was clearly worried.

"Fuck him, Dan. I'm beginning to get a bit fed up with this guy." The annoyance was clear in my voice. "Who does he think he is, anyway? I tell you something: I've been very tolerant up to now and tolerance is something I don't do very well. But I'm supposed to be in journalist mode. So I've put up with some of his bullshit. Back in England, on the street, I'd have steamed into him by now."

"I know, Norm. I just don't want you to fuck up the assignment. To be honest, I've had my own fallouts with Trent in the past. He can be a bit of an arsehole at times. I know I've only known you a couple of days, but we seem to get on well and I'd like to think that we're mates. I'm not going to take sides, but I'm just trying to avoid any awkwardness."

"I understand that, Dan. And, yeah, we do get on well together and I appreciate what you're trying to do. But pride is a bit of a fault with me and I'll only stand so much."

As I finished, Trent suddenly appeared, beetling across the plaza, his arms swinging wildly and his face a study in anger. I sat back in my chair quite nonchalantly, not at all concerned. If it came to a punch-up, I was confident I could handle him. But I didn't know what the guerrillas would make of the two of us, supposedly professional journalists, battling away right outside their office.

While still thirty feet away, Trent beckoned me to come and meet him away from the front of FARC's office. I was out of my chair like a shot.

Now it was my turn to swing my arms as I rushed towards him, serious violence firmly on my mind. "Yeah, what do you want?" I asked aggressively as I closed on him, my face twisted into a scowl.

As Trent suddenly realized that I was right on the verge of steaming into him, his attitude abruptly changed. "Hold up, hold up, mate. There's no need for this." He stopped and held his hands out in front of him, as if to ward me off.

"Well what do you want? Coming rushing over here all aggressive, as if you're looking for a row. If it's a row you want, well, let's have it."

The anger just flowed out of me. It was a combination of the jungle heat, the failing assignment and Trent's attitude.

In the event, he turned out to be all bluff and bluster. "No, Norm, it's just that I'm the senior man and you left me in the hotel." There was a pleading tone to his voice now.

"Look, mate, don't give me all that shit. It might be my first foreign assignment, but I'm not a fucking idiot. If you want to lie in bed when there's things going on, well, that's up to you. Just don't expect me to sit outside your bedroom door waiting for you. And don't treat me with disrespect, OK, 'cause I don't take that from anyone."

By now, Trent looked thoroughly crestfallen, his eyes focused on the floor, his shoes, anywhere but on mine. Suddenly, I felt sorry for him. I only wanted to put him in his place, not break his heart. "Look, Trent," I said in as conciliatory a tone as I could manage, "if we're going to get this assignment done, we'll have to work together. As far as I'm concerned, we're all equals here, Danny, me, you, because we're all taking the same chance of getting killed or whatever. So let's just start again, eh?"

As I finished, I stuck out my hand. He shook it reluctantly, but I wasn't going to make an issue out of that. I wanted to get along with him only while we were on the assignment and in the jungle. I wasn't looking to be his pal back in the real world.

We both went to sit with Dan outside FARC's office. By now, there was only one guerrilla sitting inside and he said he was too busy to do an interview. So, left to our own devices, we decided to tour the town on our own.

Again, this was where Danny's fluent Colombian Spanish was crucial. We wandered from bar to bar, in and out of various cafés, and we stopped people in the street. Everyone seemed to know that we were English journalists. In every instance, Danny put them at their ease and very quickly had them laughing.

The story that we were uniformly told about San Vicente came as a surprise. People said that, before FARC came, there were four or five murders a week, which for such a small town was amazingly high. Now there was none and the place was virtually without crime.

They pointed out the hospital and the school that FARC had built.

The most amazing thing was that, despite being surrounded by coca fields, no one did coke. Nor did they smoke the Colombian grass.

They were heavy drinkers, but there was a strong social stigma about taking drugs.

A sceptic might argue that the townspeople were so terrified of FARC that they only parroted the party line to us. But what was quite apparent was that there was absolutely no climate of fear. Unless they were all naturally consummate actors, they seemed like ordinary Colombians going about their social lives. In fact, many of the people we spoke to were in the advanced stages of inebriation, so their answers to our questions were all the more spontaneous. Further, all three of us were experienced in drug culture and the behaviour that goes with it.

In all the bars and cafes we visited, we would have seen some sign of it, but there was none.

Now, while this might have been revelatory stuff for a piece in the *Guardian*, it was bad news for *Loaded* readers. Instead of their intrepid reporters filing a gripping article from Bandit City, capital of Bandit Country, it seemed that San Vicente was one of the safest, straightest places on earth.

By now, Saturday evening was upon us and all we had to show for our trip to Colombia was the interview and photo with Lucero and scores of photos of the local roadworks. Frustrated and depressed, I agreed to join Danny and Trent for a night out on the town. In the *Loaded* article, I might have written, "But, when *Loaded* journalists' backs are against the wall, they know only one way to react: they go out on the piss." But the truth was far more mundane. I had specifically asked Danny to hold back on the little tin while we were working. I didn't want Trent getting so off his face that he couldn't take a photo. Now that I had wasted their time dragging them down to San Vicente, I might as well let them go and enjoy themselves for a night. And, even though I didn't drink due to a stomach condition, I thought that, rather than sit in the hotel room, I might as well go out and get some fresh air.

As we wandered from bar to bar, Danny explained about the Colombian culture of drinking. There was a local highly potent drink brewed out of pure cane spirit, called *aguadiente,* which roughly translated as "firewater". Each area of the country was proud of the potency of its local *aguadiente* and there was great competition to brew the most potent drink. As was to be expected, San Vicente claimed that theirs was the strongest.

I had been listening carefully to all this, trying to discern which of my many allergies the *aguadiente* would affect. But, while the fermented brew would do little to improve my yeast infection, at least it wasn't made out of anything that would trigger an allergic reaction. Reluctantly at first, I joined them, but soon I was matching them drink for drink.

Carrying a couple of bottles of the stuff, we staggered down a particularly ill-lit street and came upon a funfair. It was rudimentary in the extreme compared with British funfairs, but in a Colombian jungle town it was a rare treat, made possible only by the fact that today was one of the local fiestas.

By now, the three of us were quite drunk. Not falling-down drunk or slurring-your-speech drunk, but sufficiently affected to stagger from time to time and generally talk nonsense. We staggered out of the funfair and into the darkened street again and towards what would be a pivotal moment in our whole trip.

Suddenly, around the corner of the narrow street came a sight that was both amazing and incongruous in the extreme. To the accompaniment of whistles and bells El Gusanito, or "The Little Worm", thundered out of the darkness. El Gusanito was a kiddies' ride in the shape of a giant worm.

The head or engine that pulled the rest was a green plastic

construction in the shape of a Disney worm's head, complete with large bulbous insect eyes and waving antennae. The construction completely obscured the farm tractor that it was mounted on. Behind it were eight two-wheeled cars, again covered with bright-green plastic, that made up the worm's body. The whole ride was festooned with multicoloured flashing lights and, every so often, a loud mournful siren would sound over the clamour of the whistles and bells.

Of all the things we might have expected to encounter in the darkened streets of San Vicente this was in the outer ranges of improbability. The three of us stood there, literally with our mouths open in surprise.

As it drew close, we saw that several of the cars were occupied by young children. Almost before I knew it, Danny and Trent had grabbed me by the arms and pulled me into one of the little cars with them. As we thundered off along the street, I suddenly discovered another aspect of the ride. As they rounded the many sharp corners of the narrow street, the children would lean out of the cars, wave their arms and scream at the startled passers-by. Other children and the occasional dog ran out of the darkened hovels we passed and howled after us.

This was somewhat less than dignified behaviour for supposedly serious, international journalists. Drunk or not, I couldn't help but feel slightly ridiculous. Danny and Trent were suffering no such qualms.

Urging me to join them, they leaned out of the cars as we rounded the bends and screamed enthusiastically at the unsuspecting townsfolk.

By now I was caught up in the moment too. We rounded one particularly sharp bend and the three of us leaned out and screamed in unison at the three startled pedestrians standing on the corner. It was only as we flashed by that we noticed the jungle fatigues and automatic weapons. It was a three-man FARC patrol. In the event, they were more surprised than we were. I still have a clear picture of their startled faces as we disappeared into the darkness.

The central square acted as a terminus for the ride, and

that was enough for me. Danny and Trent expressed their intention to visit the town's only brothel, somewhere up in the impenetrable blackness of the hills above San Vicente. It wasn't for me for a whole host of reasons, not the least of them being the almost palpable presence of the vengeful spirit of Marsha *[his girlfriend]*. I staggered off towards the hotel and oblivion.

The following morning, at breakfast outside the Yokomo Café, Danny and Trent regaled me with details of their visit to the brothel. In keeping with the rest of San Vicente, this seemed to be a bizarre establishment, too. According to their account, it was run by a bearded transsexual and had only two whores. Danny and Trent had monopolized these to such an extent that they had provoked a mini riot, with outraged and impatient fellow customers banging on their room door and demanding access to the girls.

Sitting bleary-eyed and somewhat the worse for wear in the early morning sun, I was aware of a growing feeling of embarrassment. What would FARC think of us? Every bit of credibility we might have had must surely have vanished. Would they even speak to us now?

The reality, though, was completely the opposite. Guerrilla after guerrilla came up to our table, laughing and slapping us across the backs. Mauricio was effusive and the normally taciturn Nora could be seen laughing behind her hands. Lucero larked about with Danny and he had them all laughing uproariously as he re-enacted events from the night before. It was intimated that they had been very suspicious of us previously and had thought that we might be spies. They had been watching closely everything we did.

In retrospect, our night out on the piss was probably the smartest move we could have made. No doubt the CIA and MI5 train their operatives to keep a low profile. So, for FARC, whatever we were, we definitely weren't spies. The only misgivings I had about that was that they might also conclude that we weren't serious journalists either.

However, over the next couple of days we got everything

we could ever have hoped for. We were taken inside FARC's office, a place that had been strictly off-limits to us before. There, under a large poster of Che Guevara that would surely have been a cliché in any other circumstances, we had FARC's ideology fully explained to us. The access-to-the-office bit was definitely a strategic mistake on FARC's part, because after that we were hardly ever out of the place.

We went on river patrol with Mauricio and three heavily-armed guerrillas in a massive iron canoe. Afterwards, we went on township patrol. FARC definitely seemed to be popular. Everywhere we went people rushed out of their shacks to greet them effusively and discuss whatever problems they had, and, considering the degree of poverty, they certainly had plenty of those. It was all a visual feast for Trent, who was snapping away frantically in the background.

We were introduced to FARC's graffiti artist, a callow youth who would surely have been a social menace in any other society. It was he who was responsible for the literally hundreds of revolutionary slogans and icons plastered all over San Vicente. Purely as an acknowledgment to who we were working for, we got him to spray "*Loaded*" in big yellow letters on a nearby wall.

Tuesday saw a major press conference at FARC's local HQ, just down the road at Los Pozos, and we were invited. The Colombian national press had arrived in force. TV crews in vans mounted with satellite dishes thronged the main square and nearby streets.

The star of the show was Raul Reyes, a small elderly bearded guy in jungle fatigues, who was number two in the guerrilla high command.

He looked slightly bemused as he was first introduced to, then photographed with, the three English journalists from *Loaded*. The copy of the magazine had been deliberately left behind and I had instructed Danny to keep things as vague as possible, but still I saw Comandante Raul mouth the word "Loaded" a couple of times with a quizzical look on his face.

It was my first real experience of a press conference, but,

in the circumstances, I was a quick learner. I watched and listened as the representatives of the national press first introduced themselves and their media group, then asked their question. Comandante Reyes sat at a small table cluttered with microphones as dozens of heavily armed guerrillas scanned the surrounding countryside.

I just couldn't resist it. Clutching a piece from the *Independent* of a couple of months previously in which General José Serrano, the Colombian chief of police said, "The SAS have given us great help in recent times," I framed my question. Or, rather, the Colombian TV presenter who had agreed to help us did.

"Norman Parker, *Loaded,*"he said, live on Colombian national TV, as he acknowledged me standing next to him. "Bearing in mind the human-rights allegations against the Colombian Army, what evidence does FARC have of the British SAS training the Colombian military?"

Comandante Reyes confessed that he didn't have such information to hand, but promised to seek it out as a priority. I wasn't disappointed in the slightest. The late Robin Cook, then the UK's Foreign Secretary, was forever wittering on about an "ethical foreign policy". Sheer and utter hypocrisy, of course. I just welcomed a chance, however small, to embarrass him for a moment.

I also took full advantage of the close proximity to so many leading Colombian journalists, as well as several from other South American countries. Speaking off the record, they were a rich source of information. On the subject of who profits from the drugs trade, the overwhelming consensus was that every party does, FARC, ELN, the paramilitaries, the cartels and the Colombian Army.

One informed me that a former president had resigned amid claims that his election campaign had been financed with drugs money.

All claimed that the US had its own agenda beyond that of drugs.

"The last thing the US wants is a Marxist Colombia," said an Argentinean journalist. "The Panama Canal has just been handed back and there is a nationalist, reformist government in Venezuela."

"FARC are incredibly strong," said another. "They even have Stinger missiles. The Colombian military won't be able to cope and the US will have to send in troops. That will polarize the whole of South America and could well turn Colombia into another Vietnam."

It was all heady stuff, but I didn't kid myself that *Loaded*'s City-boy readership would pause for a millisecond before doing their next line of charlie. However, wars are fought with information as well as bullets, and I had managed to fire a few shots. [. . .]

At different times, FARC, ELN, the paramilitaries and the Colombian Army had all held sway here *[Barranca, Colombia]* for a while. At the moment, no one group enjoyed absolute power, but all were fighting to do so. Last year there had been 700 murders and 1,000 disappearances. Now the authorities didn't bother to report massacres involving fewer than ten people.

In any other set of circumstances one could only have concluded that Edgar *[a hired guide]* was joking. But his delivery was deadpan and absolutely matter-of-fact. As we got up to make our way back to the hotel, he added, almost as an afterthought, that it was best that we stay close together, as very few Europeans ever came to Barranca and there was a very real chance of being kidnapped. As a throwaway line, it really took the prize. As I lay in my hotel room, I couldn't help thinking, if that's what he was *willing* to tell us, what has he held back?

Disappointments were coming thick and fast now. The next arrived with breakfast. As I sat opposite Danny in the hotel dining room I could tell something was very wrong. The normal boisterousness was gone and his complexion was the same hue as the milk he was pouring on his cornflakes. "I'm scared, Norm," he suddenly blurted out. "I know this country and things are very dangerous here right now. The boatman who Edgar had hired to take us upriver has pulled out because FARC and ELN are fighting in that area."

I knew that we were going to have to make the rest of the journey by boat, because roads just didn't run through the jungle. The hotel was situated on the bank of the river. The dirty brown water flowed swiftly past the dining room window where we sat. As I gazed into the middle distance, I cursed Hollywood for making us all live filmically now. I couldn't help thinking about *Apocalypse Now* and Martin Sheen's boat trip into the "heart of darkness".

Danny suddenly brought me out of my reverie. "Edgar's managed to get us another boatman, Norm, but he says it's very dangerous and that's why I'm scared."

I wouldn't have described my own state of mind as "scared", rather as "concerned but committed". If I set my mind on doing something, I tended to accept the dangers and just focused on achieving it. But the way Dan was going on, my state of mind could soon change to "scared".

"Look, Dan, I'm scared, too, mate, but I've taken *Front*'s money now and I'm committed to go through with it." *[Norman Parker was now writing for a different magazine to the one for whom he visited the FARC guerillas.]*

Danny's reaction was characteristic. Suddenly, he burst out laughing. "I didn't say I wasn't going, Norm. I'm just saying that I'm fucking scared."

That made me laugh, too. Danny was brave enough. He had told me that he'd run with West Ham's "Inter City Firm" for a while, and you can't be a faint heart and cope with that level of football violence. He had the loyalty that went with it, too, and the more I got to know him, the more I liked him.

The atmosphere changed somewhat as Edgar joined us at the breakfast table. For the worse. Over his toast, he presented me with his scale of charges. It would be $300 to take us to our first stop, a jungle village some eight miles upriver. Then it would be another $200 for the next leg to another village. He was just in the process of detailing the amount for the next leg, all pointed out on a little map he had spread out on the breakfast table, when I stopped him abruptly.

Anger flared as I waved my hand to silence him as internationally as I knew how. "Danny, you tell this prick that

I'm not some kind of fucking idiot." The anger was clear in my voice now, and in my expression too. Edgar sat back abruptly. "I want one price for the whole trip, start to finish. I can see what's going to happen. We'll get to the last stage and it will be some sort of $1,000 to get to the prize. By then I'll be in for several hundred dollars anyway, so I won't have much choice. Tell him, one price for the whole trip, or we call it quits now."

You could tell that Edgar was impressed. He had been nodding in agreement through my tirade without ever understanding one word I said. But he didn't have to. No doubt he was a sharp cookie and knew all the moves. Now he knew that I knew them too. Apart from anything else, it was essential that I establish some sort of understanding with him right from the start. Now, at least, he knew that I wasn't a mug.

We agreed on the round sum of $1,000, an absolute fortune by Colombian standards. But, as he so rightly argued, he was risking his life for us. By now, Jorge had joined us at the table. As he heard the final stages of the agreement, his glum look perfectly matched the one Danny currently had on his face. I was paying them $700 each.

However, my irate state was enough to preclude any negotiations for an increase in their pay.

Edgar was all smiles now. He leaned across the table and shook my hand and I thought I saw a new respect there. I was frantically using all my prison-learned skills of summing a man up. I was reasonably sure he wasn't an evil bastard. If I had got an inkling of that I would have had to watch him very closely indeed. There was always the possibility of his luring us somewhere and killing the lot of us for all the money.

In this new spirit of camaraderie, Edgar suddenly pulled a small box out of his pocket and offered the contents around. They were small pills of two distinct types. He explained that one was an anti-malaria tablet and that we should take it because the river was infested with mosquitoes. The other was a muscle relaxant. It seemed that the constant battering of the boat by the river over the four-hour trip could seriously bruise your back. The experienced river traveller always took a muscle relaxant.

We collected our bags from our rooms and, with Edgar leading, trudged down the muddy bank to the boat, or, to give it its correct name, the canoe. The term boat smacked of something substantial, and there was little substantial about this craft. Basically, it was a fifteen-foot-long flat-bottomed punt with an outboard motor at the back. That it regularly functioned as a punt was evidenced by the long pole held in the hands of the boatman as he welcomed us aboard.

The boatman, an elderly black guy, was all smiles as he steadied the boat with the pole while we settled into our seats. Or rather, benches, for these were bare wooden boards without a trace of cushioning.

Muscle relaxants or no muscle relaxants, I could still see my getting out at the other end with a sore bum.

As we settled in, the boatman's assistant, a teenaged boy, scurried about helping to stow our bags. With an absolute minimum of fuss, the boatman pushed the boat away from the shore with his pole and started the outboard motor. Soon we were speeding along at about thirty miles an hour.

Now I was starting to enjoy myself. This was the start of the adventure proper. I reminded myself that, whatever the outcome of the assignment, this would be the experience of a lifetime. Barely two years previously, I had been sitting in a prison cell. Now I was speeding into the heart of the Colombian rainforest in pursuit of a cocaine factory.

I had instructed both Jorge and Danny to take lots of photos of anything of interest. The three of us sat with cameras at the ready. That was when I discovered that, stimulating as I had first thought the boat ride to be, there was very little of interest to see. For a start, there were no roads, no bridges, no buildings of any kind, no telegraph poles, no animals and no people. And, since both banks were lined by tall reeds, all you could see in every direction was a brown-green wall that served to obscure everything else.

I was soon bored. The few birds we might have seen were frightened off by the roar of the outboard, which, as the river narrowed, seemed deafening. Then there was the percussive drumbeat of the bottom of the boat striking the water as it skimmed across the waves. This was aggravated by the boatman's criss-crossing of the river to avoid the shallows. Resist it as I might, whatever position I adopted it still sent shockwaves all the way up my spine. Now I could appreciate the value of the muscle relaxants. My romantic conception of river travel was rapidly undergoing a marked transformation. Already I longed for the boat ride to be over.

But, as Edgar was quick to inform us, we had just over four hours of this before we got to our destination. This was another thing I was discovering about Edgar. Although, at first sight, he didn't seem to be a morbid chap, he was an absolute fund of disturbing information. All conversations had to be conducted at a shout, to be heard over the roar of the outboard, so there was no ignoring what he was saying.

Either he was bored too and was talking to pass the time, or he saw it as part of his duty as tour guide. However, he told us in quick succession that the river was teeming with piranha, some of them so large they could bite your hand off; there were also lots of alligators and crocodiles, some of which could grow to twenty feet or more; and there was the ever-present danger of colliding with sunken logs as we sped along the river. I briefly contemplated the prospect of some scaly, armoured behemoth pulling me from the canoe, as his smaller brethren, all snapping teeth and flailing fins, tore chunks of flesh from my bones. I resolved that the first Spanish phrase I must learn would be: "For fuck's sake, shut up, Edgar!"

Half an hour into the journey, the river suddenly widened again and there, on the bank about 200 yards away, was some kind of military checkpoint. Two soldiers wearing army fatigues, crouched over a heavy machine gun. "Don't let the soldiers see the cameras," shouted Edgar, in a determined attempt at a whisper. "If they think we're journalists, they might turn us back or confiscate the cameras."

You would have thought that, with so little else to occupy them, the soldiers would have taken the opportunity at least to search the boat and question us about where we were going. For, if Europeans were scarce in the jungle towns of Colombia, you could bet your life they were virtually nonexistent on the rivers. But not at all. Without even standing up, they glanced down into the boat, checking, I guess, that we weren't carrying weapons. Then they waved us on.

On the bank, perhaps fifty yards past the checkpoint, was the wreckage of a crashed plane. It was a small two-seater job that looked relatively intact, except for the tail section, which had broken off and was lying separately from the rest. Edgar said that it was probably a narco-trafficker's plane that had been forced down. Shielding the camera with my body, I took several surreptitious snaps of the downed plane.

The next three and a half hours seemed to pass exceedingly slowly.

Occasionally, a straw hut would break the unchanging backdrop of the wall of vegetation. From time to time, a native fisherman would stare at us as we sped by. The monotony of the unchanging surroundings, the roar of the engine, the buffeting from the boat, the heat and the mosquitoes all combined to make an experience that was little better than purgatory. The only moments of interest were when the river narrowed to such an extent and the shallows became so difficult to pass that the boatman and his assistant both got out of the boat and, waist deep in the opaque water, guided us through by hand. My thoughts firmly with the crocs and the piranhas, I wondered out loud if the time would come when we too would have to do the same. I took little comfort from the fact that Edgar didn't see fit to reply.

It was during one of these periods, when the boatmen were out of the boat and the outboard noise was just below the pain barrier, that Edgar decided to share one of his gems with us. He remarked that he had been kidnapped a total of five times by the various armed groups.

Discussing it later, Dan and I were of the considered opinion that he had left it rather late to tell us and, seeing that he had left it so very late, why did he bother to tell us at all?

Eventually, the river widened out again and there before us was El Bagre, our destination. You could barely call it a village, just a collection of wood and straw huts clustered along the river bank. As Edgar had explained to us, it was a point controlled by

FARC. It was one of them who would direct us to the *cocina*, or coke kitchen. They didn't call them farms or factories.

We made our way up the bank and Edgar introduced us to Comandante Alphonso, who was the senior FARC guerrilla in charge. Alphonso was a very laid-back black guy. He said he would phone HQ and find out what had been arranged for us. Still in a very laid-back manner, he cautioned us that if we were spies we would be shot.

Minutes later he told us that a FARC boat was on its way to take us on the next leg of the journey, as there were no *cocinas* in the immediate area. I settled down in the shade to wait, all the while observing daily life in El Bagre.

The sun was exceedingly hot and the humidity made breathing difficult at times. So all activities were conducted at a very leisurely pace. There were about thirty villagers in all and among them I saw two more guerrillas patrolling slowly between the huts. Alphonso told us that the paramilitaries had attacked El Bagre two weeks previously. A FARC guerrilla had been killed and ten villagers massacred, while the paramilitaries had lost ten of their own. It seemed hard to believe in a place that looked so idyllic.

From time to time, boats stopped at the bottom of the bank. One of the guerrillas would walk down and check the cargo, money would exchange hands and then the boat would be on its way again. Mostly they were carrying clearly visible drums of gasoline and bags of cement.

Other cargoes were hidden under covers. Edgar explained that it was all connected with the coke trade. The gasoline and cement were used in the production process and the hidden cargoes were the finished product. All cargoes were taxed by FARC before being allowed to go on their way.

Occasionally, other people arrived and came to sit around a hut that served drinks and snacks. Their city-smart shirts and slacks made them stand out quite clearly from the villagers. Danny was quite an authority on the coke trade himself. He pointed out two well-dressed, serious looking guys sitting together by the snacks hut. "They're both from Cali," he said. He pointed at two other similar guys sitting a short distance away. "And they're from

Medellín. That's something you wouldn't have seen a couple of years ago. They'd have killed each other on sight. But the big cartels have been broken up and there are hundreds of smaller cartels and people have learned to co-operate."

Dan went on to explain that these guys were here to buy the coca base produced in the *cocinas*. They would pay about £600 a kilo for it. Back in their home cities, they would process the base into its crystalline form and its price would increase to about £1,200 a kilo. Quite amazingly, though, they wouldn't take so much as a gram back with them. The actual bags of coke they bought and paid for at El Bagre would be exactly the same ones delivered to them by FARC in their home cities!

All of a sudden, the soporific effect of the heat was causing my eyelids to droop and I felt an irresistible urge to sleep. I found an empty hut that must have been used as a store and fell asleep immediately.

When I awoke a couple of hours later, Danny was standing outside, "'Ere, come and have a look at this, Norm," he urged. "See what you've been sleeping next to."

I stumbled outside, blinking in the bright sunlight. The hut I had been sleeping in was divided in half by a wall. Danny was pointing to the inside of its other half. Stacked against the wall were about three dozen clear polythene bags containing large off-white granules. "You've been sleeping right next to forty kilos of coca base, Norm."

If nothing else, it was an excellent photo opportunity. I fetched a clean *Front* T-shirt from my bag and put it on. It was a black one with *Front* printed on the front of it in big yellow letters. Then, holding several kilo bags of coke in my arms, but with the word *Front* clearly visible, I got Danny to take a dozen or so photos. I guessed that these photos alone would be worth the trip to the boys back at the magazine.

For a while I sat watching some women of the village washing clothes in the river down by the bank where we had landed. Due to the heat I had been going through clean socks at an alarming rate. It caused some amusement among the women when I joined them to wash some socks out in the river water.

I reasoned that, in the heat, they would be dried out before we went on our way.

Ever mindful of Edgar's crocs, alligators and piranha, I was paying more attention to what was going on in the nearby waters than I was to the actual washing of the socks. I didn't relax till I was hanging them on a line stretched between two huts. Suddenly, there was a loud explosion. I cringed and ducked with everyone else. All eyes turned to focus on a young city-dressed guy standing next to a group of playing children. A pistol was lying on the ground between his feet. Clearly, it had dropped from his belt and accidentally gone off. I watched as the nearest guerrilla walked across and roundly chastised him.

Almost immediately there was a flurry of activity down by the riverbank. A canoe pulled up carrying four heavily-armed guerrillas in jungle fatigues. They trudged up the bank, the bright sunlight glancing off the machine guns and bandoleers of bullets they were carrying.

Two things surprised me. First, they were ELN guerrillas. ELN were supposed to be fighting with FARC at our original destination, yet here they were comrades and friends. Secondly, they were all so very young.

They were also very friendly. Edgar did the introductions. Ernesto, their leader, was still only twenty and had been training to become a doctor before he had joined the guerrillas. I asked him, through Danny, why he had joined.

"When you see the paramilitaries come to your town and massacre people, you know it could be your turn next. It is only common sense to fight," he said with passion.

Although friendly, too, Elena said little. She was barely seventeen and clearly quite shy, but there was something more. It was as if she had retreated from the world. When we got Ernesto on his own, he told us that her whole family had been massacred by the "death squads". That was why she had joined ELN. He added that she was a fearless fighter and offered the opinion that it was very sad, because it seemed that she was searching for death.

By now, Danny, in his own inimitable way, was on excellent terms with all of them. He had Ernesto laughing heartily and even Elena was smiling.

Next thing, he had their M16s and Kalashnikovs off them and he and I were holding them over our *Front* T-shirts for another set of photos.

When they asked what we were doing here, Danny told them about our mission to find a *cocina*. Ernesto said that, if we couldn't do it through FARC, we should come to their base at a nearby lagoon in the morning and they would try to help us. I got Danny to take full details of exactly how to get there. I wanted to give myself other options, because I was becoming worried now by the lack of results at our current location.

It was as they were leaving that I suddenly realized that the boatman who had brought us to El Bagre was nowhere to be seen, and nor was his boat. Edgar said that I shouldn't worry, because his job was only to bring us here. River travel was the only way to get about here and it would be the easiest thing in the world to get another boatman to take us where we wanted to go.

Then the senior FARC *comandante* everyone was waiting for arrived. He was a serious-looking, no-nonsense sort of guy in his forties, wearing the regulation jungle fatigue and the equally regulation heavy black moustache. He moved about with an air of authority, clearly used to being obeyed. The pace of the three local FARC guys quickened visibly, as they hurried about to his barked orders.

Even with Edgar's influence, the best we could achieve was a place at the back of the queue behind the guys from Cali and Medellín. Quite clearly, the important business of the day was coke business. I watched as local growers and vendors brought their bags of coca base out for the inspection of the city guys. Quality was discussed and price negotiated. Money was handed over and delivery details given for where the coke should be delivered to. All the while, the senior FARC *comandante* supervised proceedings.

With our turn came our latest and biggest disappointment. We found out that the only reason the *comandante* had come to El Bagre was to do the coke business. He said that there were too many things going on in the area for him or FARC to accommodate our wish to see a *cocina*.

And he said it in a manner that brooked no argument. Almost before we knew it, he was back in his canoe and speeding away up the river.

So what did I do now? I looked at Edgar enquiringly, and his gaze could hardly hold mine. The reality was that I was deep in the Colombian jungle and I was no closer to finding a *cocina*. Edgar suggested that we go to see Ernesto at the ELN base in the morning.

"What's the matter with now?" I demanded aggressively, the prospect of failure looming like a spectre before my eyes.

"It's almost 6 p.m. and FARC shut the river at 6," said Edgar sheepishly.

"What?" I barked.

"It's a curfew, Norm," added Danny. "After 6 p.m., nothing moves on the river and anything that does gets shot at by FARC."

Well, that was straightforward enough. Whatever our next moves were going to be, the sure thing was that we were going to spend the night at El Bagre.

There was no such thing as a hotel, of course, just a wooden hut partitioned off into absolutely basic rooms. Luckily for us, there was one room left. Unluckily for Jorge and Edgar, it had only two beds. To be honest, I would have tossed a coin to see who slept where, but Edgar, overcome with guilt no doubt, volunteered to sleep in the cane chairs near the café. At the same time he volunteered for Jorge, too.

When I saw the room, I realized that he hadn't made much of a sacrifice. I don't know what impressed me the least: the two hammocks slung between the rough wood walls, the open gaps for windows or the bare earth floor. Before leaving us for the night, Edgar just couldn't resist imparting one last gem of wisdom. "Make sure you sleep with your shoes in the hammock with you, under the mosquito netting," he called out. "Otherwise poisonous scorpions, snakes and spiders could get in them in the night and sting you when you go to put them on in the morning."

I knew I was going to have difficulty falling asleep. I was roasting in the heat, suffocating in the humidity and my right arm was on fire from a dozen mosquito bites. Now, as I swung perilously in the unstable hammock, a sweaty trainer nestling snugly under each arm, all I could think of was the big bristly tarantula, poised at this very second to launch itself upwards and bite my unprotected bum through the hammock canvas. I briefly toyed with the idea of waking Dan up and asking him how high the Colombian spiders could jump, but I knew he wouldn't thank me for it.

I must have lain there for a couple of hours, listening to the sounds of the jungle. The myriad rustlings, chirpings, buzzings, hissings, slitherings, croakings, hummings, screechings and growlings – and Danny's snoring acting as a backdrop to the sudden sharp death cries, as nature's creatures fell upon one another in an orgy of mass slaughter.

Just as I was finally dropping off from sheer exhaustion, there was a piercing shriek ending in a throaty gurgling that brought me fully awake and nearly pitched me out of the hammock. I heard Dan stir and I called out in a breathy whisper, "Dan, what the fuck was that?"

There was silence for a couple of seconds, over which I could hear the continuing gurgling. "Sounds like someone slaughtered a pig," said Dan and, with a grunt, turned over and fell asleep again. I lay there wondering what sort of idiot slaughtered a pig in the middle of the night.

The following morning I wasn't in the best of moods. I had just spent the most uncomfortable night of my life and I had awoken to find that toilet arrangements were basic in the extreme. Residents took turns to fill a bucket from a large vat of river water, then wash in the bucket. I improvised slightly by filling several buckets with the relatively cool water and tipping them over my head. Bliss, utter bliss!

But only for about half an hour, when the cycle of sweating and overheating began again.

We ate breakfast at the café, then the four of us trudged back down the bank to where another boatman was waiting with his motorized canoe. The ELN base was located at a nearby lagoon called San Lorenzo. We sped along narrow rivers that were little more than streams, turning sharply round tight bends and sending our frothy white wake crashing into the reedy banks.

I had promised Marsha I would phone her every day. I knew that a little detail like being in the middle of a tropical rainforest would carry little or no weight with her should I not do so. There had been no phone at El Bagre, so I told Danny to ask the boatman to stop if there was a place with a phone.

The canoe slowed as we suddenly came to a junction where four small rivers met. The boatman pointed to the bank and spoke to Danny. "He said that there's a small village over there called Four Mouths and it's got a phone," said Dan in a tone that sounded not at all pleased.

"So let's pull over for a minute," I replied, puzzled. This was good news. In a few minutes, I would be talking to my dearly beloved and getting myself off the hook for another day.

"It ain't that easy, Norm." Dan's tone was still grim. "The boatman says that the 'head cutters' have been active in this area recently and they may've attacked this village."

I digested the information and conjured up two images: one was of a death squad comprising bloodthirsty cut-throats; the other was of an irate Marsha. It was no contest really. "Fuck 'em, Dan. I've got to phone Marsha, so let's put ashore, eh."

There was a large hut situated right on the shoreline, so we coasted in close by. Behind it, through the trees, could be seen similar huts with a narrow earth road between them. All was deathly quiet and it seemed as if no one was about.

It was only at the last moment that we noticed the painted slogan daubed on the side of the hut in large white letters. Danny translated, but I already knew that the letters AUC stood for "Autodefensas de Colombia", the preferred name of the paramilitary death squads. So we now knew for sure that they had been here. The burning question was, were they still about?

The five of us advanced slowly up the narrow earth road, stepping around household articles that had been pulled from the huts and left.

The inside of every hut had been ransacked and unwanted items smashed. Here and there fires had been started, as evidenced by the blackened timbers and piles of ash. Other huts had had their corrugated tin roofs pulled off. Two dozen or more chickens foraged among the ruins. Still there was no one to be seen.

Not one word had been exchanged between us since we had landed.

Treading carefully to avoid making too much noise, we were listening intently for signs of life. Although we all must have been aware that we were entering a potentially dangerous situation here, it was as if we were being drawn inexorably onwards by our desire to find out what had happened.

For myself, I saw an opportunity to save a failing assignment. In the absence of a cocaine story, photographic evidence to reveal this latest massacre to the world would suffice. That was why it was worth taking a risk. Mentally, I steeled myself against the discovery of tortured corpses and severed heads on poles.

At its end, the narrow dirt road broadened out into a large roughly rectangular open space that must have served as the village square. In the middle was a wooden hut with the remains of telephone wires running to it. The window openings were all blackened with smoke and the roof had collapsed. Wordlessly, I said goodbye to my phone call to Marsha.

On the side of another hut was some more painted writing. Once again the letters AUC stood out clearly. Danny translated. "It's a warning. It says, 'This is what happens to the enemies of the AUC.'"

He looked directly at me. "We better get out of here, Norm, just in case they're still around. These aren't people to fuck about with. They'll kill you as soon as look at you."

It was enough to bring all of us to our senses. It was almost as if I had been sleepwalking through the village. The full implications of what could happen should we bump into this group finally hit home.

Without actually breaking into a run, we hurried back to the boat.

Just as we were pushing off from the bank, an old man emerged from the trees. Edgar got out and went over to speak with him. The conversation was brief and he came rushing back, motioning for the boatman to push off as he climbed in. "The paramilitaries were here just over a week ago," he gushed. "They killed ten villagers and the rest have fled. There's only this old man now. He's lived here all his life. He says he's sad and lonely."

The old man stood in the trees, watching us as we disappeared up the river. I stared for a long time at the forlorn figure, musing that this was the real face of Colombia's civil war. A civilian population at the mercy of right-wing death squads, in league with the Colombian Army and indirectly supported by the US.

The river narrowed again and under overarching trees perhaps fifty feet ahead was a jungle-fatigued guerrilla in an outboard-powered canoe. He immediately set off with us in pursuit. At times it was almost like a chase, as we twisted and turned around sharp bends.

Until now, all the journey had been in the gloom of small rivers overhung by a canopy of trees that served to keep most of the light out. Suddenly, the river opened out into a large and most beautiful lagoon. Golden sunlight danced on impossibly blue waters, as countless thousands of multicoloured exotic birds swooped and called. It was breathtaking.

We crossed the lagoon and docked near the small group of huts that was San Lorenzo. The four ELN guerrillas we had met the day before were sitting among the trees with several of their colleagues. We pressed them on their offer to show us a *cocina* and they said they would have to ask their commanders further up the river.

A ten-minute canoe ride took us to The Point, a fortified bend in the river that served as an ELN command post. We were introduced to Comandante Julian and Comandante Aguado, the two most senior ELN commanders in the area. Both were friendly and helpful, but, in practical terms, there was little they could do personally to show us a *cocina*. However, they did say they would make some enquiries. Quite bizarrely, I then found myself discussing the finer points of Marxist ideology with them, while we awaited an answer.

All the while I was watching the comings and goings of the boats on the river. Many had the telltale cargoes of gasoline and cement. All were stopped by the ELN and all were taxed. Noting my interest, Comandante Julian suddenly asserted that the ELN were not involved in the cocaine trade. They taxed only the cattle and gold trades. Bearing in mind I realized I had seen only timber structures since I'd been in the jungle, I forbore to ask what all the cement was being used for then.

I snoozed for a while in the shade of a large tree and awoke to find Danny exercising a previously unknown talent as a film director.

Having decided that the guerrillas weren't actually doing a lot just sitting about in the shade, Dan had decided to get them on manoeuvres for a photoshoot. He had several in a slit trench pointing guns aggressively and several more were in an attacking formation down by the jetty confronting half a dozen more who were bursting out of some bushes. Meanwhile, he and Jorge were snapping away like crazy with their little cameras with both *comandantes*, Julian and Aguado, looking on benignly.

Our answer, when it came over a badly crackling radio link, wasn't helpful. ELN in that area couldn't help us find a *cocina*, but they would send us upriver to a FARC post, where there was a commander who could.

Once again we headed upriver in the canoe. A ninety-minute trip took us to Yanque, another collection of huts, but this time set atop a steep hill. The most welcoming aspect for us was the Coca-Cola sign. We sat in the village café, greedily guzzling exquisitely cold soft drinks.

By all accounts, Comandante Yasid was the most senior FARC commander we had met so far. He was a young, intense, yet friendly guy, whose fledgling beard and moustache only served to emphasize his youth. He was introduced as the commander of the whole 24th Front.

As Edgar waved his hand expansively to indicate the extent of Yasid's kingdom, I could only muse that never had one so young been in total charge of so many trees.

In a country that was at the forefront of cocaine production, it seemed amazing that, despite travelling across hundreds of miles, we had never been near or by a *cocina*. And that was exactly the situation now. Yasid said that there wasn't one in the area, but he knew of one near a village called Agua Sucio.

However, there were a number of problems. The direct route was by water to a large town called San Pablo, and we could get a jeep from there. San Pablo, though, was a paramilitary stronghold and anyone arriving from FARC-held territory was liable to be shot on sight. I had been following the conversation carefully through Danny's translation and, as we got to the stage of Yasid's telling us the alternative, I followed his pointing arm as it indicated a massive green-swathed mountain in the middle distance. Danny was suddenly uncharacteristically tight-lipped.

"Go on, then, Dan. What's the alternative?" I urged.

"Yasid said that it's a five-hour trip by mule over that mountain," he pronounced grimly.

By now, it was all becoming thoroughly ridiculous. I had expected some unusual situations, but a close encounter with a mule hadn't been among my expectations.

"And we're not used to riding mules," added Dan, stating the obvious. "An hour's ride will cripple us."

"I've got too much respect for my bollocks to spend five hours on a fucking mule," I exploded. "We're going to San Pablo by boat."

The boatman thought otherwise, though. It was only the obscene sum of £100, a small fortune by local standards, that managed to change his mind. I didn't much care for the way he crossed himself as we set off, but at least we were going by the direct route now.

We arrived at San Pablo just as night was falling. The four of us booked into a small scruffy hotel, then went in search of supper. Of all the places I had been so far, there was definitely a different feel about this place. People looked at us furtively and there was an air of fear. It didn't help our collective paranoia when we noticed a guy on a motorbike who was following us everywhere. We ate quickly in a restaurant, then retired to our rooms for the night.

Breakfast brought another drama. The guy with the jeep, whom Edgar had hired to take us beyond Agua Sucio, had backed out.

At daybreak, 600 paramilitaries had driven up the very road we were due to travel on to attack ELN positions in the biggest operation in years. The whole area had suddenly become even more dangerous than usual, ergo, no jeep driver.

Seeing the expression on my face and having already felt the force of my anger on several occasions now, Edgar was apologetic: "I did warn you before we started that in Colombia nothing remains the same. Everything changes." And, to give credit where it is due, he *had* warned me. He had also warned me about something called "locombia", a corruption of *loco*, the Spanish word for mad, and, of course, *Colombia*. The word itself meant a particularly crazy Colombian state of mind that ran through all things. This latest situation was classic "locombia".

All was forgiven, though, when, barely half an hour later, Edgar showed up with another guy with a jeep. Just outside San Pablo, our big red Toyota jeep was stopped at a heavily fortified army checkpoint.

Whatever Edgar said to the soldiers, it was enough to get us through.

Further on, special government anti-guerrilla troops waved us to the side of the road and Edgar talked us through again. A glaring irony that wasn't lost on me was that this was the road that 600 paramilitaries, the death squads, had travelled up just a few hours earlier. So much for the fiction that the regular army doesn't collude and co-operate with them, I thought.

We passed a burned-out command post that had belonged to FARC.

The driver told us that ten guerrillas had died here only the previous week. From here on, a road that had been merely impassable to cars became a four-wheel-drive obstacle course. The good news was that, where the paramilitaries had turned off, our route carried straight on.

We forded five rivers and drove around and over fallen trees, deep ruts and boulders. Agua Sucio just wasn't worth it. Fortunately, this miserable collection of huts was just another stop on the journey. We topped up with cool soft drinks and were soon on our way again. Finally, we breasted the brow of a steep hill and stopped. Our bone shaking ride had lasted over three hours.

The present stop was for Edgar to take a pee. Just before disappearing into the undergrowth, he pointed out to me the farm buildings nestling in the lee of the hill below. The sweep of his hand took in the thousands of coca plants that covered the surrounding hills.

Among them he pointed out the *raspachinos,* or pickers, working in the blazing sun.

He cautioned me about taking photos, saying that good manners demanded that we ask his permission first. Well, I'm afraid that by this stage I was clean out of "good manners", and something called "enlightened self-interest" was firmly in their place. I hadn't come all this way, risking life and limb, for some farmer to say I couldn't take any photos. I could take the best story in the world back to *Front,* but in the absence of photos it would be as nothing.

I too walked off into the undergrowth, making as if I were going for a pee. As I gazed through the lens of my thoroughly ordinary camera, I wondered what all the fuss was about. The collection of scruffy sheds in the distance could have been anything, anywhere in the world. If it really was a coke farm, then it certainly didn't look it from where I was standing.

As it turned out, the farmer was hospitality personified. He was at pains to emphasize that he was only a poor man and the obvious poverty on his farm attested to that. When asked why he grew coca, he pointed to his six children. He said that there weren't any alternatives for him. If he grew the food plant yucca, it would be too expensive to sell by the time he got it to market, because of the distance and the cost of transport.

Certainly, the economics of cocaine production at this end of the market weren't impressive. Coca was a hardy plant that would grow virtually anywhere. However, it still had to be fumigated by hand two to three times before each of the three harvests each year, to protect it from insects and worms. He usually employed 30 *raspachinos [literally, "scrapers"],* working eleven-hour days, six days a week. For this each was paid around £8 per day, with free board and lodging.

The gasoline and cement to produce the coca base had to be brought in by boat, and this was subject to taxing on the way. He paid a flat tax of about £18 per hectare to the paramilitaries who controlled the area and a further £60 per kilo tax on each kilo of coca base produced.

Finally, he would have to sell the base to the paramilitaries for about £600 per kilo. These were the very paramilitaries who operated out of San Pablo under the protection of the army!

The farmer said that we could photograph what we liked, as long as we didn't photograph him or the faces of his workers. That could bring the wrath of the paramilitaries down on them. He absolutely refused all offers of payment. I was already deeply impressed by the simple Colombian courtesy and hospitality I had experienced.

Before we embarked on the guided tour, though, there was one final ritual to be observed. After taking a boiling pot off a nearby stove containing coca leaves, the farmer poured each of us a cup of coca tea.

He said that it was good for everything, including illnesses and allergies, and would give us energy.

It wasn't for me, though. I had long ago promised myself that coke wouldn't have me in any way, shape or form. Further, abstinence had become almost an article of faith for me on this trip. I felt that, if I lived clean, then I might just get the story. And, as for the extra energy, on most days I tripped on my own adrenalin, anyway.

With two *raspachinos* as extra guides, we climbed the slopes covered with coca bushes and the two different types were pointed out to us. Both types of leaf looked identical to me, apart from the fact that the Peruvian coca leaf was much darker than the Colombian one. We were told that it also yielded four crops a year against three for the Colombian.

The actual *cocina* was on the summit of a small hill. Basically, it was a long shed with no walls, just six upright beams to hold the roof up.

Inside, two large black plastic sheets were spread out on the rough earth floor. On the first, a worker was chopping a vast pile of leaves into small pieces with a garden strimmer. On the second sheet, the chopped leaf was covered with cement powder, sprinkled with gasoline, then trodden in by men wearing wellington boots. Once it was well mixed in, it was shovelled into large black plastic drums, which were topped up with gasoline and left for two hours.

The next stage involved letting the liquid drain out of each drum into another drum below. Permanganate was added and stirred well in. The mixture was then left to stand for another two hours, when the coca paste could be seen in the form of a white viscous precipitation at the bottom of each drum. The farmer told us that his *cocina* turned out approximately fifteen kilos of base a week.

All through the guided tour, Danny, Jorge and I had been photographing everything that was remotely interesting. I was sure that we had several hundred photos between us. The worry that exercised me now was whether, since everyday Colombian life was so problematic, I would get back safely with the photos. Edgar emphasized that nobody had ever photographed a working *cocina* before.

I wanted to leave immediately, but the farmer asked us to join him for lunch. In the circumstances it would have been churlish to refuse: I ate with a tranquillity that belied by my internal mood. I consoled myself with the thought that the trip back couldn't be nearly as fraught as the trip out.

The ride back to San Pablo was without incident. The army roadblock had gone and there was no sign of the paramilitaries, either.

I paid the driver off, musing that too many trips like today's would see his new jeep a wreck in no time.

Back at the hotel, the first priority was a cool shower and a change into clean clothes. I took the rolls of film with me everywhere. Afterwards, I went to reception to get a cold drink from the fridge. Four young guys were by the reception desk. They gave me a hard stare as I came in. It was one of those "Who are you looking at?" stares that were so commonplace in London. Back there I would probably have responded in kind, but, quite strangely, because personal interaction was so polite and unthreatening in Colombia, I had relaxed considerably. However, it registered subliminally as I returned to my room.

Within minutes, raised voices could be heard coming from reception.

As I came out of my room, Danny was already in the hall. We hurried towards the reception area. The four young guys had Jorge and Edgar backed up against a wall. Both were white as sheets and literally shaking with fear. "They're taking us away," cried Edgar to Danny.

"Please help us."

It was in situations like this that Danny was worth his weight in gold.

He quickly engaged the four guys in conversation and soon had them laughing. Within seconds all the threat went out of the situation. It transpired that they were paramilitaries and they had heard that we were in town and wanted to know what we were doing here. They had thought that we were Americans.

Danny explained that we were English and made some deprecating remarks about Yanks that had them laughing again. He told them of our mission to photograph the *cocina*. They left, still laughing and seemingly satisfied.

Jorge and Edgar, though, were definitely not laughing. Still shaking, Edgar said that they were definitely on the verge of being taken away and killed. He emphasized that we must get out of town right away.

"We must leave right now or we're dead" were his exact words.

It wasn't exactly panic, but we had our bags packed and were in reception paying our bill in no time at all. The owner was relieved to see the back of us. He had been following developments from inside his office and was as white as Edgar and Jorge.

At a trot, we made our way down to the river and accepted the first boat available without bothering to negotiate the price.

Soon we were heading upstream towards Barranca. If I had thought that we were now safe, Edgar soon disabused me of that notion. "They will phone ahead to their comrades. We must get out of Barranca as soon as possible," added a still shaken Edgar. Ever mindful of the 700 dead and 1,000 missing last year alone, I could only agree with him.

We docked at Barranca and Edgar spent a couple of minutes finding a properly registered taxi. We paid him the £80 he wanted to take us to Bucaramanga. Three hours later, we were in the Melia Confort Hotel, five-star, safe and secure.

8

The Candy Machine: How Cocaine Took over the World

Tom Feiling

In "The Candy Machine", writer, documentary-maker and former Colombia resident Tom Feiling illustrates the corrosive effect of cocaine traffic around the world. As the following extract shows, large-scale smuggling operations would be increasingly impossible without the collusion of law enforcement and Customs officials, whether in the supplying or receiving country. One can only assume this will continue as surveillance technologies improve.

The Cali cartel's effects on Mexican society have been touched on in chapter 6. Durango state official George Torres, for example, describes the situation in the state's jails such as that in Gomez Palacio as "a time bomb". In the state of Zacatecas the Gulf cartel broke into a jail in May 2009 and freed at least fifty inmates. Thousands have been killed in drug-related violence and president Felipe Calderon has set aside 40,000 troops to fight the cartels. The violence is down, purely and simply, to disputes for dominance, and its influence on wider Mexican and Caribbean society is further documented here . . .

In 2006, 492 metric tons of cocaine were impounded by law enforcement around the world. This was the second highest total ever seized after the 588 metric tons seized in 2004, which was in turn the fifth consecutive record-setting bust. If supply-side interdiction isn't working, it's clearly not for want of trying. Yet the United Nations says that the profit margin on sales of illegal drugs is so inflated that the authorities would have to intercept 75 per cent of the cocaine produced to have any serious impact on the viability of the illegal drugs business. Despite years of eye-wateringly large interdictions, current efforts intercept no more than 40 per cent of cocaine shipments.

Sir Keith Morris was the UK's ambassador to Colombia between 1990 and 1994, and his experience of the war on drugs as it has been conducted on Colombian soil has made him a trenchant critic of the very idea that supplies of cocaine can be effectively disrupted. Reflecting on the cocaine wars that gripped Colombia during his term, Sir Keith told me that "the war on drugs briefings that the Americans were pumping out were basically 'My God, we've got to go on . . .'

"It's a classic law enforcement thing around the world. They're always winning battles but losing the war, and needing more resources. When I discovered that HM Customs & Excise, God bless their cotton socks, had calculated that they were getting nine per cent of the cocaine or the heroin coming into the country. Nine per cent? Why nine per cent? You begin to realize that these things are so fictitious, in a way."

This is not to belittle the notable impact that some multinational operations have had on the cocaine business. Operation Purple was launched by the DEA to co-ordinate seizures of potassium permanganate, a widely used disinfecting agent which is also one of the precursor chemicals used in the manufacture of cocaine. The operation was effective in drying up supplies from Europe and the United States, but a lack of international co-operation has stymied a water-tight prohibition. Almost half of potassium permanganate shipments are destined for Asian and African countries that do not participate in Operation Purple. Once docked, these shipments can be diverted to Venezuela or Ecuador, where the lists of controlled substances are much shorter, and then smuggled into Colombia.

A British cocaine wholesaler told a Home Office prison survey that, prior to his arrest, he was buying and selling sixty kilograms of cocaine a week. He would buy from Colombian suppliers in Spain for £18,000 a kilo, and sell in the United Kingdom for

£22,000 a kilo. Once broken down into grams for retail sale, that kilo would most likely have netted him £50,000, but, like most importers, he preferred to sell in bulk. His consignment would then pass through several pairs of hands, with the profit being distributed along the way. The difference between the wholesale and retail price of cocaine in the UK is about the same as that of most legal agricultural crops. The trickiest part of the smuggling operation, and hence the most profitable, is getting it into the European Union in the first place. It accounts for the largest part of the 15,800 per cent mark-up in price enjoyed by a gram of cocaine between the laboratory in Colombia and its retail sale in the UK. By way of comparison, the difference in the price of coffee beans between source and sale is just 223 per cent.

The same Home Office survey of cocaine smugglers and wholesalers found that attempts to disrupt the supply of cocaine into the UK have had an impact on local markets and local prices, but not at a national level, and not enough to deter dealers or importers. A major importer told the survey that he had used drug "mules" to import cocaine from the Caribbean; he estimated that one in four of his couriers would not get through Customs. An international haulier who had been importing cocaine into the UK by road estimated that four out of ten of his consignments did not get through, but despite losing half of his merchandise, he was still able to keep a healthy balance sheet.

Most of those without a drug problem don't find it hard to get into the cocaine trade once they know a dealer, and are able to rise through the ranks once they have proven themselves to be honest and reliable. The more dealers, the more competition, which keeps prices down. The majority of dealers consider the risk of arrest to be low and the threat of imprisonment not a serious deterrent, but a low-risk occupational hazard. If they are arrested and convicted, they hand the business to a colleague while they serve their term. The only real threat comes when the police take action to seize the dealer's assets.

Importing drugs is always likely to be monopolized by those with ties to countries where drugs can be bought cheaply. Until recently, Jamaican groups were most prominent in importing cocaine, cooking it into crack, and then distributing it around the UK, because Jamaica is an ideal transit point for cocaine bound for Europe from Colombia.

But as more Europeans have developed a taste for cocaine, and more cocaine comes into the EU through Spanish and Dutch ports, there have been opportunities for other nationalities to become involved.

Four out of every ten drug dealers in British prisons were born outside the UK, and they hail from any one of thirty-four countries.

Up to 250 tons of cocaine enters the European Union every year. Some European wholesalers get their cocaine directly from Central American and Caribbean suppliers, and work in concert with Colombian and local traffickers to bring it home. Most of it is hidden aboard large container ships that ply the sea lanes between the Caribbean and Spain and Portugal. As the European market for cocaine has burgeoned in recent years, pressure on one link in the supply chain has sent Colombian smugglers scrambling for suitable entrepôts. These days, a third of Europe's cocaine comes via West African countries such as Ghana, Senegal and Guinea-Bissau. From West Africa cocaine can be flown to clandestine landing strips in Spain or Portugal, or smuggled aboard commercial shipping containers bound for Barcelona, Rotterdam or Antwerp. In many West African countries cocaine seizures have gone up six-fold in as many years. In Tema, Ghana, half a ton of cocaine was seized in January 2004; another half-ton load was seized in the capital, Accra, in November 2005 and 1.9 tons was seized off the Ghanaian coast in May 2006. Ghanaian police also recorded the continent's biggest ever cocaine bust that year, arresting the Ghanaian and Nigerian drivers of a van loaded with two tons of the drug concealed in boxes of fish. A ton was seized in Kenya in late 2004, three tons were seized off Cape Verde in February 2006 and in June of the same year, more than fourteen tons of a mixture of cocaine and white cement was seized in Lagos, Nigeria. African seizures still account for less than one per cent of global cocaine seizures, which suggests that only a tiny proportion of the cocaine transiting the African continent is actually intercepted. Karen Tandy, the former head of the DEA, has said that "Africa will become, in terms of a drugs hot-bed, one of our worst nightmares if we do not get ahead of that curve now." Intent on doing just that, in 2007 the UK led eight European nations in setting up a Maritime Analysis Operations Centre, a task force of navy, police and Customs officials to target cocaine traffic from Africa.

"Among the destitute locals are scores of wealthy, gaudy Colombian drug barons in their immodest cars, flaunting their hi-tech luxury lifestyle, with beautiful women on their arms," wrote a journalist in the *Observer*. He went on to describe how "the seizure of West Africa by Colombian and other drug cartels has happened with lightning speed." This po-faced depiction of hapless Africans at the behest of unscrupulous drugs traffickers was reiterated by the Executive Director of the United Nations Office on Drugs and Crime (UNODC), Antonio Maria Costa. "In the nineteenth century, Europe's hunger for slaves devastated West Africa. Two hundred years later, its growing appetite for cocaine could do the same. When I went to Guinea-Bissau, the drug wealth was everywhere. From the air, you can see that the Spanish hacienda villas and the obligatory black four-wheel-drives are everywhere, with the obligatory scantily clad girl, James Bond style. There were certain hotels I was advised not to stay in." Few locals have been privy to the view from the air that so appalled the head of the UNODC. But I would venture that many of them would regard it as an improvement on what their country looked like before the arrival of the drug barons. The average income in Guinea-Bissau is $600 a year. The barons' development plan for Guinea-Bissau may not tally with that of the United Nations, but which is more likely to alleviate the poverty its people live in?

I met a Cuban-American called Juan Pablo by chance while having a late-night drink in a cheap bar in the old part of Bogotá. When I told him that I was keen to talk to those with first-hand experience of the cocaine business, he gave me an indulgent wink, and pulled up a chair. "The factory is usually out in the suburbs," he told me. "It's a sweathouse, eight or ten people just sitting at tables and cutting up coke that's come in directly from the farms and the labs in the provinces.

"When I was last there $100 got you about 100 grams, and it's ninety-five per cent pure." Juan Pablo then told me how he went about smuggling the cocaine back to the United States. "You make it about grape size. Compact it as much as possible. Then you coat it with wax, wrap it two or three times in the plastic, dip it in the wax again, wrap it in the plastic again. You don't want it breaking open. That's trouble.

"Three and a half ounces is about fifteen grapes. Then you swallow them.

"Don't fly out of Colombia in any way, shape or form. I took the land border to Venezuela, and from there I flew to Guatemala. Eat guava seeds. They make you constipated. You don't want to be shitting on the plane. Every time I stopped, I shit, washed the grapes, took off the outer layer and replaced that. Then I swallowed them again, and flew to the United States. That's the nerve-racking one. Going through Customs, you've just got to wholeheartedly believe that you're not doing anything wrong. If you're not doing anything wrong, people don't think you're doing anything wrong. So you make yourself the typical asshole American. 'Fucking foreigners, I can't believe their customs. I had this bad thing happen to me, but now I'm home, thank God.' You know, acting friendly. They search your luggage. 'Oh sure, I understand, you're just doing your job.' And you get through.

"Then you really shit yourself, which comes out good anyway, because you know that you just pulled off something fucking major. I can buy a kilo here in Bogota for 1.5 million pesos, which is $700. That's probably $20,000 profit if you take it to the States, but that's when it gets dangerous. The key is not to get greedy. Swallowing 100 grapes is going to hurt, and there's a lot more chance that they'll rupture, but twelve grapes is just not that much to have in your stomach. Miami, South Beach, I sold it for about $50 to $70 a gram. That's a really nice little profit."

Juan Pablo was a lone drugs "mule". Most mules work for the smaller drug-smuggling operations, and are driven by cash not glory. Thirty tons of cocaine is thought to enter Europe on commercial flights every year. HM Revenue and Customs and the Ghanaian authorities set up Operation Westbridge in November 2006 to catch drug smugglers who were using Accra as a gateway to the UK. It covered the installation of surveillance equipment, X-ray machines, swab tests and urine tests. In November 2007, two teenagers were seized with nearly four kilos of cocaine ingested in around sixteen condoms, en route for London Gatwick. The boys, one aged sixteen and the other nineteen, were from Lithuanian families living in south London. As many as sixty mules are thought to arrive in Britain from West Africa every week; in 2007, a single flight from Ghana to Amsterdam was found to be carrying thirty-two drugs mules.

Since November 2006, Westbridge has seized 356 kg of cocaine, 2,275 kg of cannabis and 1.3 kg of heroin. These operations make good copy for press releases, but they are short-term measures. As soon as the British police left Accra airport, the traffickers were able to bribe the baggage handlers to take bags past the scanning machines and straight on to the planes bound for Europe. "We don't have sniffer dogs. We don't have enough scanners. It's all about profiling and gathering intelligence and we need the British to attain that, not just temporary assistance," a Ghanaian Customs officer said.

Westbridge followed the lead of Operation Airbridge, a UK-Jamaican initiative launched in 2002 to catch mules before they boarded planes from Jamaica. Airbridge was set up after police at London's Heathrow Airport found that twenty-five per cent of passengers arriving from Jamaica were carrying cocaine. Most mules are recruited from the poorest neighbourhoods of Kingston and the city's "dungles" (rubbish dumps and empty plots of land squatted by recent migrants from the countryside). Muling is also fuelled by the fact that a lot of Jamaicans who work for Colombian smugglers are paid in cocaine: since there is only a small local market for cocaine, it makes good commercial sense to pay a mule to carry the cocaine to New York or London, where there are Jamaicans willing to sell it and locals willing to buy it.

By 2002, 400 Jamaican women were serving sentences in British prisons for bringing cocaine into the UK. I met Sharon at the Kingston office of Hibiscus, an organization set up to help drug mules serving sentences in foreign prisons, most of whom are poor women duped into carrying drugs by unscrupulous traffickers. "I was a business person, buying footwear and clothing to sell in the market," she told me. "I wanted to get more money to put into the business to buy things to sell. I borrowed some money from the small loans office to upgrade, but unfortunately, the bigger stores were selling clothes cheaper than we could sell, and I couldn't make enough money to repay the loan. I had put my furniture and my TV up as collateral for the loan and the office was threatening to repossess them. Then a friend introduced me to a man who said that he could make me a loan to pay back the first. But I realized that he wasn't a loans man. He was a drugs man. He said that if I made a trip to the UK I could make more than I needed. I said I didn't want to take that chance. What if I go to prison? 'No man,' he said. 'You have a nice appearance. They won't stop and check you.' He was offering me £2,500. We went to a hotel in the resort area, and I swallowed about fifty pellets, about 200 grams of cocaine. But at the airport in England they checked the entire flight. They made us do a urine test and then an X-ray, and I got caught. The judge gave me five years."

When a mule carries cocaine to Britain, she might expect to be home in a couple of weeks. But if she is arrested, her children can spend up to five years without their mother. The luckier ones will be brought up by friends or relatives, but many children have to fend for themselves as "barrel children", dependent on the arrival of a barrel of goods from relatives overseas. Even if a drug mule evades detection, she faces other dangers: several cocaine couriers have died in London, after being ripped off and killed by traffickers or overdosing on cocaine when the condoms they were carrying ruptured.

"I got three years nine months in Cookham Prison in Kent, and me do half. One year, ten month and two week," a cocaine courier called Angela told me. "I went to prison and me seen nuff people who me know from Kingston. Me called the drug-men back in Kingston to tell them that they lock me up, and the person said 'We don't want to hear nothing from you. Your brother's going to go down for this, and when you come over to Jamaica, you're going to go down for it too.'

"The thing that was puzzling me brain was me children, sweating that they was going to kill them off. Me come in to Cookham on suicide watch, but me get work folding and packing textiles, and me find meself start a get happy. Me get £18 a week, and me save and me send money back home to give me children. But when I called my mother a couple of months later she said, 'It looks like the drugmen killed your brother Steve.' The year following, me return to Jamaica. Soon after, they light me house afire. Me didn't tarry, me just leave immediately, and ended up living in the burnt-down market by Harris Street. Me haffi wait till the people selling in the market pack up and gone by ten at night before me can go a bed and lay down. Me can't have me children around me – me go a bed a night time, and me don't know which part they are pon di road. Last week me look pon me mother and me say me sorry the judge never give me a bigger sentence, where me had somewhere comfortable to put down me head."

When the Colombian authorities cracked down on cocaine-smuggling through their seaports, traffickers started to move more cocaine through Venezuela to the Netherlands Antilles, a self-governing region of the Netherlands in the Caribbean whose people carry EU passports. In 2000, four tons of cocaine was seized at Amsterdam's Schipol International Airport. The Dutch authorities responded to the increase in muling from the Antilles by implementing a novel strategy that they termed "100 per cent Control".

Passengers were subject to extensive searches; when cocaine was found, it was confiscated, and the mule had his or her passport confiscated for up to three years. They were then deported, but not arrested. The authorities reasoned that the threat of incarceration in a European prison would be scant deterrent to potential drug mules, most of whom are desperate for money. But by increasing the rate at which the authorities intercepted cocaine shipments, they could make smuggling unprofitable. In 2003, eighty couriers were thought to pass through Schipol airport every day, but by 2005, this had been cut to just ten a month.

In response to these crack downs, smugglers have switched their tactics again. These days, mules are more likely to be British, Dutch or Spanish residents who get paid for the loan of their stomach and get a free holiday in the Caribbean to boot. The authorities are reluctant to admit it, but their airport interception efforts are also hampered by local corruption, as Humberto told me when we met to talk about his time as an anti-drugs police officer in Bogotá. "We infiltrated a group of eight guys who were trafficking cocaine out of the airport in Bogota. I'd filmed the whole thing, and one day my boss asked to look at the tapes. I thought he was straight, so I handed them over, but he erased everything I'd shot, so when we went to the public prosecutor with the case, we found that we had no evidence. Then the smugglers started sending funeral wreaths to my house. Who had the address of my house? I ended up working up the case by myself. In the end their operation was busted, and the traffickers were charged with smuggling 360 kilos of cocaine through the airport. My boss, who'd protected their operation right the way through, got a medal. I just got more funeral wreaths."

In 2007, the Jamaicans declared, "yet another significant victory in the war against drugs," when the British Navy seized twelve bales of cocaine, said to be worth almost £50 million. In June 2008, a headline in the *Daily Telegraph* ran: "Prince William set for showdown with drugs baron on Royal Navy patrol in Caribbean." Despite these flourishes of bombast, in reality cocaine shipments heading north across the Caribbean have been diverted, rather than diminished, by law enforcement. Traffickers have learnt to evade interception by leap-frogging from island to island. Puerto Rican authorities seized a record ten tons of cocaine in 1998; Jamaica seized a record 3.7 tons in 2002; the following year it was the turn of the Dutch Antilles, where the authorities seized a record nine tons, and the Bahamas, which seized a record 4.3 tons. The Dominican Republic has become a command, control and communications centre for cocaine movement through the Caribbean, used to store cocaine before onward shipment to Puerto Rico and the United States.

Much of the construction business in the Dominican capital Santo Domingo is believed to be financed by drug money as a way of laundering revenue. Nearly all of the cocaine entering the Dominican Republic comes over the mountains from Haiti, its neighbour to the west.

The focus on supply-side interception is not only ineffectual; it is also destructive. As the North American market for cocaine took off in the early 1980s, Colombian traffickers cast around for a base in the Caribbean through which they could move their product.

Jamaica quickly became one of the main transhipment points for cocaine between Colombia and the United States. The island lies 550 miles north of the Colombian coast and 550 miles south-west of Miami. Consignments could be flown from clandestine airstrips on the north coast of Colombia to Jamaica, where the planes were refuelled for the second leg up to Miami. With the help of their British counterparts, the Jamaican authorities responded by building a radar station to track aircraft coming into Jamaican airspace. So the traffickers switched from air to sea. Kingston wharf is the biggest trans-shipment port in the Caribbean, full of ships bound for ports all over the world. The Americans have installed container-scanning equipment at great cost, but the cocaine trade is driven by poverty and a disdain for legal niceties that no amount of machinery can entirely quash. The port has plenty of low-paid dockhands and security guards keen to supplement their wages by smuggling cocaine on to the container ships.

Colombian traffickers also began to move their product in "go-fast" boats that they stole from Caribbean and Latin American ports. "Big Colombian speed fucking boats," Jah Runnings told me, gesturing from the bright blue sea to the little coastal village of Bluefields where he lives. "It usually come in at Crab Pond Point up there, two times a month. Big raas clot engine, you understand me? They're very fast they let off and they go. The coastguard is in Montego Bay and Negril, but they're not in their channel. Sometimes they intercept, but not all the while. In 2000, a Jamaica Defence Force helicopter intercepted one of the boats, but they didn't find any cocaine. They'd thrown it overboard, stashed it down the road. They've been doing it for years." The go-fast boats are typically stripped of all but their cargo and fuel tanks, run red at sixty knots an hour and are abandoned once they make land. Jamaica's 600 miles of coastline has plentiful mangrove swamps to hide boats in and see few patrols by the authorities. The Jamaican government recently bought three new go-fasts, at a cost of £750,000 a piece. Until 2005, Jamaica's Marine Unit was completely dependent on the six or seven worn-out boats that they were able to recover from cocaine smugglers every year, which they then refitted as police boats. The new boats provide a visual deterrent, but in private officials admit that the entire Jamaican police force would have to be put to sea for the authorities to stand any chance of stopping the go-fasts from getting through.

According to Jah Runnings, the main suppliers of the cocaine that came through Jamaica were Colombian paramilitaries formerly affiliated to the Autodefensas Unidas de Colombia (United Self-Defence Forces of Colombia), but he was understandably hazy about the details. "Colombians mostly stay up in Montego Bay, Ocho Rios.

"They're so sceptic, they live indoors, so you don't know them. Those guys are real mafia, they're hard to study, you know? You can't mess with those guys. They'll kill you. The big Jamaican dons work along with the Colombian dons, but the Colombians are the more don because they have the merchandise." Jah Runnings explained that Colombian suppliers employ locals to unload the boats, stockpile the drugs and send them out again from the north coast of the island, usually bound for the Bahamas. "My friend used to work with the Colombians, unloading the boats on to big trucks. He got $750,000 Jamaican [*about £5,300*] for taking 1,500 kilos from Colombia to here. A two-day run. It's small money, man. They'd have a couple of guys drive along with them to clear the way up to Montego Bay. From there it leaves to America and England, or sometimes to Cayman Islands, and link from there. Then one time, the boat come in, but intercept by the coastguard, so they take off the drugs and come hide it up in the bush. A bale of cocaine went missing, so they come back and killed my friend. Shoot him three times in his head."

Before going to Kingston, I had read that sixty-four per cent of Jamaicans believe crime to be the most pressing problem facing the country. I wanted to find out what impact the cocaine trade had had on the island and to what extent it was responsible for Jamaica's notoriously high crime rate. Things had got so bad that in 2004, Jamaica's Minister of Tourism warned that violent crime threatened to derail the island's tourism industry. In 2005, the Minister of National Security, Peter Phillips, spoke of "a criminal elite whose activities are centred on the illegal trade in drugs, which constitute the tap root of violent crime in Jamaica". Five years previously, Phillips had put the soaring crime rate down to "narco-terrorism". The Minister had requested assistance from "friendly countries with experience in fighting urban terrorism", and ordered in armoured cars of the type the British pioneered for use on the streets of Belfast.

[. . .] The most famous drug smuggler of all time must be Pablo Escobar, the founder of the Medellín cartel. But the cocaine-smuggling business has changed beyond recognition since Escobar's day. "In the mid-1980s, Miami was the focal point for all the drugs coming in from Colombia," a former smuggler called Christian told me. "The Medellín cartel started the whole thing of flying it in on little Cessna planes, throwing it in the water, and picking it up in speedboats." Cocaine is still flown over the US–Mexico border in light aircraft. In one case, a road-building crew in Texas had to make a dash for cover when a quick-thinking smuggler decided to use their freshly laid tarmac as a landing strip. But once the Americans were able to monitor flights over the Caribbean Sea effectively, most traffickers stopped using light aircraft, and these days only a tenth of the cocaine entering the United States comes in by air. "When the US government started cracking down, we started using alternative routes, like Haiti," Christian told me. "The Cali cartel took it to the next level, made it more like a corporation, sending it in by the ton on boats. All the Colombian ships were being searched up and down in the port of Miami, so they'd ship it to another country and bring it in on a Panamanian ship or a Guatemalan ship. We were hiding the stuff in concrete statues, or dissolving two or three kilos in water, soaking it into businessmen's suits, then drying them out and bringing it in that way. We were doing it the same way in plastic pipes."

By 2004, ninety per cent of the US's cocaine wasn't even coming through the Caribbean. It was coming through Mexico. The movement of cocaine through Mexico has been the source of some of the biggest fortunes yet accumulated in the history of cocaine smuggling, and the cause of bitter fighting between the country's rival trafficking cartels.

Now the Mexican army is waging a war on those cartels that overshadows even the bloody cocaine wars that gripped Colombia in the 1980s. Over 2,400 Mexicans were killed in drug-related violence in 2007. By December 2008, a further 5,600 people had been killed and the death toll looks set to go still higher in 2009.

Luis Rodriguez, the former gang member I had met in Los Angeles, told me how Mexico had become so important to the traffickers. "The DEA made big efforts to destroy the trade routes through Florida, and the Colombians started to think, 'Well, let's go through Mexico.'

"At first, the Colombians didn't want to go through Mexico, because it had some of the oldest smuggling organizations on the continent, and they'd have to pay all these old drug lords who had been there for a long time. Back then, they had mainly been growing marijuana, but I used to go to Mexico to pick up heroin too. In the nineties, there was collaboration between the Mexican cartels and the Colombian cartels, and the business became very lucrative and very violent."

There are several ways of getting cocaine from Colombia to the border between Mexico and the United States. A third of America's cocaine comes overland from Central America. A quarter comes directly from Colombia's Pacific coast ports like Tumaco and Buenaventura to Mexico's Pacific ports before it is smuggled north to the border. Another quarter leaves Colombia's Caribbean ports like Turbo, Santa Marta and Cartagena, hugging the coastline of Nicaragua and Honduras, before reaching ports on the Gulf of Mexico. The scale of the shipments is staggering. In 2000, Colombian police seized a 100-foot submarine from a warehouse near Bogota. Had it ever set to sea, it would have been capable of carrying ten-ton loads of cocaine, with a retail value of $500 million per load. In October 2007, Mexican police intercepted eleven tons of cocaine in the port of Tampico. The following month, they seized a ship carrying twenty-three tons of the drug in the Pacific port of Manzanillo. Had it been sold in grams in the United States, the shipment would have been worth well over $1 billion.

The United States border with Mexico runs from San Ysidro, California, to Brownsville, Texas, a distance of almost 2,000 miles. At the side of the main road leading into the Mexican border city of Nuevo Laredo from the south stand two giant concrete skeletons wrapped in cloaks, with sickles in their hands. Behind them are several simple chapels, filled with candles, beer cans, packets of cigarettes, and other offerings to La Santa Muerte (Holy Death), the cult of Mexico's criminals and smugglers. Nuevo Laredo is the Mexican half of the Texan city of Laredo. Six thousand trucks cross the border at Laredo every day, making the city the single busiest crossing point for trade between the two countries. Once over the border, the trucks follow highway I-35 up to Dallas, and from there fan out across the United States. They carry 40 per cent of Mexico's exports, worth almost a billion dollars a day.

The gargantuan volume of legal commerce also makes Laredo the single most important point of entry for illegal drugs into the United States. Americans consume roughly 290 metric tons of cocaine a year. Imported in bulk, this load could be carried across the US–Mexican border in just thirteen trucks. Instead, it seeps in in thousands of ingenious disguises: dissolved in polystyrene and turned into pet bedding, sewn into children's nappies, or smuggled inside pineapples. Very often such complicated chicanery isn't even necessary: most of America's cocaine crosses the border hidden in private vehicles.

The shift to overland smuggling through Mexico is hugely problematic for the authorities trying to intercept cocaine shipments bound for the United States. Smugglers need to be able to lose themselves and their precious cargoes in a crowd, and the isthmus of Central America allows them to do just that. One of the reasons for the huge profitability of smuggling through Mexico is that the chances of being intercepted are so slim. The Colombian cartels had originally brought their Mexican counterparts onboard as transporters and smugglers, but the smuggling routes running north through Central America to the border with the United States proved so profitable that Mexican trafficking groups were able to charge the Colombians fifty per cent of the value of a shipment for running a consignment through their country. This was quite a rise from the twenty per cent that the Colombian cartels were accustomed to paying Dominican and Puerto Rican smugglers when the bulk of the trade moved through the Caribbean.

But the new arrangement suited the Colombians, as many of them were facing extradition to the United States to stand trial for importing cocaine, and were happy to delegate the riskiest part of their operations to Mexican organizations.

The Mexican groups used their newfound leverage to build distribution networks of their own in the United States, relegating their Colombian suppliers to the role of wholesalers. They branched out from cities like Chicago and Detroit into the suburbs and the small towns beyond. In their wake, street gangs like the Gangster Disciples, the Vice Lords and the Latin Kings have formed new chapters in cities like Chicago, Cleveland and Detroit. Luis Rodriguez gave me an example. 'There's a family called the Herreras. They were from Mexico but they ended up in Chicago. When the Mexican cartels started controlling the business, the Herreras brought in a lot of drugs for the Chicago gangs, both Afro-American and Latino. In Los Angeles, the Mexican Mafia started making connections with the Mexican cartels, and brought in a lot of drugs from Mexico, which gave them more street credibility. Then all the gangs became drug-dealing organizations. Now the Guatemalan, Honduran and Salvadorean gangs are trying to get into taking cocaine through Mexico and into the United States. As a result of this westwards shift from the Caribbean to Mexico, even the cocaine users of Miami, where nearly all of the cocaine for the American market used to come ashore, are now supplied from Mexico.

The weakness of the economy is a big driver of the cocaine business in Mexico, as it is in the United States and Jamaica. The devaluation of the peso after the financial crash of 1994, and the introduction of the North American Free Trade Agreement (NAFTA) the same year, forced thousands of Mexican farmers to sell up. Farming families have been pulled in opposite directions. Sons have crossed the border with the United States illegally to work as gardeners, kitchen porters and fruit pickers in California and other southern states. Daughters are often to be found working hundreds of miles away, in one of the thousands of *maquiladoras,* the assembly plants that sprang up along the border after 1994 to produce goods for the US market.

The invasion and occupation of Iraq might have dominated newspaper headlines in the United States for the past five years, but domestic politics in 2007 were notable for rising hostility towards Mexican immigrants. There have been calls for a 2,000-mile-long wall to be built along the border to keep them out. Groups of vigilante Minutemen patrol the border on the look-out for illegal migrants. In border cities such as El Paso-Ciudad Juarez, as much as fifteen per cent of the population is living in the United States illegally, and many of them have suffered at the hands of officers from the US border patrol.

Many border town residents would doubtless argue that whatever their political differences, the economies of states north and south of the border are interdependent. For the businessmen of the United States to demand cheap labour, only for its politicians to score points by penalizing those who supply it, is senseless.

This is the backdrop to the rise of cocaine smuggling in Mexico, and explains why, despite the united front presented by the US and Mexican governments, in private, many Mexicans are reluctant to follow the United States' line on the war on drugs. Their scepticism finds expression in the *narcocorridos,* which offer a version of events at odds with the grandstanding of authorities on both sides of the border. The *corrido* is a genre of polka that became popular in Mexico over a hundred years ago. To the sound of the tuba and the accordion, the *corrido* singer would relate his stories of village feuds, the lives of the migrant labourers who worked the fields of California and the women they left behind when they headed north. After the Dry Law *[the National Prohibition Act, or Volstead Act]* made alcohol illegal in the United States in 1919, *corridos prohibidos* (forbidden ballads) were written about the tequila smugglers and their outfoxing of US border patrol officers. One is the "Corrido de los Bootleggers", written in 1935, which includes the verse: "The crop has given us nothing / There's nothing else to say / Now the best harvest / is the one the barrels give us." Another includes the lines: "Here in San Antonio / and its surroundings / they never catch the bootleggers / only those who work for them."

Mexico has been producing and smuggling drugs into the United States since the late nineteenth century. Today the trade is bigger than ever. A large part of the heroin distributed in the United States is made in Mexico. Shutting down *[meth]*amphetamine laboratories in the United States has only displaced them south of the border, where they are even harder to locate, so Mexico also produces most of the methamphetamine consumed north of the border. In 2005, Mexico produced more than 10,000 tons of cannabis, making it the world's second largest marijuana producer. Incredibly, around thirty per cent of Mexico's farmland is believed to be sown with either marijuana or opium poppies.

Alcohol and marijuana are widely consumed in Mexico, but until recently, most Mexicans regarded the drug that smugglers like to call "cola without the cola" with great suspicion. Cocaine smugglers met with the disapproval of the *corrido* singers, many of whose songs warned of the consequences of dabbling in what was regarded as a strictly gringo vice. The *narcocorridos* are a graphic illustration of how Mexican attitudes to cocaine have changed over the past fifteen years. Walk into any of the many record shops in downtown Los Angeles that cater to Mexican-Americans, and you can see how the *corridos prohibidos* have been revived and radicalized by large-scale cross-border cocaine smuggling.

The most famous singer of *narcocorridos* is Rosalino "Chalino" Sanchez. In the early 1990s, Chalino migrated from a hill village in the northern state of Sinaloa, where the Mexican drug-smuggling tradition is strongest, to Los Angeles (where the American drug-taking tradition is strongest). Until Chalino came along, Mexicans born in California had usually taken their cultural cues from the native urban culture, listening to West Coast hip-hop and dressing like their black neighbours. Chalino was a reserved, stubborn man with a reedy voice, but his celebration of the exploits of a new generation of drug smugglers struck a chord with West Coast Latinos. They found Chalino's stories of how a cocaine trafficker evaded detection, made a fortune, and went back to his village to build himself a house with a pool, cheering. If the trafficker then paid for a school to be built, he got added kudos for doing what the Mexican government had all too often failed to do.

Thanks to Chalino, Los Angelinos started to dress like Sinaloan drug traffickers. Out went the hip-hop gear, in came wide belts with engraved plate-metal buckles, lizard-skin boots and frilled jackets.

This is not to say that drug smuggling became cool. To understand the *narcocorridos,* or the American offshoot of hip-hop known as "crack music", as celebrations of criminality misses the point. Most of the young Mexican-Americans in the audience at a Chalino gig knew next to nothing about smuggling, but they responded to his *narcocorridos* because he didn't apologise for being a village-born Mexican.

What Chalino celebrated was not the drugs trade, but the power the drugs trade has given to the powerless. For Mexicans who have had little choice but to leave their own country to work as second-class citizens in the United States, cocaine is the hero of the piece. It has given Mexicans something that Americans are happy to pay good money for, something that miraculously *gains* rather than loses value when it crosses the border.

In 1992, Chalino Sanchez was shot and killed after a gig in Culiacán, the state capital of Sinaloa. Following his death, the *narcocorrido* genre that he had pioneered went stellar. It remains big business to this day and *narcocorrido* singers have gone on to appropriate elements from gangsta rap, posing with bazookas and AK-47s on the covers of albums that sport titles like "*Mi Oficio es Matar*" ("Killing is My Business"). As the cartels have become more powerful and their violence more extravagant, the distinction between commentator and apologist has gradually been lost, with lethal consequences for the singers of *narcocorridos*. Valentin Elizalde's "*A Mis Enemigos*" ("To My Enemies") became the signature tune of Sinaloa's drug-smuggling cartel, a tribute that rebounded in 2006, when gunmen from the rival Gulf cartel shot and killed Elizalde. In many cities of the United States, the authorities have asked radio stations not to play *narcocorridos*. The DEA has reportedly trailed the composers of the songs, as they have the composers of crack music. In some cases they have even taken singer-songwriters to court, charging them with complicity in the drug-smuggling offences they describe in their *corridos*.

Some of today's *narcocorridos* certainly celebrate the exploits of drugs-traffickers, but most offer a more nuanced interpretation of the smuggling life, one more inclined towards the tragic than the epic.

"*Los Tres de la Sierra*" by Los Norteños de Ojinaga, for example, includes the lines: "You damned Americans don't know what we go through / To get you the drugs you like so much." Drug dealers can be simultaneously proud and ashamed of their actions, a sentiment apparent in much of the music about the drugs trade on both sides of the border. In border cities like El Paso-Ciudad Juárez, where drug smuggling is pervasive, most traffickers do not regard themselves as criminals, anti-heroes or victims of poverty, but as regular citizens trying to make a living. The services they provide may be welcomed and reviled in equal parts, but this contradiction, as familiar to the migrant as it is to the smuggler, is one that many residents see as just part of the rough-hewn fabric of border town life. Many have attitudes akin to those of the illegal poachers in Africa described by James Siegel. "If a poor schmuck who is a subsistence hunter has bad luck outside a park area and then crosses into the national park hoping for better luck, he knows that he is breaking some central government law, but he doesn't see himself as a poacher *per se*. The common person sees the game warden as some stupid policeman for the state, not looking out for the community's interest at all. It becomes a game of cat and mouse, a silly and destructive contest."

Although there are nearly a dozen drug-trafficking organizations in Mexico, four are especially powerful. The biggest cartel is el Sindicato, the Sinaloa cartel, which is run by Joaquín "el Chapo" Guzmán. The Sinaloa cartel operates cells in Guatemala, Nicaragua and El Salvador, and its leaders have also established a presence in Colombia and Peru. Mexico's second largest cocaine-smuggling organization is the Gulf cartel, though its influence is on the wane. Its current *capo* is Osiel Cárdenas, who runs the business from the maximum-security La Palma prison near Mexico City. The Tijuana cartel, whose home city lies over the border from San Diego, California, has been run by the Arellano Félix family for many years, but its leaders are currently in prison in the United States, and it too is losing ground to the Sinaloa cartel. The fourth major drugs-trafficking organization is the Juárez cartel, based in El Paso-Ciudad Juárez.

Mexico's current wave of cocaine trafficking-related violence began when Osiel Cárdenas, the leader of the Gulf cartel, bribed his way out of a maximum security prison in 2001. He then bought himself an elite army regiment, known as the Zetas. This is not as hard to do as it might sound. Between 1994 and 2000, 114,000 conscripts deserted the Mexican army, and the cartels pay former soldiers much better wages than most legal employers. The Zetas were once a division of the GAFE (Grupo Aeromóbil de Fuerzas Especiales) *[Special Forces Airborne Group]*, where it is believed they received training in weaponry, intelligence-gathering and surveillance techniques from the United States Army, before being sent to the border to combat drug trafficking. With the Gulf cartel's recruitment of the Zetas, acts of brutality usually not seen outside Colombia have become standard business practice for the Mexican cartels. Members of rival organizations have been tortured, executed and their corpses burnt in barrels. Severed heads have been set on stakes in front of public buildings and in one especially horrifying incident, the heads of five rival soldiers were sent rolling across the dance-floor of a nightclub in Michoacán.

In 2005, the ranks of the Zetas were augmented by soldiers from the Guatemalan Kaibiles, one of the most gruesome military forces in all Latin America, responsible for many of the massacres of civilians committed during Guatemala's thirty-six-year civil war. Inter-cartel violence has reached such levels that even in cities like Monterrey – one of the most affluent and, until 2006, one of the safest cities in Mexico – people talk of children's birthday parties having to be protected with metal detectors, and of security guards hired to inspect the guests' presents for explosives.

Former DEA agent Celerino Castillo III was a key witness of the cocaine-Contra affair. He has become a keen observer of the drugs war since retiring to his border hometown of McAllen, Texas. He told me how extreme violence and good pay were drawing increasing numbers of mercenaries into the conflict. "A few months ago, thirty US Iraq veterans came through from all over the country. They had just got out of the Army. They'd had two or three tours of Iraq so they're fucked up already, suffering from post-traumatic stress disorder. All they want to do is kill, so they just go out looking for a bullet with their name on it. They were hired by the Mexican government to kill members of the cartels. They went down there, and they got into big fire-fights. Every single one of them was killed and buried somewhere in Mexico. Now they've got another fifty going down."

In July 2005, explosions and gunfire rocked downtown Nuevo Laredo's main shopping complex as drug traffickers spent half an hour battling each other with machine guns and grenade-launchers. The Gulf and Sinaloa cartels were fighting for control of the Nuevo Laredo *plaza*, a term that refers not to the city's main square, but to a cartel's right to smuggle drugs through a city. Since anything the security forces did that might have benefited one side would only have made them the target of the other, they did nothing. The laws against drug trafficking might just as well not have existed.

To defend such a lucrative business, traffickers have to be able to resort to terrific violence when necessary. The ability to dispense violence is an intrinsic part of running any illegal business that is both highly profitable and highly criminalized. Such lucrative cargoes, transiting such poor countries, generate fierce competition. Being illegal, and therefore unbound by any legally enforceable contract, that competition can all too easily turn vicious. Eliminating rivals and reaping the benefits can be preferable to dividing up territory and settling for less. Much of the violence of the cocaine trade through Mexico is caused by the fight for the right to run drugs through key border cities like Tijuana, Nogales, Ciudad Juárez and Nuevo Laredo.

In the late 1990s, when the Tijuana cartel and the Juárez cartel were battling for dominance of Mexico's drugs trade, one of their main battlegrounds was Ciudad Juárez, and their war generated the same violence and corruption seen in Nuevo Laredo today. Ciudad Juárez is still a dangerous city, but nothing like it was when control of the drugs trade was being disputed. *[Not that anyone knows for sure whether the epidemic of murders of young women in the city has abated, or even the total number of killings, which have occurred among the poorest, most dispossessed and anonymous. Numerous theories have been advanced featuring serial killers or orgies of copycat killings, covered comprehensively in* Daughters of Juárez *by Teresa Rodriquez. Whether or not they involve members of the drugs trade, they would probably not have happened without the lawlessness it has engendered.]*

Violence is also the product of personal vendettas between traffickers, who strike at each other's organizations to avenge the murders of family members or close associates. Once these reprisals get underway, they can quickly spiral out of control. The fight between the Gulf and Sinaloa cartels is a good example: Osiel Cárdenas was allegedly responsible for the murder of Chapo Guzmán's brother, and Guzmán's vengefulness set off a chain reaction of retaliatory killings.

Employees in the drug economy can only pray that they escape the violence. Some pray to Catholic saints, others to La Santa Muerte or Jesus Malverde, the patron saint of smugglers. Malverde was a railroad worker who was hanged in 1909 in

Culiacán, the Mexican city most associated with the drugs business, after making a name for himself by robbing the rich to give to the poor. He has since become a sacred guide for all those skirting the edges of the law. The Roman Catholic Church doesn't recognize him as anything of the sort, but that has not diminished the esteem in which the "narco-saint" is held.

"This is not an easy task, nor will it be fast," Mexican President Felipe Calderón told an assembly of army officers shortly after assuming office in December 2006. "It will take a long time, requiring the use of enormous resources and even, unfortunately, the loss of human lives." In October 2007, US President George W. Bush offered President Calderón a $1.5 billion aid package to help his government in its struggle with the drugs traffickers over the next three years. There would be funding for a witness protection programme, sophisticated scanning equipment to be installed at the border crossings, and $500 million for transport and surveillance planes. This was in addition to the $7 billion that Mexico planned to spend on "security measures" over the following three years. Bush and Calderón's package still needs the approval of their respective Congresses, and is currently mired in Washington. Even if their aid package is approved, the Americans know that they can't count on the Mexicans to give them the kind of compliance they get from the Colombian government. For much of the 1990s, Mexico refused Washington's offers of assistance in tackling the cartels, and Calderón won't allow the United States armed forces, military advisers or private contractors to carry out operations on Mexican soil.

So for the time being at least, the Americans are dependent on the Mexican army and police to do the fighting. This reliance brings other problems. Violence might be the most eye-catching aspect of the drugs trade, but by and large it is only used when local officials and policemen won't accept the cartels' bribes. The drugs trade works so well in countries like Jamaica and Mexico because all too often the very people charged with fighting the drugs trade are corrupted by drugs money. In 2002, a corruption scandal in Tijuana revealed that key officials charged with fighting the traffickers, including the city's police chief and the assistant state attorney-general, were in the pay of the Tijuana cartel. In 2005, prosecutors charged twenty-seven state, federal and city police officers in Cancún with running a drugs ring and murdering fellow officers. That year, the efforts of the city police in Nuevo Laredo were so corrupted by collusion with gangsters that the Mexican government suspended the city's entire police force and sent in the federal police to patrol the streets. Forty-one city policemen were later arrested for attacking the federal police when their units arrived in the city. Even with the city police in handcuffs, the federal police had no impact on the violence in Nuevo Laredo.

The number of drug-related killings actually rose, as once again the delicate balance of power between the Gulf and Sinaloa cartels was upended. The connections between police and criminals run so deep that many cartels have come to be seen as franchises of the Mexican police, and vice versa. To counter police corruption, the Mexican government has become more dependent on the army to go after the *capos*. But as soldiers have joined the front line, they too have succumbed to bribery. In 2002, more than 600 members of the Mexican army's 65th infantry battalion were found to have been protecting opium poppy and marijuana crops. Corruption was so pervasive that the authorities dissolved the entire battalion.

According to a report by Transparency International, an international non-governmental organization that monitors corruption around the world, Mexican judges are also particularly susceptible to bribery by drug traffickers. It cited a case from 2004, in which a group of eighteen hit men from the Sinaloa cartel was detained by soldiers in Nuevo Laredo. They were found to be carrying twenty-eight long guns, two short guns, 223 cartridges, 10,000 rounds of ammunition, twelve grenade launchers, and eighteen hand grenades, yet Judge Gómez Martínez set them free, ruling that they were innocent of charges of involvement with organized crime. A judge in Guadalajara, Amado López Morales, decided that Héctor Luis "El Güero" Palma, one of Mexico's best-known drug traffickers, was in fact an "agricultural producer", despite the fact that he too had been detained in possession of a battery of weapons.

Another memorable judge is Humberto Ortega Zurita from the southern state of Oaxaca. In 1996, he presided over the case of two men detained in a car with six kilos of cocaine. The judge absolved them, declaring that no one could be sure that the cocaine was theirs. Hearing a case of a woman who had been stopped on a bus with three kilos of cocaine taped to her stomach, Ortega Zurita ordered that she be set free because "she did not carry the drugs consciously". Shortly afterwards, Judge Ortega Zurita "committed suicide", by stabbing himself several times in the heart.

There have even been allegations that the Catholic Church in Mexico has accepted contributions from drug traffickers. In 2005, Ramón Godinez, the bishop of the central state of Aguascalientes, caused uproar when he conceded that donations from traffickers were not unusual, but argued that it was not the Church's responsibility to investigate the source of donations. "Just because the origin of the money is bad doesn't mean you have to burn it," the bishop said. "Instead, you have to transform it." He insists that the money was "purified" once it passed through the doors of his church. In considering how best to tackle the cocaine trade, Bush and Calderón neglected to address the fundamental corruptibility of Mexico's institutions of state. They would have done well to heed the warning intoned by Mexico's biggest *narcocorrido* group, Los Tigres del Norte: "Don't waste your money buying more radars / or tearing up my landing strips / I'm a nocturnal bird / that can land in any cornfield / And besides, the day I fall / plenty in high places will fall with me."

Since the earliest days of the drugs business in Mexico, official reports have linked drug traffickers to high-ranking politicians, who have long been suspected of being directly involved in the illegal trade and even of controlling it. The monolith il Partido Revolucionario Institucional (PRI) ruled Mexico from 1928 until 2000, a reign quite unprecedented in what was, in name at least, a democracy. Under the PRI, politicians, police and intelligence agencies regulated, controlled and contained the drugs trade, as they did all aspects of business, protecting certain drug-trafficking groups from the law and mediating conflicts between them. To persist in seeing a neat division between legal state, society and economy, and illegal drugs cartels, counting on the former to support a war on the latter, is naive. The only governments that have ever been able to suppress the drugs trade effectively have been extremely authoritarian: the anti-drugs efforts of China and the Soviet Union spring to mind.

An anonymous PRI official's lament to a journalist from the *Washington Post* illustrates the point well. "In the old days, there were rules," he told a reporter. "We'd say, 'you can't kill the police, we'll send in the army'. We'd say, 'you can't steal thirty Jeep Cherokees a month. You can only steal five.'" Impunity was granted to certain cartels, while others were persecuted to satisfy the politicians in Washington. In return, the cartels ensured a steady flow of cash remittances from abroad, and financed the election campaigns of prominent PRI politicians. One such grandee was Mario Ernesto Villanueva, who is currently serving a thirty-five-year prison sentence for cocaine smuggling. Between 1993 and 1999, while he was governor of the southern state of Quintana Roo, Villanueva helped the Juárez cartel smuggle between seventeen and twenty-seven tons of cocaine a month through his state.

The Gulf cartel rose and fell with the fortunes of Raul Salinas, the elder brother of Mexico's then-president Carlos Salinas. Raul is suspected of shielding the cartel's former head, Juan Garcia Abrego, and his takings from the cocaine business, estimated to run to more than £5 billion a year. Raul Salinas is thought to have made at least £500 million in the six years that his brother was president, though no wrong-doing on his part has ever been established.

For as long as anyone could remember, this collusion between Mexico's politicians and criminals was a fait accompli, but as the PRI began to lose political power, culminating in its defeat in the presidential elections of 2000, its grip on the smuggling business slackened. The election of Vicente Fox of the Partido Accion Nacional (PAN) as president in 2000 was hailed as a turning point in Mexico's development as a democracy. For years, the DEA had been telling the Mexican authorities that the root of the problem was the cartels and the official protection they enjoyed. Since the election of Vicente Fox as president in 2000, the Mexican authorities have arrested more than 36,000 drug traffickers, including senior members of nearly all the cartels.

Fox was determined to reassure the Americans that he would be a dependable partner in their war on the drugs trade. Fox also wanted to show Mexicans that the cartel s could and would be brought to book. He raised the military's profile in the anti-drug effort, gave more top soldiers positions in the judiciary, and extradited traffickers to face justice in US courts. Fox also made several valiant attempts to purge law enforcement agencies of corrupt officials, most notably the Agencia Federal de Investigación (AFI), the Mexican version of the CIA. Since its creation in 2001, more than 800 AFI agents have been investigated for drug trafficking, extortion, kidnapping, torture and murder.

Vicente Fox had swept aside the corrupt but cosy web spun by the PRI, but he failed to create a workable alternative. This became clear in the course of 2006, Fox's last year in office, when drug-related violence skyrocketed. Targeting the *capos* left a power vacuum; suddenly drug-trafficking corridors and territories worth billions of dollars were up for grabs, which the *capos'* lieutenants rushed to secure. The ensuing struggle for control unleashed terrible violence, which rival cartels vied to exploit and Fox's successors have proven unable to put an end to. The problem is that aggressive drug enforcement only increases the violence it purports to put an end to. Yet such is the authorities' faith in the law and its enforcement that they see the disputes that their policies give rise to as a positive development, however counter-productive they prove to be.

The abject failure of Mexico's anti-drug policies has yet to be fully addressed because the truth about the drugs trade has been kept hidden. The complicity of Mexican police officers, judges and politicians and their corruption by the illegal trade in drugs are rarely discussed in public because the cartels bribe and intimidate journalists, much as they do the police and public officials. In both Colombia and Mexico, "to disappear" has become a transitive verb, not something you do, but something that other people do to you. Those who don't toe the line laid down by the cartels face execution. As a result, Mexico is second only to Iraq as the most dangerous country in the world in which to work as a journalist. In 2006, nine Mexican journalists were murdered and three were disappeared. The following year was worse.

In February 2007, gunmen opened fire on the staff of the daily *El Mañana* in Nuevo Laredo, seriously wounding one person. Two journalists were killed in March for covering stories about the cocaine trade. In July, traffickers kidnapped Rafael Ortiz Martínez of the daily *Zócalo* in Moclova, a town in the northern state of Coahuila, after he reported on drug smuggling in the region. In August, Enrique Perea Quintanilla, editor of the monthly *Dos Caras, Una Verdad,* was shot dead in the northern state of Chihuahua after the Juárez cartel put a contract out on his life. In November, Misael Tamayo Hernández of the daily El *Despertar de La Costa* was found dead in a motel in the southern state of Guerrero, having been killed by a lethal injection.

Later that month, Roberto Marcos García, deputy editor of the weekly *Testimonio* in the eastern state of Veracruz, another drug-trafficking centre, was shot dead in the street.

In the climate of self-censorship that these killings have created, anyone hoping that the truth might make the light of day would have been heartened by an advertisement which appeared in a Mexico City daily in May 2006. It described the Gulf cartel's army of Zetas as "narco-kidnappers and murderers of women and children", who had bought protection from agents in the Mexican Attorney-General's office. Unfortunately, the only person with the money and the courage to place the ad was Edgar "La Barbie" Valdez, the head of the Negros.

To counter the terror tactics of the Zetas, the Sinaloa cartel had raised its own army, known as the Negros. They had responded in kind, bribing police and other public officials, killing those who would not be bought, and waging a bloody street war with the Zetas.

Vicente Fox was succeeded to the Mexican presidency by Felipe Calderón in 2006. Just days after assuming the presidency,

Calderón launched Operation Michoacán, despatching 6,500 soldiers and police to the central state of Michoacán to set up checkpoints, and execute search and arrest warrants of individuals linked to drug trafficking. Counter-drug operations have since been deployed in a further nine states, involving over 27,000 soldiers. From January to June 2007 they intercepted 928 tons of marijuana, over 5.5 tons of marijuana seeds, 192 kilos of opium gum and 3.6 tons of cocaine. They detained 10,000 people for drug crimes, including the leaders and operators of seven drug-trafficking organizations, seized money and arms, and eradicated 12,000 hectares of marijuana and 7,000 hectares of opium poppies. Drafting in soldiers to do the work of police officers was only supposed to be a temporary measure, but it has quickly taken on an air of permanence. Some legislators have even called for troops to be deployed to patrol the streets of Mexico City.

Corrupt officers are purged, new forces are created, and cocaine's kingpins are captured to be paraded before the cameras. Yet new traffickers and new organizations take the place of those killed or imprisoned, and the cartels' power and reach only seem to increase.

In a single week in May 2008, they killed a hundred people, including Mexico's acting Chief of Police, Edgar Millan Gomez, and the head of the federal police's organized crime division, Roberto Velasco Bravo.

Were they targeted because they were doing their jobs, or because they were allied with a rival cartel? Most journalists are too scared to even ask such a question. There is a growing sense of crisis in Mexico, as the solutions proffered seem to create new problems, without having the slightest impact on those they were designed to address. The cajoling and mollycoddling of the Mexican people into believing that victory is in sight is wearing thin. According to the Interior Ministry, public service announcements designed to combat drug trafficking and crime were broadcast on radio and television 732,000 times in just five months of 2007.

As the pill gets bitterer, politicians on both sides of the border insist that the medicine must be working. "Why are we having all these homicides and all these crimes on the streets?" President Fox once asked. "Because we've been winning the campaign. The more we destroy drug production and the more we catch drugs in transit, the more desperate the traffickers become and the more they challenge the authorities."

President Bush's drug tsar, John Walters, made a similar claim about the rise in Mexico's drug-related murders when he said that "unfortunately this is one of the possible signs of the efficacy of anti-drug efforts."

What to do but continue as before? Drug policy officials in Washington are genuinely worried about the escalation of the violence in Mexico. On the one hand, they had high hopes that President Fox would make significant headway against police corruption and ineptitude, and were confident that jailing top traffickers would have a lasting impact on the drugs trade. On the other hand, they view corruption as endemic to Mexico. When asked what should be done now that the army has been shown to be incapable of defeating the cartels, many throw up their hands in resignation.

Mexico's inability to control the drugs trade is already affecting the south-western states of the United States. Arizona and New Mexico both declared states of emergency in 2005. According to drug tsar John Walters, "the killing of rival traffickers is already spilling across the border. Witnesses are being killed. We do not think the border is a shield." Worse, officials in the United States aren't immune to corruption either. Investigators have discovered that drug traffickers regularly pay off border authorities in exchange for the right to traffic drugs unmolested into the United States. FBI probes have found instances of corruption in the US border patrol, as in the case of a senior agent and his brother who accepted $1.5 million in exchange for allowing truckloads of marijuana to pass through checkpoints near Hebronville, Texas. Other undercover investigations by the FBI have revealed that US soldiers have conspired to traffic drugs through south-western states. One such probe nabbed thirteen current and former soldiers taking bribes in exchange for transporting cocaine between Texas and Oklahoma. An operation called "Lively Green" indicted fifty current and former soldiers and police officers in Arizona who pleaded guilty to similar charges. The rewards on offer to those prepared to collude with the smugglers are sufficiently tempting to entice even the War on Drugs most loyal foot soldiers.

9

Druglord: Guns, Powder and Pay-Offs

Graham Johnson

John Haase and his associate Paul Bennett were apprehended at gunpoint in a very successful police action, Operation Floor, in a Croydon street. The culmination of a long-running police-surveillance operation, their arrests would have resulted in more than a few raised pint glasses in the police pubs of London and Liverpool that evening of 16 July 1993. Both the importation and distribution components of a major heroin cartel had been taken down. Operation Floor had been a great success.

In the years that followed, however, Haase and Bennett would go on to dupe British justice like no one else before or since.

Haase and his mate moved in the same circles as Curtis Warren, growing up in the same world of Liverpool graft. City centres in northern England were hopeless places in the late 1980s: in the industrial era, the unemployed had been mostly temporarily so, moving between jobs in the vast manufacturing complexes that dotted the UK. Young men of the 1980s were the first generation to graduate to employment in the post-industrial era, and the factories were gone. The devil made work for idle hands, and chasing heroin across the tinfoil wrapper of a Kit-Kat was the perfect way to while away a wet afternoon spent pondering the peeling wallpaper. You could even eat the chocolate afterwards, if you still had an appetite.

Heroin for distribution to a few mates was easily come by on credit. The suppliers – men like Haase, convicted of bank robbery in the 1970s, who had realized that the drug trade, for the most part, was a source of more regular cash – were easily confident that you would do your best to pay back their stake, for you would have seen or heard of what happened to those who didn't. How much you made above that was up to you.

Haase and Bennett distributed the heroin that was imported by a gang of Turks with a UK base in north London, to Liverpool dealers a few rungs above these. (The Manor House and Green Lane areas of London have long had their criminal connections, as well as being places where family and home are important. Turkish and Greek Cypriot together with Maltese immigration have a firm tradition here, but the Mediterranean gangs' role in the heroin trade has been to some extent supplanted by Balkan gangs in recent years. In March 2008, the Metropolitan police conducted the successful Operation Mista, raiding the drug-dealing and money-laundering activity taking place on nearby Blackstock Road and involving many of these new gangs.)

Haase and Bennett, however, hooked up with one of the Turkish gangs, seeking a source of smack they could sell up north. Reading the cold chronology of the prosecution evidence at their trial in August 1995 gives an insight into the extraordinary everyday lives of both gangs. In the early part of July, as 100 kilos of heroin were being brought successfully across the English Channel, a major Turkish importer known as The Vulcan with a right-hand man, Yilmas Kaya, flew into London and then travelled (separately from the stash, of course) to Liverpool, and met with Haase and Bennett at a club called the Boomerang to seal the deal. The Turks then shuttled back to confirm matters with their contacts in Paris, and, one assumes, to be out of the country should things "come on top".

The pair planned to return in a couple of days to collect from the Liverpudlians, however Kaya's passport in the *name of Dusanian did not hold up and he was deported to Istanbul. Meanwhile, Eddie Croker and Neil Garrett, two of Haase and Bennett's gang, were observed cutting the stash and distributing it to various Liverpool addresses, while Haase and Bennett had been seen in possession of a large plastic bag and, on various occasions, wearing surgical gloves. Police swooped simultaneously on Croker and Garrett, who were caught brown-handed with 85.7 kilos of heroin, worth an estimated £13,234,229, a figure that dwarfed the £28,000-odd thousand pounds they held in cash at the time. Even allowing for the fact that the police are known to talk up the value of a bust – and, when it comes to "face", the criminals concerned usually have more interest in seeing it talked up than down – this is a staggering amount. Haase and Bennett were arrested, and Kaya was nicked at King's Cross station, having made his way back to the UK on a passport in the name of Garo Sarkizian.*

Haase and Bennett were looking at very long sentences. Following his arrest, Haase knew that the police still had their eyes on the ultimate prize – the capture of The Vulcan (whose nickname came from a corruption of the name "Volkan"), and sought to play on it, not merely for whatever reduction in sentence his information may be worth, but for nothing less than a Royal Pardon, which could only be granted by the Home Secretary. As he commenced, he realized his actual information would not be enough. So Haase went on to organize a scam that one might think would stretch anyone's credulity, though not, apparently, that of Britain's Customs & Excise ...

Haase, Bennett, the Turks and the rest of the gang were facing massive sentences. They had been caught bang at it, as a result of the greatest victory British Customs had ever had over an international drugs ring, at a time when the Tory hard right had vowed to destroy trafficking in the War on Drugs. They were going to make an example out of this one for everyone to see, to show everyone how great they were and how well they were doing. The government was going to throw the book at them, no two ways about it, and then throw the key away. No one was getting any breaks; no one was getting anything that wasn't coming to them. Haase and Co. were going to jail for a very long time. That was a fact.

Only a comic-book miracle was going to save them now.

Pessimistic Haase did not believe in miracles. He was devastated.

Deep down he knew he couldn't face another big stretch in the shovel. He also understood, however, as a modern drug dealer schooled in the dark arts of counter-surveillance, plea bargaining and generally playing the system, that there were always options.

After all, the law was now a business. That was also a fact.

The best answer to the grave set of circumstances that faced him was the simplest one: turning grass. By ratting on the rest of the gang, including the Turks, and confessing first-hand in detail how their heroin operation worked, there was a good chance that he could buy himself some credit with the authorities and get a portion of his sentence knocked off as a reward. But there were limitations to this strategy. As the second-most-wanted prize behind The Vulcan – and considering Customs might not even need him onside because of the vast amount of evidence they had already accumulated – Haase would be bargaining from a weak position. He would be telling them things they already knew. For this, he would be risking a lot, including certain retribution from the Turks, for an outcome of which there was no guarantee. In addition, Haase knew that Customs almost certainly wouldn't let him go just like that. He'd have to serve at least some time in jail.

As the uncompromising John Haase, though, he was demanding an unconditional instant "walk out", and as far as Customs were concerned that was an outcome which they could not deliver.

The second option was to turn supergrass. The difference between a grass and a supergrass is that grasses only inform on the specific crimes with which they have been charged.

Supergrasses blow the lid on everything that they know of, relevant and irrelevant to the case in hand. Haase would have to inform on everything he knew about the wider underworld over and beyond the Turkish Connection, any crimes or criminals he could think of, any organization, friend or foe who was bang at it and of interest to the law. As a Liverpool Mafia godfather, that was potentially a lot of sensitive, valuable information. He could bring a lot of people down. But there was a problem: this option didn't sit well with his underworld code of silence. In addition, it would mean instant death or, at best, life on the witness protection programme away from his beloved villainy when he ever got out of jail.

The third option was a win–win solution, but one that was almost impossible to achieve: to pretend to be a supergrass. That would involve stunting up a series of phoney crimes, fabricating evidence to make them look real and reporting the incidents to his handlers in a bid to simply *convince* them that he was an informant. If that could be done while he was in jail on remand, and they fell for it, he might be in a position at the trial to watch the sentence-meter go into reverse. The bigger the bogus crime, the more years would be scrubbed from his time. A good word goes into the trial judge's ear and bingo, you're back on the street, a hero to all concerned. This scam had been successfully used by villains to wriggle out of smaller cases in Scotland and London for a long time, but never on such a high-profile case. If it was done right and no one realized what was going on, everyone would be a winner. Haase would get out of jail early. To boot, he would be revered by the underworld for conning the government, his reputation intact for not really grassing anyone up. (Customs & Excise and the police would not only get a result on the Turkish Connection, but on a whole raft of other "big crimes", which would make them look good, leading to greater commendations, etc. and hopefully promotions and pay-rises for all concerned. It's a no-brainer.

There was only one problem: pulling it off. The phoney crimes would have to be big and spectacular – drugs, guns, murders, terrorist attacks, underworld hits, etc. – and have to look real.

The bigger the lie, the more likely it is to be believed, to paraphrase Hitler. It would take another devious and practised liar, a criminal mastermind, no less, to organize such an audacious and preposterous scheme. Haase was certainly up to the job – even though his hands were tied to some extent, being behind bars in Manchester's Strangeways prison. That meant he would need a team on the outside to follow his orders to the letter, good communications with them and a war chest full of money to ensure that his Hollywood-style special effects were successfully put into action. The con would have to be good enough to conjure up an illusion of reality to a high degree, so much so that it would deceive the trained observers of the law.

Haase would also have to rely on the gullibility of his handlers, to an extent. How much would they want to believe it? How hungry were they for success? How desperate were they to repeat their recent achievements in smashing his gang? How much did they want to believe that they were dealing with a top villain?

How much did they want to believe that he was capable of handing them top cases on a plate? Haase figured they would go for it. He knew the psychology: in general, he believed that certain middle-ranking investigators in Customs and the police had the same motivations as the villains they chased for a living.

They were ambitious. They had big egos. They were impressed by reputations. At the end of the day, they were still boys at heart – in it for the adventure, fearful of the mundane and mediocre.

They were like desperate reporters chasing a story – success at all costs. They sacrificed a lot in pursuit of the villains they hunted: family time, seeing their kids, weekends, wives, marriages, their well-being. It was an unhealthy, unbalanced lifestyle, and one that could be exploited by someone as cunning as Haase, who was seemingly offering short cuts to success. Haase knew that they would be pleased with themselves for netting as big a fish as him.

He also knew that they would try to become his mate. Law-enforcement officers could be as guilty as villains in respecting the gangland hierarchies, in revering the big players. If he started talking, it was the icing on the cake – it would blow their minds for sure. They would put the double coup down to themselves, down to their own skill. That's just the way they were. Ego would prohibit them from suspecting that Haase was pulling a fast one.

A possible theory is that Haase chose option three and that the con was put into action with immediate effect. It makes sense that he hatched the plan within a few days of being arrested. His main worry would have been how he was going to fund the campaign, but that could be instantly sorted. His gang on the outside was still in possession of fifty kilos of heroin from the 100-kilo parcel that the Turks had given to him. Some of this was the 25–30-kilo load that Eddie Croker had been observed bashing by Customs officers the week before he was arrested. Astonishingly, this fifty kilos had slipped the Customs net during the arrest. As Haase's stand-in boss in his forced absence, Chris No-Neck had got it and was awaiting instructions from Haase on what to do with it. Haase knew he could sell it to fund his war chest.

The next problem would be choosing the right solicitor. Haase and Bennett's initial tactic seemed to be finding a brief who would actively participate in the scam – a respectable professional to front the con. The downside would mean they would have to confide their plot to the lawyer – a risky business – but the upside, if it paid off, would be that they would benefit from the injection of expert and specialized legal knowledge. It seems that they looked around for a bent lawyer to bring on board for the big win, and it didn't take long to pinpoint a possible conspirator. Colourful Kevin Dooley was Liverpool's number one mob lawyer. He was a local lad made good, able to talk to his shadowy clientele in a language they understood. The larger-than-life character was rumoured to have "washed" millions of pounds of Curtis Warren's drug money – a suspicion which hung over him until he was struck off many years later and until his subsequent death. Dooley was so close to the city's top gangsters he was dubbed "Alfonso" – a reference to his flashy suits, blingy jewellery and bullish manner.

Like so many people who love hanging around the underworld, Dooley started to behave like the gangsters he represented, throwing his weight around, issuing ultimatums and giving the impression that he was untouchable. Some of his big clients loved it, including Premiership football players, big businesses and international terrorists. Other clients did not know about his shadowy links, including many of Liverpool Football Club's top players such as Robbie Fowler, and even Colonel Qaddafi's son.

Business boomed, but Dooley refused to move his fifty-strong staff from his dingy offices in Kirkby. The down-to-earth HQ gave him even more street credibility.

According to Dooley, Bennett made contact with him with a view to retaining his services. Though Dooley was wide, he wasn't stupid. As soon as the con was explained to him, he refused to have anything to do with it. The gun-planting scheme was a preposterous perversion of the course of justice with a one-in-a-hundred chance of working. He knocked it back, without further ado. To curry favour with the Merseyside Police, Dooley later claimed that he tipped off his senior contacts about Haase and Bennett's devious intentions. Meanwhile, the pair was furious that they had been forced to show their hand to Dooley without benefit. Later, Dooley claimed that they swore revenge, to get him back for not going along with their plan. No one said "no" to John Haase. Dooley said that, as a result of his refusal to co-operate, Haase and Bennett set out to destroy him, constantly trying to ruin his reputation in a smear campaign.

The pair decided to be more careful about what they told the next lawyer. They decided to choose someone straight and keep him in the dark. Solicitor Tony Nelson was a rising star on the criminal-law circuit. He was introduced to Haase by shaven-headed Liverpool hard-man The Enforcer, a security consultant who ran most of the nightclub doors in the city. This time, Haase and Bennett were more discreet. They did not tell the lawyer about their intention to stunt up phoney crimes in which they had a guiding hand. They simply told him that they wanted him to defend them against the drugs charges and they would like to cut a deal with Customs. On top of his normal brief, would he act as a conduit for their supergrass information, passing it on from them to Customs? According to senior police sources, it is unusual for a solicitor to act as a middleman between a supergrass and the authorities. But Nelson agreed and, unbeknown to him, it was time for Haase to put his plan into action.

Over the next eighteen months on remand, Haase pulled off his massive con – mixed in with a heavy dose of alleged cash bribes – and got out of prison.

CHRONOLOGY

July 1993 – Haase and Bennett arrested in London and put on remand in prison.

October 1993 – mass gun-planting begins.

December 1994 – key gun planted at Strangeways – clincher for Royal Pardon.

February 1995 – Haase and Bennett plead guilty to heroin distribution to avoid an open court and jury.

June 1995 – mass gun-planting ends.

August 1995 – after the trial of other defendants, Haase and Bennett are sentenced to eighteen years each.

Autumn 1995 – alleged bribery begins and continues into 1996 in order to cover up suspicions over gun-planting.

June 1996 – Royal Pardons granted to Haase and Bennett by Michael Howard.

July 1996 – both men are released.

The con comprised three phases. First, Haase instructed his gang on the outside to buy hundreds of guns from the underworld. Stacks of deactivated weapons were sourced from official depots and rearmed. Plastic explosives were purchased from mercenaries. Haase's men on the outside, led by Chris No-Neck, then planted the guns in safehouses and abandoned cars.

The key element in this phase was that Haase was given the glory of telling his Customs handlers the location of the specially made caches – obviously implying that they were owned by other gangsters who were about to use them in killings or terrorist outrages. He pretended they were IRA arms dumps and weapons for use by contract killers.

Convicted heroin dealer Ken Darcy was one of the foot-soldiers paid by Haase's gang to buy and plant Semtex plastic explosive. "I got paid five grand for just two kilos of Semtex," said Darcy. "It was planted in a flat in Liverpool and later found by Customs or police."

On another occasion, Haase's gang diluted three kilos of heroin to make six, so that it would make a better find for police and Customs. Darcy said, "When the police found it, along with loads of E tablets, plus loads of guns, it gave them better credit."

Other phoney caches included 150 illegal firearms, eighty brand-new shotguns, Kalashnikov assault weapons, Armalite rifles, Thompson machine guns, Uzi sub-machine guns and 1,500 rounds of ammunition.

Former gangster Paul Ferris also admitted helping to supply between £20,000 and £50,000 worth of weapons to Haase. He said, "They were planted in a car in Holyhead ferry terminal in North Wales and a lock-up in Liverpool, and Haase said they were IRA. Customs never found out the truth."

Suleyman Ergun *[one of the Turkish gang who worked with Haase and was apprehended with him]* said, "I was told three times about the gun-planting: before, during and after it happened. The first time, Bennett told me while we were in prison that they were going to buy up guns from all over Britain and plant them in Liverpool to make Customs think that they were informants.

"He told me he'd help get me free using phoney plants."

Between October 1993 and June 1995, Haase and Bennett led police to twenty-six gun and drug caches containing 150 firearms and explosives. Phase two was the clincher for the Royal Pardon: the crown jewel of the phoney gun plants. It consisted of no more than a single pistol – but it was the location and the timing of this particular set-up that were so crucial. Haase dreamt up this stroke of genius, two-thirds of the way through the gun-planting period, in December 1994. By that time, even after offering up a series of spectacular arms finds, getting out of prison immediately was not on the table. Customs & Excise were playing hardball with their remand prisoners. They were saying that they could get a bit of time off, but a walk out was out of the question. After all, no arrests had been made as a result of Haase's intelligence. Some wise old officers were also getting a touch suspicious. And at the end of the day, Haase was asking a lot – he was asking them to wipe the slate clean on fifty kilos of gear, and on one of the greatest arrest coups they had ever achieved.

Haase was getting frustrated, racking his brains to discover a way to raise his game. Then he stumbled on it – the Royal Prerogative of Mercy. Haase found out that only this Prerogative, otherwise known as a Royal Pardon, would guarantee instant freedom. He had also found out that this ancient decree dating back to the Norman era was exclusively used in modern times to reward model prisoners who had helped save prison officers' lives in one way or another. It was a quirk of history, rather than official policy, but that was the lie of the land. Haase thought that if he managed to have one of his moody guns smuggled into a prison with one hand and then conveniently grassed it up with the other, meanwhile gently blaming it on a fellow prisoner, that could be construed by the authorities as having prevented the potential killing of a prison officer, an IRA-style breakout or a hostage situation. In December, Haase arranged for a gun to be smuggled into Strangeways prison, Manchester, the weapon hidden in a sandwich toaster. Haase told his handlers about it. The authorities pounced and Haase got the credit. Bingo! Royal Pardon in the bag. The fact that the gun was wrongly blamed on another prisoner, Thomas Bourke, was of no consideration to Haase.

A report to trial judge David Lynch later praised Haase and Bennett for "The prevention of a possible hostage situation. A prisoner convicted of two double murders was planning to escape by use of a gun. A loaded gun was recovered and the prison officer responsible for smuggling the weapon into the prison was identified."

[. . .] Using a bank of eighteen stolen mobile phones, Haase and Bennett began co-ordinating the biggest con to date on the British judicial system. The pair were in prison on remand, so legally they could only communicate with underbosses on the outside such as Chris No-Neck during official visits. The stolen mobile phones were therefore essential to the military-style operation.

They were smuggled into prison by a corrupt prison officer and paid for from a roll of fresh £50-notes which Haase carried around the wings. He was able to fiddle free airtime on the phones by keying in a special code when the contract credit hit max. That way, Haase was able to spend hours talking to his henchmen, carefully detailing where gun caches were to be stashed.

Mobile phones are strictly prohibited within prison, and inmates used them in secret in their cells. Bennett became frustrated. He needed to answer calls immediately, to thoroughly stay on top of the gun plants and to ensure split-second timing wherever he was in the prison – in the gym, in the toilets, in his mates' cells. He quickly devised an ingenious method. He stashed the phone in a Michael Jackson-style ghetto blaster which he carried on his shoulder like a break-dancer, the speaker containing the mobile phone next to his ear. When the phone rang, he was able to hear it. There was a secret panel in the plastic casing through which he could answer the phone and talk. If he was being watched and couldn't take the call, sometimes he would disappear back to his cell to call the person back.

On the outside, The Bank Manager Chris No-Neck was in charge of putting Haase's instructions into action. He was busy selling the missing fifty kilos of heroin and soon raised £1.25 million for the war chest to spend on gun-planting and alleged bribes. That's why he was known as The Bank Manager to some members of the gang; he had his hands on the purse strings. He stashed most of the money close by in the house of a straight-goer – a gangly teenager who had no connection to crime. He was dubbed The Bank Clerk, as it was his job to run around the city dropping off money from the main war chest to pay for underworld services rendered.

The first proper gun plant occurred in October 1993, when Customs recovered four machine guns, two moderator silencers, one stun gun, one revolver and 160 rounds of nine-millimetre ammunition as a result of Haase and Bennett's information. But the scheme did not move into top gear until after Christmas in February 1994 and continued until June 1995. Haase and

Bennett were staging bogus plants for a full twenty-one months, and no one in authority realized enough to raise the alarm.

Haase arranged to buy many of the guns himself. After all, he was in the perfect place – prison. He put out the word to his friends within the penal system that he would buy anything and everything that could fire a bullet, and soon gangsters from London, Scotland, Sheffield and Manchester were queuing up with batches of Kalashnikovs, shotguns and pistols.

Once they had shaken hands on a price, it was a simple case of getting his people in Liverpool to talk to their people, wherever they were, do the meets and pick up the parcels.

In Liverpool, a notorious gangster called Tommy Gilday was also supplying the gang with guns. Two of the city's most violent crime families – sworn enemies of Haase – also agreed to forget their differences and help Haase if the price was right. The real names of the other hand-picked gun-planters are known to the author, but cannot be revealed for legal reasons. They include two brothers who are protection racketeers and restaurant owners, another gangster called George, a villain called Ray, The Iceman and Curtis Warren's former right-hand man, Johnny Phillips. Phillips later died in mysterious circumstances, allegedly killed by a professional hitman team called The Cleaners. Ironically, he had fallen out in an unrelated feud with one of the crime families involved in the gun-planting.

One phoney cache consisted of eighty brand-new Italian shotguns.

The deal to buy them was helped along by gangster James Turner, a Park Road hoodlum who had helped Haase in his feud with the Ungi/Fitzgibbon crew. He said, "I know where the guns came from. I got offered them. Came off a wagon, brand new. But he got them. I said, 'John [Haase], do you want these?'" Chris No-Neck bought them on behalf of John Haase and they were planted in a McDonald's car park. Astonishingly, a nationally known crime boss from London had sussed a way of sourcing a large amount of recycled guns from a police depository. These were guns that had been used in crimes and then confiscated by police, probably deactivated at an official proof house and then stored in a secure facility. Somehow, the London gangster was able to smuggle them out or buy them at auction, reactivate them and sell them to Haase. Another gangster in Scotland, who owned a workshop and had connections to Glasgow's top hitmen, began to supply very high quality guns.

The gun plants were so convincing that even MI5 thought they were real secret stashes. To get more credit, Haase pretended that he could help seize IRA guns, ammo and explosives destined for use in atrocities on the mainland.

Haase was so devious that he knew this stash would get the authorities "drooling".

The IRA was the government's number one priority. A few months before Haase was arrested, on 24 April 1993, an IRA bomb at Bishopsgate devastated the City of London's financial centre, killing one and injuring more than forty people. The renewed campaign shocked the nation. Now the IRA was threatening other prestige targets, including the then newly built skyscraper at Canary Wharf in the capital's Docklands and, more worryingly, the under-construction Channel Tunnel. Canary Wharf was eventually bombed three years later in 1996 and a ceasefire was hastily declared before the Channel Tunnel was hit. The tunnel was one of the main British motivations behind peace.

Haase's ruse was nothing short of criminal genius. First, he bought £20,000–£50,000 worth of weapons from associates of Glasgow godfather Paul Ferris and a Manchester-based Scot called Rab, the heroin dealer once supplied by the Turks. Then Haase arranged for a car full of guns to be dumped near a British ferry bound for Ireland. To make it sing, Haase had his men go to the Republic and get Irish newspapers that were left on the back seat on return to the UK, and even cigarette stubs from pubs in Dublin, to make it seem that Irishmen had been driving the car. Haase tipped off his handlers, and an MI5 observation team watched the car for three days to catch the phantom IRA operatives picking up the guns. Of course, no one turned up, but the authorities trumpeted the seizure as a great coup in the fight against the terrorists. This equalled Brownie points for Haase. Ferris said, "They were planted in a car in Holyhead ferry terminal in North Wales and a lock-up in Liverpool, and Haase said they were IRA. Customs never found out the truth."

Haase's devious operation was nearly exposed after a close brush with the law. Some of the guns were transported from Manchester to Liverpool by two stunning women (one known as The Supervisor) who were close to Haase. The idea was that a couple of dolly birds, who looked like they had been on a shopping trip to Manchester, were unlikely to get a pull off the police. But the ladies' sports car was stopped almost immediately for speeding. The boot was crammed full of assault rifles and hand grenades. The scantily clad girls did their best to distract the traffic cop away from the boot, flashing their legs and cleavage. It worked. He let them go with a ticking off without searching the car.

In another extraordinary incident, the operation nearly came crashing down amid fears for public safety. According to uncorroborated underworld sources, Haase's men claimed they planted a cache of Semtex and several small arms in a car near a pub called Black George's on Park Road in Liverpool 8.

The pub was run by the Ungi family, and Haase hoped the find would throw some guilt by association on them, at least enough for a bit of harassment. But the plan backfired when the car was stolen by joyriders before the police could seize it. A massive police operation was mounted to find the car and eventually it was spotted by a patrol car being driven at high speed by a teenager and his pals through the streets of Walton.

The joyriders were awestruck when they were suddenly roadblocked by nearly twenty police, an armed-response unit and a bomb-disposal unit. The Semtex was found in the boot untouched. The kids hadn't even noticed it and were never told. There was a collective sigh of relief. This anecdote has not been confirmed by Merseyside Police and the validity of the information cannot be verified.

Other seizures included 7,534 Ecstasy tablets, five kilos of amphetamine, fifty-eight litres of methadone, the recovery of 100 LSD tablets *[sic]*, the locating of a skunk (cannabis) factory, 200 cannabis plants and a machine gun – all planted by Haase.

But there was only one problem – no one had been arrested,

and the lack of bodies *[arrests]* was now raising suspicions. Despite nineteen "raids", there was not one single arrest. Police invariably arrived at the location of a tip-off to find a deserted safehouse or an abandoned car with a holdall full of guns in the boot. All fingerprints had, of course, been wiped clean. All of the vehicles had mysteriously been purchased for cash a few days earlier by untraceable men, who, despite numerous appeals in the press, never came forward.

So Haase set to work in finding a criminal who would knowingly sacrifice himself for cash. In January 1995, nearly a year after the phoney gun-planting had begun and at the point when some Customs officers were becoming suspicious and demanding "bodies" to back up the Scouser's intelligence, Haase was saved from the brink. A low-level drug runner called Billy the Hamster agreed to hide three handguns in a toolbox in his house which would then be reported to the police by Haase. He would take the rap, go to jail and get a big bung for his trouble. On the day of the bust, the Hamster was arrested on suspicion while his house was searched. But then things went badly wrong. According to underworld sources, farcically, the first police rummage team failed to find the guns. And by the time of the next search, the search-warrant period had allegedly expired. The guns were found, but the evidence was inadmissible, and by this time Billy had had second thoughts about getting himself mixed up in such a hare-brained scheme, refusing to give a statement to back up Haase's plan. He was mysteriously released from custody and not charged. He then tried to blackmail Haase for £5,000, threatening to blow the lid on the gun-planting scam, but was quickly silenced and bashed up by Chris No-Neck.

In another attempt to show that "real bodies" were behind the crimes that Haase was "uncovering", Haase invented a story that The Vulcan had put a hit out on the family of Customs Officer Paul Cook. A total fabrication, but Cook and his family went into the witness-protection programme. (Customs had to take this seriously; a Liverpool Mafia heroin gang had put a contract out on several Customs officers in 1992, even firebombing one of their houses. For many Customs officers, this had been a big motivation for taking out Haase, as he was a Liverpool Mafia boss.) Haase then got the glory when he said that he used his underworld power to get the contract called off. This may have been an early attempt to meet the conditions of winning a Royal Pardon – by helping to prevent danger to a law officer.

In fact, the only people that Haase had "grassed up" up to that point were corrupt law officials – a crooked prison officer, a corrupt CPS manager, a rogue solicitor and a bent copper.

This super-selective targeting of "enemy" fall guys docked up extra Brownie points on the street. The villains were happy that Haase hadn't actually grassed any villains up. The breakout was a triple-whammy success – the most audacious escape plan since Steve McQueen went over the wall on a liberated German motorbike. Haase became an instant underworld legend.

JOHN HAASE On the outside, Bennett and me had been working overtime. When Bennett and me got nicked, we had over fifty kilos of brown [heroin], which is worth £1,150,000.

Chris No-Neck, who was an associate of ours, had control of this heroin. This heroin was sold and we used some of the money to purchase weapons which were later planted so that the police and Customs & Excise could find them. Bennett already had a couple of hundred thousand pounds of cash and so did I, so we had plenty of money.

Tommy Gilday got a lot of guns for us, but no favours were done. We paid for everything – machine guns, AKs, hand pistols. When we were first getting the machine guns, they were £2K each, but later on, when we were getting them in tens, the price was reduced. One of our main contacts was a Londoner.

A lot of our stuff was guns. This was a member of the underworld. I met him in prison when the guy was in prison doing an eighteen-year sentence for armed robbery. I can confirm that some of the guns that I bought had originated from a police depository – that is, they had been confiscated by the police in previous crimes, but then had been released back onto the streets for resale.

A lot of them were coming in from eastern Europe, especially the AKs. I was getting them in the end for £750 from my

London contact. There were loads of people involved in getting us guns. People from Sheffield, Manchester – that's the one where they found the car in a car park with machine guns in it.

We got a couple of garages, a couple of flats, eight to ten vehicles, cars and vans. One of the vans we parked in Bootle on the McDonald's [car park] with eighty shotguns in it. All this information I used to pass to Mr Nelson. All the guns were spot on. I was getting them and telling people where to put them so that I could inform Customs & Excise of where they could be found. It was a con all the way, but for some reason they were delighted to get the guns off the street.

The police wanted to get involved after the first couple of things had been found. Tony Nelson asked me could the police come and see me. I said, "No, I'm only dealing with the Customs." The Customs wanted information about anything but for some reason they were delighted – they couldn't get enough of it.

These little stashes get the deals going. For instance, there was bomb-making stuff in Lower Breck Road [in Liverpool].

Someone went out of town for me. This was because I met this guy on remand in Manchester prison. I was talking to him, got a bit friendly with him and asked him if he had any guns up there. He said, "I've got loads, what do you want?"

I said, "Whatever you can get me."

When I was in Manchester with Bennett, we had mobile phones with us so I could speak to anyone at any time. We were co-ordinating the operations and the planting of the guns using mobile phones. I also had one in Hull. On one occasion when guns were brought back from out of town to Liverpool, there was a problem. Coming down the East Lanes Road, back towards Liverpool at about eleven o'clock at night, the two women got stopped by a police car. The car had all kinds of firearms in it – machine guns, rifles, etc. A police officer came to the car, asked the lady if everything was all right. She said "fine", showed him her driving stuff and the officer waved them on their way – a normal stopping. But the guns were never discovered.

In the Southend, in Liverpool 8, we had a stash of guns in there, in an empty flat. One of Bennett 's people was told to go round and put a couple more in. They never went themselves and sent someone else round to put the extra guns inside. The story I got told afterwards was that they didn't put the right number in the alarm. The alarm went off, they couldn't shut it down so they ran away. Later, the police arrived and found the guns – so we lost them.

The next one was one of the big ones they were all drooling at. Someone went to Ireland and got an address over there.

They got some newspapers and went to pubs over there and got cigarette stumps and all bits and pieces [from ashtrays in the Irish pubs]. A car we bought in Liverpool was booked on to the Holyhead ferry. That was booked through a travel agency in Alderhay (astonishingly through the same travel agency that Haase had used to book drug runs to Ireland. A simple check may have exposed the link.) Booked on to go to Ireland.

Thousands of pounds of ammunition, rifles, etc. were put in the car and that was parked in Holyhead car park. The newspapers and cigarette stumps were also put in the car and the keys were left on the back wheel. The car was full of rifles and thousands of rounds of ammunition and many weapons.

We told the Customs about it. MI5 sat off and observed the car for three days before they hit it. That cache was planted by me and Bennett to give the impression that there was an IRA connection. This was a total fabrication. You can imagine the Brownie points Cook was getting and that's why the police wanted to get involved. [During this time] I made a tape recording of me in a [prison visiting] room with Paul Bennett, Tony Nelson and Paul Cook. I taped them in prison. The next time, I got nicked for having an unauthorized tape-recording machine.

They can't be that thick, but they are, believe it or not. How can I be in prison and know information like that? And every time it's spot on. Every time I told them, they got something.

Without knowing what's going on, I knew it was there. Lower Breck Road; I knew it was there. Loads of guns. That was ours.

There was bomb-making stuff in the Lower Breck Road one. That come from London, that. Nothing got robbed before the police found it.

So far they've [Customs] got no bodies. But I said to Bennett one day, "These are going to get suspicious here, because they haven't got a body yet." Me and Bennett are in custody, so it was left to Chris No-Neck to get a body. Billy the Hamster was nicked with some guns in January 1995. I'd like to know myself what happened because even though he was nicked, he never went to court. Chris No-Neck, Bennett and me know him – he runs drugs around for people. Chris No-Neck got this chap, Billy, to accept to have a toolbox in his house with three guns in it. Loaded hand pistols, they were. The information was passed on to Paul Cook. The police raided this man's home and found the firearms. He got charged, but never went to court. All's I know is that he got on the phone to No-Neck after he'd been arrested for the guns and asked No-Neck for £5K. I thought he'd got a bit cheeky and said he'd do something. No-Neck met him/bumped into him, bashed him up and that was the end of the episode. But still Billy the Hamster never went to court. The reason I know this is because when I got the legal papers this time, for my last case in 1999–2001, I saw the papers in the court and they said that he never went to prison.

Remember all the trouble over Cheers? I gave them information – pure 100 per cent luck on my side. We planted a car full of guns near Cheers and two days later David Ungi was shot. That gave the impression to the Customs & Excise that I had the inside track on gangland shootings. Like I said, it was pure luck on my side over Cheers, the information with David Ungi. Said there was a car parked up with guns in and that.

We started the rumour that The Vulcan, the Turkish heroin dealer, was going to put a hit on Cook's family, because they [Customs] tried to get the Turks to testify against The Vulcan, who was the main man they wanted. But the police said that the Turks were too terrified to give evidence, so me and Bennett said there was a hit on Cook's family and he went to the witness-protection programme. This added credibility to our con because the Customs said that if you're going to be a grass, you've got to grass someone up. That was us who started the rumour about the hit on Cook, not Curtis Warren, as people thought. To give it more credibility.

The Vulcan was a dangerous man. He was the main man but

they couldn't get him. I think he's done a couple of murders over here . . . Customs wanted Bennett. And they said they'd let me walk if I gave them evidence against The Vulcan. I said, "What's it worth, because he's dangerous, him."

And they went to the judge. They said, "Mr Haase does not give evidence against The Vulcan because we can understand that the man is too dangerous."

I wouldn't have done anyway, because he's a good friend of mine. Even Kaya is [my friend]. Been to Istanbul and that. Met his mum and dad.

For him [Cook], it was credibility. If I said I could get The Vulcan, it looked good for him, didn't it? I said he'd been to my house, The Vulcan. He knows where I live. The man's got plenty of money. Especially him wanting protection for him and his family. If you're going to be a supergrass, who are you grassing? You aren't grassing anyone. That's why we put the body in. That's what they wanted.

What you've heard there is about a tenth of what went down. Don't forget that this is nearly three years this is going on. We was on remand for over two years. That's why Cook kept delaying it. Kept putting it back all the time.

In a bid to ratchet up the terrorist link, Haase promised Customs they would supply information about a container of weapons on board a ship heading for Liverpool, according to uncorroborated sources. The ship was already in Liverpool docks, the container doors booby-trapped with bags of Semtex.

The bomb-disposal experts blew the doors off, revealing fifty weapons and some heroin. Then Ken Darcy was roped in by No-Neck to get more Semtex explosive and heroin to add variety to the Customs finds. According to Peter Kilfoyle MP, some of the weapons came from a West Midlands police repository and some equipment registered in North Wales had come through the repository in Liverpool.

KEN DARCY Just come out of jail [in 1991] from a three-and-a-half-year sentence for half an ounce of cocaine. Come home.

Had to move house because the bizzies *[police]* took the house, whatever. Knew Chris No-Neck for a long time, through mates.

All in all, I've known him for twenty-odd years. Done this and that with him. So I come out of jail and done a bit of this and that to get by.

Anyway, all these drugs and guns [were being planted] around the city and I ended up getting involved with that.

John Haase and Paul Bennett were away. Gets a phone call from Chris No-Neck. There was simply too much for him to do. Half the stuff [*the guns and explosives*] he couldn't get, so I come in and got what he needed.

No-Neck had a lot of the firm's money – all of the firm [Haase/ Bennett/Croker] had been nicked bar him. So he was left with all the money, the contacts, control over everything.

He was acting on behalf of John Haase and Paul Bennett. All along, they knew they weren't going to be away for a long time.

It was a scam from day one. Everyone knew that Haase and Bennett were going to get out of jail quickly. They were throwing people in [informing]. There was also the gun plants, the gun in the prison. That's what got them out.

No-Neck would have cups of tea with me, telling me he had planted guns and alarms had gone off and that. That was in the Southend [of Liverpool] where the alarm went off on the house. These two boys had put the guns in, but the alarm goes off. So the find was made by ordinary bizzies. So John Haase couldn't ring up the Customs and tell 'em about it. There was a bit of trouble over that. The boys got a hiding over that.

That's the point when I said to No-Neck, "I'll help you now. "Make a list of what you want."

He's up the wall planting guns every which where. Buying this, buying that. That's when he asks me about Semtex, when I got Semtex, firearms for him, and I did about four drops here there and everywhere.

I knew one was in Bootle Strand. I knew one was in a house in town. I just supplied the firearms, Semtex, bullets . . . I knew a couple of the locations. Got [the Semtex] off these mercenaries from out of town through a mate of mine. I done a favour a few days before for him. Then I called the favour back. Got the

Semtex, planted it on Haydock racecourse till it was time to bring it home, back to Norris Green. A man I'll call Soldier Boy came and collected it. It was gone then and put wherever it was supposed to go, and then it was found. Only one in Semtex. I got paid five grand for just two kilos. Soldier Boy come and took it from me.

I asked no questions. When the police found the guns, it usually was in the papers – big news. But it was never mentioned that Semtex was found. That was very strange; it was never mentioned in the paper. It was to be organized in a plant to make it look like a terrorist link. I asked him [No-Neck] about that. He said, "Don't worry about that. It is not a problem." It was very strange, seeing as they were going on about bazookas, guns and that.

I done about four plants over a couple of months. Only for a certain amount of time, before Haase and Bennett came out of prison. They was on remand. They'd been using fucking no-marks, idiots, before then.

There were other people high up in the city who were saying, "I can get you this or I can get you that." At the time, they [Haase's gang on the outside] had endless amounts of drugs.

Some of it was shit, but they were bashing it for more than it was. From three ki to six ki. That was done so it could be planted and it would make a bigger find for the Customs. The bizzies aren't arsed because they're getting it off the streets. Tablets were also used in the phoney plants. But at the end of the day, the gear was shite, so it was worth giving in rather than selling. That's the way they were looking at it. I did guns but one lot was a drugs plant. The drugs were got by me calling in lots of favours.

I knew all the fellas No-Neck was using [to buy and plant guns]. There were a lot of people. Money bought some, but there were also friends. Everyone in the underworld wanted in on it to get credit for it [from powerful Haase when he got out]. I had lads coming from Preston, Leyland, Manchester, Wales with six or seven guns. I ended up buying some in town.

It didn't matter if it was any good. It was just for plants so the Customs could find them. Buy anything: hand grenade, stun guns, bombs. Some of the guns were from Davy Crockett days [old-fashioned] ... but at the end of the day, a gun is a gun. As far as the Customs and police are concerned, it's off the street.

They're happy.

A lad from Manchester, a football hooligan, he had ten in a suitcase. The quicker you stashed them, the better it was for Haase. The money was no problem. Some young kid [The Bank Clerk] would drop the money off to me to pay for the guns. I'd phone him and say; "I need five grand." The five would be brought round in the hour.

Billy the Hamster – how did he get off with all them guns in the box? He said the warrant expired. I'm not having that. The bizzies came with the warrant and searched the house. There's a big steel box with guns in and they never found it. Chris No-Neck rang John Haase and told him the bizzies haven't found it. He was fuming. The bizzies went round the next day, found the box, but he got off with it because the warrant had expired.

I did a few of them. I was still carrying on doing a bit of graft at the same time. Then one day I get a phone call telling me they [Haase and Bennett] are out. Then Chris No-Neck comes round to me and says, "They're out."

And I said, "Fuck off!"

A couple of weeks later, John Haase comes round to see me.

Shakes my hand ... says, "Thanks a lot." Nice fella. No one got nicked. No one got hurt.

For Chris No-Neck, the massive logistics in organizing the fake plants – buying huge amounts of weapons and shipping them all over the UK undercover – proved to be a nightmare. Plus there was the added hassle of dealing with unscrupulous gangsters who wanted to make a profit. On one occasion, two black gangsters from Toxteth – known as The Iceman and The Security Boss – were given money to buy guns to plant for Haase. Instead, they bought a cache using Haase's money and then sold it for a profit. All-out war was prevented when The Iceman and The Security Boss got hold of a second cache and put it Haase's way.

But there were reliable gangsters including Tommy Gilday who provided many guns. It was No-Neck's job to liaise with Gilday, get him money and make sure that the guns were handed over to a runner and then planted without Gilday knowing what was going on. The cell structure ensured secrecy.

No-Neck was obsessed with getting the detail right. Sometimes, No-Neck would observe gun handovers from afar with binoculars, disguised as a lycra-clad professional cyclist.

CHRIS NO-NECK I helped John and Ben get out of prison because Ben was my best mate before John come out in 1992. I had been grafting with Ben until then – but they fucked me off when John got out. They said they never wanted me in on their graft. Now, if I had been in on the graft in the first place, they and the Turks wouldn't have got nicked. The reason they got nicked was simple – because John had the same crew that worked with me and Ben for five years before John took over.

Why didn't they break the pattern up? Where's the common sense in that? So it was their own fault – but I agreed to help because of Ben. He was the first proper friend to me. I would have died for him.

Doing the stashes was very stressful. It was severe pressure for three years, but I handled it. I went to the gym a lot to box and started running – it was that training got me through it.

That's why I ended up doing the London Marathon. I did quite a lot of gun plants. It was heavy. That's why I've gone grey. At the end of the day, what I did for them got them out of prison. And I did it because I cared about Ben – not for money, 'cos I got nothing out of it. I asked them for sixty quid [sixty thousand pounds] later but I got fuck all. But it didn't matter. Ben was an old mate.

They have never told me their innermost darkest secrets – so at first I had to make sure they weren't properly grassing. I'm not a gringo, I'm a grafter. Never crossed the line for anyone.

Never grassed for nobody. But John said he was fucking the system. I said I'd do it for my bit. Not for John, but for Ben.

It was simple – I created crimes for Ben. Then I relayed the information, via a phone box, to a mobile phone [which Bennett had in prison]. That information was then passed on to his solicitor, who then talked to whoever it may be [Customs]. The people I know [the gun-planters] went through me. I done it. I knew what I got myself into.

The things were placed in certain places. I wouldn't pass any information over to John until I knew they [the gun-planters] were well out the way. They are clear, get off now. I got 200 brand-new shotguns from Southampton, in boxes. Two hundred quid a go, a mate of mine offers me. About eight grand in total. I said, "Yeah, give us them." Got a mate of mine to pick them up. Got a mate to go disguised, go to Birkenhead in a Rascal van, put them all in a van and parked them outside a McDonald's in Bootle. We left them there for two days to see if anyone was watching. Then I phoned John up and said, "That's there now, blah, blah, blah." I did another one where I got a fella's car full of guns and dispersed them wherever. In effect, we were creating crimes. No crimes done but it looked like they were. It was a good scam. Haase has got more audacity than Saddam Hussein. And he's got some front, hasn't he?

Fucking kite [*face*] on him as well.

Tommy Gilday used to come to my house every day. Loved me, he did. I bought things [guns] off him. Not that I bought them, but Haase and Bennett would give me the money and I bought them. When I was doing the plants, Gilday couldn't fathom what was going on. He used to get me a few things but I'd plant them and that. So he didn't know about that stage.

One exchange took place between Gilday and one of my lads.

To make sure it went well, I was on a railway in Tuebrook with a pair of binoculars on my mountain bike, all the official gear, right. I looked a right plonker, but I did it. Proper *Tour de* Liverpool, it was. I goes up the embankment and I had my binoculars because I had set it up for the lad to go and pick those things up from Gilday. Gilday turned up in a red Audi. I focused in on him so I knew exactly what he was wearing, right, during the meet. When I went to see him afterwards, I said, "Everything sound?"

He said, "Yeah, yeah. Can I use your toilet?"

Then I said, "Didn't you have a loud, bright red T-shirt on, a stripy one, in your red Audi?"

That made him go right para'. He said "How did you know that?"

"Because," I said, "I was watching you."

And he said, "I had someone watching your mate as well."

Gilday was a hard-case but I clued him up that I wasn't stupid. He realized I was astute. Then he respected me for everything. In my house after that, he told me everything.

Tommy's both sides of the fence. Classic saying was "that's put to bed".

John also put a fake contract out on Cook. One day, John and Ben asked me to go to the Crown Court. They had told Cook beforehand that there was a contract out on him but they was going to stop the contract. Now, if I showed my face in the Crown Court that day, that would give Cook the signal that they had called off the contract on him. That was the shit they were giving him. But it was a lie. A fabrication. Like a lot of things I done for him. I created crimes that never existed.

Because people owed favours, whatever. That was the way their freedom was sorted.

One time, I went to visit Ben in Strangeways [to talk about organizing more plants face to face]. I never used to visit Haase. He was always on the next table with his bird. You could see his grey hair and that. Ben said, "I know these lads who have done a bit of graft."

I said, "Who?"

He said, "The Security Boss and that. Sort it. Get on with them."

That meant I had to buy guns off them for planting.

So I phoned up The Security Boss and The Iceman and said, "You want to see me?" I went down there [to Toxteth] to meet them, and him and The Iceman are there. They wanted money. So I went and got some dough off lads I know and came back to them and said, "There's our dough for our part of the bargain."

Listen to this what happened afterwards: they get the graft in but they hold on to the guns, to sell the guns. They wanted to use my people on another second trip. But I thought, "That's our dough they've used. They've got the fucking parcel there." So I goes down the Southend [Toxteth] on me own. I asked them for the money but they wouldn't give me a penny.

And these lads had a reputation, especially the one they call The Iceman. I said, "Listen, this is nothing to do with John Haase or Ben. This is my name here. I can't walk away. This is my name, my mates, my dough."

They said, "You're gonna get the dough."

But it escalated into a little underworld feud. I wasn't going to rest until there was closure on this – because I didn't want to lose face. I wanted either the guns or the money back. Later there was like a gangsters' meeting in Gilday's house. Curtis [Warren] was there. I said, "You know your mate [The Security Boss], I'm going to cap [shoot] him."

He said, "You're not going to cap him."

I said, "I'm not scared of you, mate. I'm on me own."

On your own is the best because at the end of the day, you live or die by your own bat. They have millions of pounds between them but I didn't give a fuck. I'm not a back-stabber, I said to Curtis, "I don't fear you. You could have me scrubbed.

"But you wouldn't do it yourself." Then I left. Then Gilday comes knocking on me door. He tells me that they like me, that I'm all right. That's because I'd stood up to them. I said, "I don't give a fuck whether they like me or not. They don't know me. I shouldn't have to go down there for the money, Tommy.

"I shouldn't have to do that."

Then Curtis phoned up, said, "I'll get your dough back."

But nothing happened, so I went in the jug to see Haase and Bennett, right. Sat down with Ben. Then he started backtracking, saying that I shouldn't have done business with them. He goes, "I wouldn't have done it with them."

"What?" I said. "It was you who put them on me. You introduced them to me! Now you're backtracking."

I knew I wasn't getting any sense out of them, so I just decided to sort it myself. I goes back down the Southend, right.

Had a meet with The Security Boss and The Iceman. Two of them in the car. I jump in the back of the car. They come in with caps on, plugging [intimidating] me. But I wasn't wobbling. They thought everyone else would, but I wouldn't.

Stood me ground. Then I said, "Listen, lads, I can't let this go.

"I'll die for this. And I will do because I am not having my mates calling me a fucking rat." I got the money back in the end. And I thought, "You'll never ever do this to me again."

After that, I felt that Haase and Ben had used me. But I was loyal so I carried on. They never trusted me 100 per cent.

... At the end of the day, what I done for them [Haase and Bennett] meant they walked out of prison in 1996 because of me.

That was me, right. I never got paid for it. They wouldn't give me fuck all [for planting the guns]. The money used for it all was really the Turks' cash – from the missing gear. But they didn't give a fuck about the Turks. They used their money.

Ben wanted me to meet the Customs. He asked me to meet certain people. But I didn't want to meet them. No way was I going to sit down with Cook, that motherfucker. Then Merseyside Police wanted to see Haase and Ben but they were fucked off by the Cussies *[Customs & Excise]*. They were obliged to protect them.

SULEYMAN ERGUN   I knew they were planting guns because Bennett told me on the exercise yard when we were on remand in Walton in about November 1993. Kaya and Manuk were also there. We were demanding the million pounds they owed us for the fifty kilos. But he said – and this was actually before he did it – that he was gonna plant Semtex, guns and heroin to get out and that they were gonna use it to get us out as well. It was a good plan, but I knew the bit about us was bullshit. He was only going to get Haase and himself free. He told me that Chris No-Neck was gonna be in charge, it would be in Liverpool and that they had already done one dummy run.

There was also a bird called The Supervisor who was in charge. She was the one who came into prison all the time to see him.

Haase was always on the phone to No-Neck for hours. On the dummy run, Haase said that they had told the Customs about some guns in a few boxes and that the police swooped on them straight away but there was nothing there. By that time, I had become wary of them. I didn't trust Haase so I just pretended to go along with them.

Ben later told me about planting the guns on the boat. It was supposed to have come from Venezuela, but it never actually left Liverpool docks. John Haase was the brains behind everything.

Because we kept asking about our million quid, they got themselves shipped out from Walton to Strangeways. John didn't get nicked in his cell with that vodka, Scotch, pot, the Es and the phone for nothing. That was a set-up so they could move.

Months later, a special visit was arranged for me to go to see Haase in Strangeways in the solicitor's visiting room. I got a special taxi cab from my prison in Liverpool. By then, they had done a good few plants. They had a message from a mate on the outside. It was from The Banker [Curtis Warren's boss] offering help. But I kindly refused – I didn't need it. Haase just said about the gun plants that "we're gonna do more". All the plants were a massive fucking hoax. Then they started blagging me that they were gonna help me with it. But they were just trying to play me. They had set the meeting up to persuade me to plead guilty. I later found out that they were doing that on behalf of Customs as a condition of the deal to get out. They said I was looking at fifteen or twenty years. I told them that I didn't give a shit – I was gonna go not guilty. Then they told me that they planted eighty shotguns in one go.

They told me who planted them for No-Neck. It was a lad who was on remand with us but he got out. He was all right. He did a few plants for them.

No-Neck did everything. Years later, he told me that he did the planting – that's when I fell out with him. Then Eddie Croker told me about five kilos of Semtex they had planted.

Eddie also told me that they were planting heroin. Haase had promised Eddie that he would get out as well. Eddie knew it was bull but he kept quiet because he was shit scared of Haase.

In Full Sutton, Ben was bouncing around the wings like a kid. I was getting packets and packets of trips. He was taking them and bouncing around the wings like a kid.

We knew John would fuck us over, so me and Kaya decided to do our own plants. But instead of guns, we were going to plant massive stashes of heroin in holes in a forest and then grass them up. Ten or twenty kilos at a time. But we called it off because we knew that because they had done the guns, it just wouldn't work. We didn't have a relationship with Customs.

Over a three-month period between February and May 1994, seven huge arms caches were "discovered" by police. On 4 February, a stash included a Kalashnikov, an Uzi and seven Czech machine guns. One haul unearthed on Monday, 14 February 1994 – the biggest ever on Merseyside – included eighty brand-new Italian Armi Technique twelve-bore shotguns worth £30,000 retail still in their boxes. The shotguns were the parcel bought by No-Neck with the help of James Turner and were stashed in a red Daihatsu in Bootle. They had been part of a consignment of eighty-nine that had been stolen from a lorry while the driver was asleep near Oxford six days earlier. Another stash gave up ten sub-machine guns, five silencers, three magazines and 229 rounds of ammunition. The first find, in February, yielded thirteen automatic weapons. On 31 March, buried wartime rifles were dug up in Formby. Four discoveries in April turned up pistols and a machine gun in Fazakerley, AK-47s in West Derby, a Czech pistol in Stanley Park and, among other weapons, an elephant gun in Ellesmere Port. In June, six Uzis were recovered.

The finds were sold to the public as a major coup in the fight against organized crime. Confidently, investigating officers immediately ruled out a terrorist link and said the guns were definitely heading for the criminal underworld. It was just the success that Merseyside Police had desperately been looking for. The city was reeling from a recent spate of gangland shootings. The success of Curtis Warren's drug operation was causing friction between those favoured distributors who were growing rich on his business and those gangsters who were being kept out of the loop. The rivalry would eventually lead to the shooting of David Ungi on 1 May 1995, though there was no evidence to suggest that he was involved in drug dealing.

Big photo-calls were staged by the police in which serious

looking officers posed with the staggering array of weapons they had taken off the streets. The press conferences were reminiscent of the RUC displaying captured IRA weapons in Northern Ireland. It was unprecedented on the mainland.

Experts, like celebrity cop John Stalker, were wheeled in to ominously explain how Merseyside had become a "staging post for gun-runners", but that the good news was the police were getting on top of it. A police spokesman said, "The information is proving spot on. We are trying to improve intelligence - this shows it is working."

John Haase's scam could work because Customs & Excise together with Haase and his gang all wanted it to. No one who was not guilty, apart from the hapless if unsympathetic con who found himself the victim of the gun plant, Thomas Bourke, stood to lose, and the handful of guilty were from the establishment, not the underworld.

As journalist Nick Cohen wrote in the New Statesman *in 2005, "It all sounded very secret and very important. Yet the truth was that, from the Home Secretary downwards, the criminal justice system had fallen for the simplest of cons. Real informers change their names and go into hiding."*

In November 2008 Peter Kilfoyle, Labour MP for Walton, Liverpool, made a speech in Britain's House of Commons which drew on the dogged investigative work of journalist Graham Johnson, and in which he observed that the loser was the criminal justice system itself. Along with cases such as that of Brian Charrington (a "supergrass" whose discredited evidence had implicated Curtis Warren), John Haase's activities served to finally discredit the supergrass system.

As the MP observed, "They [Haase and Bennett] were so arrogant, they thought that they could swagger around the streets of Liverpool at their old trade and nobody would notice, or at least nobody would get at them. If they had done what the judge in the original trial believed they were going to do, which was to change their identities and go to South America, nobody would have known what had happened. Nobody would have had a clue, and I wonder in how many other cases that remains so because of the secrecy that obtains in the exercise of the Royal Prerogative."

Freed after serving eleven months of their original eighteen-year sentences, Haase and Bennett were convicted in 2008, as a result of Operation Ainstable, of organizing the gun plants that secured their release. They were returned to prison for twenty and twenty-two years respectively, Bennett's increased sentence reflecting the fact that he had been on the run in the meantime.

Conspiracy theorists point to unfinished business from some further evidence in the case: that bribes were passed to unnamed officials within the court system in order to properly fix their original release. These are alleged to have totalled over a million pounds, and to have been made in five drops. Two of these are alleged to have taken place at the Forte Crest Hotel near London's Regent's Park, with sums of money left for collection on room-service trays outside a particular suite, and no one seen by either side. It's alleged that a cousin of the Home Secretary of the time, Michael Howard, a convicted Liverpool speed dealer who was known to Haase, was involved with these two payments.

However, these allegations originated with Haase, and with those close to him. It's suggested that bribes were paid after some within the police service and judiciary were becoming suspicious of the scam. But suspicion remained – Liverpool Police tried more than once to gain access to Haase and conduct their own investigation into the gun plants, but lost out to Customs & Excise in internal discussions.

Meanwhile, the Turks had not been paid. So the bribe rumours were backed up by Suleyman Ergun, who asked for the million pounds he was still owed for fifty kilos of heroin. "Bennett said the money was getting switched to big people that would help us all get out. Bennett was so happy he was clapping about it. So I put the debt on hold." The chances are those "big people" were really Haase's confidants, like Chris No-Neck, for their gun-buying trips. Far better and more convenient to suggest this war chest found its way into *the hallowed halls of the police and judiciary, where it's truly to be assumed beyond recovery.*

Home Secretaries act on briefings, rubber-stamping before they're off to the House or home for dinner, and the real scandal is, as Kilfoyle points out, that all the way up to the compiling of those briefing papers, there were no checks or balances – not a single person who had any incentive to think that Haase and Bennett's gun and drug plants might not be for real.

10

Cocky: the Rise and Fall of Curtis Warren, Britain's Biggest Drug Baron

Tony Barnes, Richard Elias and Peter Walsh

On 3 December 2009, Curtis Warren was sentenced to thirteen years in prison for his part (leading, of course) in a plot to import £1 million of Dutch dope via France to Jersey. At the time of his arrest for this offence, he had been out of Dutch custody for a grand total of five weeks, having been sentenced to seven years in 1997 for importing over £100 million of cocaine, Ecstasy and cannabis (a load of routine value for Warren), with four years added for manslaughter when he killed another prisoner in a brawl.

It would be a naive comment to say that he didn't take long to get up to his old tricks upon release – reading even a little of the literature on the drugs trade will reveal that a prison sentence is often little more than a head-office relocation, along with the logistical and communications difficulties that might present for any small-to-medium-sized company. Pablo Escobar famously deigned to commission his own prison, "The Cathedral", while Warren's fellow Scouser, John Haase, ran the complex gun- and drug-plants that would earn him a Royal Pardon from his cell (see chapter 10).

It would also miss the point that to apprehend a man like Warren having a hands-on role in an operation like this would be like watching Jensen Button take part in a Saturday stock-car race. The man had been on telephone terms with the tallest poppies of the opium trade, cocaine and synthetic-drug trades. And here he was punting a boatload of blow (in UK-English not US-English argot) in local waters.

If he was, as was claimed in his trial defence, skint enough to require another job to fund himself, then it flies in the face of the hype: Warren, the Cocky Watchman, was a Toxteth folk-hero, a robber who rose to be a multi-millionaire. Gifted at recalling names, numbers and faces, Warren was the star pupil that never was. A high-flyer in a fairer world, he was the mixed-race Scally from the streets who thumbed his nose at the establishment. Driving his Lexus around Liverpool was a show of front. But it also gave hope to other Italian-leisurewear-clad would-be gangsters, whether he intended it to or not, that one of their own had found his dolce vita, and so parts of the city took his fists and threats to their heart.

Though he famously made it onto The Sunday Times Rich List *thanks to his property empire, it's reasonable to assume that a vast portion of his wealth might be found nowhere with his name on it –but in foreign fields (literally: several London gangsters, it is reported, lost significant sums in cash they could not retrieve before the Euro-zone was created in 1998), tax-haven bank accounts or among the assets of grateful and/or threatened, awaiting its recall, perhaps with interest.*

If this is the case, then the psychology of Warren's participation provides a rich seam for criminology students to mine. What motivated him? Our common image of the gangster is that they are seeking their place in the sun, the day when they will not have to look over their shoulder, as per the film Sexy Beast. *To many it becomes clear that they'll end their days at the hands of their enemies, or even friends, thanks to what they know, or else in a cell.*

So why does anyone, especially someone of Warren's underworld stature, return to the graft and the scams? (It's not as if he wouldn't want to touch his capital, purely for investment purposes, next to the other risks involved.) And especially when he was such a marked man? Quoted after the recent Jersey conviction, Bill Hughes, the director general of Britain's Serious Organized Crime Agency, said: "Serious organized criminals don't suddenly stop just because they've been caught once. That's why when a criminal comes on to SOCA's radar, they stay there for life. Curtis Warren was a career criminal for whom prison was a temporary setback. He was already planning his next operation from inside prison, and when he was released SOCA was waiting, watching and listening." In the five weeks after his release, they recorded 1,500 phone calls, and had Warren and a co-defendant under surveillance as they visited the beach on the east Jersey shore (not to be confused with Tony Soprano's turf) on to which they planned to make their drop.

Upon his release, Warren would have known the intentions, if not the reach, of "the bizzies". Perhaps he found the stakes compulsively high – a problem gambler will invariably tell you that they remember one big win that set them on their way. Perhaps a gambler with Cocky's record of success could not but feel driven to carry on. In other words, what's life about if we can't get our kicks? As Warren confided to Stephen French (see chapter 11), *"I've got enough money to stop and I wouldn't have to work again. But what am I going to do? Fucking sit at home and watch daytime TV?"*

The following extract from Cocky: The Rise and Fall of Curtis Warren, Britain's Biggest Drug Baron *by Tony Barnes, Richard Elias and Peter Walsh (Milo Books, 2001), sheds light on how the Colombian Cali cartel's move into Europe (see chapter 6* Drug Lords: The Rise and Fall of the Cali Cartel) *was achieved, and how Curtis Warren became a major player thanks to their network:*

The point man in the Cali Cartel's new assault on the European and US markets would be Mario Halley, a personable, multi-lingual young Colombian. Halley was a natural salesman, well-connected and shrewd beyond his twenty-two years. His potential was spotted early: by young adulthood he had been sent from his native Colombia to Europe, settling in the Netherlands and successfully applying for Dutch citizenship.

There he set to work. The account of how the Colombians and the Liverpool mafia tried – and partially succeeded – in flooding the UK with cocaine is murky and complicated . . . What is not in dispute is that in Amsterdam Mario Halley met a Liverpudlian ex-boxer who was resident in Holland. Halley treated him royally, jetting him to California on Concorde, and entertaining him in Venezuela.

It was a getting-to-know-you period on both sides.

With trust established, Halley was introduced to Curtis Warren and, through him, to a shady figure named Brian Charrington.

In March 1991, the Tynemouth lifeboat was called out to rescue three men who had abandoned ship in stormy weather off the north-east coast of England and were adrift in a small inflatable. One of them was Brian Charrington. *[Unknown to Customs & Excise, Charrington, a major cannabis smuggler was also a police informant for the Cleveland drugs squad.]* He and his friends had been sailing out to meet another boat when a heavy storm struck and they were unable to get back to port. The following day, none the worse for his ordeal, he flew to Holland with a friend named Curtis Warren. How the pair first met is not known – it was possibly through mutual acquaintances on the Spanish Costa del Crime – but it seems they struck up a quick rapport. When Charrington returned from Holland, he spoke to DS Weedon, who in turn phoned DI Knaggs:

[Weedon] reported to me that BC . . . had been over to Rotterdam with a man called Curtis Warren and . . . had met a Colombian national called Mario Halley, obviously a close associate of Curtis Warren. DSW [Weedon] told me that they had been put up in an expensive hotel, seen large quantities of what appeared to be very good quality cocaine and they had been treated like royalty by Halley, who had huge amounts of money. Talk had been of a huge importation of cocaine into Europe from Colombia or Venezuela within the next five to eight months. At the time they said they already had a suitable vessel which had been purchased and was going over to South America which would have a replacement hold fitted and into which 2,000 kilograms of cocaine would be concealed and then despatched to Europe ... Halley had asked BC if he would like to go to Colombia with him to meet the organizers and possibly form part of the crew. Curtis Warren had also been invited.

The two Teesside detectives felt they had hit the jackpot. If Enigma One was telling the truth, it was the biggest job any copper could expect to pull: the largest narcotics importation into Europe ever. The Colombian cartels were the most potent criminal organizations in the world; here was an informant offering an "in" at the highest level. On top of that, the story had elements which could be checked out. Flight records showed that Warren had indeed been to Holland with Charrington. And the names of Warren and Halley rang bells; the Cleveland officers were aware that they had cropped up in a high-level operation called Bruise being conducted by their RCS counterparts in the Midlands. With a growing sense of excitement, Knaggs and his immediate boss drove down to meet officers from the number four Regional Crime Squad in Staffordshire and passed on what they had heard.

Charrington was balancing on a knife edge. "The guy must have balls of steel," said a source familiar with the case. "I think it was an ego thing with him. He thought he could outsmart everybody." The risks were brought home when he showed DS Weedon an eight-inch bundle of documents. It contained confidential intelligence reports from law enforcement agencies in England, Spain, Holland, Canada and Scandinavia and direct references to Operation Bruise. He claimed Warren had given him the file. If his claims were true, it meant Cocky had a top-level mole. For all his bravado, Charrington was deeply uneasy. When asked if he would help to target Warren specifically, he refused.

Yet that autumn, Charrington did travel to South America

with Warren. What happened there is still not entirely clear. What is beyond doubt is that somebody put together a deal to bring unprecedented amounts of Colombian cocaine into Britain.

The essentials of any large-scale smuggling enterprise are money, transport, storage and a plausible front.

The money for the deal was put up by the Liverpool mafia; in particular, the Banker. Transport and storage at the UK end were arranged by his friend Brian "Snowy" Jennings, a haulage contractor and wheeler-dealer with fingers in many pies. "Snowy was a thief but people thought a lot about him," said one source: "He was a genuinely nice guy. He was worth a fortune but dressed like an unmade bed." With the arrangements in hand, all that remained was to find a business that could appear to be making a legitimate importation.

Enter Joseph Kassar. An entrepreneur of Ghanaian birth, he graduated from Manchester Business School before starting a number of small businesses, mainly in textiles.

His acumen and ambition brought him a good lifestyle and a white mansion, with lawns sweeping down to a brook, in a middle-class Manchester suburb. Among his longest-standing contacts was a Liverpudlian who supplied him with goods ranging from wool to cocoa beans: Brian Jennings. Late in 1991, Kassar started exporting reconditioned plant and machinery to Ghana, mainly for road construction. But he was in trouble. As the recession bit, he faced business and personal debts of around £375,000 and owed £200,000 on a mortgage.

Kassar put a proposition to a distant cousin, Emmanuel Nana-Asare, known as "Joey", who lived in south London and imported fruit and vegetables. Kassar said two of his pals, "Mario and Brian", wanted help importing scrap metal from Venezuela. A profit of up to twenty per cent was promised. Kassar said he was too busy to get involved but wondered if Asare might be interested. It sounded good.

Asare set up a firm called Jena Enterprises and was given the number of the Conar Corporation in Caracas. After numerous transatlantic calls and faxes, he arranged to import forty tonnes of aluminium and eighty-five tonnes of lead in ingots. What Joey did not know – and what Kassar was later cleared of complicity in arranging – was that the ingots were an ingenious method of moving drugs.

Inside each huge lump of lead, impervious to X-rays and so thick that unless you knew where to drill you had little chance of finding anything, would be a steel box containing cocaine.

In September 1991, nine days before the load was due to leave Venezuela, Curtis Warren and Brian Charrington arrived at Dover in a new Jaguar, telling Customs officials they were going to France for a holiday. Both showed British visitors' passports, valid for one year and useable only in Europe. Both, however, had ten-year passports concealed in their pockets. From France they flew to Malaga, then Madrid, then on to Caracas, booking into the Hilton Hotel. Mario Halley was also in Caracas; Ivonne Cruzatty saw him in the Conar office with two Englishmen.

Prosecutors would later claim – unsuccessfully – that Warren was in South America to oversee the departure of the drugs. Certainly the ingots, with paperwork checked and stamped, left Puerto Cabello, Venezuela's main port, at this time. At the Dominican Republic, the containers were unloaded and placed on board a ship called the *Caraibe*, which then set sail across the Atlantic to Felixstowe, her final destination being Piraeus in Greece. Halley left for New York, while Warren and Charrington returned to Europe. In Spain they put their ten-year passports into an envelope and posted it to a flat in Amsterdam. Then they reversed their original journey, picked up the Jag in France and drove on to a car ferry, showing their visitors' passports at Dover, thus "proving" they had remained in mainland Europe the whole time.

Charrington did not initially tell his police handlers about the trip. When he did, they could scarcely believe their ears. He said he had been introduced to a druglord of unimaginable wealth, as DS Knaggs later recounted:

BC said that the man he had met in Colombia was called E [name withheld], who owned a large yacht called The *Lady*. E's yacht was anchored at La Guera and then sailed on to the

Rochas Islands off Colombia. A number of influential people were aboard the yacht and very beautiful girls, for example, Miss Colombia. After sailing, E took them by private plane into the Colombian jungle where he visited one of his drug factories – but BC stayed at the plane and he did not see the factory. Talk of E having a personal fortune of 900 million dollars buried in the jungle around the factory site. E gets the US dollars back from the US in imported partitioned water tankers.

Charrington also said a Turkish contingent who were major heroin importers had been in Colombia to meet the same people, as had a group of Italians. With the substantial caveat that Enigma One's word must be suspect, this suggested a confluence of the most influential crime groups in the world: a cocaine cartel, the Italian Mafia and the Turkish *babas*. As top-level drugs intelligence goes, this was as good as it gets. He repeated his claim that 2,000 kilograms of cocaine was heading for Europe but said he had no idea how or when it would arrive. "BC said he could give us the biggest job there had ever been but that it had to be realized that he had to be heavily involved with these people to gain their trust," recorded DS Knaggs.

"BC said he wanted a realistic reward and also some protection from smaller agencies that might be involved."

Trust was in short supply. On 8 October, the North East RCS finally disclosed to Customs & Excise that Charrington was an informant. The effect of this news can only be imagined. Not only did protocol dictate that Customs should have been told much earlier but also they had been targeting Charrington for months – in co-operation with the RCS – in the still on-going Operation Python. Customs officers were, and still are, deeply critical of the relationship between Charrington and his handlers.

They believed Enigma One should have remained Target One.

Events unfolded at increasing speed. On 16 October, Mario Halley flew into Manchester Airport for a whistlestop meeting with Curtis Warren. Two days later, the *Caraibe* docked at Felixstowe. Kassar told his cousin, Joey, who had no idea what was really going on, that the lead could be stored on an industrial estate near Liverpool's famous Aintree racecourse until they found a buyer. Snowy Jennings paid £2,000 to rent a unit. It was here, allegedly, that the cocaine would be removed from the ingots.

Warren spoke repeatedly to Kassar and Halley during this time, using two new mobile phones, while Halley, every inch the international sales executive, was calling Milan, Amsterdam, Piraeus and Caracas. The Colombian already had a Conar Corporation bank account set up in Amsterdam. Now the drugs were on British soil, it was time to pay up.

The Caracas police drugs unit first learned about Conar in October 1991. They were too busy to investigate immediately but someone did tip off British Customs that a major shipment was due to arrive, probably in a consignment of metal. So when the *Caraibe* arrived at Felixstowe, a rummage team paid particular attention to her cargo. They took photographs of several containers and examined the ingots from the Conar shipment. One was removed and an attempt made to drill into it. The drill bit was too short to penetrate to the hidden box and snapped inside the lead. The searchers gave up; anyway, they were looking for concealments within the container, not the ingots.

It was a disaster. Just inches away from them was a suspected 500 kilos of cocaine – and they missed it.

Apparently the Colombians knew that HM Customs did not possess any drill that went deeper than twenty-five centimetres and had adapted their packaging accordingly.

The containers at Felixstowe were cleared by Customs on October 30 and were sent by rail and lorry to the Aintree lock-up. The *Caraibe* sailed on with another 500 kilos still aboard. "It went on to Piraeus," said a Customs officer.

"From there, they were going to bring the drugs overland to Holland. But the Yugoslavian Civil War broke out and blocked their land route. They stopped that plan and shipped it instead."

Jesus Camillo Ortiz now arrived in England and checked into a hotel near Aintree. As Conar's deputy chairman, he knew exactly how to extract the cocaine from the ingots. Each weighed two tonnes and had to be lifted several feet off the floor to allow someone underneath to cut away the lead and reach the steel box inside. While this was allegedly going on, Halley checked into the Park Lane Hilton in London. He bought at least three BMWs for cash, planning to send them abroad – it was one way of moving a lot of money out of the country. He also picked up an English girlfriend and was having a good time.

Joseph Kassar too was suddenly flush. He gave his wife a plastic bag with £40,000 in cash stuffed inside. He also ordered new plant to be shipped out to Ghana and drew up a list of vehicles he intended to buy for his West African business. As for Curtis Warren, all anyone could prove was that he had travelled and met with certain people and made certain phone calls.

The only task remaining was to dispose of the empty lead ingots. Snowy Jennings paid his (innocent) son-in-law to dispose of the scrap metal and it was buried under tonnes of rubble. A week later it was dug up and sold, ending up at a yard in Newcastle-upon-Tyne where it was melted down. The deal's financiers could now celebrate.

They had paid £14,000 a kilo for almost-pure cocaine.

When cut and sold on the streets for around £80,000 a kilo, it would yield a profit of at least £70 million.

It seems that the authorities first knew of the importation in early November, when Charrington told DS Weedon that 500 kilos had come in and the job "had gone off perfectly right under the noses of Customs, who did not have a clue". Charrington claimed he had only learned the details of the shipment after its delivery and so could not have warned the police in advance. His involvement was to be in laundering the proceeds for Halley. On one occasion he produced a sack with £900,000 in it to prove his point. He was changing the sterling into dollars, using bureaus de change in London.

He also said the Colombians were pumping five tonnes a month in to the US and Europe, using the same method and the same shipping line.

Enigma One was playing a very dangerous game. "The Colombians think nothing of killing any official of any nationality, with life being to them extremely cheap," noted Knaggs. "BC said it was urgent we get on with it and if we were not interested in the job to tell him now so that he could get out, as anyone even suspected of informing would be murdered. BC said only a handful of people resident in the UK knew of Halley's activities and if it became obvious that the leak came from England, then the Colombians would eliminate them all."

Inexplicably, it seems that little effort was ever made to recover the drugs. "Not then, nor at any subsequent time, did the Customs or, for that matter, any senior police officers, ask for myself or DSW to pursue an investigation into the 500-kilogram importation that we had been told about by BC," recorded DI Knaggs. "Had they done so at this time, we could have had a positive result. Everyone's eyes were on the next job."

Almost immediately after the dispersal of the first shipment, a second was set in train using the same method.

Thirty-two cylindrical ingots, each four feet high, would leave for Liverpool on the freighter MV *Advisor*. They would contain another monster load of cocaine: 900 kilos, worth £150 million on the street. The Cali Cartel was going for broke. (Fourteen tonnes of cocaine would be seized in Britain and Europe in 1991, up from virtually nothing six years earlier.)

Customs were persuaded at last to meet Brian Charrington and establish what to do with him. The meeting was arranged for a hotel in the seaside resort of Scarborough. Present were Knaggs, Weedon, Charrington and an experienced Customs investigator. It did not go well. Drink was consumed and there was "an element of confrontation and argument", according to Knaggs.

Charrington made a crack about Weedon and Knaggs being on the take; it was intended as a joke but fell flat.

The Customs officer questioned Weedon's integrity and Knaggs got the distinct impression he "thought DS Weedon and myself were bent". However Customs did eventually agree to pay Charrington a reward – the figure of £500,000 was bandied around – if he helped them identify the source of the shipment. He agreed and gave them the name of the shipping company. He also revealed the drugs would again be in ingots.

That December the Venezuelan police raided the Conar Corporation and closed its offices. Nevertheless, the shipment continued, setting sail a few days later. This time it was being monitored by Customs and the police.

Charrington told them the plan was for the ingots to be unloaded at Felixstowe and then taken by road to Liverpool.

They arrived on 12 January 1992, and Kassar rented a warehouse in Derbyshire to store the ingots. Charrington continued, with official sanction, to launder money so his cover would not be blown; at one stage he even asked a Customs officer if he could get him a better exchange rate, as the bureaus de change were "pissing him off".

Before the authorities could move on the gang, there was yet another development, this time in Holland. On Saturday, 18 January, Brigadier Simon van Rijn of the Dutch police led a team of officers on a raid at a warehouse and an adjoining property. They arrested three men including Jesus Camillo Ortiz. "He was actually wearing goggles and gloves and holding a drill to an ingot when he was arrested," said one of the Dutch officers. In the warehouse were thirty-five lead ingots and a variety of metal-cutting tools. Each ingot held thirty-seven packets of cocaine, a total of 845 kilos.

According to DI Knaggs, the Colombians now contacted the "men in the UK to warn them that the consignment at Felixstowe would have to be sacrificed".

The innocent Joey Nana-Asare received a telephone call from a Liverpudlian called "John". "Don't touch the consignment," ordered John. "All my friends have been picked up in Holland. We'll find a better way of bringing it in."

Asare was mystified. Why would anyone be arrested over a pile of metal? "This was the start of my nightmare," he later recalled. "I told him, I am doing genuine business.

"But he just hung up."

Minutes later, John rang back. He was curt. "I told you.

"Forget about the consignment."

"What do you mean?"

Again the phone went dead. Shocked and intimidated, Joey found the number of a solicitor in the *Yellow Pages*.

Within twenty-four hours he was talking to Customs.

Meanwhile, Curtis Warren was spotted in Smithdown Road, Liverpool – yards from where he had previously robbed a post office – using a public telephone box to dial Joseph Kassar's home in Accra. Later that day Kassar rang Asare from Ghana. The police were listening in. Asare complained about the call from the mysterious John.

JK   *He said what?*

JNA   *He said, "Forget the consignment. All my friends have been picked up in Holland. We sent the consignment through Greece. The fork-lift driver fucked up. Now all my friends have been picked up so don't go to Felixstowe. Don't touch anything." He starts giving me orders. In fact, I was bloody annoyed.*

JK   *Joey, listen. All you have to say to him is, "Talk to Joe."*

JNA   *That is exactly what I said: "Have you spoken to Joe?" He says he does not know how to get into contact with you, so I said, "Give me a number, I can talk to you* [Kassar] *and then we can get to the bottom of this. "Then the guy says, 'Look, I've run out of money,' and that's it.*

Kassar ignored the advice to "forget the consignment". He told Asare he would come over to England and instructed him to find a new warehouse for lead. He also warned him to "stay off the phone". It was too late. Operation Singer was up and running.

That Wednesday, the lead and its hidden cargo arrived at a warehouse near Stoke-on-Trent. At night, it received a secret visit from a ten-strong police-Customs team. One of them was Customs officer Peter Hollier. "The bottom of the first ingot was cut open and revealed a tight casket in the bottom with a lipped entrance," he recalled. "I prised open the lips and inside were twenty-eight packages of cocaine. We opened another two ingots that night and they took some work because we were not exactly sure how to get into them. It was very strenuous. It took us almost three hours to get into the first ingot but we had to stop during daylight and only returned again when it was dark. There were twenty-eight or twenty-nine packages in each ingot." Officers removed 905 kilos of cocaine with a purity of between eighty and ninety per cent, the biggest single haul seized in the UK up to that time. Then they resealed the ingots and put the warehouse under observation.

At around the same time, Warren flew to Amsterdam and met Halley. He returned three days later and drove a Rover Sterling to Cheshire to meet Kassar, who had flown in from Ghana to sort things out. The ingots – having secretly been emptied – were moved again, first to an industrial estate on Merseyside and then to a storage depot in Runcorn. Staff were told that someone would be "picking up one of the ingots and taking it away for testing".

A middle-aged man from Liverpool turned up in a car followed by a friend driving a flatbed truck. The ingot was loaded onto the truck. After a circuitous route it was transferred to a lorry and driven to Huskisson Dock on the Liverpool seafront, where it was unceremoniously dumped. It was to lie on the quayside for three weeks, untouched, before being collected and returned to Runcorn.

The Liverpool gang, said Charrington, now knew there was no coke in the ingots. They were expecting "a pull" but believed there was little hard evidence against them. In March, Charrington travelled to Fuengirola in southern Spain to meet Halley and find out what was going on.

Weedon and Knaggs went as well, shadowing him. Halley never showed up; the Cali Cartel's European sales manager had been arrested in Holland, supervising yet another 800-kilo shipment, and was charged with conspiracy to import cocaine. Warren was now under massive surveillance and believed a spotter plane was following him. The unwitting Joe Kassar, however, was determined to push ahead. He booked into a Cheshire hotel with his Swedish mistress and moved all thirty-one (empty) ingots back to yet another warehouse in Stoke. With arrests imminent, Charrington decided he would be better off in Spain for a few days.

Just after 10 p.m. on Sunday, 29 March, Customs officers and police burst into Joe Kassar's room in the Kilton Inn, near Knutsford. He was in the bathroom. As he saw the officers, he tried to throw away a piece of paper with a Vodafone number on it. They had little trouble arresting the mild-mannered Kassar but Warren was considered a different proposition. He had convictions for violence against police officers, albeit when he was a teenager. He was located at a girlfriend's house in Tuebrook, Liverpool. A contingent from the Midlands Regional Crime Squad, which had been working on Warren since Operation Bruise, travelled up to join the bust. They booked into the Adelphi Hotel in central Liverpool posing as the "West Midlands County Council", saying they were something to do with the inquiry into the Hillsborough football disaster.

"We were warned Warren had a Rottweiler dog and was built like Mike Tyson," said a Customs officer. "We had an armed police team but unfortunately it was nine in the morning, with kids going to school and the binmen coming round. It wasn't ideal. I was sent round the back of the house and I thought, if he comes running out I'm going to have to hit him with the bin because it's the only way I'm going to stop him.

"Anyway we smashed our way in and he didn't try to leg it. But he was giving us a right mouthful, all kinds of abuse. Then this police inspector came in and gave him a mouthful right back. I had a quick look around, then wrote down what he was saying – which wasn't very nice – and asked him if he wanted to sign my notebook as a statement of what had happened. He was sitting on the settee and his exact reply was, 'How can I sign your notebook with my hands cuffed behind my back, you cunt?' The cops had slapped the cuffs on him and I hadn't realized. As for the Rottweiler, fortunately it was quite old and docile."

Warren had £1,000 in cash, a Bearcat scanning device for intercepting police frequencies, and an envelope with a British visitor's passport inside. Beside his bed was a mobile phone – bearing the number on the scrap of paper Kassar had apparently tried to hide. "Curtis was taken to the central detention centre. He saw one of the Midlands officers and said, 'Oh! You're with the West Midlands County Council. You were staying in the Adelphi, weren't you?' The cops got a real fucking fright. Curtis knew everything that went on in Liverpool."

Around a dozen other men were arrested. Most remained silent, though one or two who had been involved in a minor way in moving or storing the ingots did answer questions. They said they were acting entirely innocently and knew nothing of any drugs. All were charged with conspiring to import cocaine.

The trial of the Operation Singer defendants began in April 1993, having been sensationally relocated from Manchester after Stephen Mee, a defendant in another drugs case who would later go on to work with Warren, was sprung from custody in an armed raid on a prison van.

In the event, what followed was the stuff of criminal legend. The judge, Justice May, ruled that there was insufficient evidence to convict Warren and directed the jury to acquit him. This was because, although it could be inferred that the absent Mario Halley was involved in the drugs trade generally, there was "no possible evidential basis for inferring that Halley was concerned with the particular importations which are the subject of this case." It is denied by all the officers involved, but was reported in several newspapers, that as Warren left the court he remarked, "I'm off to spend my 87 million quid from the first shipment and you can't fucking touch me."

Of those tried following Operation Singer, only Joseph Kassar, who had thought he was trading a cargo of ingots, did not walk free. The Ghanaian's conviction was eventually quashed by the Court of Appeal in 2004, after eleven years of imprisonment. Meanwhile, cocaine flooded the streets of north-west England, with a twenty-eight per cent rise in seizures in 1992 and a rise in cocaine-related arrests of over fifty per cent.

Warren's spirits rose as holes began to appear in the prosecution's case. It was revealed that Joey Nana-Asare had been paid by Customs for his help – around £20,000 plus around £19,000 for expenses – though a Customs officer denied defence suggestions that the money was to ensure his attendance at court. The biggest bombshell, however, was a ruling by the judge concerning the absent Mario Halley. The court had heard how he went to Liverpool with Warren when the first load of drugs was being removed there; how he met Charrington, Warren and others when the cocaine was being sold and distributed; and how he spent the next few days buying top-of-the-range cars for export in Park Lane showrooms, paying with bundles of cash. Yet this, said Mr Justice May, was not enough.

"Whereas it might be possible to suspect and perhaps infer that Halley was concerned with drugs generally . . . there is, in my judgment, no possible evidential basis for inferring that Halley was concerned with the particular importations which are the subject of this case," said the judge. Any evidence of Warren's contact with Halley could, under the Police and Criminal Evidence Act, adversely affect the fairness of the trial, added the judge.

And with that, he ruled it inadmissible. It was a body blow from which the prosecution never recovered.

"The judge said, so what if he went to Colombia? What did he do there? There was very little left at the end of the day," recalled Keith Dyson, a Manchester solicitor who represented Kassar at the trial and currently acts for Warren.

Yet Halley was at that moment languishing in a Dutch jail, awaiting trial (or his role in the importation of 955 kilos of coke, again in ingots). The judge also excluded evidence relating to Warren's trip to Venezuela.

At the end of the prosecution's case, before a single defence witness had been summoned, Mr Justice May ruled there was insufficient evidence to sustain a conviction against Warren and instructed the jury to acquit him.

Cocky rose and left the dock. What followed has since passed into criminal folklore. According to reports in several newspapers, Warren left the modern courthouse and walked into the street. He then stopped, turned and went back. He took the lift up to the third floor, where a small huddle of shell-shocked Customs officers were gathered, and strode up to them.

"I'm off to spend my £87 million from the first shipment and you can't fucking touch me," he said.

Keith Dyson, Warren's solicitor, denies the incident took place. "The £87 million story is apocryphal. It never happened." True or not, it came to symbolize Warren's self-confidence and sense of invulnerability.

Another legend has grown up around the Cocky Watchman's return to Granby. According to law-enforcement sources, he cruised the streets in an open-topped Lexus as scores of friends and well-wishers came out to greet him. His release from custody had made him a hero in the eyes of some of the Toxteth community. He was the living embodiment of the buck ethos. He was coming to believe he was untouchable, something he would later brag about in a secretly recorded phone call to a close friend, Tony Bray:

CW   *Hey, I come out smelling of fucking roses all the time, don't I?*

TB   *You're a lucky sod, you. You've got the luck if the devil with you, haven't you?*

CW   *Do you reckon?*

TB   *Fucking telling you. You always come out smiling.*

Next, Warren and his girlfriend, Stephanie, went for a two-week holiday abroad. On his return, he was stopped by an unusually large group of Customs officers.

"Welcome back Mr Warren, is it nice to be back out?" one of them asked sarcastically.

"Yes, thanks to British justice," replied Warren.

To their chagrin, Warren and his girlfriend were taken away and searched. Nothing was found but the girlfriend was furious.

"Why did you have to answer back," she demanded.

"It just came out," said Warren.

After two days of deliberations, the jury found Joseph Kassar guilty as charged. They could not agree verdicts for two other defendants involved in the movement of one of the ingots. The men would later be cleared at a re-trial.

The rest were acquitted and walked free immediately. Fall-guy Kassar, aged forty-two, copped the lot. "One and a half tonnes of cocaine means utter degradation, both physical and moral, and perhaps death to thousands of people," the judge told him. He was jailed for twenty-four years, one of the longest sentences ever imposed for a drugs offence in the UK, for "being knowingly concerned in the fraudulent evasion of the prohibition on importation of cocaine". Yet it was scant consolation for the officers of Operation Singer.

[Kassar's conviction was quashed by the Court of Appeal in 2004, and he was freed after eleven years of imprisonment.]

[. . .]Meanwhile the stockpile of cocaine from the first shipment was pouring on to Britain's streets. Police nationwide recorded a twenty-eight per cent rise in coke seizures in 1992. In Greater Manchester, always a ready market for narcotics, cocaine-related arrests rose by almost sixty per cent. The drug landscape had been changed irrevocably. The genie was out of the bottle.

11

The Devil

Graham Johnson

An overview of drug barons would not be complete without an account of the likes of Stephen French, for Frenchie operated as a different kind of underworld aristocrat – a robber baron. Readers familiar with the HBO series The Wire *will recall how Omar earns his living – holding up drug dealers at gunpoint. The closest French's victims could come to law-enforcement, if they were "lucky", would be to call on the likes of Carlton Leach (see chapter 13) to resolve their problem.*

Because so many of Britain's street dealers in the 1980s and 1990s did not have recourse to such protection, the field was clear for guys like Frenchie to exploit them. On occasions, however, the situation could be more political than that – behind the most well-supplied and high-rolling dealers, there was usually someone higher up the supply chain in the background. The following extract deals with how French managed the politics when these situations arose. Fortunately for him, as we'll see, he was well connected.

A Scouser who grew up on the tough streets of Toxteth, Stephen French had run with the Young Black Panthers, was a member of the Federation of Liverpool Black Organizations, and walked a line between radical politics and crime, as people who think for themselves and have no assets often do. He was also a skilled martial artist, and the only value drugs themselves held for him was financial. He also understood that the mental discipline that came with learning fighting skills could, apart from anything else, help you not to lose your bottle and brown your jeans when the going gets tough. Which, as any intelligent hard man will agree, is more than half the battle and often in fact the way to avoid a tense situation turning into a fight – one which no one really wants and which could leave behind a wealth of potential prosecution evidence. A successful property developer today, he looks back on the high-rolling highs – and the very low lows – of a life in crime.

A young associate of Curtis Warren (see chapter 10), French is also included here for his insider's take on the motivations of The Cocky Watchman. As for those lows – French spent the day of his honorary brother's burial straitjacketed in solitary confinement and snotty from a prison beating – perhaps the most respectful way to play it if you cannot be there. The murder of Andrew John is covered in more detail here. A tragic case of a young man with much to live for cut down in cold blood, John's death is a sad example of the collateral damage that can follow when events that were beyond the law to begin with get out of hand.

If you are a tax accountant, you might join a professional body, such as the Chartered Institute of Taxation. They have rules to keep budding taxmen in line, such as client confidentiality. However, if you're going to be a successful taxman in the drugs world, you must learn the following.

THE CODE OF CONDUCT FOR THE STEPHEN FRENCH FOUNDATION OF TAX STUDIES

Rule 1 – Never tax the same person twice If you tax a man once, he can wear it. He may well put it down to experience, an occupational hazard, a necessary evil. However, if you tax him a second time, he *will* get angry, and it's human nature that he *will* seek revenge. This is because a frightened man is a dangerous man. If you tax him twice, he's going to think to himself, "Every time Frenchie is skint, he's going to take my money." You'll force him into taking some action against you.

I had the monologue to deal with this: "I've taken these goods from you, but you have nothing to fear from me ever again. Even if somebody asks me to do something against you in the future, I'll have to tell them that I can't do it because we have history – that I've already done something to you, and I don't want to evoke feelings of fear or panic. So, my advice to you is to wear this tax like a shirt that doesn't fit and just get on with your life."

The psychology behind this rule goes back centuries to Machiavelli. He said that men would often put up with great tragedies befalling them. Nevertheless, the same men would explode with unpredictable fucking ferocity if you managed to slight them in the smallest possible way and, as a result, would spend the rest of their lives seeking revenge. That is what my victims would see a second tax as – a slight against their honour, dignity and self-respect.

Rule 2 – Never chase dead money Dead money is simply cash that is difficult to retrieve. The best tax is when you get the goods first time – often by surprise. But if you learn of a particularly big stash and you go after it and fail, write it off. Don't bother going back for it, because you'll be going into a nest of vipers. Remember, it's only your greed that won't allow you to let go. If it's dead money, it' s likely that you could die in the process of going back for it again.

Rule 3 – Never give the goods back once you've stolen them This seems pretty self-explanatory; however, after you've taxed someone, 101 reasons to give the stolen goods back might present themselves. For instance, a gangster you know might also be mates with the victim, and he'll come lobbying to get the gear back on behalf of his pal. Or the victim or his allies might kidnap one of your gang and hold him for ransom until the goods are restored.

Nevertheless, no matter what shit comes your way, *you must hold firm*, because thems your wages.

Rule 4 Never tax someone you know I'm not even saying for one minute that you'd do it deliberately.

Sometimes it might be done by pure accident. For instance, you might not know when you tax someone that the gear is owned by a mystery third person in the background, who might turn out to be someone you know. Or you might be given some duff info about the ID of your intended victim, and when you attack the feller he turns out to be an associate. If so, you have to make amends. Crossing the line on this one can literally lead to murder, as will be later exemplified in a case study very close to home.

Rule 5 – Never leave physical evidence on the victim Following a nice touch, the difference between jail and a £15,000 holiday in St Lucia can be as minute as a molecule. Don't leave any DNA on the victim. And remember, injuries are the most compelling evidence in court.

There are two other legal factors that are related to this rule, both of which are vital to a taxman – police intelligence and police corruption, the two being interrelated. It's not what the police *know*, it's what they can *prove*. All villains are aware of this. My police intelligence file consists of at least four to five boxes of shit that police claim I've been involved in. Nonetheless, it doesn't fucking matter, because none of it can be proven. The important fact is that my actual police record is only a sheet long. So, from four or five boxes of crime, they have only ever managed to boil it down one sheet's worth of convictions. That's because I make it a top priority never to leave physical evidence behind.

Now, police intelligence can work for you or against you, and this is where the police corruption comes in. For £1,500, I could find out what sort of investigations were going on in relation to me during my taxing days, especially out of one particular police station in Liverpool. In all fairness to the Merseyside Constabulary, Norman Bettison, appointed chief constable in 1998, later cleaned up the force. He was an honest man, and if you were in tune to the nature of the beast, you could actually feel it softening when Bettison came to power. You could actually feel the beast becoming more politically correct, because law and order and fair dealing all took priority over bent officers.

So concludes the Stephen French code of conduct. However, everyone who goes to work knows that the rules regulating behaviour don't just exist in a vacuum: there's something called "office politics", a kind of invisible set of constantly changing rules that determine how we behave, and how the rules are interpreted and enforced, based upon our relationship with our co-workers.

You'll be glad to hear that the drugs taxation industry is no different from working in an insurance office or a bank.

THE OFFICE POLITICS HANDBOOK FOR THE STEPHEN FRENCH FOUNDATION OF TAX STUDIES

A – Choose your victim carefully Don't prey on criminal organizations bigger than yours. For instance, I once knew a drug baron called Jim, who was head of a powerful crime dynasty. If Jim phoned me up and said, "Some nice Charlie there. I'm going to put a ki away for you," I'd have to go down and see him, pay him for the gear and do a genuine deal. (Most of the time, the code he used was cars: "A lovely ride. You'd love to drive this. Come down and have a look.") If anyone else rang up and said that to me, I'd simply steal the gear and get off without paying. However, you couldn't mess with Jim. He and guys like him were so cocksure of themselves.

They had so much confidence in their own reputations that they would give out kilos of cocaine or heroin on tick, knowing that they would be paid. If they weren't, they would just murder the culprit. In the jungle, you won't see a lion trying to feed on a rhino. D'you get me? As a taxman, you look for an antelope that's come into the wrong part of the jungle or one who's come to the waterhole to feed. If you want to be involved in the nefarious world of drug taxing, you've got to make sure that you can hold your own.

B – Draw up clear lines of demarcation in your business plan One day, I might be taxing someone, the next I'd be doing a legitimate drug deal with some proper dealers. But don't chop and change and confuse one with the other. Get this in your head: if you're doing a deal, do a deal. Don't suddenly think, "I'm going to tax this person", 'cos you're getting greedy. People will soon stop doing business with you, and your rep will suffer at the hands of the office politicians.

In these kinds of situations, it was useful to have a good "checker". A checker was a kind of bodyguard-cum-middleman-cum-referee who made sure that a drug deal went well between two parties who did not know each other and had yet to build up trust. Everybody and his brother wanted to sell drugs, but you needed a good checker to make sure that it didn't descend into anarchy. The minnows were scared shitless of doing business with the sardines. The sardines were scared to do business with the sharks. Then there were the killer whales who wanted to eat everything. With a checker, the minnows got themselves a net – an equalizer – to make sure that the bigger members of the ecosystem didn't start biting their heads off.

Because I obeyed rule A rigidly, I became a checker myself and made hundreds of thousands of pounds in commission. During these deals, some of the sharks would turn to me and say, "What are you here for?"

"Well, I'm here to make sure that he doesn't get robbed," I'd reply.

Of course, I could have turned Turk on the minnows and robbed them. However, I had to say to myself, "When I'm taxing, I'm taxing. When I'm doing a deal, I'm doing a deal. If you double-cross the guy that paid you, you're not going to get any more work." However, by remaining consistent and not betraying anyone, people started to say, "Well, Frenchie had that £1 million in cash of my money in the room, but he didn't try and have me off." Those jobs would then keep coming.

For instance, there was a gang from Huyton that was doing business with a black gang from my area. I got a call from Jim, and he said, "Look, something's going on down there, Stephen, we need you around. Look after them lads. Them lads are all right."

It was a case of the old favour syndrome.

I said, "Well, I was going to have them, Jim, but since you've given me a call, it'll go straight." The lads from Huyton then knew that they had a checker. "We can use this guy," they were thinking. "We can sell some stuff to the black geezers through this guy, because we've got a checker on them." I did all this because I didn't want to upset my friends.

A lot of people thought that you could buy into being a checker full-time: ensure someone's deal went OK, make a living and get a good drink out of it. But suddenly checkers became obsolete. This was because the minnows turned to another form of equalizer – the gun. This was why guns spread far and wide so fast throughout the drugs game – they levelled the playing field for the barnacles and crustaceans. The crustaceans could start trading with the crocs without fear. Look at all the shootings going on now. It isn't the crocodiles and the great whites who are doing it – it's the fucking plankton. The skinny teenagers in their 4x4s – armed to the teeth.

The thing is, the killer whales can do fuck all about it. They've been rendered toothless because they've got a lot to lose, whereas the kids haven't.

C – Guard your reputation with your life This is law five in *The 48 Laws of Power*, one of my favourite books.

You've got to build your rep as a taxman with fear and violence, and then you've got to defend it. What I'm talking about here are the everyday slights made by your co-workers, designed to undermine your power. Everyone will understand what I mean when I say, "Gossip is the Devil's Radio."

I'll give you an example. In sobriety, Jim was fine. However, once he had had a line of coke and a few drinks, the horrible racist in him reared its head. His chat would be, "Niggers this, and niggers that, and they can't come down here, and they can't do this and that."

If I was out in his company, I'd say, "You can't start that Jim, 'cos I'm a nigger."

He'd then say something like, "But I don't mean you, Ste."

I'd reply, "Yeah, but if anybody knows that I'm sitting here listening to you nigger this and nigger that and nigger the other, what does that make me? And I'm no fucking Uncle Tom. So don't fucking do that, mate. Curb that, otherwise I'll get off, understand?"

You have to make sure you get on top of things like that.

D – Never show fear in front of the lads If you crumble on the job, the lads will laugh at you. They'll say things like, "Go and get the piece of wood out of that skip and strap it to your back.

Get some backbone, lad, if you want to get involved with the graft." There was a rice mill near the docks, and they'd say, "If your arse is going to go, go and get a job in the rice mill and hump bags, don't sell drugs." My fear was always under control, but I watched many fall by the wayside by lacking a good pair of town halls *[balls]*.

E – It's not all about race The reason why I was always taxing white geezers was because I didn't really know any white people, and this made them practical, risk-free targets. (See the taxation code of conduct, rule 4.) Sure, it also made it easier for me to make them suffer, as I didn't trust any white geezers in the first place – I was brought up not to like Johnnys, as in John Bull the Englishman.

However, later in life, my opinion changed. I never really had much time for white people until I met a white guy called Franny Bennett, who was a mate of the Rock Star. And another white guy called Whacker, a really sharp young lad who was also a friend of the Rock Star, had an effect on me, too. I really liked him. Unfortunately, he never realized that, because he was scared of me.

Then, finally, I met a white businessman and had an epiphany.

I equate it to when Malcolm X went to Mecca and met white Muslims. Because he was so pro-black, he never wanted anything to do with white people. However, after Mecca, he realized that race and colour were just a construction of society, and it would only take two generations to breed racism out of us all. Two generations and it could all be gone. However, as it stands, the prejudice just keeps getting carried over and handed down from father to son.

Personally, I grew into a completely different person and was more successful than I had ever been before. I went legit and made much more money than I ever did as a gangster. So, my advice is don't let your vision be narrowed by your own prejudices.

In conclusion, I advise you to follow all these guidelines to the letter, as they might well save your life. Andrew John ignored the rules. And he paid a very high price.

* * *

[. . .] The Hull connection and our protection rackets had taken off – but it wasn't enough. So, in 1989, I opened up another route smuggling cocaine. Andrew and I smashed it and made money hand over fist.

Then one day, a member of the gang called Romy Marion came to me and said, "I need two grand out of the kitty." I gave it to him, because it was fuck all to me.

A few days later, a woman came to see me and told me that Marion had been getting high on crack cocaine and that it had become a big problem for him. When I saw him next, I said to him, "Where's the fucking two grand?"

Of course, he replied, "I spent it."

Now, in hindsight, I should have left it there. Trying to get £2,000 off a crack head is chasing dead money. Also, he was a mate, so it was against two of my personal rules to do him over for it. But I couldn't let it go: two grand is two grand.

After threats were made, Marion tried to make up the loss by offering a benefit in kind. He gave me a tip-off about some potential tax work involving a drug dealer called Samuel. Marion thought that he could get himself off the hook by returning the £2,000 commission on the money I was going to tax from Samuel.

He reckoned I could score £100,000 off the guy. So, one night, I got my gloves and mask on, and went to Samuel's ken. I took a lad with me who had been asking me for some tax work – his name will go with me to the grave. Inside the flat, we searched high and low but couldn't find the money. Me being the determined individual that I am, I decided to wait for this lad Samuel to come home so I could make him tell us where he had hidden his stash. I grabbed a big knife and a baseball bat, and crouched down in the dark, ready to jump on him as soon as he walked in the door.

One hour later, I heard the key in the lock and a shaft of light poured in as the door opened. I couldn't see who it was at first, because the figure was silhouetted. However, as he turned his head, I got a glimpse of who it was. For fuck's sake! It was Val the getaway driver from the Solid Gold Posse – my old crew. He was a very old and trusted friend. I'd been given jarg info by Marion – there was no Samuel.

Now, as you will remember, one of the golden rules was that I didn't rob anyone I knew. I only robbed strangers, so I couldn't do it – I couldn't tax him. What's more, I actually liked Val. I'd been in a lot of hairy chases with him, and he'd got me away on every fucking one, thus keeping me out of prison. *I was indebted to the guy.*

I lashed the tool and the bat on the floor in front of him and said, "Don't move." That was my signal to let him know I didn't mean him any harm and that I would not take up arms against him.

If I'd been looking to rob him, I'd have whacked him senseless.

Instead, I just wanted to make off without revealing my identity.

However, he went for me. I didn't really want to fight back, so he was able to pull my mask off. "Aaaahh, it's you Frenchie, it's you," he screamed. Then, in a moment of panic, I whacked him once, knocked him out and got off.

Word quickly spread around the ghetto about what had happened. My name on the street was mud. Val was still part of the Solid Gold Posse, and they were still the main people from the black area. They were disgusted that I could do such a thing to one of our own. I was so enraged by the mess Marion had got me into, I decided that I was gonna kill him. I didn't mean just beat him up – I was gonna chop his fucking head off.

When I found him, I hit him on the back of the neck with a machete. He went down, stunned, and rolled over. I was now in prime position to chop right into his head. However, he suddenly got a second wind. It was like the crack cocaine was acting as an anaesthetic, making him immune to the pain and giving him the strength to fight back. He curled up on the floor and managed to put his leg up to protect his head, and I cut right into his flesh and bone. I kept on hacking through his arteries and sinews, but they wouldn't give way. The crack had got him bad, so I pulled back – breathless and covered in claret – and jumped into my car. As I got off, I ran him over for good measure. I thought he was dead – five chops to the head and neck and virtual amputation of his left leg. He'd ruined my reputation – I wanted him to suffer.

I then went to see Val, who was still in hospital after my attack, to argue my case – not out of fear, but because what had happened was a cunt's trick, and I didn't want my name associated with it.

"Val, I didn't know it was you," I said. "It was a genuine mistake."

By the end of the visit, I still wasn't sure whether Val believed me or not, but at least I'd got it off my chest and done the honourable thing.

Meanwhile, Marion had also gone into hospital with his savage, life-threatening injuries. He didn't fold under questioning, but the doctors reported the incident as a matter of routine. Before long, the police had launched a full-on attempted-murder investigation.

It didn't take long before my name was thrown into the frame and the bizzies started to hunt me down.

As a result, Marion had realized that the situation had got out of hand and had checked himself out of hospital. He came to my house to make peace and have his say. At first, I didn't want to know, but he kept shouting through the letterbox, "I know you're in." Eventually, I opened up, and he started backing away from me, right down the path. I guess he didn't know how I was gonna react, so he was keeping his distance. He told me that he'd had a nervous breakdown, and was using crack to try and cope with it.

However, in spite of his explanation, I still couldn't forgive him for setting me up. "You knew it was Val's flat," I said, "Val has got me away from several robberies, and the only reason I didn't twat him as soon as he came through the door was that it was him. All I was trying to do was get away, and I whacked him out of panic."

Now, little did I know, Val had also checked himself out of hospital and was on the warpath. The drugs had worn off, and, in the cold light of day, he'd rejected the explanation I had given him at the hospital. He'd gone home to get his Magnum and had vowed to kill me. In fact, at that very moment – though I didn't know it at the time – he was sitting outside my house in some bushes, right next to where Marion was making his speech. Apparently, he'd been there for a couple of hours, lying in wait for me. He was gonna zap me right there and then on the doorstep. However, his plan had been thwarted when Marion had turned up.

Finally, my pay-off line to Marion was, "You told me it was a guy called Samuel in the flat with the money, not Val. I wouldn't have gone into Val's flat, 'cos he's a mate of mine."

When Val heard this, he was totally gobsmacked. Basically, he'd heard the non-partisan truth for himself and realized that I was completely innocent. He uncocked his Magnum – it' s like a fucking hand cannon, by the way – and slipped back to the ghetto, piecing together the whole situation.

I know all this because Val caught up with me a few days later and said, "You know what, Stephen? I was in the bushes. I was gonna smoke you, but I heard the truth. If you woulda said, 'So fucking what about Val, blah, blah, blah, and I wanted to rob him anyway,' I would've wiped you clean off the path." He would have, as well, all Magnumed-up, Dirty Harry-style. Did I feel lucky? Yes, indeed I did.

Anyway, I soon got nicked for the attempted murder of Marion.

I made bail, but the police banished me to Wales, banned me from Liverpool and prohibited any contact with the community.

However, there was no way I was going to miss carnival weekend in August, a great time in the Afro-Caribbean community. Plus my brother was the organizer of the Merseyside International Caribbean Carnival, and I wanted to be there to give him some moral support. So I bought an affro wig with a beard on it as a disguise. I walked around and brushed past people that had known me for over twenty-five years, and they were none the wiser. I stood next to bizzies, but they didn't even notice. I then bumped into an old mate called Stephen Brown and said, "Yo, Brown, what's happening?"

He gave me the strangest of looks, as if to say, "Who's this guy? I don't even know him."

Then, I said, "It's me, man. It's me – Frenchie."

Well, the guy fell on the floor and burst out laughing. That's when he told me, "You look like 'Afro Man'." If you remember the song "I was going to do my work but then I got high", that's what I looked like.

This little charade taught me the beauty of disguise – the fact that you can be right on top of somebody who has known you from birth, but they won't even see you. I began to use this to great effect in my taxing by dressing up white men as police to gain entry into drug houses – my trusted friends: subterfuge and misdirection.

Anyway, it all got sorted. Someone had a word with Marion, and he withdrew his statement. He is actually my friend now, and I'm godfather to his eighteen-year-old daughter, Rebecca. People are amazed that despite our history we're close. Nevertheless, I have two words for them: crack cocaine. This drug can turn the most normal of people into the vilest of creatures. It can turn a devoted schoolteacher into a violent abuser of his pupils, a priest into a molester of his own flock and a middle-class student girl into a prostitute.

[. . .] A lot of the top hard cases gave it the "Big Time Charlie Potatoes" in the shovel. However, I kept my head down, didn't mention I was a world-champion kick-boxer and defo didn't mention I was the Devil. However, some inmates took my low-key demeanour as a sign of weakness.

As I'm a big, athletic man, the claustrophobia of prison soon started to wear me down. My only escape was the visits. One day, my mum came to see me and said, "I'm glad you're in here."

"What?" I gasped, hardly believing my ears.

"You're in jail for a reason, and I know it's for the good," she continued.

No way. I couldn't believe it. My ma *wishing* the shovel on her son. Deep down, I knew that it was just the Irish in her – she's a bit of a psychic, and I think she said this because something inside her had told her to. *Her* spider senses had triggered for an as yet unknown reason. Nonetheless, for me, it was a sledgehammer. It robbed me of my only asset: hope.

When I got back to my cell, I started crying my eyes out,

thinking, "No one fucking cares. Even me ma's glad I'm in fucking jail."

My cellmate turned to me and said, "I thought you were supposed to be a hard-case Scouser. What's all the fucking tears for?"

Before he'd finished his sentence, I'd got him by the neck and lifted him so his feet were off the floor. It was only a bit of a go-around, but the NF guard *[self-identified]* ran into the cell, jumped in and immediately gave me a cuffing. He then got some other guards to bash me up, and I was subsequently moved to B wing.

After that incident, I decided that I was going to kill the NF guard. Luckily, I had fallen in with a lad called Dillon, who was connected to a big family of London gangsters. He persuaded me to lay off the bad screw. "You don't have to have him," he said.

"I'll get my family to sort it out."

Three days later, the NF guard knocked on my cell door and said, "Mr French, I won't give you any more aggravation. I won't ride you any more. I didn't realize . . ." blah, blah, blah. True to his word, Dillon's family had boxed it for me.

One Sunday morning in early 1991, I was doing the 7.30 a.m. slop out when some lad on the fours shouted over, "Frenchie, some lad's been killed from your neck of the woods. Do you know him?"

A murder still made the national news at that time. These days you'd be lucky to find a few lines about it in the *Echo*. I went back into my cell and listened to the 8 a.m. bulletin on Radio One, hoping that it was one of my enemies who had been ironed.

There was nothing like starting off the day in jail knowing that great tragedy had befallen one of your rivals.

Suddenly, the relevant story came on and gave a bit more info – a karate champion had been gunned down. A feeling of dread came over me. "What's his name?" I whispered into the tranny, biting my lip. The announcer shot back, "Andrew John, shot dead in Liverpool."

I looked at my cellmate and said, "That's my brother."

He said, "What?"

I said it again, "It's my brother. He's been shot."

I was shocked and numb but not crying, as I hadn't taken it in yet. My cell door then opened, and the wing governor and a doctor walked in. The jail had already been phoned from the outside and told of the connection between me and Andrew. OK, he might not have been my blood brother, but everybody had classed us as siblings. We may not have come out of the same woman, but we had lived like brothers for a long time.

The doctor tried to give me some tablets. I said, "I don't want no fucking medication." A priest then came into the cell, but I fucked him off as well and said that I wanted to make a phone call. I phoned Stephen's mum and asked her, "Who killed him?"

"Val, the getaway driver," she said.

Val, who I had knocked out during the mistaken taxation of his ken. The same Val who had been waiting in the bushes for me with the piece. Maria filled me in on the details. After I had whacked Val and we had made up, I had given him two grand in compensation to see him all right. He had taken the money off me, saying, "I now believe you didn't know it was me, which is why I didn't shoot you."

That should've been the end of it, but, apparently, after I had gone inside, Andrew had reignited the dispute. He had said to Val, "You fucking cunt, taking two grand off my mate in the jug after he didn't even know it was you." Andrew had then made out that Val had threatened to go to the police if I hadn't compensated him. He said, "You took two grand off him, otherwise you were going to the Old Bill. What kind of a fucking villain are you? Let's have it right."

Anyway, he kept riding the guy and eventually got the two grand back off him. However, he then wanted more and more dough. He started taxing Val, taking a Mercedes from him. Val was terrified and humiliated. Even his family were ashamed of him.

Apparently, Val's dad had wound him up even more by saying, "Val, if you were back home in Jamaica, you would have to do something about him. Andrew John just thinks you're a bitch."

So, Val had his dad telling him he was a bitch, and he had

Andrew John pressuring him. He was coiled up in fear for his life – a terrified animal. So what did he do next? He lashed out and shot his tormentor. He sneaked up behind Andrew and put four bullets in his back. He didn't face him and shoot him from in front, because he was so scared.

At that moment, everything became clear to me – it was like a lightning bolt of truth, searing down from Heaven. *That* was why my mum had said I was in jail for a reason. As I was the cause of all this, Val had more reason to kill me than Andrew. Also, if I had been on the outside, he would have assumed that I was pulling Andrew's strings, egging him on. The only reason I'm alive today is that I was safe in a prison cell.

When I hit the street in March 1991, there was no partying – it was straight down to business. Financially, I was down to my last twenty-five grand – my lowest net worth since 1980 when I had returned from London and lost all my dough to those card sharks. After Andrew had been killed, I'd bought his ride – a top of the range Saab – for sentimental reasons, but I had to sell it to get some money together.

When a professional criminal is facing a sure-fire spell in jail, he will do one thing: try and make as much money as he can to support his family in his absence. Up until that point in my life, I'd always considered myself to be on the periphery of the drug-dealing scene. OK, I'd imported and sold a lot of drugs, but I had never just been a *professional* dealer. I had always had other strings to my bow. The Hull connection had been so fucking simple, half the time I hadn't even touched the gear. I had never immersed myself fully in the drugs culture. First and foremost, I was a taxman.

Now I had come out of jail, was on bail and only had around twenty-five grand left to my name. I had mortgages to pay, families to keep and the possibility of six years of bird ahead of me. Thus, I made the conscious decision to become a full-time drug dealer – to live, breathe and sleep narcotics. I would personally bring it in by the armfuls if necessary. I would become a one-man drug-dealing machine on an industrial scale. I would flood the streets with as much heroin, cocaine and cannabis –

not forgetting our old staple Ecstasy – as was humanly possible. Get paid – end of story.

I had made my decision; I just had to find a way of executing it. I am always planning ahead, looking sixteen to eighteen months down the road. On that occasion, my timing couldn't have been more perfect.

My old friend and rival Curtis had gone from doing fifty-kilogram to 1,000-kilogram shipments, making him *the* single biggest drug trafficker in Britain according to official documents which were later published. Warren had first been identified by the police as a rising star in the drugs game in 1991, according to their files, which later came out in the media. His name had come on to the radar during Operation Bruise, a crackdown on a Midlands-based smuggling ring. At that time, they had Warren pegged as a middle-ranking operator. Within months, he had shot up to become the wealthiest criminal in British history, worth an estimated £250 million.

As you may remember, I had started Warren off on his criminal career at the age of eleven when I'd recruited him into George Osu's burglary gang. From then on, we'd both drifted in and out of each other's lives whenever it suited us. Both of us were tough, bright lads, and neither of us wanted to play second fiddle to the other. So, for the most part, we ran in our own little separate outfits, bumping into each other from time to time around the barrio, doing business together when we had to. But there was always friction between us. Even so, deep down, I still wanted to be his partner.

[. . .] I'd grown real close to my tax accountant Sandy. Her boyfriend Rodriguez, a Venezuelan, turned out to be a gangster in London, although he was very low-key. And, apparently, Curtis Warren's reputation preceded him, even in the upper echelons of London's criminal society.

Rodriguez and I quickly became friends and partners. One day, Rodriguez asked me if I knew Curtis. When I told him that we used to do burglaries together as kids, it was as though I'd told him I was a personal friend of Tony Blair. Totally awestruck, he said, "You personally know him? So you could ask him to do some work with you?" Who was he talking about here – Bill Clinton?

Curtis was a solid platinum underworld legend, and I didn't even know it.

"I wouldn't like to, because it's not that kind of friendship," I replied but Rodriguez forced, pressured and cajoled me into getting Curtis on board.

However, when I thought about it, I realized it could be the perfect scenario. If I could, I would score off Curtis and ship the drugs to Rodriguez to sell. I told Rodriguez that I would put up the money, but he would have to do all the work, for which he would get half the profits. It's a business principle that's worked for me ever since. Even today in my property empire, I will supply the cash to buy the land and the materials to build the houses, but my contractor partners have to supply the labour, and we split the profits between us.

As I thought this over, I realized that Curtis and I were very similar. Like me, he had a sixth sense. One time, he went to Burtonwood Services to collect a £40 million consignment. On an itch of his nose, he allegedly turned his back on it because he had smelled a rat. Now how much money do you have to have to be able to do that?

As it turned out, no one got nicked that day, and Curtis reportedly had to cover the £40 million loss himself. If you're in the drugs game, there is something called a "yellow pedal" that usually gets the dealer off the hook in the event of a bust. Say, for example, that the £40 million consignment had been discovered by the bizzies. This would certainly have made the papers. Curtis could then show his international suppliers a press clipping to prove that the goods had been seized through no fault of his own.

This clipping was called a yellow pedal, because the suppliers would often be shown a yellow charge sheet to prove that someone had been nicked and that they weren't getting ripped off. This meant that everything could be substantiated, and there was no bill to pay.

After the death of Andrew John – in a strange, grudging way – all our mutual friends were pushed closer together. Whatever the history had been between us, I knew approaching Curtis was worth a try. I had decided that Curtis Warren was to be my saviour.

I phoned Curtis. "Curtis, you all right?" I asked.

"Who's that?" replied the voice on the other end of the line.

"It's the long fella."

"Oh, the long fella, what do you want?"

"I need to see you," I said.

"See me about what? Do you want me to come to your house?"

"You don't know where I live, Curtis."

"Yeah I do," he replied. "You've got those three swords over the mantelpiece."

Even though we hadn't spoken for ages, Curtis was letting me know that he had me pegged. The subtext of the conversation was: "You think I don't know where you live? Warning: don't try anything clever with me." So much was said without being said.

One of Curtis' key phrases was, "Sometimes information is more valuable than gold."

After the initial verbal fencing on the telephone, I told him that I was on bail, and it wasn't safe for me to meet him in Liverpool.

I said that I was moving to Dublin in Ireland until things cooled down. Curtis said that he was frequently in Dublin doing business, so we agreed to meet the following week.

"You all right, lad?" Warren asked.

"Yeah, I'm all right," I replied. "You OK? How's things?"

"Oh, I'm surviving. You?"

"Surviving."

I then launched into a brief history of the blackmailing of the Chief. I told him all about the statements that I had made to get us out of the police station. The pay-off for telling him all this was that I wanted him to think of me as being a man who he could work with. However, this confession would later come back to haunt me.

Anyway, I told him that I had twenty-five grand left. He said, "I'll do you a ki for that." I asked for more on scrap, so we reached a compromise – buy one get one free. I was getting fifty grand's worth for fwenty-five grand to get me up and running. After that, I'd have to pay for everything up front.

In a matter of days, I was back for more, and business boomed from then on. My out-of-town connection would bake up the gear so that we got £1,200 for the ounce. That meant we made seventeen grand on every kilo. From April 1991, we started doing a kilo every three days. That was seventeen grand every three days – roughly thirty grand a week – and we kept that up solid and steady until the end of July. Bam, Bam, Bam. All I had to do was meet Curtis in Dublin, get the goods off him, organize the courier and send them out of town.

Now, the amazing thing about Curtis Warren was that he would actually serve me up himself. He was Interpol's number-one target, the biggest drug dealer in Europe, with NCIS, MI5 and Drug Squad tracking his every move, but he would still take time out to come and sell me a couple of kis in person. Normally, he would have sent a bottom-feeder around with such a paltry amount.

However, this deal was special to him. He was back working the street again. This was two kids from the neighbourhood doing business together. No international phone calls, no helicopters in the jungle, no Swiss bank accounts – just two lads from Liverpool grafting in a backstreet.

He would arrive in his own hire car, park two streets away, walk up to the back door of the house I was renting and say, "There you go, Stephen. Where's my money?" He would then take his dough and leave. It was as raw and upfront as that. He actually believed he was untouchable. I guess he had his sixth sense to guide him.

We both had systems in place to arrive at my safe-house. To this day, I go around a roundabout four times, even if I'm just going out to buy a pint of milk. It's just habit. I once went on a private detectives' course and learned about three-car surveillance – the authorities' preferred technique. However, three-car surveillance is easy to spot if you know what you're looking for. I learned how to travel southbound on a carriageway and all of a sudden switch to a northbound carriageway. This meant breaking a few driving regulations, but if somebody mimicked my move, I instantly knew I was being followed.

I also had special mobile phones that allowed me to switch between several numbers without changing the handset. Curtis loved that. He never feared my physical prowess; he feared my intelligence when I showed him things like that.

Everyone in our network kept logs of suspicious cars and detailed descriptions of undercover officers – information that we assiduously shared and disseminated. One day, a dark-haired man from a police unit in the UK was hovering around near my safe-house. I had a kilo of cocaine on me that had just been served up by Curtis. He was trying to appear nonchalant, but I could feel him watching me to see where I was going. I knew that I needed to get off the road, because I was going to get nicked any minute.

I walked towards a railway bridge, but there was nowhere to hide.

It was a forty-foot drop from the bridge to the ground below. People actually used to commit suicide by jumping off it.

Suddenly, a bend in the road gave me the opportunity I needed.

I was out of his sight for a few seconds, so I took full advantage. I jumped over the wall and dropped the forty feet down to the railway lines. Martial arts had given me incredibly strong legs, and because I knew how to drop and roll, I could do it. You'd be amazed how far a young body can actually jump. I was a world-class athlete at that time, and I could actually vault a six-feet-high wall in a single go. One of my nicknames was "Frenchie Lightfoot". You're not catching me – I'm too fast, like the fucking wind.

I scrambled up the grass embankment and relieved myself of the parcel on the way, stashing it carefully. I knew that he hadn't seen where I'd gone. At the top, I slipped through a fence and deliberately came back into view. The whole daredevil exercise had taken less than ninety seconds.

As soon as I got home, they swooped on me. Whoosh. There were three unmarked cars and about seven or eight officers, all in plain clothes. "Freeze," they shouted. "Get your hands up. We want to search you." Some of them were Irish police, others were intelligence officers from the UK. They frisked me and searched the car but found nothing. They were completely perplexed.

"Where is it?" they asked.

"Where's what?" I replied.

"We know who you've just met."

"Who've I just met?" I enquired.

Nine times out of ten, the authorities jump quicker than they should. With them, it's all a matter of timing: should we hit the suspect now, or should we do it a bit later? Then again, a few of us top criminals had a major advantage: a sixth sense that saved us time and again from total annihilation. Kenny Noye had it.

Curtis Warren had it. And I had it.

I gave Curtis a call to warn him. We never talked on the phone – one ring on a mobile phone was the signal for us to both go to a pre-arranged phone box. I used to change my mobile phone every three weeks as a precaution.

Later that night, at around 4 a.m., I got dressed into my black SAS-issue combat gear. I crept into my backyard and carefully took the bricks out of the bottom of the wall, wide enough for my body to fit through. I'd learned that trick after watching a film about a gangster called *The General*. He had dug a tunnel out of his own garden, because the police were watching his front door.

He would go out and rob banks and then come back into his ken through the tunnel. I slithered out into the night, stayed off road all the way to the railway embankment, collected the gear and sold it for forty-two grand.

Although I was living in Dublin, I frequently commuted back to the UK to see my family. If I was home, I'd stay in London and train at a very well-known boxing gym in the capital. I kept my training hours religiously, so Curtis would come to the club to see me when he was passing through London. Villainy goes hand in glove with boxing, right back to the Krays.

On one occasion, we were discussing my near miss with the police. "That wasn't your heat." Curtis said, "that was my heat." He then explained how the authorities were fast closing in on him.

We were standing by a wall outside of the gym and steam was coming off my sweat. "Why do you do it, lad?" I asked. "You've got hundreds of millions of pounds. I do it because I'm going to jail and I need the money."

Another rule in *The 48 Laws of Power* states:

> Never outshine the master. Always make those above you feel comfortable and superior. In your desire to please and impress, do not go too far in displaying your talents or you might accomplish the opposite – fear and insecurity. Make your masters appear more brilliant than they are, and you will attain the heights of power.

I was doing this shit instinctively, without even having read the book at that time.

I said, "Fucking hell, Curtis. How do you do it, lad? I've only had one bizzy on me, and my fucking arse is like that – gone. I don't know how you can cope with having a whole division on you."

A sick-looking grin spread across his face. Inside, I could see he was thinking, "I can do something Frenchie can't and Frenchie is supposed to be the hardest bastard in Liverpool and far beyond." I reinforced my point "You do this fucking 24/7, like it's nothing."

He said, "I've got enough money to stop and I wouldn't have to work again. But what am I going to do? Fucking sit at home and watch daytime TV? I do it 'cos it' s something to do, lad."

He was taking the patriarchal position with me, and I allowed him to, because I was making seventeen grand every three days from the geezer. I was trying to be useful to him, providing him with technology and so on, so that I could continue to curry favour in his court. I was trying to align myself with the king. It's what you're supposed to do as a courtier. You're supposed to align yourself around power but not make it too obvious. Machiavelli had written about it and now I was putting it into action.

Curtis then told me that his motives went beyond the money.

He said, "If I spent fifty grand a fucking day, I couldn't go broke."

He used to drop little lines like that on you to make you start counting up his money, but he never told anyone what he had outright.

I respected what he did, despite the problems I'd had with him over Andrew John. He had outwitted some of the smartest that the opposition had to offer. Also, he followed the rules of engagement: never grassed or compromised himself. I've had it said to me that Curtis Warren's a grass, and I think, "Go and kiss my granny." He's just anti-establishment and has been from the day he was fucking born. He was born kicking and screaming, but envious people have said that he couldn't have got to where he did and be as big as he did without being a grass. I would say to those people, "No, he paid people to get there, and he had the bizzies in place."

We could have gotten real big together, but there was a fundamental mistrust between us. He knew it was there, and I knew it was there, but we didn't talk about it. Two bulls can't live in the one pen. However, I've still got a massive, grudging respect for the guy. Later, when he went to prison, he did his bird without bitching and screaming. In contrast, when I was in jail, he spread this rumour that I had had a nervous breakdown. He said, "Frenchie isn't a proper criminal." That was because I had been to university, had a job and was doing things. My comeback was that I considered myself a twenty-first-century criminal, whereas they were still lagging behind in the twentieth century. The funny thing was that it was still only 1995. There were five years to go until the twenty-first century. I always was ahead of my time.

So, anyway, there we were outside the boxing gym, and I was having a little bit of a cool down. I asked him, "If I want to start up again, can I come and see you?"

He said, "Your money is as good as anybody else's, Stephen."

When I paid him, I always ensured that my money was in five-grand bundles – never a penny short. Curtis loved that, because he counted every penny he got. I'd watched him count his money from the other dealers, and he'd explode if it was short. He'd say, "That cunt. He gave me a bag with twenty-five grand in it, and there was only £24,980. The cunt kept £20 for ciggies." That's how I knew he counted every penny of his money.

Curtis told me that one of his turn-ons was counting money.

I've seen bundles of money the size of a couch – four-feet long and three-feet wide. He allegedly used to keep cars in inner-city streets, miles away from Liverpool 8, with bags the size of a man crammed with £10- and £20-notes in the boot. However, no one would look at these cars twice, 'cos they were bangers. I've seen him reduce the bulk of £100,000 in sterling to the size of a laptop by converting it into 1,000-guilder notes. This was a common practice among international drug dealers, who were always trying to reduce the physical size of their huge piles of cash by converting it into high-denomination foreign notes. A 1,000-guilder note was worth about £300, and Curtis was thought to have 1,000-guilder stashes all over Holland. According to underworld rumours, he had so much English money buried that there wasn't enough time to dig it all up when the notes changed, rendering millions obsolete. But fuck it. There was tens of millions more, reportedly wrapped up in businesses all over the world.

So, that was that. I had made a lot of dough, and I was ready to face prison. Bring it on.

12

The Happy Dust Gang

David Leslie

Brian Doran and Andy Tait involved themselves in supplying cocaine to their fellow Glaswegians in the 1980s. Supplied by a mysterious figure called The Parachutist, they were cautious, and the drug back then was hardly the social problem that crack would become. Their customers came from the middle classes – the butchers, bakers and candlestick-makers of a major British city – people who loved a good party but had enough to lose by way of their own reputations as to give Doran, Tait and their erstwhile colleagues the Bartlett brothers a sense of security.

It's easy to forget that cocaine was more of an aspirational product back then than it is today, to be offered with a discreet whisper, a gesture to show the recipient they'd arrived, as far as the giver was concerned. Doran and Tait's motive was financial, but social too – they were big guys in their city, legitimate businessmen of the kind that might be recognized around town, people worth knowing. The following extract deals with how the gang were busted, and the consequences for Tait and Doran. Andy Tait, a successful baker who supplied the pies for sale at the Ibrox Park football ground among other things, did his time and went back to straight life, taking the opportunity to step off the roller-coaster ride he had found himself on and grateful perhaps that he had not gone deeper and was not obliged to spend the rest of his days looking over his shoulder, for either the cops or other gangsters.

Doran, however, went deeper into the drugs trade and closer to the barons . . .

It was just before six on the night of Saturday, 13 February 1982. In the East End of Glasgow, there was an air of despondency because that afternoon Celtic had been knocked out of the Scottish Cup, losing by a solitary goal at Aberdeen while along at Govan there was jubilation thanks to Rangers blasting out Dumbarton by four goals to nil. In May, the two victors would meet in the final, the Dons take the trophy 4–1 after extra time. There was a light-hearted air in the offices of the drug squad with the day shift about to go home. Some of the officers, including Ronnie Edgar and Joe Corrigan, already had on their hats and coats when the telephone rang. It was picked up by Edgar, who heard the voice of a woman at the other end of the line.

"I don't want to give you my name, but I have information as to where the police can find a lot of cocaine. It is there now."

He was about to ask the standard questions, but experience told him this was one of those situations where it was best to let the informant have her say first – sometimes even a single question at the wrong moment could scare off a valuable caller and instead of listening to pure verbal gold an officer might hear only the burr of a line after the receiver had been hung up mid-sentence. So he let her continue.

"Go to the home of Alan and Ronnie Bartlett on Highburgh Road in the West End of Glasgow. There is cocaine in it now. At this minute. Go to Alan Bartlett's flat."

Then she was gone. Ronnie Edgar looked at Joe Corrigan.

"Joe, keep your coat on, but we're not going home. We need a warrant. Immediately."

Following her instructions was not so straightforward.

It meant scouring lists to find a Justice of the Peace who was available. Fortunately for the police, they were in luck.

But it was almost eight o'clock before they had sworn on oath that they had information about the whereabouts of cocaine, specified where they wanted to search, got together a team of seven or eight officers and arrived at Highburgh Road. There the problems were only beginning. Their caller had not given the exact address of the Bartlett flat and the detectives had to hunt about before they found it in a luxury Victorian terrace. Alan's name was on a bell outside, but they could not afford to ring the bell and wait for him to answer. In any police raid on a drug dealer, the emphasis is on surprise and speed. Once a suspect knows the police are about to pounce, it takes only seconds to flush gear down a toilet or throw it out of a window and thereby destroy the evidence.

They forced the outside door but inside found there were four flats, none of them showing the name of the occupant.

Time was of the essence and so while the detectives waited outside each door, Ronnie Edgar told one of his men to go outside and push Alan Bartlett's bell. They then listened for the flat in which it sounded. The idea was to bang on the door and order him to open up. If he didn't, they would burst the door down. However, as soon as they knocked and shouted, "Police," it was opened straight away. And immediately Alan admitted he had cocaine.

In the kitchen on a table was a tiny spoon they had been using as a measure and some pieces of paper for wraps. He even helpfully told them how much a level spoon would weigh. His then girlfriend Pamela was in a bedroom, unhappy at being told she was being arrested along with the brothers. She was carted off nonetheless. As police were making the arrests and carrying out a search of the flat, an officer keeping watch on Highburgh Road reported that Brian Doran had appeared to motor up but, seeing police activity, drove off without stopping.

The brothers and Pamela were taken to Turnbull Street and placed in cells, where the men were visited by their father, who advised them to come clean and tell everything they knew to the police. Pamela was given a procurator fiscal's release the following morning and was never charged with any offence. Their lawyer, Len Murray, was called in. Also being Doran's lawyer, the police wondered if, in telling all they knew, the brothers would implicate Doran. Mr Murray advised them to say nothing, but they insisted that, on the instructions of their father, they would make full confessions.

When they made their initial appearance in court, the fiscal decided to carry out a judicial examination, a procedure not normally done at a first appearance. Under it, an accused person can be brought before a sheriff at a very early stage in the proceedings to be questioned by the prosecutor. But Ronnie Edgar was anxious to question Alan Bartlett himself before this was done, and sent a note into the fiscal asking for permission to do so. Bartlett had indicated he wanted to tell all and the detective wanted to strike while the iron was hot. Later on, police would agree the accused man had answered everything he was asked truthfully.

Meanwhile, on the happy dust grapevine, Doran had been given word of the Bartletts' arrest and telephoned, asking to see Ronnie Edgar and Joe Corrigan. The meeting was arranged at the Blue Sky Travel offices after the rest of the staff had gone for the day. When Edgar and Corrigan arrived, they discovered Doran was alone. He offered a deal in which he would implicate those responsible if any likely charges against him were dropped. During the discussion, he dropped in the name of Andy Tait.

At a further meeting at Blue Sky, Tait joined Doran, the businessman proposing to spill the beans. In the light of what was being suggested, the officers visited their boss, Charles Rogers, to seek permission to continue speaking to Doran and Tait. He gave the green light and another meeting was arranged for that evening at the Sherbrooke Castle Hotel. Doran arrived with the two officers, walked in with them, went up to the reception desk, asked for his "usual room" and was handed a key. It was clear he regularly used the hotel and the officers suspected it was usually to take girlfriends back there. During the discussion, Doran told the policemen he realized they knew who they were after and in answer to their question who, named George Duncan and Thomas Sim. He promised the officers they would get "the actual time, date and place where they could get Duncan and Sim in possession of a substantial amount of cocaine". When the detectives asked how much cocaine, they were told "hundreds of grammes".

It was, for them, an exciting and astonishing offer. This would be the biggest capture of its type, a mega hit.

They knew cocaine was flowing into the country but had not realized the scale of the smuggling. It was at the Sherbrooke that arrangements were put in hand for the Aldwych Café arrests.

That day, as Tait arrived, a policewoman, her face partially but deliberately obscured by a headscarf, was already in place sipping coffee. It had been decided none of the officers who Duncan or Sim might recognize should be inside. The arrangement would be for Tait to find out if the two had brought the kit and, if so, to signal to the policewoman, who would in turn signal to the officers waiting outside, who would jump in. When it was over, detainers and detainees alike were taken to Govan police station.

"I know I've been set up by Doran and Tait," Duncan told Edgar and Corrigan. "One bad turn deserves another."

The detectives remained silent. Words were unnecessary.

It was all too obvious what had happened. A former drug squad detective said, "After George Duncan had been released on bail, Ronnie Edgar arrived at his office one day to be handed a message asking him to call a Glasgow telephone number. When he dialled, he recognized George's voice telling him he wanted to see him. They met and he offered Ronnie information about the exact importation details, and the number of times deliveries had been made and cocaine brought into the country on behalf of Doran.

George had even kept counterfoils of receipts for tickets used during his journeys so he could be sure of exact dates, places and times. One of the features of cocaine is that when you are in a tight spot, your resolve goes and you pass the buck.

It has the effect of loosening your tongue. Strictly speaking, because he had been charged, the police should not have been talking to him and to cover their backs the officers approached [The Procurator] Fiscal Len Higson to tell him of the offer.

The fiscal had been involved in the case of the Bartletts, so he knew the background. He was also aware of the effect a full statement from George Duncan could have on Tait and Doran. The policemen submitted a report and at the end of the day an arrangement was arrived at whereby George Duncan and Thomas Sim would plead guilty to effectively reduced charges and make statements after being sentenced. But it was of such significance, and potentially such a legal hot potato, that eventually the matter was decided by Lord Mackay of Clashfern QC, the Lord Advocate himself, who gave the go-ahead for the deal.

The Lord Advocate is Scotland's principal law officer and has the ultimate responsibility for criminal prosecutions.

For him to intervene in action being taken in a lower court was unique, but in this case it was justified because he was effectively giving permission for the case of Duncan and Sim to be downgraded from one of High Court level. As a result, immediately the two men from Holland pleaded guilty in front of the sheriff and were sentenced.

"Ronnie and Joe were free to interview them. They were brought from Barlinnie prison to Turnbull Street in Glasgow and George, in particular, spent an entire day making a copious statement. It was extremely detailed and absolutely nothing was left out. He even told them of the banks and building societies where he had exchanged the money paid to him by Doran and Tait into Dutch guilders. From the police aspect, the atmosphere was amiable. There was a feeling everyone just wanted the whole thing out in the open and finished with.

"Andy Tait had been arrested by this time. When the police came for him at his home, he was crestfallen. Andy was a big guy, who became caught up in the whole thing, sucked into a circle in which he was out of his depth, and was carried along on a wave of near hysteria.

"In the police's eyes, one of the few people to come out of the whole business with any credit was Tom Ferrie [*a local radio DJ*]. Ronnie and Joe sat outside the BBC studios in Glasgow one night listening to his show on the car radio. When it was finished and Tom came out of the building, they followed him home then knocked on his door, showed him a warrant and searched it. They found him a thoroughly nice guy and still listen to him."

While Doran was on the run, the police, of course, knew where he was. It was never a secret and, in any case, all they needed to do was to read the newspapers from time to time and see his name mentioned among the criminal community that had bedded down in Spain. In between house moves, he would book into hotels, such as the four-star Andalucia Plaza in Puerto Bonus, and occasionally receive a telephone call from Ronnie Edgar. The policeman made sure Doran was aware of the fate of Andy Tait after the baker's trial.

"Hello, Brian, how's the weather?"

"Warmer here than where you are, I bet."

"How are things?"

"Look, you didn't ring me to pass the time of day. It's about Andy, isn't it?"

"Thought I'd bring you up to speed."

"What happened to him?"

"Guilty, possessing and supplying."

"And?"

"Two years for one and four on the other."

"Concurrent?"

"Yes, but I gather he'll appeal."

"I know."

"You and he been keeping in touch?"

"You know we have, you've been tapping his phone."

"Wrong there, no need, as well you know. Anyway, I thought I'd pass on some advice."

"Meaning?"

"It may get too hot for you there, if you're not careful."

"What do you mean?"

"They're not going to allow guys like you to stay there forever."

"Well, the time to worry about that is when it happens."

"What are you up to these days?"

"I have one or two things going."

"Not drugs, I hope. They're very hard on people they catch running gear there."

"I'm not involved in drugs and never have been."

"Well, why not come home?"

"After what happened to Andy? No way. I won't get a fair deal and I'm not going to sit around in Barlinnie waiting to find that out."

*   *   *

[. . .] As for what had gone wrong, among the smart set it was acknowledged that the wheel of fortune had fallen off with the anonymous telephone call to the police, telling them the Bartletts had cocaine at the Highburgh flat. That had sparked the concatenation that led Big Andy to jail and Doran to self-imposed exile. So who made it? And, more importantly, why?

Theories abounded. Had the police told the truth in saying the call came from a female? If this was correct, then it possibly ruled out the natural suspect, Doran himself.

He had already been arrested and, in the web of double-dealing and deceit which followed, it would have been only natural for him to save his own skin by making it appear someone else had handed over the others. He could easily have organized one of his many women friends to make the fateful call. And, crucially, apart from him and the Bartlett brothers, who else knew about the drop? But if he had been so helpful, why the need for flight? Surely, as part of any deal with the police, he would have ensured for himself what the brothers and the men from Utrecht *[Dutch police involved in his extradition]* had arranged: an appearance before the sheriff and lenient treatment. In fact, those closest to Doran would put his absconding down to nothing other than vanity. One remembers, "Nobody who really knew Brian blamed him, but there were many who did, saying he did the dirty on his pals then saved himself."

In normal circumstances, he would have swallowed the pill and taken a fine, but he was such a big face in Glasgow he was convinced any scandal would have finished him. He probably believed that to bow down to the law would be to lose face. To many of his hangers-on, Brian was bigger than the law. Yet, if he had taken the fine, no one would have thought the worse of him. Instead, he chose to go in the other direction – he thought he was unbeatable and had suddenly discovered he was as vulnerable as the next man or woman.

"One or two suggested that at the time of the call, he and the police had not put their heads together, and he was probably thinking that if he was lifted why should the others not suffer also? But he was intelligent enough to know that if the Charlie was found, the Bartletts were the weak link, and the real extent of what the Happy Dust Gang had been up to would emerge and that could only worsen the trouble he was in already. Some wondered if it had come from a wife whose husband had become hooked on cocaine and was blowing the marriage and the family fortune. Or had it come from a woman whose husband had gone off with some girl he'd met at a party where gear had been flowing and she wanted revenge on those she saw as responsible?

"There were countless possibilities, but what many saw as the most likely explanation was that the call came from a girl who had been given a full nose of Charlie and while she was in seventh heaven had got her kit off for a string of men, something foreign to her nature. She'd only remembered what she'd done the next day, or even the one after, and had asked the Bartletts when the next drop was being made so she could get kit. Maybe she even sat and watched while Brian delivered and then put the call in to the police. Who knows? Of course, there were yet others who maintained there had never been a tip-off, that the police had simply been following Doran but used the call as an excuse for getting a search warrant to look over the flat.

These were the imponderable questions that would plague the party circuit for months to come.

As for the principals, Duncan and Sim went back to Utrecht, but not before the drug squad had reminded them that when – not if – Doran was brought to trial, they would be needed back to give evidence. The Bartletts threw themselves into learning the vegetable business. Andy Tait had a meeting with his legal team after which an appeal was formally made against his conviction and a successful application made for him to be given bail until the hearing.

Meanwhile, Brian Doran was setting about rebuilding his life. If he had hoped that would be with his family around him, he was in for a disappointment. Mary and he had tried their best to help the children settle. Their new surroundings would have made the youngsters the envy of their pals in Glasgow – a swimming pool in the garden, ever-present sunshine, beaches to play on and sea to swim in – but they missed their friends back home. And when Michael had to return for treatment, his mother and brothers and sisters went with him, leaving their father to fend for himself. It was a heartbreaking and distressing parting.

In Glasgow, it was agreed things were not the same without Whacko *[Doran, nicknamed from his wares rather than his nature]* and the Parachutist around, the latter being missed for the pleasure he brought and the former for his generosity. And people really did see Doran as both kind and generous. One of his Blue Sky clients remembers, "Brian went to work for an older chap who ran the agency and was such a good worker that the owner took a real shine to him and eventually left him to operate the business. He exuded an attitude that nothing was too much trouble – he was effectively Mr Holidays in Glasgow. If you wanted a decent holiday abroad, the first person you tried was Brian, and when he dealt with you personally you left the agency feeling as though you had been in the presence of royalty.

You'd go along and enquire about a holiday that would cost around £100 and if you were a friend he'd let you have it for £70. The point was everybody felt they were his friend."

He had properties in Magaluf, which he rented out and even arranged flights to them. No wonder he was rich.

"There was a rumour that one of his employees had been bragging of having been with Brian one night when he worked out his share of the proceeds from the travel company for the week and it came to £14,000, an absolute fortune then. In those days, there were no credit cards, everything was in cash, so it was difficult for the taxman to keep an eye on how much he was due. When Brian skipped to Spain, even the police were losers because they were among his biggest customers. They would think they were being given a special cut-price rate because of who they were – he would do a deal and tell them to keep it to themselves, but they didn't realize that was what he said to everyone."

So prolific was the package-holiday business that flowed through the Blue Sky offices that in the early stages of the investigation into the source of the ever-increasing quantities of cocaine circulating in the west of Scotland, some police officers wondered if flights from Spanish resorts were being used by smugglers. It was a reasonable theory. Spain was a source of the drug and the man who ran the holiday trade at the Scottish end seemed to have become suddenly and sensationally wealthy, able to spread largesse at will. Whether it was mere guesswork or carefully conceived supposition, it was a suspicion that came close to hitting the bullseye.

Other demonstrations of his generosity would be missed too. One of scores of stories illustrating his thoughtless beneficence concerned a character well known among the upper echelons of Glasgow society as a provider of high-quality regalia. Some unkindly spoke of this individual as being a dealer in "dodgy" goods – the word frequently being misunderstood to suggest his offerings might be fake, whereas this was far from the truth: they were very much the genuine article. The dodgy element came in their source. It was considered impolite to ask from where they had been derived and definitely bad form to use the expression "nicked" in his company. One evening, Brian Doran was seen in concentrated conversation with the dealer. It would later transpire he had bought two Cartier watches, one costing £3,000, the other £1,500, with the total being paid over in ready cash. Brian gave the more expensive to a female friend and the other to his very pretty wife Mary, though his actions brought a rebuke from an older confidant. "Fuck's sake, Brian, I don't understand you doing that," complained the man. Doran anticipated moral outrage. "Don't you know how life works? Give a bird a present now and again, but always give the most expensive item to your wife because that way you know whatever happens it is going to stay in the family."

However, it was in the party world that Doran and George Duncan were missed most of all. Wherever there had been cocaine, there had been a party, and wherever there had been a party, there had been Brian Doran. It was a remarkable situation. In his early thirties, having sired six children, created a fortune, built a reputation that was the envy of business rivals and associates everywhere, he ought to have been putting his feet up to enjoy the fruits of his loins and his labours.

It was rumoured that he had been introduced to cocaine by a friend who had himself discovered the drug and its effects in a bizarre way. One afternoon, this man had decided to splash out and give himself a rather special and private treat. He entered the New Solar sauna off Argyle Street, Glasgow, and hired the establishment's only two available prostitutes. They had locked the door and adjourned to a cubicle, where all three quickly removed their clothing, the customer having paid to watch the women perform a lesbian sex act he had seen in an American pornographic film and which he now described in detail to them. The girls were willing but wondered if their lack of enthusiasm might be too obvious until one briefly left and returned with a tiny packet from which she invited the others to sniff.

"What is it?" the man asked.

"Cocaine," one of the girls replied.

Soon afterwards, the pair was able to give a virtuoso performance and their clearly satisfied spectator now wondered if he had been on a short trip to paradise.

"Where did you get it?" he asked.

"On a weekend in Amsterdam."

"Got any more?"

"Not enough. If you're caught bringing it in, you're in trouble. Ask somebody going there to bring some. You'll pay about £50 a gramme but tell them not to get caught."

He mentioned the experience to a business colleague who had connections in Belgium and several weeks later was telephoned by a Dutch lorry driver who had arrived in Greenock after a journey via Hull suggesting they meet up.

After doing so and taking delivery of cocaine from the driver, when he next met up with Doran he offered a sample to the travel agent, who had been instantly hooked. [. . .]

In Spain, Doran busied himself buying into a club, running his property business and making contact with the men who ran the drug-smuggling trade along the Costa del Sol.

He knew how the Happy Dust Gang had made fortunes, certainly George and, to a lesser extent, Sim. Buying drugs in bulk was the way to riches and having been in business, successfully, he knew the bigger the outlay, the bigger the return – accepting, of course, that the same applied to the risks involved. Like any clever criminal, he was conscious that when a chance came, it had to be taken. There was no gain in pondering what might or could be.

A man who would become a close confidant in the years ahead, one of the richest drug dealers to have been born in Scotland, had become a multi-millionaire simply by grasping such an unexpected opportunity. The man's name must remain anonymous because he has never been charged with the offence that set him on his path to plenty, so we will call him Del. Del was an associate of many of those who enjoyed the company of the Happy Dust Gang but because his occupation was humble and lowly paid he could not afford the escape from the humdrum cocaine brought. He supplemented his meagre income by stealing cars and had a reputation for being skilled and reliable in this field. He was approached one day and asked to keep his eye open for two Land Rovers, vehicles that were much sought after at the time. They were wanted by a man based in southern Spain, who had made it clear he had buyers for them and would pay handsomely. But they would have to be delivered to him. Late one afternoon, a friend of Del's happened to be collecting his car from a garage where it had been serviced and was putting the key in one of the doors when it fell through a drain grating. He was unable to recover it and returned to the garage, which advised him of a nearby locksmith, one of whose specialities was providing keys for all types of motor vehicles. The locksmith, whose integrity had at times come under suspicion by the police, explained that the vehicle had a code specifying the type and number of key required and detailed where this code could be found. The car owner returned, searched for the code, found it and the next day was provided with a new key. He told this story to Del, who had kept an eye on two brand new Land Rover vehicles in a Glasgow garage compound. On the pretext of buying one of these, Del approached a salesman and asked to look it over. He was allowed to do so at his leisure, during which time he ensured he found the key code. The following day, a sidekick did likewise with another Land Rover. The locksmith was then approached and asked to cut the relevant keys, being promised a handsome bonus in the process.

That night, the locks securing the compound were cut and the Land Rovers driven away. Disguised with fake registration plates, the cars crossed into Europe the following morning by ferry from Dover and were taken to the buyer in Spain. He had been caught unawares by their arrival and had only a portion of the agreed fee but offered to complete the deal by making up the remainder with hashish. Del was reluctant at first, but eventually agreed and returned to Glasgow with the drug in a suitcase. He sold it at an enormous profit, decided his future lay in drug dealing and set off back to Europe. In Spain, he made a base from which he talked his way into the leading European hash-smuggling gangs, several times evading capture by various police forces. He is still at large but has maintained a reputation for courtesy and discretion, plus a remarkable ability to think on his feet. As for the Land Rover vehicles, for many years they proudly wore the insignia of the Moroccan police authorities, having crossed the Strait of Gibraltar to their new owners.

Like Del, Doran was ready to seize his chance, but until he was established and secure there were other more pressing matters to resolve. His priority remained his family. Mary and the children made it out to the Marbella villa whenever they could, but Michael's *[Doran's son]* deteriorating health made these trips increasingly difficult both practically and emotionally.

Mary confided to a neighbour at the time, "The ideal situation would be for Brian to be home with us. But it's something I just have to live with. He knows how much everybody misses him, as he misses his friends in Glasgow."

As Doran headed back to Marbella, technically still under investigation but for all practical purposes a free man, the storm clouds were gathering for Brits ensconced on the Costa del Crime. A century earlier, the government of Benjamin Disraeli had signed an agreement with Spain aimed at preventing the country from being a safe hiding place for UK villains. Piqued over the British refusal to hand over Gibraltar, Spain had ended that arrangement in 1978.

However, after overtures from London, the Spanish had decided to offer up a compromise: future runaways would be handed back, while those already in their country could stay on, for now. It became clear time was running out for the exiles. Talks were already under way about banishing all fugitives back to their native soils.

Just a couple of weeks before Doran's arrest and that of the others on the hash-smuggling allegations, police had arrived from England to witness the wedding of Ronnie Knight and his bride Sue Haylock at one of Brian's favourite watering holes, the El Oceano Club in Marbella. It was more likely that they were watching the guests, but the gossip at the reception was that the officers were familiarizing themselves with faces of men they would be handcuffing shortly themselves when they were urged off flights arriving at UK airports from Spain.

Doran had every reason to worry about what the future held. He was adamant his arrest had been a set-up and if that was the case, then it meant the Spanish police were out to get him. That possibility was not only of concern to him.

He had built up a useful network of contacts among major drugs traders; these were men who could not afford to have their activities coming under the scrutiny of the police. That someone close to them was in that unhappy position was a worry. There had been major alarms when Doran was arrested: some realized that had his vast knowledge of the smuggling network made its way into police files, irreparable harm would have been done to a series of carefully worked out operations. The gangs and cartels waited: arrests or raids would be put down to his having talked. Nothing out of the ordinary happened and that fact alone was enough to raise Doran's reputation to great heights. To have spent six months in Spanish jails without squealing or begging for a deal was a considerable feat and his loyalty would be remembered.

However, it was assumed that El Latigo and his men [the Spanish police] had their eye firmly on the Scot, monitoring his every move and taking special note of those with whom he associated. It was a situation that could potentially endanger friends and a number took a pace backwards from their relationships with him. Doran was not a man to complain; he understood. But as the months of 1988 began passing by, he could have used some friends. The strain of maintaining a lavish lifestyle in Spain while supporting his family back in Glasgow was draining his resources. In Puerto Banus, he had been running Rokkos restaurant, but, as with most other bar owners along the Costa del Sol, he had to survive through the lean winter months until the tourist trade picked up in late spring. And while Rokkos provided a living, it would never fetch the sort of returns he had been making during the heyday of Blue Sky Travel.

In Marbella, he was conscious of the police presence and warnings from other exiles that time for them there was running out. The advice to get out would prove sound, some skipping to other European or North African countries, others leaving it too late and having to begin a seemingly endless round of prisons and lawyers' offices as they fought to stave off extradition. As for the police, Doran had not heard the last of the Scourge.

Towards the end of the year, Brian decided it was time to move on. He had been in Spain for almost six and a half years. Friends suggested he ought to get out of Europe altogether, but he could never abandon his family or go further from them. He looked about for a new haven and picked Amsterdam, the cocaine capital of the Continent.

In Glasgow, Doran might have been long gone but he was by no means forgotten. The police had never given up their quest to recapture him. Ronnie Edgar, by now promoted to detective inspector, was especially determined that the last of the Happy Dust Gang would be brought to heel. He had kept in regular contact with Duncan throughout his travels in Holland. George was now back in Utrecht involved in the building trade and the clubbing business, and the two men would occasionally chat. When George's wife Rosa told him there was a telephone call from Glasgow, he knew it was the detective ringing to ask how he was making out and the conversations would always end with a reminder that when, not if, Doran was brought to trial, George would be needed to give evidence against him as he had been a witness against Tait. It was a situation the man in Utrecht was not happy with. He felt Doran had been punished enough, having missed watching five members of his family growing up and the funeral of a sixth. It was terrible just imagining the grief of that alone.

Doran took over an apartment on the fringe of Amsterdam's red-light district, an area in which it is easy to lose oneself. The city was also home to many Colombians, some who had been advised that a trusted friend was moving there from Marbella. In particular were members of the Ochoa family, one of whose number, Jorge Luis, had spent time in Spain trying to persuade hashish traffickers to switch their networks to the far more lucrative cocaine. The Ochoas were impressed with Doran, who knew he had an open invitation to visit them in Colombia any time. They admired his fluency in Spanish and his ability to pick up other languages with little difficulty. And they liked that he could think big – in quantities of cocaine and millions of pounds. Like him, they realized Spain was becoming too congested. There were too many criminals and too many Colombians – at one time, the Spanish government complained it was paying for the upkeep of 700 Colombian nationals in its prison system. The Ochoas asked contacts in Holland to keep a friendly eye out for the Scot.

His departure from Marbella had not gone unnoticed by others. It would always be officially denied, but the telephone line to 122 Terregles Avenue in Glasgow had been tapped.

That made it easy for police in the city to keep tabs on the movements of Mary Doran's husband. He had regularly rung home from Spain, then the calls began coming from numbers in Amsterdam, sparking alarm bells. Police there were given the numbers and asked to look out for Doran, the Glasgow officers pointing out he was the subject of an international arrest warrant. The request came not from the drug squad but from the Scottish Crime Squad for, by now, the former had become the latter, so serious had the growth in drug traffic become. What the Happy Dust Gang had started, others had continued, recognizing the huge profits that were seemingly there for the taking. Of course, there were risks, but some viewed the prospect of three or four years in prison as well worth it when there were tens of thousands of pounds to look forward to spending once they were released.

In early February 1989, Dutch police contacted their Scottish counterparts to confirm they knew where Doran was living. They were then asked to put him under surveillance. This was not a request made lightly. Police forces in general constantly complain of being short-handed – to monitor a suspect requires a team of at least ten to a dozen men, so to ask the police in Holland to take such a step was to seek a huge favour; it might mean police there having to shelve one of their own major inquiries. In this case, officers came to an understanding that the watch would only be necessary until the Glaswegians could get together the necessary paperwork to seek their man's extradition.

They had the documentation prepared by the middle of the month and a further call was made to Amsterdam asking for Doran's arrest. It was a move that came as a relief to the police there, who were inundated with pleas for help from forces all over the world, trying to track down runaways who always seemed to head for Holland.

Police who made the arrest would later say Doran appeared neither surprised nor particularly disappointed that his long journey had finally come to an end. "When are they coming from Glasgow?" was all he asked. The only response they could think to give was "possibly tomorrow".

It would turn out to be unduly optimistic and Doran was to spend several weeks in prison, waiting for the courts to decide whether the strict and often nit-picking rules of extradition had been followed to the nth degree.

It was ironic that after fleeing about Europe for so long, he should have finally settled just a half-hour car drive from the homes of the two men whose meeting with him that night in Charlie Parker's *[Glasgow nightclub]* had started off the Happy Dust Gang. The arrest did not rate a mention in the Dutch media and merited only a paragraph back in Scotland.

As the weeks began to drag in the Amsterdam jail where Whacko was held, his lawyer, by now Mr Robert McCormack, flew from Glasgow for talks with him. Having recovered from the initial surprise of being lifted, he had determined to fight the attempt that would undoubtedly be made to haul him back to a belated appearance in the dock, where he had been expected to stand alongside Andy Tait.

By the beginning of June, almost four months after his arrest, he had fought the fight, lost and was now pinning his hopes on an appeal. That turned out to be as successful as it had been for Big Andy *[Tait, i.e. unsuccessful]* but for a different reason. Newspaper reports at the time revealed his Dutch lawyers had forgotten to lodge the necessary appeal papers within the required two weeks of the decision by a judge to extradite him to Scotland. As a consequence, it was now simply a matter of not if but when he would be turfed out of Holland.

When the two men spoke during a telephone conversation in 1983 about coming home, Ronnie Edgar had reminded Brian Doran, "You'll have to face up to it sometime."

"We'll see," was the runaway's response.

"I know we will, Brian," the policeman replied.

Six years on, the prediction came true. On the 28th of the month, two officers from the crime squad boarded a flight to Amsterdam. Fittingly, one was Ronnie Edgar and in his briefcase were documents formally requesting the handover of the prisoner. He and his colleague, Detective Sergeant Tom Sneddon, were not expecting to be out of the country for long. In fact, they had been booked on the next flight back. At the same time as they were fastening their seat belts, a prison official in Amsterdam was calling at the cell where Brian Doran had sat in frustration for months to tell him he would be leaving shortly and to collect his belongings. There was no need to mention the destination.

Doran knew the worst. At Schiphol, the two officers were met and taken to a high-security police area within the giant airport. To save time, Doran had been driven under escort from the prison and was brought in to meet his old foe. In a brightly painted office, he was formally exchanged for the paperwork.

"Hello, Ronnie," he said. "You won't believe this, but I'm glad to be going back. I've been on the run too long."

As they took their seats at the back of the aircraft, the prisoner turned to his captors, singling out his old foe Ronnie Edgar. "Ronnie, how about a drink?"

"No way."

"Why not?"

"I'm on duty, remember?"

"Yes, but I'm not."

"No drinks."

"Bastard."

In Glasgow, he was driven in a police car to the remand wing of Barlinnie prison, but, before leaving, he made it plain he knew his rights. "Remember, I am here as an extraditee. You can't put any more charges to me," he said.

He was right, of course. The Dutch had agreed to return him only to face the specific charges listed on the extradition request; to have attempted to add further offences now would have been to risk an international legal row.

Getting their man back was only one hurdle to be crossed by the police. Now the real work began, getting hold of witnesses who had given evidence in the Tait case in April 1983, more than six years previously. They would need to be tracked down, interviewed once more to make sure their stories had not changed, and then visited by precognition agents acting for the defence, who needed to know what their evidence was likely to be. It was pretty much a formality. A visit to Glasgow's excellent Mitchell Library and a browse through newspaper reports of that trial would be enough to tell Doran's team what they were up against.

But Ronnie Edgar had one very important call to make.

As soon as Doran was safely in Barlinnie, he returned to his office, picked up the telephone and dialled the familiar number in Utrecht.

"Hello, George," said the voice.

"Mr Edgar?"

"Yes, it's me. Have you heard the good news?"

"No, what news is that?"

"Brian Doran has been arrested. He's in Barlinnie."

"When did this happen?"

"Today. George, we'll need you for his trial."

"When will that be?"

"There's no date yet, three or four months' time. I'll let you know."

"OK."

George Duncan did not regard this as good news. He confided to a friend, "I have the feeling that the police have been patronizing me for years. They want me for their star witness, but I decided a long time ago that if they ever caught Brian they wouldn't get me to speak against him.

"I told myself that when they got him to court, I wouldn't go and hopefully the case against him would collapse. The police keep telling me how this man had to be brought to justice but to me it's more a personal vendetta between them and him. They think they will further their own careers by putting him behind bars. I told myself while I was sitting in Barlinnie with Simmy serving our six months that they could go fuck themselves, but I played along with what they said they would want me to do when he was caught. Hasn't the guy suffered enough?"

Sporadic calls from the police to his home continued until he was told Doran's trial had been fixed for the High Court in Glasgow on Monday, 9 October 1989. "We'll want you to come over no later than the day before," they told him.

There were those in Glasgow who were disappointed and dismayed at the prospect of Brian Doran, the one-time highly regarded and respected modern languages teacher at St Margaret's High School in Airdrie, facing a long stretch behind bars. But even greater was the sympathy being felt for Mary – they met while she was teaching there – especially after all the humiliations heaped on her in the past by her husband's roving eye. And had not their children suffered?

Weren't they being punished unfairly for the crimes of their father? It may have been just those who felt sufficiently in unison with the Doran family who were determined to take positive steps and end the misery.

Five days before the trial was due to open, George Duncan arrived home from work to be told by Rosa he had visitors.

"Who?" he asked.

"They'll tell you themselves."

"What do they want?"

"They didn't say but asked to speak to you in private."

"Where are they?"

"In the park at the end of the road, waiting."

"Didn't they want to wait in the house?"

"No, they were very polite but said they'd prefer if I wasn't involved in what they had to say."

"Male or female?"

"You'll see."

George Duncan went out to meet his unexpected visitors.

He was surprised by their identities but not wholly by what they had to say. The conversation lasted less than an hour.

During it, he was offered £110,000 not to appear at Doran's trial. He reiterated to them what he had told a friend in the past – that he had determined years earlier not to be a witness against Brian – and he explained why he had reached this conclusion. The visitors pointed out that he might still change his mind at the last minute and fly to Glasgow, but he was adamant, he had made up his mind and would not alter his stance. They also noted, unnecessarily, that £110,000 was a lot of money: when the police arrived to take Duncan to Scotland, as they undoubtedly would, it would guarantee him the means of being elsewhere. His guests did not look unduly disappointed when they left, refusing his offer of a meal, saying they felt they had to get back to Scotland. Duncan had suspected that something of this nature would occur from the moment he had received the telephone call from Ronnie Edgar saying Brian Doran had been recaptured. He was not surprised at the offer of so much money not to appear at the forthcoming Doran trial. What he found funny was that he was being offered a fortune to take a course of action he had already committed himself to. Why lose out by speaking up?

The awaited call from the police arrived, as he had known it would. But his wife had been well primed and told them she and George had split up and he was working away from home. Under pressure, she agreed he should telephone reasonably regularly and promised to pass on a message to him to ring

Glasgow at the first opportunity. When he did not, the officers flew over to Amsterdam. It was Saturday and the trial would begin promptly on the Monday morning.

They desperately needed their vital witness and sought collaboration from police in Amsterdam, who called Rosa with an instruction that she was to make sure George rang the city headquarters. He did, and a young Dutch inspector told him, "You must come to the police station. This is something that cannot be discussed on the telephone. It is most important that we have a word with you."

To stall for time he agreed to a rendezvous the following evening at 7 p.m., saying he was working on a contract with a harsh penalty clause attached if it was not completed in time. He was told to finish his work and then come in, but advised, "Make sure you do. This is important." That meant a day the police couldn't afford to lose had now been wasted.

He never had any intention of attending the meeting, at which he knew he would be handed a citation ordering him to attend court in Glasgow. Once it was in his possession, he had to comply otherwise he would be in contempt of court.

This meant that on further visits to see friends and family at home he would get no further than passport control at Glasgow airport before being huckled off to the nearest police station in handcuffs. So, instead he used a coin box to make a telephone call to the inspector. "It's George Duncan."

"George, why aren't you here? The arrangement was for a meeting at seven."

"I'm still at work," he lied.

"OK, we'll wait."

"Out of the question, it will be too late."

"Well, why not come in tomorrow?"

"What's this all about?"

"Come in and we'll explain."

"Listen, inspector, you have two police officers from the city of Glasgow sitting opposite you in your office right now.

"Put one of them on the phone."

"George, it's Ronnie Edgar. Where are you?"

"Ronnie, I'm not coming in. I cannot get time off work.

"You think I am a yo-yo at the end of your string, but I have done my time and you have a statement from me. I won't be there in the morning to back you up."

He rang off, chuckling to himself and reckoning that as far as the police were concerned the penny had dropped. He was deliberately stalling and had no intention of going to Glasgow to be a witness for the prosecution. At the same time, he knew the matter would not end there. Ronnie Edgar was an old-style cop whose motto was "We always get our man", and now there was a chance his quarry, Doran, was going to get off lightly because the main witness was not going to show. He had wanted the police to know he had fucked them, and now, having conveyed that message, realized they would be furious. He had been tempted to say to Ronnie, "I know you're upset, take an Alka-Seltzer," but wisely did not do so. The game of wills had yet to be played out.

Next morning, as Glasgow awoke, four Dutch police officers arrived at Rosa's door with their Scottish colleagues.

Angry and afraid, she telephoned George.

"The police have been here and have put a letter through the door. The letter is from the police in Glasgow. It's a citation."

"Rosa, throw it back into the street."

She did so, but minutes later there was a loud knock at the door. When she opened it, she was handed a letter. She rang her husband again.

"What do I do now?"

"Throw it back into the street and if they call again tell them I no longer live there."

She followed his instructions, but it was clear the police were not giving up. They had waited more than seven years since Doran went on the run and were determined that when they flew back into Glasgow, the chief witness would be with them. They had worked long and hard and would not risk their case being weakened.

"George?"

"Yes, Rosa."

"The police are still outside the house."

"Don't worry, leave it to me."

He telephoned a relative of his wife's in Utrecht and told him, "Go up to the house and the next time they put the letter through or hand it to anyone, tear it up and throw it into the street so the Dutch police will clearly see I haven't received or read it."

Two hours later, the telephone jangled. It was Rosa to say the police had finally left.

On the aircraft taking him back to Glasgow, Doran had cursed when Ronnie Edgar had refused to allow him a drink. But that anger was nothing when compared with the fury of Edgar at his failure to persuade Duncan to travel to Scotland for the trial. His evidence was crucial and, in the eyes of the police, overwhelming in the more serious allegation of trafficking in cocaine, a charge that had earned Tait four years. Now, without him, there was no real likelihood of the prosecution succeeding. There had been frustration, too, at the fact that the Dutch police believed their own hands were tied by legislation barring them from actively supporting their Scottish colleagues.

Dust had gathered on the court papers during the long wait for the trial of Brian Doran, but even now, as the pink ribbon around them was being untied, it almost did not go ahead. Doran thought himself lucky to have secured Donald Findlay QC, widely thought then, and still now, to be the top criminal lawyer in the country, to defend him, but Mr Findlay was heavily committed to another trial that had overrun considerably. At the eleventh hour, he had to stand down from the Happy Dust case. Doran must have felt the odds stacked against him for, if that was not bad enough, when he tried getting his trial postponed for a month to allow Mr Findlay to be there, the request was thrown out. It seemed a strange decision, implying haste in settling a matter that had been in abeyance for such a long time. The Faculty of Advocates, realizing the unfair position in which this left Whacko, asked another eminent silk, Alexander Philip, to help the accused man, but this offer was turned down, Doran arguing, with some justification, that a month was not long enough in which to brief a replacement counsel. This left the legal system in an embarrassing quandary. It was not

Doran's fault he found himself in the position of a goalkeeper under attack from a well-drilled team and with no centre-half to protect him. Yet it was he who came up with a solution: he would defend himself.

The antiquated judicial set-up meant only recognized advocates could speak in the High Courts, unless an accused was given permission by the judge to conduct his own defence. There were many who believed this was but a form of self-protection for members of a very well-paid section of the legal profession. It certainly ruled out many brilliant solicitors from actively and publicly doing a better job of representing clients. The problem now was that Doran – an intelligent man perhaps but one at a definite, and possibly decisive, disadvantage when it came to arguing legal points – was the equivalent of a draughts player facing a chess master. The eventual solution was to allow his lawyer, Robert McCormack, to sit in court and pass on advice when it was requested. It was a bizarre situation and one that did the legal system no credit whatsoever.

Doran pleaded not guilty to three charges. The initial two had seen the downfall of Andrew Tait, alleging first that he was involved in smuggling cocaine into Scotland between December 1980 and March 1982 through ferry terminals at Sheerness, Hull, Dover and Harwich and alternatively that he came into possession of the drug after it had been brought into the United Kingdom illegally; and secondly that he supplied cocaine or was involved in its supply to a number of people in Glasgow between the same dates. In the third charge, he was accused that "being conscious of his guilt, he absconded and fled from justice and failed to appear for trial at the High Court in Glasgow on the 11 April 1983".

If some in the public gallery experienced a sense of *déjà vu*, it was no surprise. For many of the witnesses were the same ones who had helped condemn Tait and there was a familiar ring about their versions of what had transpired.

Alan Bartlett admitted he had used cocaine at his luxury flat in Hyndland. Had he ever received anything from Brian Doran, the Advocate Depute Alexander Wylie wanted to know? "Cocaine," was his reply. When asked how many times, he responded with

"Two or three." The Advocate Depute continued, asking if Doran had ever sold him cocaine. "Once, in mid-1981 I was sold a gramme for £50 or £60," Bartlett said.

Had Doran ever given him the drug for free?

"Once, in Charlie Parker's."

Had he ever bought cocaine from George Duncan? He replied that at about the end of 1981, Doran said Duncan was coming from Holland with cocaine and George met up with Doran and Tait at The Pantry before all three moved on to the Highburgh Road flat where he bought twenty grammes from Duncan for £1,000.

Had he used the drug, Mr Wylie asked.

"Some of it, usually sniffed through a £5 note."

The judge, Lord Murray, then asked if a £10 note or £1 note could be used?

"Yes, but not a £1 coin," Bartlett replied.

He then spoke of the night he had been arrested. Doran left cocaine at the flat, said he was off for a haircut and would be back in a couple of hours. Later, he was asked during a telephone call from either Doran or Tait, he could not recall which, to give two grammes each to two customers, one of them the broadcaster Tom Ferrie. Doran never returned; instead it was the police who called.

His version was challenged by Doran, who was allowed to cross-examine Bartlett, and accused him of "telling porky pies", himself suggesting the cocaine had been left by a "Thomas Jackson". The fruit-and-vegetable businessman further rejected a claim he had done a deal with police to get a light sentence in exchange for incriminating Doran.

Ferrie said he had made a radio programme about heroin use and decided to follow it with one on the theme of cocaine. "I spoke to a number of people in the city and eventually made contact with Brian Doran," he said. The accused man, with whom he had booked holidays, handed him a piece of folded magazine paper, he explained. When he opened it up, there was a white powder inside, which he flushed down a toilet. Doran had given him the powder for free, but he bought similar packages from Tait at his bakery and from

Alan Bartlett, in both cases also throwing the powder into a toilet bowl.

"Was it not a strange way to carry out an investigation, by flushing the evidence down the toilet?" Doran wanted to know.

"I had enough for my purpose. I was going on the premise that it was cocaine."

But, the judge asked, could it have been bicarbonate of soda? "Yes," replied Ferrie.

Tait said he spoke to Doran about knowing of a man in Holland who could get cocaine and the travel agency boss told him to call him and "get it". Three weeks later, George Duncan had arrived with 100 grammes. After being tested, it was hidden in his shop and paid for as a result of the three men – Bartlett, Tait and Doran – chipping in £1,500 each. When he had sold the drug, the three men shared some of the proceeds, using the rest to buy more happy dust. In the months that had followed, more cocaine had come over from Holland, but he did not know how much he had bought or paid for it. "I was using it myself at the time, snorting it through rolled-up £5 notes."

The big man looked a shadow of the smart, confident playboy whose company had once been so sought after by the Glasgow jet set. Now, the one-time supplier of the Ibrox pies looked crestfallen, especially when he had to describe himself as the "former" owner of The Pantry. Asked by his ex-Happy Dust Gang colleague, "Is it true that despite knowing you were guilty, you pleaded not guilty?", he replied, "Yes, I maintained I was innocent to try to stay out of prison."

The courtroom was hushed when Doran began giving evidence. His story was the one most of those present had waited many years to hear and his version of what had happened was very different from that of the others. He told the jury that when Duncan and Sim heard he was facing charges over the activities of the Happy Dust Gang, a meeting was arranged between himself and Duncan who offered to pin the blame on somebody else to get off. Their asking price was £15,000, but he refused and told the police about the proposal. He heard nothing more and went off to Spain on holiday with his family. While they were there, his lawyer telephoned with news that shocked him.

The police, he was told, intended charging him with trying to pervert the course of justice.

"After speaking to my lawyer on the phone, I decided to stay on in Spain and not go back for the trial because I felt that for some reason the police were out to get me," he said.

"They were trying to frame me. I admit freely that I used cocaine but purely on a social basis and never took money for it."

By giving evidence, he was open to cross-examination by the Advocate Depute, during which he maintained that Tait and the police had lied. "At no time did I ever supply drugs for money. I would never have dreamed of charging anyone for cocaine. It was like taking someone to a restaurant for a meal. It is not something you take money for. It is between friends." At Alan Bartlett's home, he snorted cocaine with friends. "I would put my cocaine on the table and anyone who wanted could have some. Others did the same. It was like a gang hut in a childish sense."

"A den?" asked Lord Murray.

"Yes, my lord, but not of iniquity, " he replied.

That little exchange produced laughter but in the hours that followed, Doran was in tears, openly weeping as he begged the jury not to find him guilty. "I have been away from my wife and family for more than six years. All I ask is the opportunity to return home to them. You may ask yourselves why, when I had done nothing wrong, I did not just return to Scotland to face my accusers. The answer is simply that I did not want to have to sit idly and uselessly in Barlinnie prison for 110 days before I was given the chance to prove my innocence. I went to Holland from Spain to learn if there was a way in which I could legally return to this country and live once again with my family, but in Holland I was arrested. I was brought to Scotland and what happened? I was forced to sit in Barlinnie for almost 110 days before being given the opportunity to tell my side of the story. Now, it is within your grasp to fulfil that dream of togetherness for us."

His tears did win over some of the jury members because it was only by a majority verdict that they found him guilty of supplying cocaine. The charge of absconding was dropped and, on the direction of the judge, the jury unanimously cleared him of importing the drug. Doran waited nervously as the judge shuffled through his papers, examined his notes and looked solemn.

Two minutes later, he was heading down the steps from the dock to the cells below, a sentence of two years ringing in his ears. It could have been considerably worse. It had been backdated to his arrest in Holland in February 1989, which meant that as he would be required to serve only two-thirds of the sentence – provided he behaved himself in jail – he would be freed in June 1990.

In jail, Doran was bitter at the outcome of the case. "I never took money for cocaine from anyone," he maintained.

"Others might have been out to make a profit, but I gave it away. This is how those I thought were my friends have repaid me. This is the trouble with being successful. Once you have climbed the ladder, so many want to see you toppled."

Few were listening. They had heard it all before: every hard-luck story going, every frame-up, every lying witness, every bent policeman, every jury incapable of understanding the simplest of facts. In fact, most were surprised at his being sent down only for two years, especially bearing in mind the cost of keeping tabs on his movements during the years he had been on the run. And there were those whose many experiences with the law had left them considering themselves somewhat expert on the subject. They pointed to the comment of Lord Ross when he had jailed Tait in 1983: "I accept that Doran played a major role and yours was subordinate." Surely that was an indication that if and when Doran was apprehended, he would be in for much more severe treatment, being classed as the worse of the pair. But Lord Murray said the jury had convicted Doran of the same charge for which Tait had been jailed for two years and he would impose the same sentence. No mention was made of his learned colleague's observation.

It was purely coincidental that at the same time as Whacko was pleading with the jury for mercy, in an adjoining courtroom in the same building another jury was hearing the consequences of a different cocaine deal. Five men were accused of murdering Bristol drug courier Paul Thorne on bleak Fenwick Moor, south of Glasgow. He had delivered £30,000 worth of heroin and cocaine in October 1988, was treated to a fish supper, then forced to trudge across the moor carrying a spade and dig his own grave before being blasted in the back of the head. A mattress was dumped over the body and the spot filled in. Thorne's body has never been found. Twenty-four-year-old Glasgow hard man John Paul McFadyen was sentenced to life for the murder and to a total of forty-seven years for other drug offences. Spaniard Ricardo Blanco, twenty-six, a former Foreign Legion soldier, was ordered to spend fifteen years behind bars. Underworld gossip had it that Thorne had been attempting to steal some of the consignment he was paid to take to Scotland, then sell it and keep the proceeds.

His assassination was carried out as a warning to others not to mess around. No one would ever know the truth.

The Happy Dust Gang had operated on what was, at first, a friendly basis, which had then turned sour. At least the enmity that followed had not resulted in his having to dig his own grave, even if Doran, for one, felt he had been buried by those he looked on as friends.

As Doran was settling down to prison life, the telephone was ringing in the home of George Duncan. Unthinking, he picked it up.

"George Duncan."

"Hello, George, " said a familiar voice, one he recognized from a Glasgow police station and elsewhere. "Are you back with your wife again?"

"Yes, but what do you want?"

"Heard about your old pal Brian Doran?"

"No, why?"

"Found guilty."

"What did he get? I know the police reckoned he could be looking at a twelve."

"Two years. He only got two fucking years."

"Two years? That's bad enough."

"He got two years because the main witness stayed away.

"How much did he pay you, George?"

"Listen. It was the police who wanted to get Doran, not me. I have put all that behind me. The Happy Dust Gang is in the past, long gone. The Brian Doran story ended with me years ago. I told the police that if they wanted me to come to Glasgow, they had to get in touch with me and give me sufficient time to make the proper arrangements. But they didn't do that. Instead, they turned up on my doorstep and expected me to drop everything immediately. If it went wrong, then that's the responsibility of the police, not me.

"I'm just not responsible any more. I've had no contact with Brian Doran. The police fucked up their own case because they wouldn't listen."

He hung up, turned to Rosa and told her, "You know, I've never felt so good in my life."

13

Bloggs 19

Tony Thompson

Theories now abound about the killings variously described as the Rettendon murders, the Essex Range-Rover murders, or a combination thereof. Essex Boys, *starring Sean Bean, was loosely based on surrounding events, and Julian Gilbey's* Rise of the Footsoldier *is based on the career of Carlton Leach and therefore also features them. Tony Tucker, Craig Rolfe and Pat Tate were blown away by shotgun blasts on the snowy evening of 6 December 1995. From their poses in death, they had been relaxed and at ease, expecting to meet someone they trusted – or at least not expecting violence – on the deserted country farm track. Not that they would have bottled meeting anyone else, but they would have been armed.*

The land was used as a pheasant shoot, and the sound of shotgun blasts would not have raised eyebrows in the surrounding area, be it day or night. This is just one of the ways in which the killings were coolly and professionally achieved, whether or not it was a professional hit. (Hit-people usually use more than one shot, to be sure of having achieved their intended result. Then again, they don't usually use shotguns.)

To be frank, none of the three murdered men were ever likely to be up for a Nobel Peace Prize. As their then-associate, one-time doorman Bernard O'Mahoney writes, "We were living like kings, but behaving like animals." Tucker, Tate and Rolfe were involved in meeting the needs of Essex's clubland, distributing Es, cocaine and cannabis from London's East End, throughout Essex towns such as Basildon and Colchester, and out to the coast. Well-known to the police, Tucker and Tate were bodybuilding steroid fiends whose rages only served to enhance the idea that you'd really be better off letting them into your club (not that they didn't have their own to go to – Raquel's in Basildon). Tucker and Rolfe are now thought to have killed one young street dealer who got on the wrong side of them, his body pumped full of drugs such that the inquest returned a verdict of suicide, while Tate had, not long before, seriously assaulted the assistant in a pizza take-away who had had the temerity to inform him that their toppings could not be mixed.

Tucker dealt in significant quantities to dealers inside the clubs, and police estimate that he had made at least a million pounds in the year leading up to his death. He had recently bought himself a large house in a quiet Essex village.

After a long Old Bailey trial, Mick Steele and Jack Whomes were convicted of the murders and jailed for life. (Single life-sentences perhaps reflected the esteem in which the victims were held by the bench.) They have been protesting their innocence ever since. Darren Nicholls, who claims to have driven them to and from the murder scene, is the former friend turned supergrass on whose evidence they were convicted. It's Nicholls' story that's told in Bloggs 19 *("Bloggs" being the term police assign temporarily to such an informant, until they are properly given a new identity).*

Steele and Whomes' solicitors point out that Nicholls had turned informer some time before the killings, having been caught with £10,000 of cannabis (that came from Steele) in the boot of his car. Charged with conspiring to import cannabis, he was sentenced to fifteen months after his willingness to turn Queen's Evidence was taken into consideration, and, once time served was taken into account, left court for resettlement under the Protected Witness Programme as free as a man can be who fears retribution for him and his family.

Steele's case is now with the Criminal Cases Review Commission, which has the power to refer cases to the appeals court, with Whomes' case set to follow, and new mobile phone evidence is being presented that could undermine Nicholls' story, which is the only real evidence against the men. That, together with news of a secretive police disciplinary hearing concerning Nicholls' original handler, and a Daily Mail *story that Nicholls had confessed to a fellow protected witness that his story was "a pack of lies", provide further grounds for doubt as to the safety of their convictions. The witness, known only as "Mr P", was quoted as saying, "I thought there were forensics, witnesses. I could ignore Darren's perjury because I thought it was just the cherry on the cake. Now I realize Darren wasn't the cherry on the cake – he was the cake."*

In 2007, the BBC reported that a new witness had come forward, a local resident, who placed the shooting as having occurred around midnight rather than between 7 and 9 p.m. as per the prosecution's case. Moreover, four months before Nicholls told police he had been the driver, an East Ender, Billy Jasper, claimed he had been paid to drive another London villain, Jesse Gale (who was to die in a car-crash in 1998), to Rettendon that evening, and had only noticed on picking him up that he was armed. Like Nicholls, he claimed to have been unaware of the real purpose of the journey. But police were already working on links to Steele.

Steele was a major cannabis importer who was paid a per-kilo fee by Tucker for bringing his merchandise across the English Channel. He had a track record as reliable in his field as Eddie Stobart do in theirs. Nicholls suggested that these two alpha males had fallen out over a woman, and that Tucker had sold Steele down the river over £120,000, which was to be invested in a Dutch dope deal, telling his investors that Steele had kept the money – and putting his life in danger – when in fact Tucker had. Bernard O'Mahoney suggests that this situation occurred between Tucker and Nicholls (whatever their differences, Steele was after all fairly indispensable to Tucker), and that Steele was in fact the one brought in to resolve it. The prosecution case was that Steele killed Tucker rather than be killed by him. But could it be that Nicholls was the one already in fear for his life?

The allegation is that Steele travelled with his three victims to their deaths, while Whomes lay in wait, but only one set of footprints was found around the Range Rover (which don't match either man) and it certainly didn't leave the scene for anywhere other than a crime lab (where, ghoulishly, it was transported for forensic purposes with the bodies still inside). This evidence was made little of at The Old Bailey, where Steele did not help himself by listing his string of previous drug-smuggling convictions – a gesture with which he hoped to convince the jury of his honesty, but which of course backfired. It seems that interpretations of this ageing case can even today still shift like the changeable marshlands of the Suffolk/Essex coastline that Steele knew so well.

Jasper's information concerned a Canning Town firm that Tate and Tucker had been in negotiations with over the sale and distribution of a cocaine consignment expected by the East Enders. In fact, it's rumoured the cocky country boys had been "rolling" other gangs for some time, had already taken two members of the Canning Town cartel for £20,000, and had recently invested in a sub-machine gun with robbery in mind. In reality, they were in deep with firms whose intelligence they sorely underestimated. If you fancy yourself as a drug baron, it's all very well throwing your weight around your local clubs, where most of those surrounding you will be youngsters like tragic Essex girl Leah Betts (who had dropped a pill sourced from Craig Rolfe the night she was taken ill), out to enjoy themselves. But don't let it go to your head. For settling scores, for those who care little enough for the risks, may not be as hard as you think.

With Steele and Whomes ineligible for parole because they have not "faced up to their crimes", and with sufficient new evidence to perhaps provide the necessary grounds for an appeal, we can be sure that we haven't heard the last of the infamous Essex Boys triple murder, perhaps more sure than we can be of the resulting convictions.

Whatever the truth behind these six disrupted lives, the following extract deals with how Mickey Steele operated his daring cross-Channel smuggling business in the period leading up to this carnage. It captures an atmosphere of growing resentment, rivalry, stilted conversations and power-play that's worthy of a Pinter play. Told from Nicholls' point of view, this much we can rely on ...

NICHOLLS   I was seeing quite a lot of Mick *[Steele]* now and would often drop in on him if I was in the area. About a week after Pat *[Tate]* had gone back to prison, Mick called me up and asked me to go round to see him. I found him at Tate's house, where he was building a low wall and laying a driveway in the front, just as a favour to his friend.

Mick said he had something to show me and we both went to sit in the front of his car. He then pulled a bar of cannabis resin out from a bag and asked whether I thought I could sell it for him. Now, believe it or not, I'd never touched cannabis in my life. My wife smoked it all the time but I'd never even tried it – I was always more of a drinker than anything else. I told Mick that I really didn't think I could do anything but he told me to take it anyway and see how I got on. If I had no luck, I could just give it back to him. If I did sell it, however, it was down to me to fix the price. Mick wanted £600 for the bar. Anything else I made was mine to keep.

As I was leaving, Mick explained that Pat Tate had been working on some drug importations and, now that he'd gone back inside, he'd asked Mick to look after them for him. If I did manage to sell the stuff, there was plenty more available.

I went back to Braintree and made a couple of phone calls and a couple of appointments. And that was it: I had become a drug dealer. Not only that, I seemed to be pretty good at it.

It turned out that virtually everyone I knew either smoked dope or knew someone who wanted some. Once I'd put the word around, people starting coming in out of the woodwork all over the place. I'd let them try a little bit and once they realized it was good stuff, they'd all buy some. I'd sold the lot within a couple of hours and made about £200 profit.

Any doubts or dilemmas I had about getting involved in the drug trade vanished the moment I felt that money in my hand. I took Mick at his word so far as the supplies were concerned and went to see him the next day. And the next and the next.

Mick Steele also offered Nicholls work of a more conventional nature, though even that eventually revolved around drugs.

Having rented a little factory unit in Brightlingsea, Steele asked Nicholls to wire it up for him. He explained that he was buying a boat so that he could get back in to smuggling and he needed the unit to make a few adjustments.

The boat was a twenty-one-foot black and orange Humber Attack, a type that Steele had owned before and knew well. Once in the unit, his first job was to build a trailer so that he could tow the boat around with his truck. Steele could have bought one for about £2,000, but he decided to build one himself so it would meet his exact specifications.

It was the same with the boat itself. Having bought it for £13,000 cash (in a false name through a friend to prevent Customs from finding out), Steele ripped out the insides and built his own seating and navigation console from sheets of stainless steel. Then he bolted on a 150-horsepower Yamaha engine and built some extra fuel tanks, again from stainless steel. The tanks were pressure-tested to ensure they wouldn't leak and baffled to prevent the fuel from slopping around too much.

Finally he sprayed the whole lot dark metallic blue. "I saw it when it was finished and it looked absolutely brilliant," says Nicholls. "It was a total work of art."

Despite dropping hints like crazy, Nicholls wasn't asked to take part in the sea trials. Instead, Steele took Jack Whomes and Jackie Street down to Clacton and put the boat through its paces. It performed brilliantly, the only cloud on the horizon being the engine which, while powerful, used far more fuel than expected. An extra tank would be needed. At one point in the trials, Jackie Street needed to use the toilet, so Steele docked his boat at the marina so she could use the one in the nearby yacht club. While he and Jack were waiting, they started chatting to a man on the other side of the jetty who had a smaller, less powerful speedboat.

"I like your boat," said the man. "What do you use it for?"

"Diving. Made all the console and the tanks myself," said Steele. "Your boat's pretty good too. What do you do with that?"

"Ah, this is the firm's boat," the man replied. "We're testing this one to see what it can do and how fast it is." As he spoke, three other men in dayglo waterproofs walked down the jetty and got into the man's boat.

"What is it you do?" asked Steele.

"I'm a Customs officer," came the reply.

It soon became Steele's favourite anecdote and a constant source of amusement. "If that's all they've got," he would tell whoever was willing to listen, "they'll never catch me."

Smuggling with a boat was a return to the old ways for Michael Steele.

He had started out in the early eighties with a thirty-three-foot motor cruiser, which he would sail over to Ostend once a fortnight or so with his friends Peter Corry and Paul Gwinnett.

Once there, he'd buy up to a ton of Old Holborn from a small tobacconist shop near the harbour, load it in the boat and then sail back to Britain. A skilled navigator, Steele had no trouble finding his way from Belgium to a remote part of the Essex coast in the middle of the night and he never even came close to being caught. It became such a regular thing that the harbour master knew all the gang by name (he thought they were simply moving the tobacco up the coast to another shop) and Steele, ever the ladies' man, ended up having an affair with the wife of the shop's owner.

Once the route and technique were well established, Steele switched to smuggling cannabis. Steele rarely bought the drugs himself. Instead, he worked as a kind of import agent, smuggling on behalf of others and charging them £330 per kilo, regardless of the size of the load. For the sake of easy mathematics, he preferred to bring cannabis into the country in loads of 333 kilos. That way, each trip netted him and the rest of the gang a cool £100,000.

Customs had been aware of Steele since 1987, when they received a tip-off about his tobacco smuggling, but it was only when Steele used the profits from his cannabis trips to invest in a £38,000 single-engine Cessna and started making lots of short flights to Holland that Customs decided to take action.

Having discovered that Steele was now a major player in bringing tons of cannabis to the east coast, Operation Waterski was launched and Steele became the target of a major surveillance operation.

But "Mickey the Pilot", as he had come to be known, was too clever for them. Realizing that he was being watched, he devised a cunning plan to outwit his pursuers. With pressure on their own resources, Customs couldn't afford to follow Steele all the time: the plan was to catch him red-handed flying in a consignment of drugs so all that they had to do was watch his plane. Steele's next move was a masterstroke. He bought a second plane and kept it at a different airstrip. He would leave his house and see the Customs car tailing him in his rear-view mirror. Then, as they saw he was travelling in another direction from the airstrip, they would break off the pursuit and leave him be. Within just three hours, Steele could fly from the other airstrip to Holland, pick up a consignment of drugs, land in a field somewhere in East Anglia and be back at home with Customs thinking that he had probably just popped out to the supermarket or something.

Steele's humiliation of Customs finally came to an end in May 1989 as Steele arrived at the Albert pub in Colchester to hand over his latest consignment, which he had transferred from his plane into a white Fiat van. A two-man team in a single car had tailed him since he had landed, but a split second before the back-up could arrive to arrest him Steele spotted the officers and sped off. The Customs team tried to ram Steele off the road but he managed to get away from them, crossing the central reservation and driving the wrong way down a dual carriageway at up to eighty miles per hour.

Steele spent weeks in hiding and might have avoided capture forever were it not for his mother having a heart attack.

Steele's mother is the archetypal little old lady who goes to church every Sunday and, since the death of his father, the two had grown incredibly close. When the police discovered she was unwell, they suspected that Steele would be willing to risk everything to see her and began staking out the hospital.

They were right. When Steele reached the ward, dozens of policemen were standing around on guard. One came up to him.

"Who are you?" he asked.

Steele didn't miss a beat. "Oh I'm Jeff, I was just looking for my wife."

The policeman stood aside. "Okay son, off you go. We're looking for someone else."

"I hope you catch him," said Steele, walking off towards the door.

Steele was in sight of freedom when another officer who had paid more attention to the briefing suddenly went ballistic.

"That's him, you fuckwits. Grab him now."

In court, Mick was charged with ten counts of smuggling.

He pleaded guilty to one – the one he had been arrested for – but denied the other nine and, in a classic display of honour among thieves, swore that Jackie Street, Paul Gwinnett and Peter Corry, who had been captured on film helping Steele unload the goods, had truly believed he was bringing in tobacco. As a result they were all acquitted and Steele was geared up to take the rap for the whole lot. As the case unfolded, Customs produced surveillance pictures that they claimed showed Steele at work, but Steele pointed out that they were wrong. The pictures couldn't have been taken where or when Customs said they had been. In fact, it looked as if some of the pictures had been taken weeks later than it was claimed. Slowly the evidence against Steele started to collapse, to the point that the only case remaining against him was the one he had pleaded guilty to.

He could never be sure, but Steele could not escape the feeling that if only he had pleaded not guilty to all the changes against him, he might have got away with it.

The judge sentenced him to nine years and ordered that the courts seize £120,000 cash, half his former marital home, £15,000 from his mum's house, his thirty-three-foot motor cruiser, his £38,000 aircraft and his Toyota Land Cruiser. And as he stood in the dock listening to the judge take away his liberty and everything that he had worked so hard for, he swore to himself that if he ever ended up in court again, he would never go guilty. No matter how strong the case against him seemed to be, he would always deny everything and fight, fight, fight until the bitter end.

NICHOLLS I'd been hinting to Mick that I wanted some kind of active role once he was back in the drug-smuggling business.

Selling the stuff had shown me how easy it was to make money at that end and I knew that the profits from smuggling were going to be much higher. Mick seemed to be doing very well out of it and I wanted some of what he had. I told him I wasn't interested in doing anything too heavy, just something to earn some extra money, but to be honest I would have done anything if the price had been right, and Mick knew it. Prison certainly didn't scare me any more, so I felt I had nothing to lose.

But Mick had some doubts. He was worried about the fact that I'd never been abroad before – I'd only got a passport for the first time in my life about a month earlier and had planned to use it on one of those cheap daytrips to France, but I hadn't got round to it yet. Mick had pretty much decided that he was going to at least start off with his usual team, but then fate lent me a helping hand. A guy called Paul Gwinnett was under arrest for breaching a warrant banning him from entering Belgium. He had just been caught out by a routine Customs check as he was getting off the boat and they discovered he was the subject of a ten-year ban. It all meant that the gang was one man short for the trip. So Mick called on me.

My first job was to pick Mick up from his home in Aingers Green. I arrived in my battered old VW Golf Cabriolet, expecting to head straight for the coast, but he gave me directions to a pub near Clacton. As we pulled up, I saw a bloke standing in the car park wave at Mick and make his way over. He was in his forties, around six feet tall, with greying hair.

He actually looked a bit like a slimmer version of Mick, sort of like a younger brother, but without any of the charisma.

He sat in the back and was introduced to me as Peter but he didn't really say very much. I remember that he had a bag with him and that he seemed really nervous, but that was about it.

I remembered that Mick used to talk about a Peter Corry that he used to smuggle drugs with, so I assumed this must be the guy, but it didn't seem the time or the place to start asking questions, so I just drove.

As we made our way to Folkestone to catch the ferry, Mick told me that he wanted me to go to Amsterdam with him to meet Dopey Harris, his main contact over there, because with Gwinnett in prison I'd be making the trips over there to complete the first stage in the smuggling process.

All I had to do was to pick up the drugs in Amsterdam, having negotiated a good price, then drive them all the way to Belgium – there was no border between the two countries so I didn't have to worry about being stopped unless I did something really stupid or unless I was just plain unlucky.

Once in Belgium, Mick would meet me at the beach in his boat. I'd load the drugs in and he'd set off back to England.

After that, I'd be free to make my own way back on the ferry and, even if I did get stopped and searched, there would be nothing to incriminate me.

I have to admit, it sounded like a pretty good plan and the £2,000 a time he promised me for the work sounded even better. We got to Folkestone and Mick pulled out a bundle of cash from his bag to cover the cost of the tickets. "How much you got in there anyway," I said, as a joke really. Mick looked at me. "Eighty grand." He said it so casually; I tried not to sound like I'd never seen that much money before in my life. "Oh. Right. Drinks are on you then."

You had to fill in some personal details on the form for the ferry tickets and I went to put his name down but he stopped me. "My name's too well known among the Customs people.

"Just put your name down."

We got a cabin on the boat and chatted about nothing in particular until we were bored of each other and got a bit of sleep. We finally got to Ostend in the early hours of the morning and I drove all the way to Amsterdam along the coast road. By the time we pulled into the centre of the city and Mick told me where to park, I was absolutely knackered.

We walked to Stone's Café, which is on a road that runs parallel to the Damrak and is nearly opposite a police station.

When we arrived Dopey Harris *[their regular connection]* wasn't there and we waited in the bar. Amsterdam is a weird place anyway and all the coffee bars like Stone's where you can legally buy and smoke small amounts of cannabis are weirder still. They're usually full of French and British students stoned out of their brains, even at nine in the morning. This place was just the same with loads of people giggling and the air thick with that funny pong.

But what made Stone's different was that it was also full of groups of English blokes just like us. And in every group there would be one bloke holding a bag just a little bit too carefully. And slowly I realized that everyone there was waiting for Dopey Harris – who got his name because of his business interests, not because he was thick – to go off and do a deal. Harris was a friend of the café's owner and hung out there when he wasn't dealing so he liked to meet all his contacts there. I don't think the owner had a clue what was going on.

Harris invited us all to a flat close to the cafe. The place was full of masses of video equipment, with loads of cameras trained on the front door and stairway. Apart from that the room was very basic, with a large table, one big corner sofa, a couple of chairs and a ski-machine for exercising. Apart from drug deals, it didn't look like much else went on there.

Behind the smiles and the chirpy conversation, you could see that both Harris and Mick were being cautious, sizing each other up, wondering how much they could trust the other, but slowly the tension eased and they started to get more familiar with each other. We all sat around drinking coffee and chatting about drugs and exchange rates because everything there was bought in guilders. He also explained that he had no drugs to buy and could not say when there might be some as there was currently a shortage across the whole of Amsterdam. He simply didn't know whether it would be soon or not. Mick decided that he couldn't take the money with him back to England so he decided to leave it with Harris – I guess he trusted the guy completely by then. It was left that Harris would contact Mick and then I would go over and do the deal with Harris to ensure the exchange rate was correct.

After we'd finished talking business proper, the conversation dried up so we decided to leave. I was still knackered from driving through the night, so Peter volunteered to take over the wheel. Rather than going back the way we came, Mick was really keen on the idea of coming back through the Channel Tunnel, so we headed off towards Calais.

I was well up for it and neither Mick nor Peter had been through the Tunnel before, so it was something we were all looking forward to. I went to the duty-free shop at the terminal and bought some perfume for the wife and a case of lager for myself while Mick and Peter stocked up on cigarettes. When we finally got on the train I was still really tired, so I decided to have a quick kip before we set off. Mick woke me up in Dover – I'd missed the whole thing. I've always believed that bad things happen in threes, so that was number one. As I drove back from Dover to the Dartford Tunnel, it soon became clear what number two would be.

The petrol gauge on the Golf was getting pretty close to empty. I suggested we stop off and fill up but Mick was really keen to get home. He insisted that he'd work out what mileage we'd done and there was still loads left, no matter what the gauge said. We hit the A12 to Ipswich and passed another petrol station. "Keep going," they said, "keep going."

Then we passed the Brentwood garage. "Keep going," they said, "keep going." And we did, for at least a mile until we ran out of petrol and ground to a halt. "That's two," I thought to myself.

It was pitch black and freezing cold as I walked along the A12 back to the Brentwood garage. I didn't have a petrol can in the car so I had to buy one, fill it up and trudge back. I kept trying to cadge a lift, but no one stopped, so I just kept on walking. Then my mobile phone went. It was Mick. "We can see you," he said. "You're about half a mile a way. But, you're getting closer all the time." His voice sounded really strange, I'd never heard him quite like it before. Then Mick burst into a massive laughing fit and put the phone down. About ten minutes later, he phoned again and did the same thing. "I've got my binoculars and I can see you coming towards us," he said before collapsing in a fit of giggles again.

I didn't find it funny at all and couldn't work out why Mick was behaving in such a strange way; it was really out of character. It's not so much that the guy didn't have a sense of humour, it's just that he was always so serious. It was only when I got back to the car that I found out why they were so happy – they'd got bored of waiting around so they'd broken into my cases of lager and drunk the lot. That was three.

I was pissed off in a major way and really tempted to tell them to fuck off and find their own way back, but I was also only too well aware that, in the next week or so, Mick was offering me the chance to earn £2,000 for eighteen hours work. So I drove them home. I didn't get back myself until well after ten that morning and had to go straight to bed. In less than thirty hours I had gone from never having been abroad in my life to having been on a ferry, through three European countries and the Channel Tunnel. As far as I was concerned, I was a seasoned traveller. I'd actually really enjoyed it.

A couple of days later, Mick rang to say that the drugs were ready to be picked up. It was time to go abroad again.

This time I decided to take my Peugeot 405 because I thought it would be a lot more comfortable. I drove over to

Mick's and then followed him in his car to the pub where we had met Pete Corry the last time round. The three of us then went to a cashpoint in Clacton, where Mick took out £250 – money to cover our expenses.

Peter went for a piss – nerves probably – and Mick took the opportunity to take me to one side and explain that, even though he'd given me the marine radio to contact me when we got close to the coast, Peter was in charge. After all, Peter had made the same trip dozens of times and knew exactly what he was doing. If there were any problems, I should do exactly what Peter said. And if there weren't any problems, then I should do what Peter said anyway.

Unfortunately, the only thing that Mick didn't tell me about Peter was that he was a total prat. As we drove down to Folkestone, he kept on going on about what a big man he was and how people across Clacton where he lived were really scared of him. It was like he was really trying to impress me for no reason; after all, I was just there to do a job of work, the same as him. But it was all, "If you're ever in Clacton, just mention my name and you'll be all right. It's my town, I virtually run the place."

It was another overnight ferry so we took a cabin, which gave Peter the chance to get on my nerves at right close up.

He spent the whole journey saying things like, "If we get stopped by the police, tell them I'm a hitchhiker you've just picked up." Basically his attitude was that if we got caught out, I should take the blame for everything so he could go back and explain the situation to Mick.

Peter was so anxious about being able to use the hitchhiker excuse that he refused to drive the whole time.

Then, on the way to Amsterdam, the radiator sprang a leak, giving him another chance to panic. We couldn't find a garage anywhere and we were running low on diesel as well.

In the end, we parked up on a garage forecourt at around five in the morning and got a couple of hours' sleep while we waited for it to open.

Having sorted out the radiator and filled up, we finally got into Amsterdam proper at 10 a.m. and met Dopey Harris.

We agreed a price of £1,150 per kilo, which gave us just under seventy kilos of top-quality cannabis resin. The drugs themselves weren't kept at the café so we had to wait for them to be brought to us. One of Harris' business partners pulled up outside the café in a brand new Merc about three hours later with the drugs in his boot. Rather than just taking them there and then, I asked him to guide me to the main road out of the city so I didn't end up driving round in circles for hours.

Once I knew where I was, he pulled over and we swapped the drugs over from the boot of his car to mine and then I set off towards Belgium.

We only made one stop on the way – at a payphone to call Mick and let him know that we were on our way to Blankenberg. He had a four-hour journey across the English Channel and wasn't particularly keen to leave unless he knew we definitely had the goods. I could hear the excitement in his voice as I told him that everything was fine and that we'd meet up with him as planned. It was the first time he had done any proper smuggling since he'd been sent to prison back in 1990. As far as he was concerned, the good old days were back again.

We made really good time and got to the Blankenberg about three hours early. The area had been chosen because it had a perfect ready-made smuggling spot that Mick had taken advantage of many times in the past. If you stand on the pier and look out to sea, on your left is a beautiful, ten-mile-long sandy beach. On your right there are three or four really ugly great concrete pipes, which take sewage or something into the sea. The pipes stick up out of the water a good few feet and Mick was planning to bring the boat up by the second pipe on the right; that way he'd be hidden from the beach and the pier.

Up until now I'd been putting up with Peter, mostly by ignoring him and just going off into my own little world, but once we got to Blankenberg, he became completely impossible to deal with. I said we should just go in the main car park by the beach, like every other person in the area was doing, wait till it got dark and near the rendezvous time, take the drugs from the boot and head for the water. But he wanted to treat the whole thing like some big military operation. Park miles away, walk to the beach to check the coast was clear and then walk back for the drugs. But the problem with that was we'd parked so far away we had no idea if the coast would still be clear by the time we got the drugs. It was stupid, but that's the way we did it because Peter was in charge.

One long walk later, Peter decided that it was time to drive close to the beach and take the drugs out. He changed into his waterproofs – he'd be going back on the boat with Mick – and we took the drugs and hid ourselves in some grassy sand dunes about 200 yards from the waterline. We were sitting there in the dark with these three sports bags stuffed full of cannabis and people were walking right by us, either taking their dogs out or going for a cold swim. None of them seemed to be paying us any attention though.

We had the Marine Band walkie-talkie tuned to Channel 14. The idea was to wait until the allotted time and then switch it on. Once we confirmed that Mick was there, we'd flash a torch to give him a bearing. He was navigating in the dark using this miniature satellite link, but it was only accurate to within about twenty metres, so he still needed guidance for the final approach.

There were a couple of minutes to go and Peter turned on the radio. All we got was some fisherman muttering in French. That sent the big man from Clacton off into a right panic. I was trying to explain that it probably just meant that Mick was still a little far out. Once he got nearer, he'd override the other signal. He'd stressed that we should always wait for him to call first rather than give the game away – until there were drugs in his boat, he'd always be able to bluff his way out of trouble by saying he was fishing or something so, if anything was going to go wrong, it was important that there was no link between the three of us, otherwise we'd all get done for smuggling.

So we waited. And waited. And waited. When it got to fifteen minutes past the meeting time, Peter was practically having kittens. "I'll tell you what we're going to do," he said.

"We're going to take the bags and move down to the beach."

I couldn't believe it. "No way," I told him. "No way am I moving from this well-hidden bit of grass to sit on the beach like a fucking idiot with eighty grand's worth of dope on my lap." But Peter was unstoppable. He grabbed one of the bags and made off.

Just then, the radio crackled into life. "Sparky, Sparky, are you there?" It was Mick using my call sign. "Zulu, Tango, Xray, Tango – receiving you loud and clear," I replied. Mick then asked me to give him the signal. I shouted for Peter to stay still and flashed the torch a couple of times. The radio crackled into life one last time. "Gotcha," Mick said. After a minute or so I could just about hear the boat's engine so I grabbed the bags – it turned out that Peter had left me with the two heavy ones – and headed down to the water.

I met Peter down by the sea and we soon saw the silhouette of the boat come into view. We packed all the drugs in and then Peter climbed on board. Mick turned to me, a big grin on his face. "Call Jack, tell him that it's all going to plan but we're twenty minutes late." The boat had come so far into shore that it had virtually been grounded, I had to push it back out to sea and the water was coming up to my chest. I pushed the boat as hard as I could, but it just couldn't seem to break free of the waves that were pushing it back to shore. Then suddenly, the propeller caught and it shot off into the darkness. I was soaking wet and walked slowly back to the car, where I changed into my tracksuit bottoms and trainers. It was absolutely freezing and so was the water, but I was so worked up with the adrenalin that I couldn't feel the cold at all. I was shaking, but it was with excitement.

All my nerves and fear had gone and all I could think was, "Fuck, I've done it. I've got away with it." I've got to admit, it was a great feeling.

Blankenberg is just down the road from Ostend, but when I arrived there a little later that evening, I discovered that I'd missed the last ferry. The next one wasn't until 7 a.m. which meant I wouldn't get home until the middle of the afternoon.

I didn't fancy that. I knew there was a ferry at 2.30 a.m. from Calais and, looking at the map, it didn't seem to be that far, so I decided to drive the rest.

When I reached the French–Belgian border, I got pulled over by one of the guards and asked where I was going. They searched my car and found my wet clothes in the boot and asked what I'd been up to. I was feeling confident and cocky; after all, there was nothing at all to link me to any kind of drug smuggling. I had nothing to fear. I told the guard that I'd been playing around in the sea earlier that day and I'd missed the last ferry home from Ostend, so I decided to go back via Calais so that I'd still be home the following morning. He looked a bit suspicious but checked my passport, ran my name through the computer and let me go.

I got to Calais and, on my way to the boat, got pulled over by French Customs. "Fucking hell," I said. "I've already been searched once tonight." The guy's face didn't even break into a grin let alone a smile. "Not by me, you haven't."

He proceeded to give the car a really good going-over but, of course, couldn't find anything, so he let me get on the boat.

I tried to get to sleep on the ferry but I couldn't because crossing was so rough. Once we got to Dover, the only thing on my mind was getting back home and going to bed as quickly as possible.

I drove the car off through Customs and, as sod's law would have it, I got pulled over again. I was so tired, just so totally exhausted, that I just couldn't handle it. I freaked out.

I was swearing and shouting and going on about the fact that I must have some kind of guilty sign stamped on my forehead because I'd been pulled over twice already. In the end I think they felt sorry for me. They just photocopied my passport and let me go home.

The next day was even more exciting – pay day. I'd already been planning what I was going to spend the money on and I was really looking forward to seeing all those notes in my greedy little hands

I got there and told Mick I was there to pick up my wages. He went into the boot of the car and then laid a bar in my hands. "What the fuck's that?" I said. "It's a kilo of puff," he said. "Over here that's worth £2,200. That's your wages apart from the £200 which you now owe me."

Fuck. This was not the way things were supposed to happen. One of the main reasons I wanted to get involved in the actual smuggling operation was so that I wouldn't have to sell drugs any more because it was such a pain in the arse lugging the stuff around town and then getting the money off people. But thanks to Mick I was right back where I started.

Within two weeks, Nicholls had sold all the cannabis he'd helped to smuggle into the country and was knocking on Steele's door to get some more. He had an extensive customer base, supplying dealers across Braintree and the rest of Essex as well as London and Cambridge, but he kept it restricted to friends and colleagues. Despite steady sales, the new venture failed to be the boost to his income he had hoped.

NICHOLLS I had to be very careful about who I sold to and I never wanted to get out of control. I was only too well aware of the fact that I fitted the profile of a typical drug dealer – I had several cars, albeit it all of them old and tatty, I seemed to live beyond my means and had a large number of visitors each day from my wife's large family, friends and the people I employed. And that was even before I started to actually be one. But selling to people that you knew made it harder to keep it as a proper business. I was giving people credit and discounts. The money was coming in dribs and drabs. I'd expected to have £2,000 in my hand and be able to buy a decent car or something. Instead I just got a few quid here and there and a load of hassle. On paper I was doing well but I had no idea how long I was going to have to wait for the money to come in, so I was pretty stuck.

Nicholls paid off a few bills, bought his kids some clothes and took his wife out to the cinema, but by the end of the month, he was just as broke as ever. So when Steele called in October and asked him to do another run, he was more than up for it. He got even more keen when Steele explained that, because Corry was

on holiday, he wanted Nicholls to be in charge and find someone
to go out to Amsterdam with him. A specific amount of money
was never mentioned, but Mick implied that, as he was taking
on more responsibility, Nicholls would be paid a higher fee.

NICHOLLS As soon as I found out we were off again, I went
out and bought a pair of chest waders. I'd got really soaked
the last time from trying to push the boat back out to sea and
didn't want it to happen again. Over the next few days, I kept
asking Mick who would be in the boat with him – the whole
scam about coming back into the harbour having dumped
the drugs off relies on having at least two people in the boat.
You can hardly claim to have been out diving on your own,
can you? Mick said he was sorting it out.

The day before we were due to set off, Mick called me
up on my mobile and said that he couldn't find anyone to
come back in the boat with him, so would I do it. He could
tell I wasn't keen so he launched into this big thing to try
and convince me. He was going on about how he wanted to
expand the business, how he wanted to go back to using two
boats and how he needed someone who would be able to get
across the Channel on their own. Basically, he was saying he
wanted me to experience it so that I could see if I liked it.

And, if I did, well, that's where the real money was. " It'll be
worth your while, Darren, promise." Either I was blinded by
greed or just feeling in a generous mood. I said yes.

The next day Mick gave me £70,000 and gave me strict
instructions to try and get grass rather than resin, even
though it was bulkier and a lot harder to handle. There was, of
course, method in his madness. Mick charged £300 per kilo
to import drugs; it didn't matter what he was importing, that
was the amount he charged. Because grass was a bit cheaper
per kilo than resin, it meant that we came back with an extra
thirty or so kilos, which meant that Mick earned an extra
£9,000 for taking exactly the same risk. Clever boy, old Mick.

I took my mate Christian and we took the overnight ferry
from Felixstowe to Zebrugge and then drove to Amsterdam.
Mick told me he had phoned Dopey Harris a couple of

days earlier to tell him to expect me, so when I got to the bar and he wasn't around, I knew he'd be on his way.

Harris arrived on his push bike at around 10 a.m. looking a bit mean and serious, guided me up to the flat above the bar and then started tearing into me. He was ranting and raving about the fact that Mick was gonna get us all arrested, that he was not being careful enough on the phone and making it too obvious what he was doing.

"That loud-mouthed fucker is going to get us all arrested one day," he said. "For a bloke with his kind of background and experience, he doesn't half run his mouth off. When you get back, you tell him to watch what he says, otherwise he's gonna have to find himself another supplier."

Once the bollocking was out of the way, we got down to business. We agreed a price for the grass and then Harris asked me what car I was driving and where I'd parked it. I told him; then he asked for the keys. "Now piss off and enjoy yourself for a couple of hours," he told me.

When we got back, the car was in the same place. I went to see Harris and he said everything was fine and gave me back my keys. And that was that. We set off for a bit then stopped off down a side street and checked the boot – three nylon laundry bags full of grass – so I called Mick's mobile and told him we were on our way and headed off to Blankenberg.

Mick and the boat arrived at the rendezvous at dusk, sticking out like a sore thumb because it wasn't as dark as it was the time before. But Christian and I loaded the boat and I got in.

I was trying to pretend that I was really cool about it, but the truth was I was really excited about being in the boat at long last. I was a bit pissed off that I'd missed out on the sea trials, but I was hoping that this would more than make up for it. I wasn't disappointed. When we sped off it was the most incredible sensation. There was loads of noise and spray flying up all over the place and, because we were so low down, it felt like we were going at a million miles an hour.

Mick was in front and I was directly behind him. The sea

was really calm, as flat as a pancake, and in the half-light you could see for miles. It was like being on some gigantic pond.

Absolutely fantastic.

After about ten minutes, when we were well out of sight of Blankenberg Beach, Mick stopped the boat and started fishing around in a bag. "Here, put this on," he said, handing me a buoyancy aid. "The weather's not too clever ahead so you'd better wear it. Unfortunately, I've only got the one life jacket and I'm wearing it."

As I put the buoyancy aid on, I had a good look at Mick. I saw that as well as the lifejacket he was wearing a full dry suit – proper boating clothing. He also had a safety line attached to the console, so if he fell in, he wouldn't end up separated from the boat. If I fell in, my waders would have filled up with water and I'd have sunk to the bottom in seconds. All I could do was hold on. And pray.

We set off again and Mick told me that, rather than sitting down, I should straddle the seat directly behind him; that way, if the boat left the water for a second and came down with a bang, my legs would act like suspension springs.

After about half an hour, the land behind me was vanishing fast – and so was my excitement about my first ever trip in a RIB (a rigid inflatable boat). The waves were getting quite rough now and we were bouncing up and down like a trampoline. We'd started out speeding along at about 33 knots but now we were down to about 12 knots. I decided the best policy was just to keep my eyes shut and use my ears instead. I knew that when I heard the engine note change, the boat had come out of the water and the whole thing was airborne. That was my signal to hold on extra tight and brace myself for the landing. I was concentrating really hard but one time, I don't know, I must have just lost my focus for a second, because I slipped and nearly went over the side. That's when I started to get really scared. I was just about to ask Mick to slow down even more when I heard the engine roar again.

I braced myself, but this time, when the boat landed it hit a wave that was travelling sideways and rolled right over to one side. I fell and just managed to grab the edge to stop myself going over. I was rolling all over the place and I was bawling like a baby until Mick stopped to have a look at what was going on.

I was really shaken. I was convinced that I was going to die, that I was going to fall out of the boat and that Mick would be miles away by the time he realized and not be able to find me before I went under.

We set off again, this time a bit more slowly and with me holding on tighter than ever, but I'd already decided that there was no way I was ever going to be making this trip again.

"How far is it across, Mick?" I asked.

"About seventy miles."

"Seventy miles! Fucking hell, I always thought the Channel was about twenty-two miles wide."

"Only between Dover and Calais," Mick explained. "Not between Blankenberg and Point Clear."

"Okay. Well tell me when we're halfway."

"Why?"

"Just tell me when we're halfway."

Then, about half an hour later, "Okay Darren, we're halfway across now. Why the fuck are you so interested anyway?"

"Well if I do fall in, I want to know which way to swim."

Slowly, the weather started to improve, so I started to play the maritime equivalent of "Are we there yet, Dad?" I'd see lights and I'd say, "Hey, look over there, Mick. Is that land?"

"No, it's a boat."

Five minutes later, "Hey, how about that, is that land?"

"No, that's a boat too."

Then I saw a flashing white light. That wasn't land either but some kind of marker buoy, which meant the shore was about twelve miles away. I was starting to feel much better and much braver. The big waves had all gone and we were getting closer to home. We were still going fairly slowly, so I was actually starting to enjoy it when I fell over again. I stood up for a minute, but then I fell again. I just couldn't seem to get a grip properly with my feet. My first thought was that we must have sprung a leak and the boat had started shipping water. I tapped Mick on the shoulder and pointed to the floor.

We stopped, switched on a torch and saw immediately that the main fuel tank had split. We couldn't see the actual hole, but we could see the fuel slowly leaking out. Naturally, I started to panic. After all, I didn't have Mick's experience – this was all new to me. But what really freaked me out was the fact that Mick started to panic as well. He said we'd have to sit on the seats – even though it was more dangerous and made the boat less stable – and that we'd have to go as fast as possible to make sure we hit the shore before we ran out of fuel all together. He reprogrammed the GPS so that we headed for the nearest bit of land rather than Point Clear. If we could get close enough, he explained, then Jack Whomes, his back-up man for all his new smuggling ventures, could always come out and get us in his speedboat, but if we ran out of fuel where we were, we'd have to call the coastguard and that would mean dumping £70,000 worth of drugs over the side.

We were flying along and I was absolutely terrified. Mick was trying to work out where we were, but the GPS was playing up. He reset it to read the depth of water rather than location so he could try to work out how close we were, but somehow he fucked it up. The whole screen went blank.

So there we are in the pitch black with no guidance system, totally fucking lost and with a boat that's pissing away fuel going round and round in circles. Then Mick perked up and pointed to some poxy little light he could see in the distance. He said it was definitely Clacton Pier, or maybe Walton Pier, and that he knew where we were, probably. Either way, he reckoned we were only four miles from the coast. I was just gearing myself up to feel a bit more confident when, right on cue, the engine died and we ran out of fuel completely.

We switched to the reserve tank, but that was empty too.

We primed the carbs on the engine by hand and it started up, went about fifty yards, and then stopped again. We kept on doing it and I had to rock the boat from side to side – the last thing I wanted to do – to try to get the last remaining splashes of fuel into the pipes.

Then Mick managed to get the GPS working again; I don't

know what he did. I don't even think he knew what he did. I just heard him say, "Fuck me, it's working again," and at last we were going in the right direction. We had to kangaroo-hop all the way with the engine firing and dying every few yards, but when we got about half a mile from the spot where Jack was, we realized it was just about shallow enough for me to get out and push the boat to the shore. So I did.

I'd never been so happy to see Jack as I was when I saw him sitting on the beach waiting for us. I could have kissed him. He helped us drag the boat up to his Range Rover and we started unloading the drugs. But the problems were far from over. The plan, as always, had been to unload the boat and then take it back out to sea so we could come in to Felixstowe and pretend we'd been out fishing or something.

But with a split tank there was no way that was going to happen and the trailer was back at Jack's workplace so we couldn't even move the boat.

Mick and I were pacing around, telling Jack about our nightmare journey and trying to work out what the best thing to do was. We were so caught up in our own problems that we hardly heard Jack say that there was a problem with the Range Rover. It turned out that Jack had driven it down on the beach and gone over a pole stuck in the ground, which had wedged in his axle. He was totally stuck.

Mick was furious. Only a few minutes earlier we'd radioed him and he told us it was safe to come into shore. "What exactly is your definition of safe, Jack?" Mick was saying.

"Because I don't think being stuck on a beach with no car and no boat and a load of drugs fits in with my definition of safe."

We took the drugs out of the Range Rover and hid them a bit further up the beach. Mick then stormed off to his mum's house, which was about a mile away, to borrow her car.

While he was gone, Jack and I set about trying to get the pole out of the axle, but didn't have any luck.

Mick came back at about 3 a.m. and took the drugs to go and hide them in his mum's garage – so that was the main worry off our shoulders – and then went off to get a chainsaw to try and cut the pole. In the meantime Jack and I tried a different technique, wedging bricks and stones underneath the wheels as they went into the air. It worked.

By the time Mick came back, the Range Rover was free.

Mick had to take his mum's car back and Jack was going to follow him and then take him up to Ipswich where the trailer was and then bring it back so they could get the boat off the beach. In the meantime, they wanted me to sit around and stand guard. Great. Mick had picked up a few sandwiches and a drink from a garage, but I wasn't really in the mood for a picnic.

I was fighting a losing battle to keep my eyes open and terrified that I'd drop off to sleep and the boat would be washed away. I ended up tying the rope from the boat around my ankle, then I curled up on the stones and fell asleep. I woke up a bit later to find my feet in the water and the boat tugging at my leg. The tide was starting to come in.

I dragged the boat up the beach and fell asleep again, only to be woken up by the water lapping at my feet once more. I was cold and miserable, I ached all over and I felt like I'd been there for days.

It was just getting light when they finally came back. Mick had a go at me for dragging the boat up on the rocks because I'd scratched the base, but I just didn't care. All I wanted to do was get home.

Jack dropped me at Mick's house and I borrowed his Renault to drive home, nearly falling asleep at the wheel a couple of times. That meant that even though I was freezing cold, I had to drive with the window open.

I was knackered by the time I finally got to bed – I didn't wake up until the middle of the afternoon and I took Mick's car straight back to pick up my money. Once again he paid me in drugs, explaining that he needed his cash to pay to get the boat fixed. And he ripped me off again by only giving me just over two grand's worth of grass. He said the shipment wasn't as big as he planned so he couldn't pay me more, but he'd make it up to me next time. "And don't forget," he said. "you owe me £200 for the drugs."

I sold it all almost as quickly as I did the time before and was rapidly building up a reputation as a quality supplier. I took a load more orders and went round to Mick's to pick up some more. Only there wasn't any. Pat Tate – along with Tony Tucker and Craig Rolfe – had worked out some deal and bought the whole lot in one go.

14

McMafia

Misha Glenny

In his comprehensive overview of organized crime, veteran writer on the Balkans, Misha Glenny, illustrates how the global growth of gangsterism – mirroring the globalization of the straight world – has been responsible for increased social harm in individual nation states. He demonstrates how crime crosses borders not only in terms of smuggling routes and in how ill-gotten money is laundered and legalized but, owing to patterns of globalization, now via a third way, too. For a complex global network of organized criminals, many from the countries featured in this book, seem to have come of age in the twenty-first century. Not only have they created smuggling routes along which, thanks to a complex web of allegiances, debts and loyalties, end-to-end reliability can be guaranteed as much as possible, they have also begun to broker goods between each other in a way that can immeasurably extend the reach of any single organization that has proven itself capable of rewarding such investment.

Drug dealers are often paid in kind – a smuggler getting to keep a portion of the drugs, for example, and drugs often bartered between gangs for other commodities. Given the suspicion large amounts of cash can generate, this is often preferred. Drug transactions were traditionally binary, relying on a disparity in the availability and price of a drug between one place and another, and extending no further than a single arrangement between one gang and another (however many different growing, smuggling and distribution gangs might be involved in any single supply chain), because that was as far as trust and reciprocity could be guaranteed. Howard Marks, for example, realized that hashish was at such a premium in California compared to weed that it was worth his while exporting it there from Europe or North Africa even when he paid retail. Relatively simple – a supplier on one side and a buyer on the other.

Today, gangsters live in the "global village" probably even more than the rest of us, and the complex web of proxy activity they generate makes it much harder for law enforcement to determine who its ultimate beneficiaries are. Ted Leggett, who works at the UN Office for Drugs and Crime, based in Vienna, here discusses the phenomenon from the starting-point of South African cannabis: " ... some sort of international barter is going on, with our dagga *(weed) being traded for more potent drugs overseas ... We don't have to trade* dagga *directly with Afghanistan or Burma in order to get heroin back, because international brokers service a complex network of supplies and demands at once. These syndicates may even service demand for non-drug products, such as cell phones and automobiles. Cash is taken from countries with hard currency, and commodities are shuffled between the rest."*

These global uber-*fixers can access a diverse range of products, such as exotic animals in which it is illegal to trade, whether across the world or just in the nation from which they come, for example, those from Africa with uses in the Chinese herbal market, or Beluga caviar now that the Caspian has been overfished. These are the real drug barons of today, those who trade in other products too, in a department store of crime – if it's illegal, they'll have it, and they're never knowingly oversold.*

Sadly, therefore, prohibition has made drugs, which except in tragic cases of misadventure, are invariably more victimless than any other criminal activity (if all goes according to plan, the farmers are paid and the users are happy), part of a bundle of activities such as people-

trafficking, in which gangs from the Balkans, former Soviet states, China and Vietnam have all been found to participate.

As well as, obviously, granting a monopoly on the drugs trade to those who think they're hard enough, prohibition also has the effect of keeping prices at a certain level, making it worth their while. Distribution networks which are large enough can factor in busts as a business cost much as a store will factor in the costs of shoplifting without seeing it as an overall threat to their activities.

Equally, smuggling continues on its age-old linear model. Much of the UK's supply of brown street heroin, for example, comes into Europe via the Balkans, where it is sourced via Turkey from the traditional growing region of southern Afghanistan. It is here that Ahmed Wali Karzai, brother of president Mohamed Karzai, is the most powerful figure outside of the Taliban.

The following extract deals with the anomalous situation that exists between British Columbia and the US when it comes to "BC Bud" – the Canadian province's hydroponic product that puts grins on the faces of smokers in the American West – already a demanding and spoilt market. The US has a schizophrenic attitude to the drug in several instances, not least in California, where city ordinances in San Francisco, LA and Oakland, in the East Bay of San Francisco, have legalized the sale of medical marijuana for those with a medical card. A medical interview to assess a California resident for a cannabis card costs around $150, and the bar is not set particularly high when it comes to the severity of medical disorder required to qualify an individual for receipt, and for every worthy MS sufferer there's a waiting room filled with those suffering a list of often indefinable medical conditions.

The shops themselves, a handful of which, in Oakland's case, cluster around the city's Broadway, are more in the manner of head shops than clinics, full of buds so strong that their sticky-sweet smell wafts onto the street, even though actually smoking any on the premises is prohibited under the ordinance (passed by the city in 2005 in accordance with California's state-wide proposition 215, or Compassionate Use Act of 1996). Pot-leaf logos and joss sticks to the fore, these establishments have collectively branded the area "Oaksterdam", and exist alongside hydroponic stores where those who can produce their card can buy the paraphernalia to grow their own. Being California, there's also an abundance of highly evolved equipment which rivals the complexity of Italian espresso machines and is designed to make consumption healthier, such as vaporizers which allow the THC to be absorbed in water vapour rather than smoke. There are space-cakes and elaborate bongs – none of the joylessness we northern Europeans would probably seek to impose were we to permit medical marijuana. (In Britain, when it has been mooted as a Parliamentary possibility at all, it has been in pill form.) There are around 400 such "cannabis clubs" statewide.

Possession of a reasonable personal supply is legal in the state when accompanied by a card – as long as it's a California state or city cop you're talking to. As states-rights issues in American history go, it's preferable to slavery, however it demonstrates the kind of anomaly that the US federal system throws up on occasion. As Supreme-Court Justice Sandra Day O'Connor observed, states are often "laboratories" for federal law. Given the varied opinions and level of confusion that exist in the US towards the question of whether or not to legalize "the kind bud" and for whom, it seems futile that the US nonetheless seeks to punish British Columbian dope growers in the same way it punished Colombian cocaine traffickers ...

"Open the back for me, please, Dan." Quiet yet firm – that's how they speak around Metaline Falls. Dan Wheeler walked around his pickup truck and unbolted the tray. "Let's clear away all that stuff, please, Dan." Wheeler started hauling the grubby but neatly piled strips of chromium that were lying on the flat-bed. The Customs officer at the border crossing into Washington State helped by shifting the snow chains, toolbox, rags, oil cans and the detritus common to an artisan's vehicle, "I'd like a look at the propane tank, please, Dan." Wheeler skipped under the car to unbolt the steel frame and thick weld mesh that shielded the tank – a mesh that another border official had recommended to Dan as a means of reducing the chance of an explosion if the truck were back-ended.

Stooping deliberately, the US customs officer positioned his nose just above the propane tank's outlet valve. A jet of noxious gas flew up and the guard straightened smartly. Then he tapped the fuel gauge, which shimmered gently – the normal reaction.

"Thank you, Dan. What fuel is the truck running on right now?"

"I'm not sure. Gasoline, I think."

"Switch it over to the propane, please, Dan, and turn on the engine."

Dan switched the fuel supply and started cranking the engine.

Nothing. He tried again. Then again. Third time, the Liquid Petroleum Gas (LPG or propane) reached the carburettor and the motor burst into life. The officer bent down and breathed in the exhaust pipe – he could tell from the fumes that this was propane; it has a very different odour from gasoline exhaust. He had ascertained what he needed to know: Dan Wheeler was not smuggling BC Bud, one of the most popular and potent brands of cannabis in the world, from Canada into the United States. These elaborate tests were necessary – the only other way he could have established Dan's innocence would be by sawing open the LPG tank. And the resulting explosion would have blown apart him and everything else within a 500-yard radius.

"Okay, Dan. Just come on into the office to fill in the forms and you'll be on your way!"

Wheeler fumed, "Hey, can you at least give me a hand with reloading the car?" The officer turned and grimaced before helping reluctantly.

As he headed away from eastern British Columbia through the spectacular evergreen forest of Colville National Park towards the slush and wooden shacks of Metaline Falls itself, Dan's mood darkened.

How many times had he been through that damn border?

And how many times did he have to take his whole truck apart? And he knew that they liked him. There weren't many of their regulars who could talk with such authority about the things those boys loved – guns, hunting and fishing. "I guess that's why they're so good at their job," Dan thought. He was sincerely impressed by their thoroughness, even though it inconvenienced him most times he travelled.

By the time he arrived at the storage compound in Spokane, Washington State, Dan's spirits had brightened, but he was on alert.

After entering the pin code to the main gate, he started unloading the chrome strips into his rental lock-up under the arbitrary gaze of the CCTV cameras. Finally, he drove the truck into the space, closed the door and hooked up his lamp to the cigarette lighter. "With my tool kit, I dove underneath the truck, careful to place a little blanket underneath so I didn't pick up too much dirt – it's those little touches which make the difference between professionals like me and the amateurs who will at some point get caught." Removing the weld mesh as he had done at the border, Dan then unbolted the propane tank and swung it around ninety degrees so that he faced the semi-spherical end.

Telling me the story inside his voluminous garage and workshop, Dan demonstrated the routine with the propane tank. "You can't tell by looking at it, but if you chisel away at the right place with a screwdriver and a hammer, you bust away this glass-fibre body filler, which I use to cover up a socket," Dan explained. He then started to unscrew a small square nut. Pang! "There we go!" he exclaimed with a broad smile. And the end of the tank comes off.

There was no mighty explosion. Instead, I saw small-bore copper tubes inside, which ran from the external sniffer valve, gauges and fuel pipe to a small cylinder of propane used to fire camping stoves.

"The truck actually runs for fifteen klicks on the camping propane, and of course if anyone checks the sniffer valves or the fuel gauge, everything appears to be normal," said Dan proudly.

When he followed this procedure in the Spokane lock-up, the remainder of the tank was stuffed with fifty pounds of Bud from Beautiful British Columbia or God's Country, as the locals like to honour its wealth of natural beauty and resources. "That compound was my hot zone," Dan recalled earnestly, "Even when you've taken every precaution imaginable, you can still hear the squeal of the Feds' tyres in your mind. There was no retreat from the lock-up and no possibility of talking your way out of fifty pounds and $200k in cash."

In BC fifty pounds of Bud is worth US$55,000 at wholesale prices.

In Spokane, two and a half hours from the border, its value had almost doubled to $100k. If Dan could be bothered (which he often could), the trip to California added another $50k to his haul. If he drove it to Kentucky, he could sell it there for $200,000, almost four times the value in BC.

The turnover of Dan's business was $100,000 a week with minimal capital outlay. As Stephen Easton of the venerable Simon Fraser Institute in Vancouver has noted, the profits from this trade are seductive even for its most junior participants. "For a modest marijuana growing operation of 100 plants, harvest revenue is from thirteen kilograms of marijuana sold in pound blocks out the back door valued at $2,600 per pound. This amounts to slightly less than $20,000 per harvest. With four harvests per year, gross revenue is nearly $80,000. A conservatively high estimate of production cost is about $25,000. The return on invested money is potentially high: around fifty-five per cent. For the ordinary folk of western Canada, nothing competes financially.

For the pros, like Dan and his buddies, it comes close to being a licence to print money. "I was part of a three-man team," Dan continued. "Marty co-ordinated all the grow ops to deliver the fifty pounds per week – that's no easy job. Much of it came from his own farms, but some smaller ops sold to him, and you have to maintain the quality, hey. This is a highly competitive market and the guys we sold to, they knew their shit real good." Michael, the third partner, co-ordinated sales in the United States. "Look," said Michael, whose laid-back appearance conformed much more to the hippyish stereotype than Dan's just-back-from-felling-an-entire-forest look, "there are a lot of problems not just the question of your clients' reliability, but the security issues.

"God knows how many cell phones we use – we only use 'em for a week or so, then we chuck 'em away. There's a real damn problem – remembering all the different phone numbers."

Michael conceded that Dan was in many ways the linchpin of the operation. "The bottleneck has always been in getting the stuff into the US. But that's the big market – there's thirty million Canadians, but everyone in Canada either grows it themselves or has a buddy who does, even in Vancouver or back east. There's close to 300 million Americans and that's a massive market. Taking it to market – that's the real pro work and that was Dan's niche."

Marty, Michael and Dan are part of an industry that the BC Organised Crime Agency valued at $4 billion in 2001. At the time of writing, it is worth one-third more, according to most estimates, which means that it is responsible for more than five per cent of BC's GDP. Around 100,000 workers are engaged both full-time and part-time in the cultivation, distribution, smuggling and retail of marijuana, compared to 55,000 working in the traditional sectors of logging, mining, oil and gas combined. Only manufacturing employs more people – and this is all according to official statistics of Canadian law enforcement.

Although BC remains the main producer, the farming of marijuana has been spreading steadily eastwards over the past ten years and most provinces now boast a flourishing industry.

The implication of these figures is stark: western Canada is home to the largest *per capita* concentration of organized criminal syndicates in the world. In turn, Canada has become one of the biggest law enforcement headaches anywhere – organized crime has broken out of the ghetto of marginal communities and conquered the middle classes. "In a town like Nelson," says Dan, "I would estimate that about thirty per cent of households are involved in grow-ops of some size or other, but in the Slocan valley, I reckon between half and seventy per cent of the households will be involved."

From atop the reassuring slopes of Elephant Mountain (so called as it clearly resembles a dozing pachyderm) I gaze across the west arm of the Kootenay Lake at Nelson's rooftops. As they stack prettily up a steep green incline, they look ripe for transformation into the image on a cheesy jigsaw puzzle. In the background beyond looms the sharp peak of Silver King, the mountain whose precious metal deposits attracted large numbers of immigrants from southern and eastern Europe at the turn of the nineteenth century. To this day, this twee settlement resembles the idealized images of small-town America before it was blighted by unregulated advertising hoardings and fast-food joints. Almost every store in Nelson has a picture of its manager or owner with their arms around Steve Martin and Daryl Hannah, in commemoration of the time when the town was indeed transformed into America for the filming of *Roxanne*, a feeble update of *Cyrano de Bergerac*. Hollywood likes Nelson: for its unspoilt looks; for the Kootenay's stunning countryside; and because, of an evening, the crew gets to smoke Cuban cigars and fat joints packed with BC Bud.

But despite these attractions, Nelson and the surrounding area have been in steady economic decline for a couple of decades. Although its tourist and media industries are growing, these have not yet compensated for the slow demise of the traditional mining sector and the crises that have afflicted the logging industry. President George W. Bush dealt the most punishing blow to BC's economy in recent years by bending to pressure from the American lumber industry and imposing a twenty-seven per cent tax on Canadian softwood sales into the United States. Regulators of the North American Free Trade Agreement (NAFTA) and the World Trade Organization (WTO) subsequently ruled that this was an outright violation of America's free-trade responsibilities. The Canadian Government calculated that in three years after the imposition of the tariffs in May 2002, 7,000 jobs were "permanently lost in logging, sawmilling and remanufacturing across BC . . .

"Including indirect impacts, job losses have risen to a reported 14,000.

"A common myth assumes that these impacts will disappear with a settlement in the softwood dispute and that jobs will come back to BC communities. This is not the case, as our communities continue to witness mill closures." As indeed has been the case.

Many of those who once worked in the traditional industries have moved into marijuana. The trade in weed has attracted large numbers of highly skilled workers who, as I discovered on a trip in to the BC interior, have been quick to redeploy their skills into producing vast quantities of marijuana. Three of the four annual harvests are produced exclusively indoors (products of the summer outdoor harvest are often sought-after by connoisseurs, but your average consumer can usually be counted on not to give a damn). But the word "indoors" does not quite do justice to the extraordinary installations in which some of the plants are grown.

As our 4×4 embarks on the forest road, I am reminded of the train ride in Friedrich Dürrenmatt's dark surrealist novella, *The Tunnel.* As the train goes deeper into a tunnel, the dank bricks wrap themselves ever tighter around the carriages, forcing the travellers to confront their worst nightmares. At first BC's interior is not quite as threatening as Durrenmatt's trip through a hellish Swiss tunnel – the leaves are not so dense as to block all the sun as we rush northwards for an hour, maybe two, through the towering evergreens. But eventually the sun is bound to set and there are no cell phone signals here. If the vehicle breaks down, then the living nightmares of British Colombia's infinite interior will appear. Trekking home is out of the question – the terrain is littered with a plant known as the devil's club. These tough stalks three to four feet tall are topped by a ball covered in vicious spikes. As you walk through them, the club swings back and rips deep into human flesh. But the great fear is the grizzly bear. The world's most powerful natural predator, the grizzly plays cat-and-mouse with its victim, breaking its bones and its will, then laying it in a shallow grave before returning three days later to munch on the body after it has softened up. Thank God I've come here with a group of three professionals.

The men look, smell and move like loggers, their senses finely attuned to the outback. As well as scanning for the telltale signs of grizzlies, they keep their ears open for the distant twittering of helicopter rotors – "Could be game wardens, could be RCMP [Royal Canadian Mounted Police], could be DEA," one mutters. They talk like loggers, too, which is almost never.

I thought it was tough terrain for the 4×4, but when we finally arrive at the clearing that is our destination, I am rendered speechless by the vision of an idle mustard-coloured industrial digger with its bin resting triumphantly upwards. How do industrial diggers travel to the middle of nowhere? But even more impressive are the two seagoing containers, each forty feet long, which are sunk into an enormous hole in the forest. Accessible only through a door reached by some makeshift stairs cut into the ground, they are easily covered over by earth if necessary. The containers are humming. Cables lead away into the forest. "Proximity to a power cable is an important factor in the location," said Jim, who had rigged up the electric supply. An engineer with BC-Hydro, Jim formerly worked on constructing the dams that have helped turn Canada's most westerly province into one of the world's biggest power suppliers. "Basically, in order to get the power from the main cables, I have to build a series of sub-stations capable of reducing the voltage until we reach the grow-op."

Inside the two sea containers, hundreds upon hundreds of freshly planted cannabis saplings are starting to crane towards the equally numerous halogen lamps. This facility also has a system of CO_2 injections, as one of the horticulturalists explained to me. "You are much more in control of the environment by introducing CO_2 at the right time of the day and night. The more CO_2 you give 'em to deal with, the more they like it and they grow into fatter, healthier plants. Increases their potency and you can double the yield and beyond."

At the beginning of the 1990s, the best yield from indoor grow-ops was about three-quarters of a pound per one-kilowatt lamp. The most recent advance in cultivation techniques has more than doubled this to over two pounds per harvest cycle. Aeroponics is a still more efficient way of channelling nutrients to the plant than hydroponics. "If you circulate the nutrients through liquid, which is what hydroponics is, you lose efficiency because not all the particles are small enough to enter the roots. But by misting the roots – and it's a very fine mist – the intake of nutrients is still higher. This cultivation method is without peer."

Of the many things BC has in abundance, space and electricity have been decisive in transforming it into one of the world's great marijuana farms. Space, because the RCMP and the US's DEA just cannot find the great majority of the largest grow-ops (especially after they are hidden deep underground in sea containers). "The DEA may have unlimited access to BC," Senator Larry Campbell, former Mayor of Vancouver, told me, "but do you know how many logging trails there are in the Kootenays? I mean you can bring in every Blackhawk helicopter you want – forget the haystack. You're looking for a needle in a jungle!"

As for electricity, the lamps feeding the cannabis may need huge amounts of power by normal domestic standards, but by the standards of BC's vast hydroelectric capacity, the amount is negligible.

Back home in the Slocan valley at the end of another tough day, Dan places one of his favourite shows in the VCR. "You're going to love this," he says. "This'll show you just how dumb Americans can be!" he adds in gleeful anticipation.

Presented by Rick Mercer, the CBC TV show is called *Talking with Americans*. The host travels across the length and breadth of the United States and encourages Americans to give their reactions in the spirit of neighbourliness to fictitious events in contemporary Canada. "Congratulations, Canada!" an attractive New York woman gushes, "On your first 100 miles of paved highway!" Or "Congratulations, Canada! On opening your first university!" In one show, Mercer persuades an Ivy League English professor to denounce in all sincerity Canada's supposed annual ritual of setting its elderly citizens adrift on ice floes as a method of demographic control. And even the Governor of Arkansas *(not* Bill Clinton) is gullible enough to send his best wishes on camera to Canada's Prime Minister for having constructed the world's first parliament made from ice.

Popular resentment towards America and the intellectual insularity of Americans is part of everyday life in Canada. It is persistent, low-level, sometimes dumb and sometimes funny. It also reflects the inferiority complex tinged with irritation that characterizes many Canadians' relationship with their southern neighbours. Within a few days of my arrival in the country, I – like many foreigners before me – have been invited to play "Name the famous Canadian", before the host reels off a legion of celebrities from Michael J. Fox through Shania Twain to Glenn Gould and J.K. Galbraith – luminaries whom a majority of Americans believe to be as authentic as Apple Pie, but who are in fact Canadian, at least by birth.

This social anti-Americanism assumes a more serious form when economic interests are at stake, as demonstrated by the very different attitudes towards the United States in two neighbouring provinces, BC and Alberta. The latter's economy is heavily dependent on investment from American companies, first and foremost because of Alberta's burgeoning oil industry. Already Canada is the largest single supplier of petroleum to the United States, ahead of Mexico, Saudi Arabia and Venezuela. The province's potential reserves are estimated at a gigantic 175 billion barrels of recoverable petroleum, but this is in the form of so-called oil sands, an intense mix of hydrocarbons, sand and clay from which it is expensive to extract oil. For this Alberta needs the co-operation of American oil companies, their most fervent customers. And the benefits are considerable – in 2004, the oil yielded US $10 billion in taxes and royalties to the provincial government, contributing to the transformation of Alberta into the fastest-growing economy in the country and the new centre of affluence.

Of course that wealth is the consequence of America's hunger for gasoline, and this has fused with Alberta's traditionally close ties with the US to confirm the province as the most pro-American in Canada by a long chalk. The quintessential representative of Alberta is Canada's Prime Minister, Stephen Harper, who built his political career in the provincial business capital, Calgary. In the 2006 general elections, he led the Conservative Party to a clean sweep in Alberta for the first time.

A firm friend to President George W. Bush, he is the most vocal supporter of closer ties with the United States in Canadian politics.

Although right next door to Alberta, British Columbia presents a very different political profile. Here a majority of the seats in 2006 went either to the Liberal Party, the traditional centrist grouping, or the New Democratic Party, a left-leaning party. Most strikingly, in the key marijuana-growing areas, parties supporting the decriminalization or legalization of marijuana won huge majorities. In the Southern Interior of BC, a constituency that includes Nelson and the Slocan valley, the parties won eighty per cent of the vote as opposed to the Conservatives' twenty per cent, whereas in neighbouring Alberta constituencies, the Conservatives received an average vote of just under sixty per cent.

BC, and indeed Ottawa, have locked horns with the United States over the softwood dispute and, equally importantly, over marijuana.

These two issues have contributed decisively to the emergence of a more virulent anti-Americanism in BC than in the rest of Canada.

To be sure, British Columbians often appear confused about where their loyalties lie; after all, BC has always nurtured secessionist sentiments that rail against the perceived bureaucratic behemoth in the federal capital, Ottawa. Indeed, in the BC interior there is a strong gun culture that shows affinities with the militia mindset common in Washington, Montana and other neighbouring American states.

But the issue of cannabis is defining attitudes to the United States in BC and Canada with ever greater clarity. About sixty per cent of Canadians now favour decriminalization or legalization of marijuana possession. BC, however, is way out in front – more than seventy-five per cent of British Columbians want a relaxation in the law relating to cannabis possession. In doing so, BC has entered into a collision course with the United States.

Similarly, cannabis is also influencing attitudes in Washington towards Canada – Vancouver in particular. In 2003, the then

Canadian Government announced its intention to introduce legislation decriminalizing the possession of less than fifteen grams (about half an ounce) of weed. This would not make possession legal, but the offence would attract a small fine and the recipient would not be encumbered with a criminal record. The US reaction was swift. "You can't wall this off, saying, 'We're only talking about a little cannabis,'" exclaimed David Murray, special assistant to Washington's Drugs Czar, John P. Walters. He then added an apocalyptic afterthought:

"Our experience is they [various narcotics] come together like the Four Horsemen!"

Since his appointment in December 2001, Drugs Czar Walters has placed the issue of BC's cannabis trade close to the top of his agenda.

"Canada is at risk, I believe, at a very great risk," Murray told me in his Washington office, "more than they have been willing to acknowledge.

"The level of crime is in certain provinces really undermining the legitimacy of their own institutions. The issue seems to be a certain Canadian complacency, a sense of self that is disastrously innocent, absolutely unwilling to acknowledge – they find themselves in opposition to us."

As the tension between the US and Canada over marijuana has surfaced, it has again highlighted one of the most controversial, difficult and dangerous aspects of global organized crime: the United States' policy on, and policing of, the international trade in narcotics.

In 1987, US paratrooper Steve Tuck suffered a serious spinal injury when doing a jump in Central America. Invalided out of the army, he spent a year and a half at the renowned Walter Reed Army Hospital in Washington, DC. Twenty years and another twelve operations later, he remains in severe pain and on the same dose of morphine he was given at the time of his accident. His body was remoulded into a sack full of metal. On medical advice, he turned to marijuana for pain relief and was soon growing the stuff for himself and friends in northern California. In 2001, just as John P. Walters was acquainting himself with his new role as Drugs Czar in Washington, Tuck did a runner from justice after the police came after his cannabis farm – his easiest escape was a hop across the border to Vancouver. The Canadian government welcomed Tuck and even licensed him to sell marijuana seeds to be used in research. At around the same time, the US began extradition proceedings against Tuck.

In November 2002, the thirty-six-year-old was relaxing by puffing on a large spliff at the New Amsterdam Café in East Vancouver. It had been a tough day – Tuck had been protesting outside the hotel where John Walters himself had been staying during his first official visit to Vancouver. Walters intended to acquaint himself with the severity of the narcotics problem in BC's economic capital. The two men had been sparring in the media. At a press conference Walters described Tuck and his friends as "darker angels of society" for advocating the use of marijuana for medicinal purposes. Tuck had countered in an interview that was transmitted countrywide on the Canadian Broadcast Company by denouncing Walters as a liar.

After the rigours of such a day, the New Amsterdam Café and its gentle clientele provided welcome relief for Tuck. That night was music night and so people had dressed up. "It looked like any yuppie bar in any major city," recalls Steve. "Then several men in black, all with the same standard-issue trenchcoats, with the ear-pieces and the high-powered mikes marched into the café. I knew straight away they were secret service." The visitors were bad karma enough for the café's laid-back customers. But worse was to transpire as the agents fanned out. "I recognized him immediately – John P. Walters, the President's Drugs Czar!" Walters strode up to Tuck as if he knew him. "It was surreal. He obviously knew who I was and just started saying that this was a disgrace and then, pointing right at me, 'Arrest this man!'"

Walters stared at the joint and Tuck's stash. *Of all the gin joints in all the towns in all the world, she walks into mine . . .* "But he was staring me down and shouting at me, and so I just took a toke of my joint and blew the smoke right in his face!"

For a split second, the atmosphere in the café turned nasty – the other customers were rising through the fog of smoke in anger at the presence of this unwanted guest. The bouncers were beginning to wrestle with the Secret Service men, while the chief of Vancouver's police was explaining to Walters that he would not be arresting Tuck as he was doing nothing illegal.

Tuck tried to calm things down. He announced to the other guests in the café that this was the famous John P. Walters. He advised everyone to sit down and talk. But that did not prevent the Drugs Czar from continuing to berate his hosts, the guests at the café and above all Steve Tuck. Finally, the police persuaded Walters to leave.

Tuck felt vindicated, but two years later Walters' spirit returned in the form of Canadian police, who forcibly removed Tuck from a Vancouver hospital, with a catheter and IV tubes still attached, before bundling him into a car, hooded and manacled, and handing him over to US federal agents a couple of hours later. He was slung into jail and left there, suffering excruciating pain because of the embedded catheter.

Tuck's encounter with Walters was not the only surreal moment of the Drugs Czar's visit. The voters of Vancouver, or Vansterdam as it had also become known by now, had unexpectedly just elected a mixed bag of environmentalists, leftists, vegetarians and dope smokers to run the municipality. Standing proud at the head of this woolly-jumper invasion was Larry Campbell, the city's coroner, best known for his consulting role on Canada's smash-hit cop show, *Da Vinci's Inquest*, whose plots often unfold in Vancouver's drug-addled quarter of Downtown Eastside.

But apart from serving as coroner, Campbell had for many years been a senior officer of the Royal Canadian Mounted Police's Drugs Squad. Like a minority of former RCMP officers and DEA agents, he ended up questioning his role in busting addicts come what may. "It wasn't really until I became coroner that my position started to shift," he told me in his parliamentary office in Ottawa, "because in that position you start to worry less about enforcing the law on the users, and to worry more about how you keep these damn people alive. Vancouver was always a high drug-usage area, but in the 1990s there was a glut.

"Afghanistan was rocking. The Golden Triangle was rocking. In 1976, when I was on the Drugs Squad and we took down a pound or a key, it'd have a big effect on the street. They weren't even cutting the stuff then. You had to go hunt the addicts to find 'em. By '96, they were all over the city – outside the back door, in the parking lot, in the parks, on the streets. One day we just woke up in Vancouver and said:

Holy Jesus, this place makes Needle Park look like a children's playground.

We gotta do something!"

After his encounter with Tuck, John Walters was heading off to see an even more sordid den of iniquity – Insite, the clinic set up in Vancouver where they administered heroin to addicts under medical supervision. For while cannabis was the recreational drug of choice for most of British Columbia's users, heroin (which was strictly illegal) had gained a stranglehold over large parts of inner-city Vancouver and other urban areas in BC. This was not only a serious law-enforcement issue, it was first and foremost a public-health issue. And Larry Campbell and the new administration were determined to come up with effective solutions to the problem.

Campbell and his allies visited Europe and acquainted themselves with a system called harm reduction, developed particularly in Holland and Switzerland, which replaced traditional drugs programmes that sought in the first instance to punish drug users with ones that sought to assist and rehabilitate them. Vancouver went on to deploy their version, known as the Four Pillars. Essentially, this assumes the drug user to be a victim rather than a perpetrator, and seeks ways in which the health and social services can embrace the addict as a way of minimizing risk to him or her and to the wider society. A critical element of the programme is needle exchange, whereby the state provides unused needles to addicts to reduce the infectious spread of HIV, Hepatitis C and other communicable diseases. Similar programmes have been hugely successful in Europe, especially in high drug-usage cities like Zurich, Amsterdam and Edinburgh.

But Mayor Campbell went one further than this. In 2003, he sought and received the approval of the Federal government to open an injection site at a BC medical facility in Downtown

Eastside, where addicts could receive professional help in administering heroin.

And if this were not enough, the Federal Canadian government announced at the same time its intention to decriminalize possession of cannabis.

For Walters and his Office of National Drug Control in Washington, DC, Sodom was being built just miles from the US border. It was time to issue a warning, so David Murray was dispatched to explain to the Canadian government that the US "would have to respond" to decriminalization, implying that border traffic between the two countries, which enjoy the most profitable commercial relationship anywhere in the world, might be disrupted. Murray warned that decriminalization would result in "the loss of the mutual co-operative partnership we've had with Canadians regarding our borders, regarding the integrity of the hemisphere, regarding our commerce, regarding the implications of trade and value to ourselves; the loss of that would be something truly to be regretted".

Larry Campbell said he got a still clearer message from a higher authority. "Walters told us that he could shut the border down," he said. "And so I made some offhand comment about it being a shame to see LA in the dark." Campbell offers a mischievous smile as he alludes to California's partial dependence on electricity and natural gas from BC.

The debate between Washington and Ottawa and the future course of narcotics policy have enormous implications for the global shadow economy, for trans-national organized crime, for international policing, and for domestic policy across the world. They impact on governance, on international relations, on social and health issues, but most crucially on economics – especially if the UN is correct that seventy per cent of financial resources available to organized crime derives from the narcotics industry.

But if economic globalization has enabled this huge expansion, cultural globalization has also played a part, advertising the pleasures offered by narcotics in regions that were opening up as markets. Rave culture, for example, and the accompanying use of drugs such as amphetamines and Ecstasy, swept across the world, reaching Japan, Thailand, South America, Israel, Russia and elsewhere. It was transported effectively by backpackers and the Internet alike. Very soon, chemists from Serbia, Bulgaria, Thailand and Israel were learning the tricks of the trade from their counterparts in Holland – production of the new generation of drugs was no longer confined to the slopes of the Andes or the remote fields of the Golden Triangle (not that the coke- and heroin-traffickers didn't benefit from the dozens of new and unmonitored commercial routes springing up around the globe).

The upshot of this was increased supply and increased competition in the market, which resulted in lower prices and thereby increased demand for virtually every mass-produced recreational drug. There was, however, no comparable increase in the capacity of the world's police forces to deal with this expanded activity in the drugs market.

Indeed in some countries, like Russia, the police's ability to control illicit markets collapsed, especially since the military was frequently involved in the distribution of narcotics from Central Asia into Moscow and beyond. And when the drugs market expands, so does related criminal activity. In its first major assessment of the global narcotics industry, published in the mid-2000s, the UN pointed out "that in Britain seventy-five per cent of serious crimes are associated with drugs; that seventy per cent of the income of the criminals who are drug addicts is generated by theft; that drug addicts need £43,000 a year to support the addiction. In surveys most addicts cite theft, fraud, begging, prostitution and drug trade as their main sources of income or are prepared to tap such sources." This, of course, puts a huge additional burden not just on the police, but on the entire criminal-justice system.

With support from the great majority of its members, the United Nations Office on Drugs and Crime advocates a policy of uncompromising prohibition on drugs – a policy that confers the right on the state to deploy its full police resources to intervene and destroy the narcotics market. With a commodity such as fissile material (where police forces have a fighting chance of tracking regions of production and constituencies of demand), prohibition has a real chance of achieving its stated goals. But with narcotics, where demand is immense and relentless, prohibition drives the market towards the only place capable of satisfying that demand and regulating the industry: organized crime.

Lev Timofeev, the former Soviet dissident mathematician turned analyst of Russia's shadow economy, has written one of the most comprehensive economic studies of the drugs market. His conclusions are stark:

> Prohibiting a market does not mean destroying it. Prohibiting a market means placing a prohibited but dynamically developing market under the total control of criminal corporations.
>
> Moreover, prohibiting a market means enriching the criminal world with hundreds of billions of dollars by giving criminals a wide access to public goods which will be routed by addicts into the drug traders' pockets. Prohibiting a market means giving the criminal corporations opportunities and resources for exerting a guiding and controlling influence over whole societies and nations. This is the worst of the negative external effects of the drug market. International public opinion has yet to grasp the challenge to the world civilization posed by it.

From an economic point of view, a person's decision to enter into the drugs trade as a producer, distributor or retailer is entirely rational, because the profit margins are so high. This is all the more compelling in countries like Afghanistan and Colombia where chronic levels of poverty are endemic. Time and again, narcotics-traffickers have demonstrated that their financial clout is sufficient to buy off officials even in states with very low levels of corruption, as in Scandinavia. In most countries, traffickers can call on combined resources of billions of dollars, where national police forces have access to tens or hundreds of millions (and are further hamstrung by a complex set of regulations constraining their ability to act).

On the whole, governments do not argue that drug prohibition benefits the economy. They base their arguments instead on perceived social damage and on public morality. On the contrary, it distorts the economy because it denies the state revenue from taxes that might accrue from the purchase of a legal commodity (not to mention the immense costs of trying to police the trade and the incarceration of convicted criminals). This huge financial burden is one reason why so many economists, like Timofeev, and indeed one of the great organs of the British establishment, *The Economist* magazine, are adamant in their support of the legalization of drugs. "Ultimately," argues Ted Galen Carpenter, Vice-President of the venerable American right-wing think tank, the Cato Institute, "the prohibitionist approach is an attempt to repeal the economic law of supply and demand, and therefore it is doomed to fail."

Timofeev has identified a further problem. With the manner of a boffin who seems permanently distracted by some knotty intellectual conundrum, he outlined his findings to me in his wooden dacha just outside Moscow. He is a man as far away from the world of drugs and its related social evil as one may imagine. "The growth of funds available to the drug business," he argues, "along with its enhanced managerial capability make it possible to diversify their risk assets by transferring capital to other markets. This is precisely what the organized-crime groups do when they are shifting their assets from one illicit activity to another. For instance, the Sicilian mafia invested proceeds from smuggling cigarettes and emeralds into the drug business. In the 'hot spots' across the world (such as Afghanistan or Chechnya) drug dealers invested a considerable proportion of their income into illegal arms shipments."

Prohibition is also a godsend to terrorist networks. Organizations like the Taliban and Al-Qaeda fund their activities through the narcotics trade. In this respect, the inability of the NATO-led force in Afghanistan to pacify anything beyond the centre of Kabul since the invasion of 2001 has been a disaster. Cultivation of the opium poppy had sky-rocketed by more than 1,000 per cent within the first year of Afghanistan's occupation. It was not long before the Taliban was re-arming itself by taxing this opium harvest. Attempts by Western governments and agencies to limit the poppy harvests have been an abysmal failure.

The only way you can prevent the Taliban and others from sustaining their military capacity through drug sales is to legalize narcotics.

When a punter buys some grass, crack or Ecstasy on the streets, only a tiny percentage of the money covers production costs. The great bulk goes towards paying off the distribution network for assuming the risk in bringing an illegal commodity to market. This was demonstrated irrefutably by the economics of alcohol prohibition in the 1920s and 1930s. Then, as now, Canada, which dumped Prohibition a few years before the US, became a key supplier of the illicit substance. By 1933, the world's largest producer of alcohol was Seagram, a Canadian company, and its success was not accounted for by Canadian drinkers.

Some argue that there is a cultural difference between today's illegal narcotics and alcohol. There may well be a *cultural* difference, but with regard to the relationship between drugs and organized crime, the economic argument is central – and here there is absolutely no difference between illicit alcohol and illicit drugs. The astronomical profits generated by drugs lie in these commodities' illegality. There is no institutional regulation that might influence the value of the commodity, and so the price comes down purely to what the consumer is prepared to pay. The only indirect involvement of the state lies in its deployment of policing methods to break up the smooth functioning of the market.

[. . .] If a country supports prohibition, it is also *guaranteeing* that on the supply side all profits will accrue to underground networks; and on the demand side it is *guaranteeing* that any social or public-health problems associated with drug-taking will only come to light in the great majority of cases once they are out of control. If the UN is right and drugs account for seventy per cent of organized criminal activity, then the legalization of drugs would administer by far the deadliest blow possible against trans-national organized criminal networks. [. . .]

Lev Timofeev argues that prohibition tends to distort the market, favouring cartels and monopoly tendencies. This is because, he continues, larger organizations are more efficient at enforcing their monopoly than smaller ones. Translated into the vernacular, this means that big criminal groups can beat the shit out of smaller ones.

In 2005, Dan Wheeler decided to break up his partnership with Michael and Marty. There was no falling out between the three of them, but Dan was unhappy about the direction of the trade. "I was offered the opportunity of doing a trip to Miami," he said. "It was a new kind of deal – for every one kilo of Bud I delivered in Florida, I would be paid one kilo of pure cocaine, the idea being that I'd then bring it back here." Dan was silent for thirty seconds. "No way . . . No fucking way.

"What you have to understand about weed is that it attracts people who have a healthy attitude to life. It never promotes aggression, and most of the people I've come across involved in the trade on both sides of the border are thoroughly decent people. The people who handle coke are very different, and in the past few years I have seen coke and its entourage make ever deeper inroads into places like the Kootenays."

The purveyors of cocaine in BC are also becoming increasingly interested in expanding into rural areas and competing in the profitable BC Bud market. In BC and Vancouver, the most powerful and visible organized-crime syndicate is the Hell's Angels.

There are two reasons for the strength of Vancouver's Hell's Angels.

The first is common to most chapters of the movement worldwide: organizational discipline. They have a strict hierarchy and place a premium on absolute loyalty. It takes many years before an aspiring Angel can get anywhere close to the centre of power. Trainees, or "prospects", are expected to carry out any orders handed down from the full-patch members – instructions can range from clearing up after a meeting to engaging in extortion by the threat or use of physical violence. Because the aspirant must be prepared to accept years of drudgery and hanging around before he (I use the gender advisedly) might be considered a member, Hell's Angels are impossible to infiltrate, sharing a security system that is as effective as the Chinese triads.

Infiltrating the Mafia, the Colombian cartels, the Balkan or Russian mafias is, by contrast, like falling off a log.

The second source of the Vancouver Hell's Angels' power is the group's control over the city's port. "The Hell's Angels are involved with bringing in whatever's profitable – marijuana, cocaine or precursors," said Brian Brennan, chief investigator for the drug squad of the RCMP. "They still have influence in the ports – their influence on cocaine is still strong and we are now seeing them in synthetic drugs."

The Hell's Angels exert that influence through friends, business associates and corrupt officials, and control of the port has meant control of cocaine. Vancouver is used to import cocaine both directly from Latin America and from the United States, but it is also used as a transit point for cocaine going into the US. "What you've seen in recent times," Brennan continues, "is an increase in violence as the struggle for control of the grow-ops heats up."

The Hell's Angels established themselves as a major criminal group decades ago, and in that time the RCMP can count the number of convictions on the fingers of two hands. "Is the problem big?" asks Brennan rhetorically. "Absolutely – it's huge. The number of grow-ops is beyond the capacity of law enforcement as a whole, not just the RCMP. And the money being made by the organized groups, like the Hell's Angels, means that they can walk away from properties that they own without batting an eyelid. We're talking about a house worth $500,000 on the lower mainland of British Columbia, and if the police go and seize a thousand plants in that house, they'll just walk away.

"Because they are making so much money that they don't care about losing that investment."

The RCMP co-operates closely with the DEA in trying to stem the flow of marijuana to the US, but as I speak to Brennan, I detect for the first time a note of irritation creeping into his voice – not when talking about the DEA, but when talking about Washington politicians and their criticism of Canada's drugs policy. Because this rhetoric implies that the RCMP is doing a poor job in holding back that flow. "The US," continues Inspector Brennan, "has a legitimate concern that the amount of marijuana from north to south is growing – there has been an increase in seizures, so maybe we're getting better at the border – it's hard to measure. But I must stress that only two per cent of what is domestically consumed in the United States comes from Canada. They make a lot of a fuss about it, but it's down to the fact that the relationship between the two countries is really good, the border is very long and so it is likely to be porous. It's big news if something like the tunnels are discovered in Canada, but in the last year, they found about twenty-seven tunnels between Mexico and the US."

It took me a while to understand the implication of what Brennan was saying. BC Bud is a $6 billion industry. According to the RCMP, between seventy-five and ninety per cent of marijuana produced in BC makes its way on to the American market. But the US and Canada confirm in their official Drug Threat Assessment that this amounts to a mere two per cent of America's cannabis consumption. Even I can do the maths on that one. One might legitimately ask what in God's name are they smoking in the US? Frankly, there are no accurate figures as to what it is or where it comes from – the only thing we all do know is that there's a hell of a lot of it!

The Mammoth Book of Casino Games
By Paul Mendelson

ISBN: 978-1-84901-271-3
Price: £7.99

Do you want to gamble or do you want to win?

Paul Mendelson offers an indispensable guide to beating the odds
in just about every gambling game, both in casinos and online. He
reveals how to shift the odds in your favour as he clearly explains
every game and analyses optimum strategies in detail with the aim of
helping you to win.

Other chapters show you how to:

• get the best out of your casino – pick up free drinks, meals, hotel
accommodation, thousand-dollar shopping trips, room upgrades,
flights, bonus money etc.

• make the most of your trip to Las Vegas or anywhere else –
casino information, the best places to gamble (for each game),
recommended hotels and attractions

• win online – which sites to avoid and which can be trusted, a
discussion of every game from poker through to online bingo,
including bonuses, incentives, play-through data and the best
strategies to use.

Visit www.constablerobinson.com for more information

The Mammoth Book of Cover-Ups
By Jon E. Lewis

ISBN: 978-1-84529-608-7
Price: £7.99

**Everything 'they' never wanted you to know –
and were afraid you might ask**

Who really assassinated JFK? Was Princess Diana murdered by MI5
despite the denials? Do the Illuminati covertly rule the world?

Historian Jon E. Lewis explores the hundred most terrifying cover-
ups of all time, from the invention of Jesus' divinity (pace *The Da
Vinci Code*) to Bush's and Blair's real agenda in invading Iraq.
Entertainingly written and closely documented, the book provides
each cover-up with a plausibility rating.

Uncover why the Titanic sank, ponder the sinister Vatican/Mafia
network that plotted the assassination of liberal John Paul, find out
why NASA 'lost' its files on Mars, read why no-one enters Area 51,
and consider why medical supplies were already on site at Edgware
Road before the 7/7 bombs detonated…

**Just because you are paranoid, it doesn't mean that they
aren't out to conspire against you.**

Visit www.constablerobinson.com for more information

The Mammoth Book of Jack the Ripper
Edited by Maxim Jakubowski and Nathan Braund

ISBN: 978-1-84529-712-1
Price: £7.99

Jack the Ripper – all the evidence, all the key theories

An updated and expanded edition of the fullest ever collective
investigation into Jack the Ripper and the Whitechapel Murders.

This volume includes not just all the key factual evidence but also
twenty different arguments as to the identity of Jack the Ripper.
Contributions are from the world's leading Ripperologists, including
Patricia Cornwell, William Beadle, Melvyn Fairclough, Martin Fido,
Shirley Harrison, James Tully and Colin Wilson.

The many suspects include Montague John Druitt, Walter
Sickert, Aaron Kosminski, Michael Ostrog, William Henry Bury,
Dr Tumblety and James Maybrick. The only certainty is that
Ripperologists have not found an invididual on whom they can all
agree.

The essays are supported by a detailed chronology, extensive
bibliography and filmography.

Visit www.constablerobinson.com for more information

The Mammoth Book of Killers at Large
By Nigel Cawthorne

ISBN: 978-1-84529-631-5
Price: £7.99

Reason to be afraid – over fifty unsolved cases of serial murder

Murderers and serial killers do not always get caught. Behind every
headline of a newsworthy conviction lie other cases of vicious
murderers who got away, and who remain somewhere among us.
Here in one giant volume are more than fifty of the most serious serial
killings and other murder cases that continue to remain unsolved.

The cases covered in this alarming book include:

• **Argentina's crazed highway killer,** responsible for mutilating
and killing at least five people since 1997, and dumping their bodies
along remote highways

• **The 'Green River Killer',** believed to be a middle-aged white
man, who has claimed at least forty-nine lives to date in the Seattle-
Tacoma area

• South Africa's **'Phoenix Strangler',** suspected of killing twenty
women in the province of KwaZulu Natal.

• **The 'Twin Cities Killer'** – either one or several people
responsible for a series of over thirty murders on the streets of
Minneapolis and St. Paul, where the victims were mostly prostitutes

• **Costa Rica's elusive 'El Psicópata'** (The Psychopath), thought
to have murdered at least 19 people in this small quiet Central
American country

• **'The Monster of Florence',** responsible for a series of fifteen
sexual slayings just outside Florence

Visit www.constablerobinson.com for more information

The Mammoth Book of Best British Crime 7
Edited by Maxim Jakubowski

ISBN: 978-1-84901-197-6
Price: £7.99

The cream of UK crime – a new collection of short stories in this award-winning series

Leading critic Maxim Jakubowksi's must-have collection of the year's best new short crime fiction, from the UK's most outstanding writers, is back. Bringing together stories of every kind, from noir and hardboiled to ingenious mysteries and lovable amateur sleuths, it's a treat for all lovers of crime and mystery fiction.

The collection features a brand-new Inspector Morse mystery from Colin Dexter plus new stories from top crime writing talents such as John Harvey, Tom Cain, Ken Bruen, Val McDermid and Peter Lovesey.

'Jakubowski is the doyen of British crime-fiction editors, and any collection edited by him is assured of quality.' *Good Book Guide*

'A page-turning compendium of British talent that has captured the imagination of readers around the world.' *Crime Time*

The Mammoth Book of the Best of Best New Horror
Edited by Stephen Jones

CLIVE BARKER, HARLAN ELLISON, NEIL GAIMAN, STEPHEN KING, PETER STRAUB AND MANY MORE

ISBN: 978-1-84901-304-8
Price: £9.99

A twenty year celebration of *Best New Horror*

For the past two decades the annual *Mammoth Book of Best New Horror* series has been the major showcase for superior short stories and novellas of horror and dark fantasy. This World Fantasy Award, British Fantasy Award and International Horror Guild Award-winning series has published more than 450 stories by around 200 of the genre's most famous and acclaimed authors, as well as many just starting out on their careers.

To celebrate the anthology's twentieth anniversary, the editor has selected from each volume one story that he considers to be the 'best' by some of horror's biggest names, including RAMSEY CAMPBELL, CHRISTOPHER FOWLER, ELIZABETH HAND, JOE HILL, GLEN HIRSHBERG, CAITLÍN R. KIERNAN, TERRY LAMSLEY, TIM LEBANON, BRIAN LUMLEY, PAUL J. McAULEY, KIM NEWMAN, MARK SAMUELS, MICHAEL MARSHALL SMITH, LISA TUTTLE, and SIMON KURT UNSWORTH.

"Horror's last maverick." Christopher Fowler

"Stephen Jones . . . has a better sense of the genre than almost anyone in this country." Lisa Tuttle, *The Times*

"The best horror anthologist in the business is, of course, Stephen Jones." Roz Kavaney, *Time Out*

The Mammoth Book of CSI
Edited by Roger Wilkes

ISBN: 978-1-84529-478-6
Price: £7.99

**When only the evidence can tell the truth –
over thirty real-life crime scene investigations**

With the technology available to forensic science, crime scene
investigators can answer questions others never even thought to
ask. This fascinating collection presents over thirty classic cases
of forensic detective work. Genetic fingerprinting, blood spatter
analysis, special photography, toxicology, ballistics analysis – the
whole range of forensic techniques is featured. These investigators
trust only the evidence to speak for those who cannot speak for
themselves: the victims.

The cases featured include:

• The killing of a six-year-old beauty queen JonBenét Ramsey,
found covered in a blanket with a handwritten ransom note and an
extraordinary cast of suspects

• Robert Thompson and Jon Venables, the killers of James Bulger
identified when CCTV pictures taken in a shopping centre were
technically enhanced

• Sam Sheppard, whose murder trial based on blood evidence
inspired the TV series *The Fugitive*

• Colin Pitchfork, eventually trapped by DNA fingerprinting
evidence for the rape and murder of two fifteen-year-old girls

• Barry George, convicted of murdering television personality Jill
Dando, a case in which a single microscopic particle provided
compelling evidence

Visit www.constablerobinson.com for more information

The Mammoth Book of Bizarre Crimes
By Robin Odell

ISBN: 978-1-84529-781-7
Price: £7.99

You couldn't make it up!

A gripping collection of stories of human criminality at its most bizarre. These unusual, sensational murders recall not only gruesome historical crimes, but also touch on shocking and macabre modern murders. Included are details of ground-breaking advances in crime detection, law enforcement and forensic science. This is the top-secret report on the most grisly, and unusual, criminal activity of our time.

Incredible and bizarre true crimes include:

Kyrstian Bala: Polish writer who killed a rival, then used the murder as the plot for a novel

Alexander Pichushkin: Russian man stopped one short of killing the 64 victims he needed to "fill a chess board"

John Lee: "the man they could not hang", who survived three attempts to execute him at Exeter Prison

Robert "Rattlesnake" James: Californian barber who used two snakes in a box to kill his wife

The Mammoth Book of Travel in Dangerous Places
Edited by John Keay

ISBN: 978-1-84901-311-6
Price: £7.99

First-hand accounts of exploration by David Livingstone, James Cook, Meriweather Lewis, Ernest Shackleton, Roald Amundsen, Sir Edmund Hillary and many others

The romance and danger of the great explorers' daring expeditions captured the public imagination and the world's headlines to an extraordinary degree. Journalists vied for their stories, and publishers rushed their first-hand accounts of exciting and dangerous journeys into print for a wide and voracious readership.

Acclaimed travel historian **John Keay** introduces this selection of the best of these first-hand narratives, including those of:

- **David Livingstone's** exploration of the headwaters of the mighty river Congo, and **Henry Stanley**, the *New York Herald* journalist who went in search of him

- **Alexander Mackenzie**, who made the first recorded crossing of the North American Continent

- **Hiram Bingham**, who discovered the magnificent Inca city of Machu Picchu

- **Wilfred Thesiger**, who crossed Arabia's forebidding Empty Quarter with Bedouin company

Visit www.constablerobinson.com for more information

**The Mammoth Book of Perfect Crimes
and Locked Room Mysteries**
Edited by Mike Ashley

ISBN: 978-1-84529-337-6
Price: £7.99

Presenting thirty impossible mysteries and bizarre crimes guaranteed
to fascinate and intrigue. The delight in these stories is unravelling
the puzzle and trying to work out what on earth happened.

Stories include:

- A man alone in an all-glass phone booth, visible on CCTV and
  with no one near him, is killed by an ice pick.

- A man sitting alone in a room is shot by a bullet fired only once
  and that was over 200 years ago.

- A man enters a cable-car carriage alone and is visible the entire
  journey but is found dead when he reaches the bottom.

- A man vanishes at the top of the Indian rope trick and is found
  dead miles away.

- A dead man continues to receive mail in response to letters
  apparently written by him after he'd died.

The anthology includes several brand new stories never previously
published, plus a range of extremely rare stories – from such names
as **Robert Randisi, Edward D. Hoch, Joseph Commings,
Peter Tremayne, Bill Pronzini and Gillian Linscott.**

Visit www.constablerobinson.com for more information

The Mammoth Book of Sex, Drugs and Rock'n'Roll
Edited by Jim Driver

ISBN: 978-1-84529-808-1

'Hail! Hail! Rock'n'Roll!'
The lives and times of the revolution that
turned Western culture upside down.

This wonderfully eclectic collection of journalism and essays on the
highs and lows of rock'n'roll ranges from the first blues recordings
to Amy Winehouse. Featuring top writers, such as Allen Ginsberg
and Tony Parsons, it tours with The Beatles, Rolling Stones
and Sex Pistols, and recalls the shock demise of rock stars Jimi
Hendrix and Michael Hutchence. It joins Jagger in bed – and in the
aftermath of Altamont; visits Paris with Iron Maiden; and meets the
Brothers Grim – aka Oasis – Pete Doherty and the new bands of the
next rock'n'roll millennium.

'Several entries in this anthology would merit the entrance price for
their inclusion alone: Michael Braun's fly-on-the-wall account of
The Beatles in 1963; Nick Coleman on Keith Richards ('the only
man ever to look good in a guitar'); Jenny Fabian's afternoon in bed
with Syd Barrett; Phil Kaufman on his illicit cremation of Gram
Parsons.'
Independent

'Driver has condensed the very best of irony-free rock writing into
one handy reference work...Essential reading for every budding
Keith Richards.'
Big Issue

Visit www.constablerobinson.com for more information